HELLENISTIC CIVILISATION

HELLENISTIC CIVILISATION

W. W. TARN

Third Edition revised by the Author and

G. T. GRIFFITH

A MERIDIAN BOOK
NEW AMERICAN LIBRARY
TIMES MIRROR

W. W. TARN

Sir William Woodthorpe Tarn is a Fellow of the British Academy and Honorary Fellow of Trinity College, Cambridge. Among his other books are *Hellenistic Military and Naval Developments*, *Alexander the Great*, and the monumental *The Greeks in Bactria and India*. *Hellenistic Civilisation* was first published in 1927; a revised edition appeared three years later. The present thoroughly revised edition was first issued in 1952.

Reprinted by arrangement with St. Martin's Press, Inc.

MERIDIAN TRADEMARK REG. U.S. PAT. OFF. AND FOREIGN COUNTRIES
REGISTERED TRADEMARK—MARCA REGISTRADA
HECHO EN FORGE VILLAGE, MASS., U.S.A.

SIGNET, SIGNET CLASSICS, MENTOR, PLUME, MERIDIAN and NAL BOOKS *are published by The New American Library, Inc., 1633 Broadway, New York, New York 10019*

FIRST PRINTING/WORLD PUBLISHING COMPANY, JULY, 1961
FIRST PRINTING/NEW AMERICAN LIBRARY, JANUARY, 1975

4 5 6 7 8 9 10 11

PRINTED IN THE UNITED STATES OF AMERICA

PREFACE TO THE THIRD EDITION

WHEN this book was first published in 1927 I called it 'an attempt to get a general picture of the civilisation of the Hellenistic period', a period which at that time had been much neglected by British scholars. Even in 1927, to get the work into any reasonable compass, I had to omit the Greeks in the West (Italy and Sicily) and those in the Farther East (Bactria and India); the limits taken were, in time, the conventional ones of 323 B.C. (death of Alexander) to 30 B.C. (Augustus), and, in place, the world between the Adriatic and the Persian desert, including Egypt. A second edition, with notes and a few additions, was published in 1930, and has been running ever since. Meanwhile, apart from new discoveries, there has been a vast outpouring, in many languages, of special studies and monographs concerned with this period; and while a third edition, revised, of this book had become overdue but was prevented by the war, the attempt to get a general picture in a reasonable compass, which remains the object of the book, has become more and more difficult. Of longer comprehensive works now available in English I might mention Professor M. Cary's *History of the Greek World from 323 to 146 B.C.* (1932); the relevant chapters in the *Cambridge Ancient History*, vols. VI–X, which cover the whole ground except the Farther East; and Professor M. Rostovtzeff's magnificient *Social and Economic History of the Hellenistic World* (3 vols., 1941), exhaustive for the subjects of which it treats.

In this new edition of *Hellenistic Civilisation*, while much has been revised, added to, recast, or rewritten in the attempt to get it more nearly up to date, there is also a good deal which has not been altered; it is a new edition, and in no sense a new book. As circumstances had made it impossible for me to do a new edition alone, I was fortunate in securing the co-operation of Mr. G. T. Griffith, who has indeed pulled the labouring oar throughout and taken a quite undue share of the work off my shoulders, for which I am most grateful.

Generally speaking, we share the responsibility for statements made in the book, but there are exceptions: Mr. Griffith disagrees with the view expressed on page 49 on the highly controversial question of the motive for Alexander's deification in his lifetime, and prefers to suspend judgment on the question of Alexander's conception of a human brotherhood (page 79). Again, the book as I wrote it in 1927 was a very personal affair, and I used the first person singular rather freely; after due consideration we decided that this must remain as it was, or we should be stating as facts what was only my personal interpretation of facts, or maybe of conjectures; and for my personal interpretations my collaborator is naturally not responsible. Most of the scholars to whom I expressed my indebtedness in 1927 are dead; but we should like to thank Professor A. D. Nock of Harvard for his kind help on certain points in the revised section on Religion. We desire to thank Messrs. Edward Arnold and Co. both for undertaking to publish this new edition and for having kept the 1930 edition alive by successive reprints; and in particular we desire to thank Mr. B. W. Fagan for the interest and help which he has accorded to the preparation of this edition, and especially in connection with the maps, which are a new feature.

W. W. Tarn

Muirtown House, Inverness
Midsummer, 1951

CONTENTS

MAPS

LIST OF ABBREVIATIONS

Abbreviations for titles of periodicals, or of publications of inscriptions or papyri, are included in this list only when they differ materially from, or do not appear among, those listed in Liddell and Scott, *Greek-English Lexicon*, ed. 9.

Archiv	Archiv für Papyrusforschung.
Arnim, *S.V.F.*	H. von Arnim, Stoicorum veterum fragmenta.
C.A.H.	Cambridge Ancient History.
C. d'É.	Chronique d'Égypte.
Ditt.[3]	W. Dittenberger, Sylloge Inscriptionum Graecorum, ed. 3.
F.H.G.	C. Müller, Fragmenta Historicorum Graecorum.
F. Gr. Hist.	F. Jacoby, Die Fragmente der griechischen Historiker.
G.G.A.	Göttingische Gelehrte Anzeigen.
G.G.M.	C. Müller, Geographici Graeci Minores.
Heichelheim, *Wirtschaftsgesch.*	F. Heichelheim, Wirtschaftsgeschichte des Altertums.
J.D.A.I.	Jahrbuch des deutschen archäologischen Instituts.
Mitteis, *Chrest.*	See Wilcken.
P.W.	Pauly-Wissowa-Kroll, Real. Encyclopädie der classischen Altertumswissenschaft.
Préaux, *Écon. royale*	C. Préaux, L'économie royale des Lagides.
Rostovtzeff, *Kolonat.*	M. Rostovtzeff, Studien zur Geschichte des römischen Kolonates.
Rostovtzeff, *Large estate*	M. Rostovtzeff, A large estate in Egypt in the third century B.C.
Rostovtzeff, *SEH*	M. Rostovtzeff, Social and economic history of the Hellenistic World.
Schubart, *Einführung*	W. Schubart, Einführung in die Papyruskunde.
SGDI	H. Collitz, Sammlung der griechischen Dialekt-Inschriften.
S.V.F.	See Arnim.
Tarn, *Alexander.*	W. W. Tarn, Alexander the Great, I Narrative, II Sources and Studies.
Tarn, *Ant. Gon.*	W. W. Tarn, Antigonos Gonatas.
Tarn, *Bactria.*	W. W. Tarn, The Greeks in Bactria and India.
Wilcken, *Grundzüge,* and Wilcken, *Chrest.*	L. Mitteis and U. Wilcken, Grundzüge und Chrestomathie der Papyruskunde.

CHAPTER I

HISTORICAL OUTLINE

THIS book aims at giving, in brief outline, a sketch of the civilisation of the three Hellenistic centuries, from the death of Alexander in 323 to the establishment of the Roman empire by Augustus in 30 B.C.[1] These limits are of course conventional, for the germs of certain phenomena of Hellenism begin to appear before Alexander, and in some respects Augustus represents no real break. But they do serve to emphasise two facts: the creative impulses evoked by Alexander's career forbade anything ever to be quite the same again as before, and, after the Hellenistic world had finally gone down in the ruin of the Roman civil wars, with the Empire it began to be built up afresh on different lines; civilisation became Graeco-Roman. Throughout this book Rome and Roman history are taken for granted, and we are concerned simply to see what Hellenism was and what kind of world the Roman Republic found when it came eastward. Unlike the Empire, that Republic, in its contact with Hellenistic civilisation, was purely receptive; the Greece that taught Rome was not the older Greece but contemporary Hellenism, and so far as modern civilisation is based on Greek it is primarily on Hellenism that it is based.

What now does Hellenism[2] mean? To one, it means a new culture compounded of Greek and Oriental elements; to another, the extension of Greek culture to Orientals; to another, the continuation of the pure line of the older Greek civilisation; to yet another, that same civilisation modified

[1] All dates and centuries throughout the book are B.C. unless otherwise stated.

[2] 'Hellenism', though incorrect in form, has long done duty as the substantive of Hellenistic, Hellenisticism being an impossible word in any language. It is too late to coin another.

by new conditions.[1] All these theories contain a truth, but none represents the whole truth; and all are unworkable the moment one comes down to details, such (for example) as that Hellenistic mathematics were purely Greek, while the sister-science, astronomy, was Graeco-Babylonian. To get a true picture we must look at all the phenomena, and Hellenism is merely a convenient label for the civilisation of the three centuries during which Greek culture radiated far from the homeland[2]; no general definition will cover it all. Moreover, in some respects, these three centuries represent, not one phase of civilisation, but two: the earlier phase creative in science, philosophy, literature, political state-forms, and much else, with an independent Graeco-Macedonian world extending its civilisation to Asia; the later phase distinguished by the exhaustion of the creative impulse and the reaction, both spiritual and material, of the East against the West, while the Graeco-Macedonian world is caught between that reaction and Rome, until Rome, having destroyed the Hellenistic state-system, is ultimately compelled to take its place as the standard-bearer of Greek culture. The two phases cannot always be definitely separated; but the lines of the evolution of any particular matter are easier to understand if the above broad distinction be kept in mind. There are, however, many respects in which the Hellenistic period does form a connected whole, and as such we may for a moment glance at it.

The world of Hellenism was a changed and enlarged world. Though the particularism of the Greek city-state was to remain vigorous enough in fact, it had broken down in theory; it was being replaced by universalism and its corollary, individualism. The idea emerges of an *oecumene* or 'inhabited world' as a whole, the common possession of civilised men; and for its use there grows up the form of Greek known as the *koine*, the 'common speech', which was

[1] R. Laqueur, *Hellenismus*, 1925; see Berve, *Phil. Woch.* 1926, 329; Jüthner, *G.G.A.* 1926, 76; Schubart, *N. J. Kl. Alt.* 1926, 633.

[2] One school would include under Hellenism the contemporary civilisation of the Roman Republic. It is not so included in this book; but I am not expressing an opinion on that view.

also used by many Asiatics; Greek might take a man from Marseilles to India, from the Caspian to the Cataracts. Nationality falls into the background; common speech and education promote a common culture in every city of the 'inhabited world'; literature, learning, above all philosophy, do to some extent envisage a larger world than Greece, and the upper classes in Rome and parts of Asia come to feel that Greek culture is a thing a man must have, at least in externals. Commerce is internationalised. Most of the barriers are down: thought is free as it was not to be again till modern times; race hatred is a thing of the past, except perhaps among some native Egyptians and some Jews; religious persecution on religious grounds is unknown (for Antiochus' attack upon the Jews was a political measure); morality is a matter for science, not for authority. The personality of the individual has free scope. It is an age of specialists, from the scientific worker to the carpenter who makes a door but requires another man to hang it; when Poseidonius tries for the last time to take all learning for his province, as Aristotle had done, his superficiality in certain fields is apparent. And even the creative third century differs from its forerunners in this, that, though the Greek spirit was still of supreme importance, it can no longer be said that every fruitful idea was Greek; for, quite apart from religion and astronomy, the single greatest creation of the age, the Stoic philosophy, originated with one who, whether he had some Greek blood or not, was certainly to his contemporaries a Phoenician.

The resemblance of this world to our own is at first sight almost startling. There was the same complex of states, big and little, with different state-forms, some more advanced than others, working within the bounds of a common civilisation; and, beside some of the phenomena noticed above, there were many others which look very modern. Such are the eternal trouble of prices and wages; Socialism and Communism, the strike and the revolution; the growth of ideas of humanity and brotherhood combined with savage quarrelling; the emancipation of woman and the restriction of population; questions of franchise and (possibly) representation, of emigration and the proletariat; exact learning and crass superstition side by side; a vast literature dealing with every sphere of human activity, often competent, but no longer producing writers equal to the great names of the past; the spread of education, resulting in the manufacture of masses of the half-educated; the more conscious emergence of propaganda; the growth of all the half-worlds that cling to the skirts of science, of history, and of religion. I am not much concerned to draw parallels with the modern world, and have usually left this to the reader. But such parallels must not be drawn too far. Though many things had a certain likeness to the things of to-day, they were seldom the *same*; for example, there is little resemblance between an Egyptian and a modern strike, or between modern and Stoic Communism. And underlying everything were two radical and crucial differences: it was a world empty of machines and full of slaves. This last fact cannot be over-emphasised. To see Hellenistic society as it existed, the slave background must never be lost sight of; and such aspirations as freedom and brotherhood—even the very revolutions—too often convey a sense of unreality when it is remembered that a large part of the population was, by most people, excepted from their scope.

The Hellenistic period has often been treated as one of decline, even of decay; but probably few would now care to argue that this was true of the third century. Such terms can only apply, if at all, to what I have called the later phase; and even then it must, I think, largely depend on the point of view. For example, if physical science, or art, be all-important, then the later phase was one of decline; but if the emergence of certain religious instincts and feelings, such as might pave the way for something greater, be at least equally material, then it was one of growth. What we *do* seem to see in the later phase is a mass of contradictions; for example, which really represents the late second century, the slave-market at Delos or the manumissions at Delphi? Are we to argue from the peripatetic magician, or from the

Stoic who believed that virtue was its own reward? I myself venture to entertain considerable doubts whether the true Greek, the racial aristocracy of the Aegean, really degenerated. This is not the more usual view; but I have given the facts as they appear to me, and they should enable the reader to form his own conclusions. Much too which at first sight looks like decline can be accounted for by two general considerations. One is the steady diminution in the numbers of the true Greek after *c.* 200, combined with the intrusion, or admixture, of alien stocks, which, whatever their latent capabilities, often had not at the time the intellectual, political, or social energy of the Greek. The other is the behaviour of the Roman Republic, which tended to break the Greek spirit and probably ended by convincing many people beside the kings of Syria and Egypt that efforts doomed beforehand to be fruitless were not worth while. Mere subjection by greatly superior force, by whomsoever wielded, naturally has no bearing on the question; it is not the business of history to cheer for the big battalions.

One remark needs making here about the literary sources. More important than their fragmentary nature is the fact that they are so often hostile to what they are describing (Plutarch is an exception); even Polybius has small claims to impartiality. To copy out party propaganda, such as is represented by (say) Pausanias on the end of the Achaean League or Justin on Ptolemy Euergetes II, and call it history, is merely misleading; we are still some way from a proper answer to the question: What is much of the tradition *worth*? There are plenty of figures and events in this period which, I imagine, we do not see at all; we see only a literary smoke-screen. But we have one steadily increasing source which can be trusted, the contemporary inscriptions and papyri; and the smoke does gradually tend to clear.

* * * * *

Alexander's empire at his death embraced Macedonia Egypt, and most of Asia south of the Caucasus-Caspian line from the Aegean to the Punjab, except Arabia, Armenia, and northern Asia Minor: most of the Greek cities of Asia, except those on the Black Sea, were his free allies,[1] while his relations with those of old Greece were regulated by the League of Corinth. He left no heir, and had made no arrangements for carrying on the government. Once the uprisings of Greece in the Lamian war and of the Greeks in the far east were defeated, a struggle for power started among his generals, in the shape of war between the satraps (territorial dynasts) and whatever central power aimed at general control; the battle of Ipsus in 301 definitely decided that the Graeco-Macedonian world could not be held together, and that world presently returned very much to the political shape it had before Alexander, though under different rulers and a different civilisation. By 275 three dynasties, descended from three of his generals, were well established; the Seleucids ruled much of what had been the Persian empire in Asia, the Ptolemies ruled Egypt, and the Antigonids Macedonia. A fourth European dynasty, not connected with Alexander, the Attalids of Pergamum, subsequently grew up in Asia Minor at Seleucid expense, and became great by favour of Rome. In 212 Rome began to take part, at first tentatively, in Hellenistic affairs, and ultimately absorbed the whole Mediterranean world, the last independent state, Egypt, coming to an end in 30 B.C.

The complicated story of the struggle among the generals down to 301, largely waged with mercenaries of every nationality, can only be briefly indicated. The arrangements made by the army after Alexander's death vested the kingship jointly in his idiot half-brother Philip III and his posthumous son by Roxane, Alexander IV: his general Perdiccas had the effective control in Asia, and Antipater in Europe, where he had been governing Macedonia and supervising Greece for Alexander. Various satrapies were allotted afresh among the generals; in the division Ptolemy, a wise and far-seeing man, secured Egypt, Antigonus the One-eyed, satrap of Phrygia, obtained further territory, and Lysimachus received Thrace. War broke out in 321 with a

[1] Tarn, *Alexander* II, App. 7.

combination of Antipater, Antigonus, and Ptolemy against Perdiccas, who professedly stood for the kings but was accused of aiming at the throne; he was ultimately murdered, and the united Macedonian armies made Antipater regent. He was the last of the generals of Philip II, and the universal respect felt for him enabled him to hold the empire together till his death in 319; during this time Antigonus, who, as his general, commanded a large force, crushed Perdiccas' party till only one leader survived, the Greek Eumenes of Cardia, Alexander's secretary. On Antipater's death Polyperchon was locally elected regent in Macedonia; Antigonus began to work for his own hand, and Eumenes joined Polyperchon to uphold the kings. War blazed up again; in Asia the protagonists were Eumenes and Antigonus, who was supported by Ptolemy and others; in Europe, Polyperchon and Antipater's son Cassander, who was Antigonus' ally. The war in Europe ended in 316 with the complete success of Cassander, a man of remarkable ability, who became master of Macedonia and much of Greece, including Athens; Philip III and Alexander's mother Olympias perished in the struggle, and Cassander obtained possession of the young Alexander IV. The fight made under great difficulties by Eumenes, resourceful and absolutely loyal, is one of the romances of history; he captured Babylon, secured the help of the far eastern satraps, and defeated Antigonus more than once, but early in 316 he was betrayed to Antigonus by his own troops and put to death. With his death the cause of Alexander IV was definitely lost.

Antigonus, a man of enormous capacity and unlimited ambition, now held the strongest position of any of the generals, and claimed to stand in Alexander's place; he began by striking down the eastern satraps, and Seleucus, satrap of Babylon, only saved his life by escaping to Ptolemy. The smaller men were by now largely eliminated, and the principal rulers—Cassander, Ptolemy and Lysimachus—formed a coalition against Antigonus, on the ground, which was true, that he was aiming at the empire; but the war (315–311) was indeterminate, though in 312 Ptolemy restored

Dardania
PAEONIA
ILLYRIA
Dyrrhacium
R. Strymon
R. Axius
MACEDONIA
Amphipolis
Pella
Thessalonica
Chalcidice
R. Haliacmon
Pydna
Cassandreia
Dium
Mt. Olympus
EPIRUS
Phoenice
Tempe
Magnesia
Corcyra
R. Peneus
Larisa
Dodona
Pindus Mts.
THESSALY
Cynoscephalae
Demetrias-Pagasae
Pharsalus
C. Sepias
Ambracia
R. Achelous
Phthiotic Thebes
Actium
ACARNANIA
Thermopylae
Histiaea
Heracleia
EUBOEA
AETOLIA
Thermum
Elatea
PHOCIS
Delphi
Chalcis
Ithaca
LOCRIS
L. Copais
Eretria
Naupactus
Chaeronea
BOEOTIA
Patrae
Aigion
Thespiae
Thebes
Oropus
Cephallenia
ACHAIA
Dyme
Eleusis
Cynaetha
Pellene
Megara
Sicyon
Athens
ELIS
Corinth
Aegina
Piraeus
Zacynthos
Olympia
ARGOLIS
Epidaurus
Mantinea
Argos
Methana
R. Alpheus
ARCADIA
Tegea
Troezen
Phigaleia
Megalopolis
Messene
Sellasia
MESSENIA
Mt. Taygetus
Sparta
LACONIA
R. Eurotas
Gythion
Melos
C. Malea
Cythera
Cydonia
English Miles
0 10 20 40 60 80 100
42
40
38
36
20
22
24
24 East
A.C.

GREECE, THE

ESTERN ASIA MINOR

Seleucus to Babylon. Antigonus however in 314 secured the moral support of the Greek democracies by a proclamation, which for years he carried out honestly, that all Greek cities should be free, ungarrisoned, and self-governing; it was a revival of Alexander's policy, directed against Cassander's system of governing the cities through oligarchies and garrisons (Chap. II). One result was that Delos revolted from Athens, and remained free till 166. After the peace of 311 between Antigonus and the coalition, which left Antigonus master of Syria, Asia Minor, and Mesopotamia, he attempted to crush Seleucus, but failed, though he half-ruined Babylon, and Seleucus subsequently secured everything east of Babylon, though he had to cede the Indian provinces to the Mauryan Chandragupta; in return he obtained a large force of war elephants.[1] In 310 Cassander murdered Alexander IV, a step which the other dynasts had invited by the terms of the treaty of 311; and all now became independent rulers.

In 307 Antigonus and his brilliant son Demetrius, a man of great and varied talents but unstable character, began a second struggle to secure the whole empire, a struggle which ultimately involved the entire military strength of every part of the Hellenistic world. Since 317 Cassander had governed Athens through Demetrius of Phalerum, a Peripatetic; the city had had peace and prosperity, and Demetrius had made laws in Aristotle's spirit, but his government had favoured the well-to-do. In 307 Antigonus' son Demetrius freed Athens and restored democratic government, and in 306 utterly defeated Ptolemy in a naval battle off Salamis in Cyprus and secured the command of the sea; his father and he, who trusted each other absolutely, thereon each took the title of king, as joint-monarchs of Alexander's empire. But Antigonus' attempt to invade Egypt and destroy Ptolemy failed, and in 305 Ptolemy and the other dynasts also took the royal title, as kings in their separate territories; and a year wasted by Demetrius over his famous and unsuccessful siege of Rhodes enabled Cassander

[1] Tarn, *J.H.S.* LX, 1940, 84 on the origin of the legendary number 500.

to begin reconquering Greece. Demetrius drove Cassander off, freed most of Greece, and in 303 re-formed Alexander's League of Corinth with his father and himself as Presidents in Alexander's seat. Cassander, Lysimachus, and Ptolemy then secured Seleucus' help, and in 302, while Demetrius moved on Macedonia with a great force, Lysimachus, with reinforcements sent by Cassander, crossed to Asia. Antigonus, who failed to crush him, had to recall Demetrius, and in 301, at Ipsus in Phrygia, the two gave battle to the combined forces of Lysimachus and Seleucus, who had most of his elephants in action; Antigonus was defeated and killed, but Demetrius escaped.

The victors divided the spoils, Lysimachus taking Asia Minor north of Taurus and Seleucus Mesopotamia and Syria; Ptolemy however had occupied Syria south of Aradus and of Damascus during the Ipsus campaign, and Seleucus, who never forgot that he owed to Ptolemy both life and kingdom, did not demand its retrocession, though he preserved his claim. Cassander, the soul of the coalition, was content with Macedonia; Demetrius still ruled the sea, and held Tyre and Sidon, some cities in Asia Minor, and parts of Greece. The mutual distrust of the victors was of advantage to Athens, still the greatest of Greek cities except Syracuse, and Cassander's forbearance left her her liberty till Demetrius conquered and garrisoned her in 295. Cassander died in 298,[1] and quarrels between his sons enabled Demetrius in 294 to seize the throne of Macedonia, a throne he held for six years, during which he reduced most of Greece except Sparta, Aetolia, and Pyrrhus king of Epirus, and built his name-city Demetrias (p. 68). The position of the parties in the Greek cities meanwhile clarified, and henceforth, while the democracies usually stood for national independence, the wealthy looked to Macedonia for support, as later they were to look to Rome. Demetrius, however, though he could conquer, could not govern; he compared badly with the statesmanlike Cassander, and never secured his people's affection, for he treated Macedonia merely as a

[1] W. S. Ferguson, *C.P.* 1929, 1, on *P. Oxy.* 2082.

base for the reconquest of Asia. In 289 his naval preparations alarmed the other kings, and they combined against him; in 288 Lysimachus and Pyrrhus overran and partitioned Macedonia, Athens revolted with Ptolemy's aid, and Demetrius was again reduced to some Greek cities and his fleet. Nevertheless he invaded Asia, flung himself without much success against Lysimachus, his bitter personal enemy, and finally, driven over the Taurus, became engaged in a heroic struggle with Seleucus. At one moment it looked as if he would yet rule Asia; but he fell ill, his army deserted, and in 285 he was forced to surrender. Two years later the most brilliant of Alexander's successors had drunk himself to death in his captivity.

On Demetrius' fall part of his fleet went over to Ptolemy, who with it secured Tyre and Sidon, the Island League (p. 70), and the command of the sea. But Lysimachus, who in 285 expelled Pyrrhus from his half of Macedonia, gained most; master of Macedonia, Thessaly, Thrace, and much of Asia Minor, he was now really stronger than Seleucus. He was a cautious statesman and an excellent general and financier; though he ruled his Greek cities after Cassander's fashion he was not always unpopular, and he fostered trade, particularly in the Black Sea, which possibly he hoped to make his lake. His capital was at first his new city Lysimacheia, near Gallipoli; later he probably transferred his seat to Macedonia. Demetrius' last campaign had revealed a growing distrust between Lysimachus and Seleucus which foreshadowed a contest for the lordship of Asia, and in 283 Seleucus made overtures to Antigonus Gonatas, Demetrius' son by Antipater's daughter Phila, who was ruling his father's Greek cities.

Ptolemy's house played its part in Lysimachus' ultimate fall. Ptolemy had married Antipater's daughter Eurydice, and her long struggle with her maid-of-honour Berenice, who was Ptolemy's mistress, had ended before 287 in Ptolemy repudiating Eurydice and marrying Berenice. Eurydice's son Ptolemy, afterwards called Keraunos, the Thunderbolt, was exiled, and when in 283 Ptolemy died—the only

Successor who died in his bed—his son by Berenice succeeded peacefully as Ptolemy II. Keraunos went to Lysimachus, who had married as his third wife Ptolemy II's sister Arsinoe, Berenice's daughter; and round him centred the obscure intrigues which ended in Lysimachus murdering his eldest son Agathocles, and driving all discontented elements in his kingdom into Seleucus' arms. Seleucus ultimately crossed the Taurus, defeated and killed Lysimachus in 281 at Corupedion in Lydia, and for a moment, last and most fortunate of Alexander's companions, saw all Alexander's empire except Egypt at his feet. But early in 280 he was assassinated by Keraunos, whom Lysimachus' army accepted as Lysimachus' avenger and made king of Macedonia. Keraunos managed to hold his kingdom against his numerous rivals, defeating Antigonus Gonatas at sea, winning over Pyrrhus by help for his Italian expedition, and getting rid of Arsinoe, who held Cassandreia, by first marrying and then expelling her. Antiochus I, Seleucus' son by his Sogdian wife Apama, was fully involved at home: Ptolemy II, who had a footing in Caria, was threatening him, Northern Syria was in revolt, and he was cut off from Europe and the Black Sea by the Northern League, a combination of Heraclea, Byzantium, Chalcedon, Cius, Tios, the Persian prince Mithridates of Pontus, and Nicomedes of Bithynia, who were fighting for their independence. He was also attacked by Antigonus from Greece.

This was the situation when the migrating Galati, Gallic tribes who had followed the Danube valley, reached the Macedonian frontier, bringing their families with them. Early in 279 a body under Bolgius burst into Macedonia and defeated and killed Keraunos, but subsequently retired with their plunder; but a second body under Brennus had entered the country and, failing to establish themselves, passed southward late in the year to invade Greece. Brennus, who cannot have had over 30,000 fighting men, successfully turned the defenders of Thermopylae, but failed in an attempt to raid Delphi with a flying column, while his main force was checked and then driven north with heavy loss by the Aetolians, who acquired a well-deserved reputation as the saviours of Greece. The danger to Greece induced Antigonus and Antiochus to make a real peace, and their treaty (autumn 279)[1] remained for long a cardinal point of Hellenistic politics; it bound Antiochus not to interfere in Macedonia and Greece, or Antigonus in Thrace and Asia; and for long the two dynasties remained friends. In 278 three tribes of Gauls, the Tolistoagii, Trocmi, and Tectosages, 20,000 strong, reached the Dardanelles, and were taken into service by Nicomedes and Mithridates to attack Antiochus; they ravaged Asia Minor for two years and created a panic, but in 275 Antiochus, having settled Syria, gave the country some rest by defeating the Gauls with the aid of 16 elephants sent by his general in Bactria. Nicomedes and Mithridates then settled the Gauls in northern Phrygia (Galatia) as a buffer against him. Meanwhile another body had invaded Thrace; in 277 part of these reached the sea and were destroyed in battle near Lysimacheia by Antigonus. With the prestige of this victory Antigonus entered Macedonia, which was in anarchy, was accepted as king, and by the end of 276 was master of the kingdom and married Antiochus' half-sister Phila. Apart from Galatia, the Gauls managed to found two kingdoms which affected Greek history, that of the Scordisci in Serbia and that called Tylis in Thrace.

In the two generations that had passed since Alexander's invasion of Asia the Macedonian and Greek peoples themselves, responding to the political and military needs of the dynasts, had been widely redistributed over the area which was to form the Hellenistic world. These kingdoms were not won and lost without soldiers, and though men of all races were employed, it was natural that both the military prestige and the political maturity of Greeks and Macedonians should have been in the highest demand. There is no point in guessing at the number of men who left their homes in Europe and in the end settled permanently in Asia or Egypt to form the nucleus of a Seleucid or Ptolemaic

[1] On the date see now M. Launey, *Rev. ét anc.* XLVI, 1944, 228.

regular army.[1] Still less can we guess at the numbers of these who sent for wives or relatives from the home country. But it is certain that many of even the first generation of *epigonoi* in the new settlements must have had Asiatic mothers. Though the Wars of the Successors, with their swift changes of fortune, give the impression of creating chaos and peril for all who took an active part in them, in practice the veterans of Alexander's wars, and no doubt others, soon became professional adventurers who took things coolly, and did not hesitate to take their families and goods about with them on the greatest campaigns.[2] Isocrates had written of the soldier population of Greece (soldiers because otherwise unemployed) who could be used to colonise Asia Minor[3]: and the resettlement by Timoleon of Syracuse and other cities of Sicily had proved already before Alexander that there were in reality (and not only in the arguments of an orator) thousands of Greeks who were ready to fare far afield to get a new start in life. This was their great chance. These Greeks and Macedonians settled abroad continued from generation to generation to act mainly as soldiers and administrators, with an importance to their rulers out of all proportion to their numbers, comparatively numerous though they may have been. They were the ruling race, not as a result of any theory or prejudice, but because their qualities suited the needs of the kings themselves.

From 275 we can follow the history of the three Macedonian dynasties as separate units; Lysimachus' kingdom never revived, and in the Black Sea he had no successor. Of the new kings, Antiochus I was a great city-builder and administrator whose history is lost. Tradition makes Ptolemy II a valetudinarian and dilettante; he was really, though no general, a strong ruler of aggressive ambition, highly educated, an able diplomatist and skilled organiser. Antigonus, the second founder of Macedonia, was a blunt

[1] M. Launey, *Recherches sur les armées hellénistiques*, I, 1949, 6 ff. How far the reduced citizen population of Athens can be explained by this cause can only be conjectured: cf. A. W. Gomme, *Population of Athens*, 1933, 19.

[2] Rostovtzeff, *SEH* 143, gives a good picture of the armies of this period.

[3] Isoc. V, 120; cf. *ib.* 96; IV, 168; VIII, 24, &c.

straightforward character, of dogged tenacity and with the full family loyalty of his house; friend and pupil of the philosophers Menedemus and Zeno, his Stoic sympathies made him the first king whom philosophy could claim as her own. Egypt's foreign policy, which aimed at the empire of the Aegean and its coasts, and her great strength, were bound to bring her into conflict with the other two kingdoms, while the Seleucids could not forget their claim to southern Syria, which Egypt held. This province, important economically for its products and for the trade which passed through its cities, was even more important strategically to both the great ruling houses, if they had cause to mistrust each other. The result was the long series of the so-called Syrian Wars between Egypt and the Seleucids, conjoined with wars between Egypt and Macedonia. These wars helped to prevent Greek civilisation establishing itself as firmly in Asia as it might otherwise have done.

It was Ptolemy II who began the long struggle; probably he became aggressive as soon as Seleucus was dead, for Miletus, Seleucid in 280, was Egyptian in 279. This obscure war[1] was followed by the one called the first Syrian, when in 276 his army invaded Seleucid Syria, but was defeated and driven out by Antiochus I, who then allied himself with Magas, Ptolemy II's half-brother who governed Cyrene. In winter 276–5, however, Ptolemy repudiated his wife (Lysimachus' daughter Arsinoe I) and married his full sister Arsinoe II, widow of Lysimachus and Keraunos, probably because he needed her brains. Arsinoe took the lost war into her strong hands, turned it into a sweeping success, and ended (273 or 272) in possession of all Phoenicia and most of the coast of Asia Minor from Miletus to the Calycadnus in Cilicia; she was to receive unexampled honours both as woman and goddess. The years till her death in 270 were Egypt's golden age, and Callimachus prophesied that Ptolemy would rule the world from the rising to the

[1] W. Otto, *Beiträge zur Seleukidengeschichte* 1928, ch. I; Tarn, *J.H.S.* XLVI, 1926, 155; *Hermes* LXV, 1930, 446; *J.H.S.* LIII, 1933, 62 n.50; Otto, *Philol.* LXXXVI, 1931, 400.

setting sun.[1] Arsinoe wished to make Ptolemaeus, her son by Lysimachus, king of Macedonia, but she died too soon; she had, however, prevented Antigonus interfering in the war by subsidising Pyrrhus, who had returned from Italy and desired to attack him. In 273 Pyrrhus momentarily conquered Macedonia, but quitted it for adventures in Greece; he tried and failed to take Sparta, and was finally killed (272) in street fighting at Argos, leaving Antigonus arbiter of Greece.

Antigonus showed moderation. His position in Greece depended on holding Corinth, which prevented Greece uniting against him (for a united Greece would have been stronger than Macedonia), and Piraeus, which ensured that Athens should informally be his spiritual capital; he conquered enough to ensure their communications with Demetrias, but sought no further possessions in Greece (p. 65). In 267, however, Athens, Sparta, and other cities, encouraged by Ptolemy, allied themselves with Egypt to attack him; this severe struggle (266–262), called the Chremonidean War from the Athenian statesman Chremonides, ended in Antigonus' victory and the capture of Athens, which henceforth ceased to play any prominent part in politics. The leading men of Antigonus' party also seized power as tyrants in Argos, Megalopolis, and other Peloponnesian cities, and acted in his interest and with his support as a check on Sparta. Antigonus, a good ruler, subsequently restored Macedonia to its fullest boundaries and gave his dynasty a position in the country which nothing could shake. In 262 Antiochus I died, after losing Ephesus to Egypt.

His son Antiochus II and Antigonus, probably in alliance, took their revenge on Ptolemy II in the Second Syrian War (259–255)[2]; Antiochus recovered Ephesus, Miletus, much of the coast of Asia Minor, and Phoenicia down to Berytus, while Antigonus defeated Ptolemy's fleet off Cos and secured the Island League and command of the sea; for a time his half-brother Demetrius the Fair ruled Cyrene. But

[1] *Hymn to Delos*, 166 *sqq.*

[2] 255, not 253, as Otto *op. c.* ch. II; reasons, *C.A.H.* VII, 714–15.

the revolt *c.* 252 of Alexander, his general in Corinth and Euboea, with Egypt's support, crippled him at sea, and he only recovered Corinth in 246 after Alexander's death; while Ptolemy in 253 won over Antiochus, who sent away his wife Laodice and married Ptolemy's daughter Berenice. On Antiochus' death (late 247) a struggle began between the rival queens; Berenice and her son were killed, but their deaths were concealed, and in 246 Ptolemy III (son of Arsinoe I), who in January had succeeded his father Ptolemy II, occupied northern Syria and Cilicia, made a military parade through the distracted kingdom professedly as champion of the rightful king, Berenice's son, and reached Seleuceia on the Tigris. He met little resistance, but he described his exploit as the subjection of Seleucid Asia. In the ensuing war, the Third Syrian or Laodicean (to 241), Laodice's son Seleucus II recovered Cilicia, northern Syria (inland), and the east, but failed to recover Seleuceia in Pieria and Phoenicia, and again lost the coast of Asia Minor, along which Ptolemy later extended his power and even occupied the coast of Thrace. Ptolemy's fleet, however, was defeated by Antigonus off Andros (246 or 245); Antigonus recovered Delos and some islands, and Egypt was never again supreme at sea, but apparently the Island League broke up. Subsequently the Seleucid empire was paralysed by civil war between Seleucus II and his brother Antiochus Hierax, who allied himself with the Galatians. Cappadocia had already become an independent native kingdom; and during this period Bactria, Parthia, and the provinces beyond Parthia were finally lost,[1] and the victorious Galatians again became a threat.

That threat brought Pergamum into prominence. A eunuch from Tios, Philetaerus, half a Paphlagonian, governor of the fortress of Pergamum, after betraying Antigonus I and Lysimachus in turn, had made himself semi-independent under Antiochus I, and on his death in 263 left a little principality on the Caïcus to his nephew Eumenes, who in

[1] See now E. J. Bikerman, 'Notes on Seleucid and Parthian chronology', in *Berytus* VIII, ii, 1944, 79.

241 again bequeathed it, considerably enlarged, to his nephew Attalus I. The eclipse of Seleucid power in Asia Minor gave Attalus his chance; he challenged the Galatians by refusing the tribute which they exacted even from the Seleucids as a condition of refraining from raids, broke them in two battles (before 230), took the royal title, and then drove Hierax out of Asia Minor and from 228 to 223 ruled the whole Seleucid territory north of Taurus. Seleucus II, who was trying to reconquer Parthia, died in 226 and his son Seleucus III in 223 without having been able to deal with him.

Meanwhile Greece had been witnessing the growth of the two great Leagues (Chap. II). Aetolia, already mistress of Delphi,[1] began to expand after 279; she promised Antigonus her neutrality and kept her promise, and as compensation began to include in her League the little Amphictyonic states; she apparently met with intermittent opposition from Phocis and Boeotia, but in 245 she broke Boeotia's power at Chaeronea, and that country never regained its former importance. The expansion of the League of the eleven Achaean cities began in 251, when a young Sicyonian exile named Aratus surprised Sicyon by night, expelled its tyrant, and for security joined Sicyon to the Achaean League. Aratus was a strange character, a compound of heroism and nervous weakness, unscrupulous, but with an amazing power over his fellow-citizens; for a generation he almost *was* the League, whose general he became every alternate year from 245 onwards. In 243 he embarked on the crusade which was his life's purpose, to free the Peloponnese from Antigonus and the tyrants he supported; he surprised Macedonia's key position, Corinth, by night in time of peace and captured Acrocorinthus. Antigonus died in 240–39 without recovering Corinth, and the two Leagues at once went to war with his son Demetrius II. Demetrius curtailed Aetolia's influence, but did not damage her badly; but the Achaeans won over city after city, including Megalopolis and Argos, whose tyrants laid down their power and became League officials.

[1] Cf. R. Flacelière, *Les Aitoliens à Delphes*, 1937.

In 229 Demetrius II died, after being severely defeated by Macedonia's northern neighbours the Dardanians, who invaded the country. Philip, his son by his second wife, the Epirote princess Phthia, was a child, and the army ultimately crowned Philip's guardian Antigonus Doson, son of Demetrius the Fair, an able ruler; he drove out the Dardanians and restored Macedonia. But the Leagues had seized their opportunity; in the confusion of 229 Aetolia was able to stretch from sea to sea (p. 72), and now regarded herself as Macedonia's equal, while Aratus expelled every trace of Macedonian influence from the Peloponnese. By 228 the Achaean League had reached its zenith; it comprised Achaea, Sicyon, Corinth, Megara, Aegina, Argos and the coastal cities, Megalopolis and most of Arcadia, *i.e.* practically all of the Peloponnese which Cassander and Demetrius I had ruled; it had none but willing citizens, and was completely independent, for its nominal alliance with the now inactive Ptolemy III did not shape its policy. These years mark the culmination of the federal movement; Doson did not meddle with the Peloponnese, and contented himself with obtaining Aetolia's neutrality. Athens also recovered her freedom on Demetrius' death; none interfered with her, and except for the one episode of Philip's attack she fought no more wars till 88; she was almost as it were neutralised by universal consent, for she was a brilliant University town and the cultural centre of Greece, whose honours were sought by many kings as the highest expression of civilised approbation.

But the Achaean League could neither conquer nor win over Sparta; on this rock it was ultimately to founder. The young king of Sparta, Cleomenes III, quarrelled with the League, enrolled mercenaries, and in 227, having thus secured the necessary force, carried through his revolution (p. 123), restored (as he thought) Lycurgus' Sparta, and enormously increased his country's strength. He then invaded Achaea, and his victory at Hekatombaion laid the League at his feet; city after city, including Corinth and Argos, seceded to him, for the common people everywhere thought he would carry out social revolution and give them the land. In reality he was intensely ambitious, and was aiming at the headship of Peloponnese; as a beginning he demanded the generalship of the League, which he would have made the kernel of a new confederacy. To save what remained of the League, Aratus, who was desperate, made the great betrayal[1]; having expelled the Macedonians from Peloponnese, he decided to bring them back. He asked Doson's help, which Doson gave in return for the cession of Corinth, henceforth again a Macedonian fortress. Doson re-formed the League of Corinth as a Hellenic League of Leagues (p. 69); but as it did not include the Aetolian League, Sparta, Athens, Elis, and Messenia, Greece was really split in half, though Doson's conception was statesmanlike. Cleomenes made a good fight, but was defeated by Doson at Sellasia (222) and fled to Egypt, where he died. Doson occupied Sparta, never before taken, undid the revolution, restored the old régime, and made Sparta Macedonia's ally. In 221 he died, a heavy loss to Macedonia; he had taken care to secure Philip's succession.

Polybius' history formally begins with the accession of new kings in all the kingdoms; in Syria Antiochus III, the younger son of Seleucus II (223); in Egypt Ptolemy IV Philopater (221); and Philip V in Macedonia. Ptolemy III had allowed his army to decay, and his son Ptolemy IV was an art-loving voluptuary, who left the government to his strong and unscrupulous minister Sosibius. Antiochus III, later called 'the Great', young, energetic, and sensible, found a shattered kingdom, which he set to work to restore; by 220 his cousin Achaeus had reconquered Seleucid Asia Minor from Attalus, and he himself had suppressed a revolt of his generals in Media and Persis; once master in his own house, he set out to wrest southern Syria from the inactive Philopator. But the Syrian fortresses delayed him, and Sosibius held him off by negotiations while he brought

[1] This, the usual view, seems sound. *Contra*: A. Ferrabino, *Il problema della unita nazionale nella Grecia*, I. *Arato di Sicione*, 1921; F. W. Walbank, *Aratos of Sicyon*, 1933, who make him an opportunist throughout.

generals from Greece and created an army; he, or Philopator, also took the dangerous step of enrolling 20,000 native Egyptians in the phalanx, no native having borne arms since Ptolemy I's experiment in 312. This war, the Fourth Syrian, ended with the battle of Raphia (22 June 217); Philopator left his pleasures to take command, and a hard-fought day was decided by his leadership and the bravery of the Egyptian phalanx. Philopator retained southern Syria and Phoenicia; but for his dynasty the victory was not all gain, since from it dates the resurgence of the native element in Egypt against the Greek.

In Macedonia the accession of Philip V, gifted and attractive, roused high hopes; the unbridled temper which was to mar his life only revealed itself later. The Aetolians under Scopas had broken loose on Doson's death, and in 220 their raids on other states brought on the so-called Social War (War of the Allies), in which they and their allies Sparta and Elis opposed Philip and his Hellenic League. Philip, who was watching the actions of Rome in Illyria, did not want war, but loyally defended his allies; he made one daring raid on Thermum, Aetolia's federal centre, which he sacked. The war, which produced no result, ended in 217 with the peace of Naupactus, the peace conference being notable for the appeal made by the Aetolian Agelaus for Hellenic unity in face of the 'cloud rising in the west', the ultimate victor in the war between Carthage and Rome. The popularity of Philip, the 'darling of Hellas', in 217 was so marked that for a moment he seemed to have a better chance of unifying Greece than any of his predecessors; but he threw the chance away, if chance it were, and Aratus' death in 214–13 removed his best counsellor, for Aratus seemingly had learnt through misfortune. In 215 Philip allied himself with Carthage and attempted to expel the Romans from Illyria; the result was that alliance of Rome and Aetolia (212) which ushered in the First Macedonian War. This was the Social War over again, with one great difference: Aetolia was aided by Roman and Pergamene squadrons, Attalus having joined Rome's alliance, while Philip's new allies, Carthage and Prusias I of Bithynia, gave him little help. The once powerful Macedonian fleet had decayed, and Philip was helpless at sea; all his activity could hardly counter enemies who struck where they would. His one gain was that Philopoemen of Megalopolis reformed the incompetent Achaean army. Philopoemen, a soldier and little more, had fought with distinction at Sellasia, but had then, with a curious lack of patriotism, gone to Crete as an adventurer; he returned in 210, and in 207 the new Achaean army under his lead defeated Machanidas, who had seized power at Sparta, and thus gained confidence. One other consequence the war had: the Greek world, accustomed to Macedonian warfare, which had grown relatively humane, saw with fear or anger how Romans treated a captured city. In 205 the inconclusive war ended with the general peace of Phoenice.

Debtor and creditor troubles at once broke out in Aetolia; Scopas tried to cancel debts, failed, and went to Ptolemy, to command his army. Sparta, left masterless by Machanidas' death, was seized by Nabis, a distant collateral of the royal house; the revolution he carried through (p. 123) again strengthened Sparta enormously, and he secured some sea-power by Cretan alliances. Whatever his misdeeds, he was very popular with large classes, and it is our loss that we only possess hostile notices. The decay of the Macedonian fleet had left the Aegean masterless, and by 200 Rhodes had seized the vacant position and created a new Island League under her own presidency.

Ptolemy IV died in (probably) 205,[1] leaving as heir a child, Ptolemy V Epiphanes; Polybius has left a wonderful picture of the rising in Alexandria which overthrew the hated minister Agathocles and gave the child new guardians. Philip and Antiochus, whose dynasties had both suffered much at Egypt's hands, at once started an attack upon Egypt's foreign possessions. Antiochus had a fixed purpose, the restoration of Seleucus' empire; after Raphia he had

[1] See, on the confused chronology of his death, and his son's accession, F. W. Walbank, *J.E.A.* XXII, 1936, 20; E. Bikerman, *C.d'É.* XXIX, 1940, 124.

recovered Asia Minor from his revolted cousin Achaeus, and had then made his famous eastern expedition. He had conquered part of Armenia, made Arsaces of Parthia tributary, defeated Euthydemus of Bactria, and penetrated the Paropamisadae; and he had shown statesmanship by leaving Euthydemus his throne as a necessary bulwark of civilisation against the nomads. He may now have claimed Cyprus and the Cyclades, but more important to him was southern Syria, for the original Seleucid claim to this country (p. 11) had never been abandoned; in 202 he invaded southern Syria (the Fifth Syrian War), defeated the Ptolemaic general Scopas in 200 at Panion near the source of the Jordan, and thus became master of the whole country (including Phoenicia), which his dynasty was to retain. Philip, having built a fleet, attacked the Straits in 202, took Lysimacheia, Chalcedon, and Cius, and destroyed Cius with a brutality displayed later at Abydos and Maroneia; he was trying Roman methods, and evoked general distrust, even hatred. In 201, secure to the northward, he turned south and seized Samos; but he had foolishly antagonised Rhodes by stirring up Crete against her, and the Rhodians, to whom he had promised to spare Cius, now combined with Egypt's friend Attalus against him. Their united fleets fought a hard but indecisive battle with him off Chios,[1] and though he subsequently managed to defeat the Rhodians alone at Lade, and conquered part of Caria, he never really recovered at sea from his losses at Chios.

The conquest of Carthage in 202 had freed Rome's hands, and in 200 Egypt, Rhodes, and Attalus appealed to her for help; it was not unnatural, but it gave Rome that position of arbiter in the Eastern Mediterranean which she was never again to quit. Rome had as yet no deliberate purpose of reducing the east, and so far her interventions had been provoked; but she had henceforth a consistent block of supporters—Egypt, Pergamum, Rhodes, and Athens. Athens desired peace only, Egypt self-preservation, Rhodes the

[1] Polybius' account, which makes Philip defeated, is a Rhodian version, contradicted by events. See Tarn, *J.R.S.* XXXI, 1941, 172.

freedom of the Greeks and of the sea; but Pergamum, to whom Seleucid power was a standing threat, was usually ready to egg Rome on. Macedonia, the Seleucids, and subsequently Aetolia, came to represent the more nationally-minded opposition to Rome's advance. Rome in 200 had no grievance against Philip, but seemingly she was afraid—afraid that Philip and Antiochus would conquer and control Egypt and its resources, and launch against Italy all Alexander's empire. It was a chimaera; the two kings profoundly distrusted each other, and Philip would never have allowed Antiochus to cross to Greece. Rome's plan, to meet the imagined danger, was to free Greece and make it her outpost against the kings; she declared war (the Second Macedonian) and sent a large army to Illyria. The Aetolians, Philip's consistent foes, joined her in 198, and Philip even made an enemy of peaceful Athens, who welcomed Attalus, and whose suburbs Philip cruelly ravaged. The Achaeans deserted him, and his other allies were of little account. He held out for two years; but Macedonia was becoming so exhausted that in 197 he could only raise 26,000 men by enrolling boys and greybeards, and was decisively defeated at Cynoscephalae in Thessaly by the proconsul T. Quinctius Flamininus and the Aetolians.

The Aetolians clamoured for Philip's destruction; but Flamininus refused. Philip had to give up his fleet, surrender the 'fetters of Greece'—Corinth, Chalcis, and Demetrias—withdraw altogether from Greece and Thessaly, give up his cities in Asia, which became free, and pay an indemnity; and he became Rome's ally. Rome paid for this alliance with Aetolia's scarcely-veiled hostility, for Aetolia did not obtain for her League all the cities she claimed. But Flamininus kept his theatrical master-stroke for the Isthmian games of 196, when to a great concourse his herald proclaimed that all Greeks formerly subject to Philip or members of the Hellenic League should be free. It resembled the proclamation of Antigonus I in 314; like Antigonus, Rome acted from political motives, not sentiment, and meant what she said—at the start. The enthusiasm in Greece was enormous, the subsequent disillusionment correspondingly bitter. Doson's Hellenic League was thus dissolved, and its constituent members, including the Achaean League, became Rome's allies, as did Acarnania; the synoecism of Demetrias (p. 68) was broken up, and the Magnesian cities again made autonomous and united in a League with Demetrias as federal centre; other new Leagues now formed were the Thessalian, Perrhaebian, and Euboean.

There remained Nabis. Philip had tried to win him during the war by giving him Argos; Nabis took Argos and concluded an alliance with Rome. The loss of Argos, however, made the inextinguishable hostility between Achaea and Sparta blaze up afresh; both were Rome's allies, but Flamininus declared for Achaea. He paid Nabis, who had raised 15,000 men, the compliment of calling up all Rome's Greek allies; he ultimately had 50,000 troops in Laconia. Nabis made a good fight, and when the Romans finally tried to storm Sparta (195) his general Pythagoras fired the threatened quarter and drove them out; but Nabis lost his nerve and made terms. He surrendered Argos and the coast, but kept Sparta; Flamininus neither 'freed' the city nor restored the Spartans exiled in the revolution. The reason of his forbearance was partly his desire to settle Greece before a successor could interfere, and partly Antiochus.

Antiochus, far from helping Philip, had used 197 to conquer the coast of Asia Minor from Cilicia to the Hellespont; he also annexed the acquisitions made by Attalus, who died that year, and left to Attalus' son, Eumenes II, only the original Pergamene territory; naturally Eumenes became and remained his bitter enemy. In 196 Antiochus crossed the Dardanelles and began to subdue the Thracian coast. Both Greeks and Romans exaggerated his strength; he had had a career of singular success, ruled an enormous territory, and represented to Rome the danger of the unknown. Roman envoys met him at Lysimacheia with a demand that he should evacuate Europe. Antiochus replied that he was only reoccupying Seleucus' possessions: he did not interfere with Italy, and Rome must not interfere with

Asia. For three years negotiations continued, with the same deadlock; Antiochus only wanted to be let alone, and Rome, her hands full in Spain, did not desire war. But two powers did desire war: Eumenes, who feared Antiochus, and Aetolia, who wanted vengeance upon Rome. The Roman armies had quitted Greece in 194; the country had suffered greatly, if merely from feeding such large forces, and the democracies were disillusioned, for it was the well-to-do who favoured Rome, as they had once favoured Macedonia, and everywhere Rome had brought them to power.

In 193–2 Antiochus married his daughter Cleopatra I to Ptolemy V, and secured Bithynia, Cappadocia, and Galatia as allies; but, though Rome in 193 sent him an ultimatum, he had made no real preparation for war when an Aetolian embassy arrived, described the feeling in Greece, begged him to cross, and promised him Philip and Nabis as allies. Hannibal, who had taken refuge with him when exiled from Carthage in 195, naturally urged him to attack Rome in Italy; but Antiochus, as was also natural from his own standpoint, was not inclined to convert the defence of Thrace into a life-and-death struggle, and favoured the Aetolian plan; his minister Menippus in turn made Aetolia absurd promises. Aetolia struck at once; she surprised and secured Demetrias, a sensational event, but failed to surprise Sparta. However, she killed Nabis, and Philopoemen seized the opportunity to force Sparta into the Achaean League; in 191 he also incorporated Elis and Messenia, and the League embraced all Peloponnese, but Sparta and Messenia were unwilling members and merely sources of weakness. Antiochus, once a sensible man, but deceived by Aetolia and Menippus, exercised no foresight; his army was not ready, but in 192 he crossed to Demetrias with 10,000 men, enough to provoke war but too few to wage it. The battle-cry was the liberation of Greece from the Romans; but the promised upheaval did not take place, and though Antiochus secured Euboea and part of Thessaly, both Philip and Achaea held to Rome, and in 191 a Roman army, co-operating with Philip, recovered Thessaly and destroyed Antiochus' force at the usual death-trap, Thermopylae, the king escaping to Asia almost alone.

In 190 the consul L. Cornelius Scipio, accompanied by his brother Africanus, the conqueror of Hannibal, as the real commander, prepared to invade Asia; they were greatly aided by Aetolia requesting a truce, and with Philip's help advanced through Thrace, while the Roman fleet appeared in the Aegean and was joined by those of Eumenes and Rhodes. Antiochus' admiral, the Rhodian exile Polyxenidas, fought well; he was defeated at Corycus by the Romans and Eumenes, but subsequently destroyed a Rhodian squadron, and in the final battle of Myonnesus, probably the only sea-fight ever fought by Rome against odds, he might have defeated the Romans alone, but the skill of the Rhodian contingent with them turned the day. This battle ended the predominance of the Macedonian kingdoms at sea, which had endured since the downfall of Athens' navy at Amorgus in the Lamian war (322). Meanwhile Antiochus had collected his army, but after Myonnesus he lost his head and abandoned the defence of the strong Lysimacheia and the Dardanelles; he seems to have believed that Fortune had deserted him. With Eumenes' help the Scipios crossed the Dardanelles and late in 190 Antiochus was completely defeated at Magnesia, much of the credit belonging to Eumenes. In 189 a Roman force entered Phrygia and overthrew Antiochus' allies the Galatians, while in Greece Philip and the Romans were conquering Aetolia. The heroic resistance of Ambracia secured for Aetolia moderate terms; she again became Rome's ally, but her League was considerably curtailed, and she lost Delphi. In 188 peace was made at Apamea between Antiochus and Rome; Antiochus had to surrender all Seleucid Asia Minor except Cilicia, give up his elephants and fleet, and pay a large indemnity. Rome also demanded Hannibal, who escaped to Bithynia.

The peace of Apamea altered the face of the Hellenistic east; Rome was now the predominant power, and in Greece itself no state was really independent of her. The naval disarmament clauses of the three great peace treaties of 202, 196 and 188 had made the Mediterranean a Roman lake.[1] The time that followed was one of constant Roman interference; every weaker disputant, every person aggrieved, appealed to Rome, and Roman commissioners were perpetually travelling eastward; and in the cities the democracies, which stood for national independence, at least internally, now tended to look to Macedonia, while the well-to-do favoured submission to the wishes of Rome. Eumenes reaped his reward at the peace; he received Seleucid Asia Minor north of Taurus and the Maeander, with parts of the Pamphylian and Thracian coasts and many cities; but he could never master the wild country of Pisidia and the Taurus. He reached the Black Sea at Tios, and held his enemy Bithynia in his arms. He had a war with her, which in 183 Rome settled in his favour; Rome then again demanded Hannibal, who took poison to avoid being surrendered by Prusias. Eumenes also fought with Pharnaces of Pontus, who however took Sinope and made it his capital; but Eumenes made himself suzerain of Galatia—a success perhaps commemorated by the great altar at Pergamum (p. 319)—and extended his influence even to Cappadocia and Armenia. His relations with his Greek cities are noticed elsewhere (p. 165). He grew great, but was everywhere disliked as being Rome's jackal, the traitor to Hellenism. Rhodes received Lycia and Caria south of the Maeander; she had now reached her zenith, was head of a powerful city confederacy, and ruled the sea; but the Lycians revolted again and again, and were an open sore in her side. Antiochus, for all his losses, still retained a great empire, though his suzerainty over Parthia naturally lapsed; but he had trouble over raising the indemnity, and in 187 was ingloriously killed while trying to plunder a temple in Elymais (Elam). His son Seleucus IV waged no wars, the best thing he could do, and was murdered in 175 by his minister

[1] Griffith, *Cambridge Historical Journal*, 1935, 1. On the effects of Roman sea-power in general, see now J. H. Thiel, *Studies on the history of Roman sea-power in republican times*, 1946.

Heliodorus, who apparently also removed the son who succeeded him. His younger son, Demetrius, was a hostage in Rome, and the crown was seized the same year by his gifted brother Antiochus IV Epiphanes.[1]

The Achaean League, like Rhodes, now enjoyed a high reputation; Philopoemen stood for friendship with Rome but complete independence outside the League's obligations as Rome's ally. But, as Lycia to Rhodes, so Sparta was an open sore to Achaea, and in 188 Philopoemen attempted to settle the matter by brute force; he took Sparta, razed the wall, restored the men exiled by Nabis and his predecessors, abolished the Lycurgan institutions, removed many of Nabis' new citizens to Achaea, and sold as slaves 3,000 who refused to go; he thus manufactured more exiles, who began appealing to Rome. In 183 Messene revolted and was not subdued till she had captured and poisoned Philopoemen; Lycortas continued his policy, and it was Lycortas' young son, the historian Polybius, who bore Philopoemen's urn when his ashes were brought home. In 181 Rome intervened on Sparta's behalf, and Lycortas' opponent Callicrates, head of the Roman party in Achaea, at Rome's behest restored all the Spartan exiles, the wall, and the Lycurgan institutions. Polybius naturally has little good to say of Callicrates; but some settlement of the Spartan troubles was forced on Rome, and was one of her most justifiable acts.

Philip during the war with Antiochus had by Rome's leave retaken Demetrias and parts of Thessaly and Thrace; Demetrias he kept, but Rome ordered him to retire from Thrace and Thessaly. He obeyed, with bitter hate in his soul. He had helped Rome greatly, and had received what was to become the usual reward of her friends. All that had happened to Macedonia itself had been defeat in one battle; and Philip sat down to prepare for a second war. He still had his outbursts of madness—the massacre at Maroneia

[1] I retain the number IV for Epiphanes, as is usually done to avoid confusion, even if the name of the murdered son of Seleucus IV *was* Antiochus. See Otto, *Heliodoros* in P.W.; E. R. Bevan in *C.A.H.* VIII, 497 *sq.*, 713.

when he quitted it, and the murder of his younger son Demetrius for favouring Rome, the first murder in the Antigonid house; and he became more arbitrary than ever. But his talents showed brighter in misfortune than in fortune; he restored Macedonia to strength and prosperity, stopped infanticide, introduced settlers, opened new mines, acquired large control in Thrace, and when he died in 179 he left to his son Perseus a Macedonia better populated and wealthier than she had been since Cassander's reign. One plan was cut short by his death; he meant to use the friendly Bastarnae, a powerful Gallic[1] confederacy on the lower Danube, to destroy the Dardanians, and then employ them and their relatives the Scordisci to invade Italy while he reconquered Greece. Owing to his death only part of the Bastarnae started, but Greeks were alarmed and Perseus was accused of designs upon Greece; thereon he withheld the expected support, and the Dardanians defeated the Bastarnae and for a time broke their power.

Unhappily Perseus was the least gifted of the Antigonids, with a lack of decision and will-power. But he soon attracted universal goodwill; he married a daughter of Seleucus IV and the Rhodian fleet escorted the bride; all the national or democratic parties in Greece looked to him, and he had much support even in Rhodes and Aetolia. Eumenes alone was irreconcilable, and in 172 went to Rome in person to urge her to destroy Macedonia. Doubtless it looked to Rome as if Perseus might form a great confederacy; she had no grievance against him, but she listened to Eumenes (p. 124), and when on his way home Eumenes was nearly murdered in some private quarrel, Rome accused Perseus and welcomed the pretext for war. Eumenes was believed to be dead, and his brother Attalus took his kingdom and his wife Stratonice; he surrendered both on Eumenes' return, Eumenes merely remarking that he had married in some haste (p. 40).

Rome declared war in 171, and called out all her allies; by 168 she had 100,000 men in Macedonia and Greece,

[1] Possibly they included also one or more German clans.

against Perseus' 43,000. Perseus only allies were Cotys of Thrace, Epirus, and later Genthius of Illyria. Their governments kept the Greek states quiet; their real interest lay, not in Perseus' victory, but in his survival to balance Rome. Perseus has been accused of irresolution and miserliness. Possibly however he believed that defeating Roman armies would only harden Rome's resolve, and that his one chance was to conserve his resources and protract the war till Rome wearied of the useless effort. For three years, aided by minor victories and Roman incompetence, he was successful, and only at the end of 169 did the consul Q. Marcius Philippus cross his frontier from Thessaly. But in 168 Rome sent to the army of Macedonia a better man, the consul L. Aemilius Paullus, while Perseus lost the invaluable help of 20,000 Bastarnae by haggling over their pay. Paullus manœuvred Perseus out of his impregnable position, and at Pydna succeeded in inducing him to make a premature attack. The Macedonian phalanx swept the Roman advance-guard before them, and Paullus confessed that he trembled as they came down on him, tossing his men aside on their spear-points; but the attacking formations were not properly synchronised, some Roman troops thrust in between the phalanx and the hypaspists, and taken in flank the phalanx was helpless; the end was massacre. Perseus fled while the Macedonians were dying, and lost all standing with his people; he did not even destroy his papers, which incriminated many Greeks; finally, forsaken by all, he surrendered, was led in triumph, and died miserably in a Roman prison.

Both the growing deterioration of the Roman character and the temporary eclipse of Roman philhellenism were reflected in the settlement. Macedonia was forcibly broken up into four republics, and further weakened by economic restrictions. The national parties in Greece, who had only aided Perseus with good wishes, suffered heavily, and many men everywhere were exiled; even from Achaea, which had offered Rome her army, 1,000 leading men, including Polybius, were transported to Italy. The Aetolian League was dismembered, Aetolia reduced to her original boundaries, and the whole Council exiled. Epirus, in revenge for Pyrrhus' invasion of Italy, was ruined for ever; the multitude sold as slaves was so great that an Epirote could be bought for a few shillings; three Greek cities which had joined Perseus were also sold up. Perseus' fleet had used Delos, which Delos was powerless to prevent; she was punished by being given back to Athens, who exiled the Delians and colonised the island with Athenian cleruchs. Rhodes, a consistent friend of Rome, was tricked by the consul Philippus; he suggested she should offer mediation, which she did, and for this Rome deprived her of most of her possessions on the mainland, and ended her commercial predominance by making Athenian Delos a free port. Even Eumenes, Rome's more than ally, suffered for having grown strong; on the suspicion that he had intended to offer mediation—the facts are obscure—Rome incited the Galatians against him; when he went to Italy to plead his cause he was turned back unheard, and when in 166, after a severe struggle, he broke the invading Galatians, Rome promptly declared them autonomous; in 163 P. Sulpicius Galba sat in Pergamum for ten days listening to complaints against him. No service or subservience to the Roman Republic could secure the genuine friendship of that immoral State; and few of the excesses or injustices of any ruler of Macedonian blood can compare with the practice of that Republic in its later days. The effect of Rome's anger was to render Eumenes less unpopular with the Asiatic Greeks. In 160–59 he died; his brother succeeded as Attalus II, and again married Stratonice.

Ptolemy V, after mastering for the time the native revolts which culminated in his reign, was poisoned in 181–0, leaving three small children. The elder son, Ptolemy VI Philometor, subsequently married his sister Cleopatra II; the younger was afterwards Ptolemy VII Euergetes II. In 173 the boy-king's ministers made preparations for recovering southern Syria; but Antiochus Epiphanes anticipated their design. Antiochus, the 'Saviour of Asia', was one of the most remarkable men of his house.[1] He had lived 14 years in Rome, and was her convinced friend and imitator; he was an Athenian citizen and a passionate admirer of things Greek; he adorned Athens and many other cities with gifts of temples and buildings, added to Antioch, refounded many towns as Greek cities (Chap. IV), and brought in new settlers. Magnificent and munificent, ready to play the democrat or the jester, but popular and a king, some called him mad; but he raised his kingdom to a high pitch of efficiency, and the reorganisation he attempted later was no unworthy one. In 169 he invaded Egypt, took Pelusium and Memphis, and extended his protectorate over Ptolemy VI. He then returned to Syria (for his relations with Judaea see Chap. VI); but the Alexandrians made Euergetes king, Philometor recognised him, and Egypt had two kings together. In 168 Antiochus returned and besieged Alexandria, and took the royal title as Philometor's guardian. But Pydna had been fought, and Rome, following her consistent policy of weakening the Seleucids, intervened; the envoy C. Popilius handed Antiochus the Senate's order to quit Egypt, drew a circle round him in the sand with his stick, and told him to decide before quitting the circle. It was an unheard-of insolence, though perhaps matched later when Scipio Aemilianus made Ptolemy Euergetes II accompany him on foot through Alexandria and deliberately walked too fast in order to shame his unwieldy host before his subjects. To challenge Rome was not Antiochus' purpose; he quitted Egypt, and devoted himself to his real plan, to reconquer Bactria from the Euthydemid dynasty, and to crush the growing power of Parthia before it was too late. But in 163, with success in his grasp, he died, and with him ended all chance of his empire playing any further part as a world-power.

Rome took advantage of his son Antiochus V being a child to demand the destruction of the Syrian war-fleet and elephants; the sight of the ham-strung elephants so moved the populace that one Leptines murdered the Roman envoy

[1] For Antiochus see W. Otto, *Zur Gesch. d. Zeit des 6 Ptolemäers*, Abh. d. Bayer. Akad. ,1934; and, on different lines, Tarn, *Bactria*, ch. V.

Octavius, an incident Rome merely saved up for future use. But the boy did not reign long. In 162 Demetrius, son of Seleucus IV, escaped from Rome with Polybius' help, easily overthrew the unpopular regent Lysias, and took the crown as Demetrius I Soter. He displayed energy, recovering Babylonia from the general Timarchus, who had revolted and been recognised by Rome, and setting up a new king in Cappadocia in place of his enemy Ariarathes V. But he was unpopular with his people; Attalus II restored Ariarathes, and the two combined with Philometor of Egypt against him; and a pretender appeared, one Alexander Balas, who claimed to be a son of Epiphanes. Rome and Philometor both recognised him; with Egyptian support he invaded Syria, and Demetrius was defeated and killed (150).

In Egypt the joint reign of the brothers Philometor and Euergetes was brief; in 163 the Alexandrians drove out Philometor. But Rome gave him some help, a change of opinion brought him back, and under Roman mediation the kingdom was divided, Philometor obtaining Egypt and Cyprus, Euergetes Cyrene and Libya. The tradition makes Philometor one of the best Ptolemies. Rome, with her own difficulties, was ceasing to be interested in Egypt or the Seleucids, provided neither grew too strong; and Philometor turned his thoughts to Syria. Having supported Balas, he gave him after his victory his daughter Cleopatra Thea, and virtually exercised a protectorate over the Seleucid kingdom. But Balas was incompetent, and Demetrius' son Demetrius II came back with Cretan mercenaries and disputed the throne. Philometor occupied the Syrian coast himself, but fell out with Balas and transferred his patronage and his daughter to Demetrius. Balas attacked him in 145, and was defeated and soon afterwards killed; but Philometor died of his wounds, and Euergetes thereon became king of the whole Egyptian empire, and married his sister Cleopatra II, Philometor's widow. Greek tradition makes him a blood-stained tyrant, who committed many crimes. Much of this is obvious propaganda, poorly attested, and completely contradicted by his great series of decrees,[1] which cannot be gainsaid; though possibly his character, like Augustus', changed in later life. Much of his reign was occupied in civil war with his sister, an obscure subject which has now been elucidated.[2] He married Philometor's daughter, another Cleopatra (III), and both Cleopatras often appear with him in official acts; the problem of whether the elder nominally remained his wife also, and what were the real changes in the relationships of the three, has now been unravelled.[3] But the interest of his reign lies in other matters than personal questions (Chap. V). He died in 116, the last of the great succession of the Ptolemies.

In Syria the excesses of Demetrius' Cretan troops at once provoked opposition, and Balas' general Diodotus set up as king Balas' young son Antiochus VI; in 142 he murdered the boy and himself took the diadem and the name Tryphon. Demetrius could not overthrow him; he left his wife Cleopatra Thea as regent of Syria and turned eastward, where Mithridates I of Parthia had extended his rule from the Purali to the Tigris, and had in 142 taken Babylonia.[4] The Greek cities had called on Demetrius for help, and doubtless he hoped to return with resources sufficient to overthrow Tryphon. He found much support, and rescued Babylonia, but was finally captured and held in honourable captivity by Mithridates, and married to his daughter; and Mithridates again annexed Babylonia. But Thea held out, and in 139 Demetrius' brother Antiochus VII Sidetes came to her from Rhodes, married her as her third husband, and disposed of Tryphon. Sidetes was the last strong man of his line; the only fault attributed to him is drink. He unified and strengthened his kingdom, subdued the long-lost Judaea (p. 235), and finally crossed the Euphrates with a large army. The Greek cities received him with enthusiasm; he reconquered Mesopotamia and Babylonia, drove the Parthian

[1] Set out, E. R. Bevan, *Hist. of Egypt*, 315; see Otto-Bengtson (see p. 239 n.1), 109 *sqq.*; Rostovtzeff, *SEH* 878 *sqq.*, 893 *sqq.*

[2] Otto-Bengtson, *passim*. [3] Otto-Bengtson, *l.c.*

[4] 142, *C.A.H.* IX, 579. N. C. Debevoise, *A Political History of Parthia*, 1938, 22, makes it 141.

king Phraates out of Media, and seemed about to restore the empire of Antiochus III. But early in 129 the Parthian surprised him in his winter quarters, defeated and killed him, and recovered his conquests; our last document from Seleucid Babylon is dated in June 130. Phraates sent Sidetes' body home, and Syria made a great mourning, as though she knew that the effective history of his dynasty was ended.

Macedonia after Pydna had a troubled existence for some years, till a man named Andriscus claimed the crown, asserting that he was Perseus' son Philip, who had really died in Italy. Rome, fully involved in Spain, paid little attention to the 'false Philip', who secured support in Thrace and in 149 invaded Macedonia, whereon the whole country accepted him. He invaded Thessaly in 148 and defeated a Roman force; but he had alienated the Macedonians by playing the despot, and was defeated by the praetor Q. Caecilius Metellus, taken to Rome, and executed; and Macedonia, first of the Hellenistic states, became a Roman province, which dated from 148 as her era.[1] Another 'false Philip' did appear, but had little success; and the history of the province was chiefly one of repeated incursions by the northern barbarians, which culminated, though they did not end, with the great invasion of the Scordisci and Thracians in the first Mithridatic war, when they destroyed Delphi and Dodona. The Roman failure to keep out the barbarians contrasted badly with the record of the Antigonid kings in this respect.

Greece found it hard to recover from the chastisement she had received and the loss of her best men by exile; in some districts, too, the increase of the Greek population was becoming insufficient to balance losses. But there was one fight still to come. The last struggle of the Achaean League is obscure; most of Polybius, here frankly pro-Roman, is lost, and Pausanias' account merely reflects the view-point of Rome's partisans, though fortunately inscriptions help; when we hear that the League was deteriorating and the leading men corrupt it is well to reserve judgment. For

[1] On this era and 146 (p. 39), M. N. Tod. *B.S.A.* XXIII, 206; XXIV, 54

years Callicrates was the leading statesman, and worked entirely in Rome's interest; but by 150 the surviving exiles, 300 only, had (except Polybius) returned from Italy and the democrats captured the government and made general Diaeus of Megalopolis, who stood for independence; Callicrates died that year, and Rome's difficulties in Spain, Macedonia, and Africa seemed to afford the hope of a revived policy. There was again trouble with Sparta, who formally seceded in 148; the League declared war, and Rome intervened and summoned both parties to a congress at Corinth in 147. There the Roman envoys announced that the League must give up, not only Sparta, which would have been fair enough, but Corinth, Argos, and Orchomenus, for generations integral parts of the League; the League had consistently supported Rome, and Rome now meant to destroy it as she had destroyed the Aetolian. The Achaeans threatened the envoys, but the story that they assaulted them is recognised as untrue. In spring 146 the League voted war; it could do nothing else, unless a small country has no right to fight for its liberties against a big one. It was a people's war; a moratorium was proclaimed, men enlisted freely, and clubs of 'patriots' appeared in the cities; at Troezen, and doubtless elsewhere, the members put all their property at the city's disposal[1]; even Polybius admits that feeling ran like a torrent. Boeotia, Euboea, Phocis, and Locris joined Achaea. The general Critolaus advanced northward to join his allies, but was defeated and killed by Metellus, who hurried from Macedonia; the defeated took refuge in Corinth, where the consul L. Mummius took over command from Metellus. Diaeus, who succeeded as general, raised a general levy, ordered 12,000 slaves to be freed and armed (an order never carried out), and hastened to Corinth with 14,600 men, perhaps the largest army the League ever raised. He defeated Mummius' advance-guard, and this induced him, though heavily outnumbered, to give battle; the Achaean phalanx fought desperately, but were defeated by the superior Roman cavalry laying bare their

[1] *I.G.* IV, 757.

flank; Diaeus, who escaped, committed suicide with his family. Achaea had no cause to be ashamed of her last fight, and she was not ashamed; the cities set up their rolls of honour, and we happen to possess that of Epidaurus,[1] 156 dead in the battle from one small town. Mummius occupied Corinth and, though it had not resisted, treated it like Carthage; the men were killed, the women and children sold, and the city razed to the ground. It was a deliberate warning to Greece (p. 263), like Alexander's destruction of Thebes. Chalcis and Thebes also suffered heavily; but in many places Mummius did not behave badly.

Greece after 146 became a Roman protectorate, supervised from Macedonia; some documents date from this year as an era, but Greece was not yet a province. Polybius now obtained leave to return, and did good service by mitigating the first severity of Achaea's fate and afterwards superintending the transition period. Greece had no more wars or foreign politics, except boundary disputes. Timocracies—governments of the wealthy—were set up in many cities, and attempts to alter the constitution prohibited. Antigonus I had once claimed, in certain cities, to 'reprehend and punish' those who proposed laws which he considered inexpedient,[2] but Rome now made 'new laws' punishable by death,[3] an illustration of the difference between Roman and Macedonian rule. Nevertheless in Greece, if anywhere, the Roman Republic for a time justified itself; it gave peace and prosperity, even if enforced. Some territories—Corinth, Euboea, Boeotia—were taxed; but Athens, Sparta, and some other cities were tax-free, and probably there was no general system of tribute till after 88. Athens enjoyed an Indian summer of material wealth, and the facts known about Messene (p. 112) suggest a widespread well-being by *c.* 100. There was too a religious revival[4]; to this period belong the great legislative decree for the mysteries of Andania (91),[5] the restoration of the oracle and service of Apollo Koropaeus,[6] the publication at Lindus in 99 of its

[1] *I.G.* IV, 894. [2] Ditt.[3] 344 l. 55. [3] *Ib.* 684.
[4] A. Wilhelm, *Jahresh.* XVII, 83. [5] Ditt.[3] 736. [6] *Ib.* 1157

religious records, the 'Lindian chronicle'. Athens and Boeotia led the way; the Boeotian Ptoia became quadrennial, and Tanagra founded her Serapieia (p. 114); Athens revived at Delos the great quadrennial Delia,[1] omitted since 314, and at intervals sent to Delphi magnificently equipped religious processions, the Pythaids,[2] to bring back the sacred fire to purify the city. All these things helped to re-establish the national consciousness.

At Pergamum the reign of Attalus II Philadelphus, a good ruler, was uneventful, save for the usual war with Bithynia; but his fleet supported Rome in 148 and 146. Under him the kingdom reached its greatest prosperity. He died in 139–8, and was succeeded by Attalus III, probably a natural son of Eumenes II, legitimised by him and adopted by the childless Stratonice[3]; Attalus II may have married Stratonice, who was not young, in loyalty to Eumenes, to safeguard his son's succession,[4] which would explain the haste he showed in 172 and Eumenes' lack of resentment. Attalus III was a man of disordered nerves, both vain and cruel, who put many prominent men to death and confiscated their estates; subsequently, perhaps through remorse, he lived in retirement, practising sculpture and studying poisons. He died childless early in 133, leaving a famous will: he gave freedom to Pergamum and probably to his Greek cities generally, and bequeathed his kingdom to Rome, which means that he gave to Rome the King's Land, the royal treasure, and the right to act as king of Pergamum vis-à-vis the other elements in the country. His reason is conjectural; hatred of his heir, his half-brother Aristonicus, has been suggested, or perhaps the

[1] F. Durrbach, *Choix des Inscriptions de Délos*, I, ii, p. 191.

[2] Ditt.[3] 696–9, 711, 728; G. Colin, *B.C.H.* 1906, 161; A. Boethius, *Die Pythais*, 1918.

[3] Theories as to who Attalus III was are collected in E. V. Hansen, *The Attalids of Pergamon*, 1947, App. 1.

[4] Precisely as Doson married Philip V's mother, Demetrius' widow Chryseis, to safeguard Philip's succession: Tarn, *Phthia-Chryseis*, in *Harvard Studies in Class. Phil.*, Suppl. Vol. I, 487. The silly story (Plut. *Mor.* 489 E, 184 C) that *both* kings accordingly killed their own children (Stratonice was about 50) proves parallel circumstances.

bequest, like that of Ptolemy the Younger at Cyrene in 155, was conditional on the death of Attalus occurring while he still had no son to succeed him, an outcome which he would presumably intend to forestall.[1] Or it may be that he merely anticipated the fact that Rome would take the kingdom when she chose. Rome accepted the bequest. The Pergamenes, fearing a slave rising, enfranchised large classes (p. 170); but in 132 Aristonicus raised a national revolt against Rome and threw in his lot with the slaves. He easily defeated Rome's allies, the rulers of Pontus, Bithynia, Cappadocia, and Paphlagonia; and though Pergamum itself forsook him, he had success enough to overrun Caria, besiege Cyzicus, invade the Chersonese, and early in 130 destroy the consul Crassus and his army. But the new consul, M. Perperna, defeated and shut him up in Stratonicea; he had to surrender, and was taken to Rome and killed. Even so, the war was not over, and in 129 the consul M'. Aquilius had hard fighting both in Caria and Mysia. The interest of this war lies in the theories which Aristonicus sought to translate into action (p. 125).

The war freed Rome from Attalus' will; she had conquered the kingdom, and in 130 she made part of it the Roman province of Asia. The cities which had aided Aristonicus became subject and were taxed; but many, like Miletus, were free and Rome's allies. Following Hellenistic precedent, Rome eased taxation at first; subsequently it was reimposed by the Sempronian law of C. Gracchus. The status of the individual cities, however, often altered, for better or worse; the ambition of all was to obtain immunity from Roman taxes. Those taxes themselves were not oppressive; what was oppressive was the manner of collection. Instead of being collected by responsible officials, they were farmed out, *i.e.* the collector (*publicanus*) bought the right to collect the taxes from a district, and what he actually collected was limited only by his own greed: it was

[1] F. E. Adcock, *L'Antiquité classique*, XVII, 1948, 11. The object of such a bequest was to warn his enemies that it was useless to kill the reigning monarch.

the worst system ever devised, especially as the publican on the spot was often only the agent of a company in Rome. Down to 88, however, some restraint was exercised, and the cities as a rule, especially the free ones, continued to prosper.

In 88 there opened the struggle which presaged the ruin of Hellenism, the first war between Rome and that remarkable barbarian, Mithridates Eupator of Pontus. These wars belong to Roman history; all that can be noticed here is their effect. Round Mithridates crystallised all the hatred felt for Rome and the Roman publican; when in 88 he overran the province of Asia many Greek cities joined him, and when he ordered a general massacre of all 'Romans' it was largely obeyed. There were cities, like Rhodes, which saved the Romans and their honour; but great numbers perished—80,000 or 150,000 in the tradition—largely inoffensive traders and their families; Mithridates' general Archelaus killed 20,000 more in Delos and the islands. Even in Greece Mithridates found allies—Achaea, Laconia, Boeotia, and, most notable of all, the Athenian democracy. Athens had had an oligarchic revolution *c.* 103, and the democracy desired to recover power; but the city, harmless and historic, had made no pretence of waging war for generations, and its open espousal of Mithridates' cause is as eloquent of the hatred felt by Greeks for their Roman masters as the massacre in Asia. Athens fought desperately when besieged by Mithridates' conqueror Sulla, and never fully recovered from the consequent ruin. In Asia, Mithridates' deportation of the Chians caused many cities to desert his cause, and he attempted to regain them by stirring up social revolution in his favour; he proclaimed abolition of debts, enfranchisement of metics (aliens without the franchise residing in a city), and liberation of the slaves; he imitated Aristonicus in trying to use revolution as a weapon with which to fight Rome.

With Mithridates the material reaction of Asia against western rule, begun by Cappadocia and Parthia and continued by Judaea and Armenia, came to a head; and Rome, who had done so much to weaken or destroy the Graeco-

Macedonian states, was ultimately forced to take their place as champion and protector of Greek civilisation in the East. But Hellenism had first to pass through a stage of distress and destruction. Caught between Rome and Pontus, and suffering heavily from both, both Greece and Asia were badly damaged; beside actual war exactions and losses, Sulla plundered temples at Olympia and elsewhere, Archelaus sacked Delos, and Mithridates' barbarian allies Delphi; the Cilician pirates, who aided Mithridates, added to the general misery. Sulla's exactions in both countries were severe, as were later those of M. Antonius Creticus in the Cretan war; and in all these wars Greek cities had to provide the Roman fleets. Before any recovery was possible, the Greek east was inextricably caught in the Roman Civil Wars.

Greece itself had no chance. Whole districts were half depopulated; Thebes became a village, Megalopolis a desert, Megara, Aegina, Piraeus heaps of stones; in Laconia and Euboea individuals owned large tracts, perhaps worked only by a few herdsmen; Aetolia, like Epirus, was ruined for ever. Relief ultimately came when in 27 Augustus made the country the province of Achaea. Two new trading cities, Caesar's Corinth and Augustus' Patrae, were to flourish; Athens was still to be a leading university; Elis and Boeotia ultimately regained some material prosperity, and Boeotia still had enough vitality to produce Plutarch; various cities were partially to recover. But for Greece, taken as a whole, Augustus' peace came too late.

Heavily as Asia Minor suffered, its fate was to differ from that of Greece. The intermediate period was bad; many cities lost their freedom after 88; a new generation of publicans, perhaps not unnaturally, showed themselves more oppressive than the old. Whereas under some Greek laws a debtor's person could not be seized, debtors were now sometimes not only seized but tortured, and their children sold. Provincial governors extorted great sums; Cicero expounds the difficulties incurred by one who favoured common honesty. Some cities, having exhausted their temple funds, were driven to borrow from Roman bankers at usurious rates; Lucullus checked usury for a moment, but in the civil wars it returned in full force. None of the contending generals except Caesar (who temporarily abolished tax-farming) cared for anything but their own success, while all needed money; a few instances of the extortion practised are noted elsewhere (p. 113). But the great cities were not actually destroyed, and short of that were too strong and too wealthy to go under; and once settled government returned they more than recovered their prosperity.

The other countries of Asia Minor fell to Rome one by one, the transition sometimes being smoothed over by the rule of a client king. Phrygia was added to Asia in 116. In 74 Nicomedes IV, imitating Attalus III, bequeathed Bithynia to Rome; and after Mithridates' final defeat Pompey made it a province, together with part of Pontus. In Galatia, where Mithridates had massacred most of the nobility, one Deiotaurus made himself king; in 36 his secretary Amyntas secured Antony's favour and the kingdom, which he greatly extended to the southward; in 25 he fell in battle with the Homadenses of the Taurus, and his kingdom passed to Rome. Another of Antony's kings, Polemon, ruled Pontus from the Iris to Colchis and founded a dynasty; his kingdom only became Roman in A.D. 63, and Cappadocia, the last quasi-independent state, under Vespasian. The complicated details and changing boundaries of the Roman provinces in Asia Minor need not be noticed here; what matters is that Augustus partly returned to the Seleucid system (Chap. IV). Much land had become *ager publicus* under the Republic, and some Romans had seized great estates; Augustus made it Crown Land again, abolished the publican, and collected the taxes through government officials as the Seleucids had done.

Seleucid rule survived Sidetes' death for 46 years; but Commagene and Edessa were lost, and the line became a local dynasty in North Syria, which tore itself and the country to pieces in domestic quarrels. Phraates had released Demetrius II before Sidetes' defeat; he recovered Syria and his former wife Cleopatra Thea, who had meanwhile borne

Sidetes five children. But the over-married and disillusioned woman could not endure Demetrius' incompetence after his brother, and when a pretender, Alexander Zabinas, defeated him she apparently prevented him escaping to safety. She now meant to hold the power herself. When her eldest son by Demetrius seized the throne she poisoned him; subsequently she set up as co-ruler the second, Antiochus VIII Grypus, who anticipated his fate by killing her first. Endless civil war followed between Grypus and Sidetes' son Antiochus IX Cyzicenus and their respective descendants; the great cities had to look after themselves, petty tyrants and Arab chieftains established principalities throughout the country, the Ituraeans of the Lebanon raided where they would, and for a time the advancing Nabataeans even held Damascus. In 83 Tigranes, who had united all Armenia, conquered most of the country and ended Seleucid rule; though unpopular, he at least supplied a government, but after his overthrow by Lucullus there was sheer anarchy, and it was well for the sorely tried Hellenism of northern Syria when in 64 Pompey made the country a Roman province.

Though no king of Egypt after Euergetes' death was in any way distinguished, the country still produced wealth and possessed many elements of strength, as is shewn by the continued exploration and advance southward (Chap. VII). Euergetes' widow, Cleopatra III, and his sons, the colourless Ptolemy VIII Soter II (Lathyros) and Ptolemy IX (Alexandros), ruled Egypt and Cyprus with various changes and combinations till 81–0; Cyrene he left to his illegitimate son Ptolemy Apion, who in 96 bequeathed it to Rome. The death of Lathyros' daughter in 80 ended the legitimate line, but the Alexandrians made Lathyros' illegitimate son king as Ptolemy XI Neos Dionysos, nicknamed Auletes, the Fluteplayer; in the tradition he was a vicious dilettante of Nero's type, who by servility towards Rome ruled till 51, after losing Cyprus in 58. Two of his children, the young Ptolemy XII and his eldest sister Cleopatra VII, jointly succeeded. The boy-king and Alexandria between them made a good fight against Caesar and came near to ending his career; but a unique glamour has been thrown over the fall of the dynasty by the name of Cleopatra. Much has been written about her, but little that gives any real idea of the woman who, whatever her crimes and her faults, was great enough to make Rome fear her and who in her own fearlessness and her ambition had something of Alexander's spirit—the woman of whom prophecy foretold that after overthrowing Rome she would raise her up again and inaugurate a golden age in which the long feud between Europe and Asia should end in their reconciliation and the reign of justice and love. Her aim was to be empress of the Roman world; had Caesar lived she might have been, but he died and she was compelled to fall back on Antony as a second-best. She did finally win him over to her audacious plan of trying to conquer Rome by means of Romans, but not till it was too late; the defection of his fleet at Actium (31) shattered her dream of empire, and with her suicide next year the last Macedonian line virtually ended, and Augustus sat in the seat of the Ptolemies.[1]

[1] For Cleopatra see Tarn, *C.A.H.* X, 1934, chs. 2, 3; also *J.R.S.* XXII 1932, 135 (the prophecy) and XXI, 1931, 173 (Actium).

CHAPTER II

MONARCHY, CITY, AND LEAGUE

THE old Macedonian monarchy had retained some of the characteristics of the heroic monarchy, known from Homer and the Teutonic sagas.[2] The god-descended king, with his subject princes and his free peers, ruled a national kingdom, but claimed an allegiance as much personal as patriotic; Alexander's Companions were the last remnant of the heroic retinue; the old bond of union, the idea of the Kin, was not yet quite dead in his time.[3] The original meeting of the free men in arms, the army, remained, and they clung tenaciously to their powers; in Macedonia these powers were possibly older than the monarchy, which was not absolute, but limited by the rights of the people under arms; it has even been called quasi-constitutional.[4] The king could not appoint his successor; on his death the vacant crown passed to the army, who elected the new king; naturally this was generally the eldest son, but not necessarily so. Were the king a child, the army alone could appoint a regent or guardian. In a trial for treason, where the king was virtually a party, the army represented the State, heard the case, and gave judgment. As the army elected the king, it could also depose him, though with a strong king this might entail going over to the enemy. But over policy the army had no voice; if they wanted one, they could only get it by mutinying, as sometimes happened.[5]

[1] V. Ehrenberg, 'Der griech. und der hellenist. Staat', in Gercke-Norden III, 3, 64 *sqq.*; Fr. Heichelheim, 'Griech. Staatskunde', 1902–32, in *Bursian Suppl. Band,* 250.

[2] H. M. Chadwick, *The Heroic Age.*

[3] Arr. *Anab.* VII, 11, 6.

[4] Ferguson, *Amer. Hist. Rev.* 1912, 34.

[5] The army's powers are deduced from events. Cf. Curt. VI, 8, 25; and now F. Granier, *Die makedonische Heeresversammlung,* 1931; F. Hampl, *Der König der Makedonen,* 1934; Tarn, *Alexander* II, p. 137, and p. 379.

The army was fully representative of the people, as all free Macedonians served, but these did not officially constitute part of the Macedonian State; subject to their powers above indicated, the king was the State, and alone represented Macedonia in its foreign relations. Thus in the League of Corinth Alexander held a double position, not always understood: the League was composed of the Greek states and of Alexander, who was officially the Macedonian State, while the man Alexander, King of Macedonia, was President. This position endured until Antigonus Doson, who made the Macedonian people the 'Commonwealth of the Macedonians',[1] and therewith made them part of the State, which was now no longer, in official language, 'King Antigonus', but 'King Antigonus and the Macedonians'.[2] It was only a name, and gave the people no extended rights; indeed Philip V sometimes acted more arbitrarily than any other Macedonian king.

The Macedonian conquest of Egypt and Asia brought new problems.[3] During the wars of the Successors the Macedonians in the armies abroad maintained their rights for a time, but probably these were lost after 300, the Macedonians having become only small minorities in mixed armies of mercenaries; and the absolute monarchies of the Seleucids and the Ptolemies exhibit no Macedonian constitutional traits of any kind, unless it be the right of petitioning the king, known in Egypt.[4] If under the later Ptolemies their army sometimes interfered, its interference was that of a Praetorian Guard, and had nothing to do with the old Macedonian constitution; indeed it would hardly

[1] Ditt.[3] 575; Philip V's bronze coins with *Μακεδόνων*. Later references Diod. XVIII, 4, 3; Polyaen. IV, 6, 14; Arr. VII, 9. 5; see Tarn, *J.H.S.* 1921, 16.

[2] *I.G.* XI, 4, 1097; Tarn, *J.H.S.* 1909, 269 *sqq.*

[3] On the theories, beside the general works, see E. R. Goodenough, 'The political philosophy of Hellenistic kingship', *Yale Class. Stud.*, I, 1928, 55; P. Zancan, *Il monarcato ellenistico*, 1934, esp. the Seleucid chapter; C. W. McEwan, *The oriental origin of Hellenistic kingship*, 1934; A. Heuss, *Stadt und Herrscher des Hellenismus*, Klio Beiheft 39, 1937.

[4] P. Collomp, *Recherches sur la chancellerie et la diplomatique des Lagides*, ch. III; O. Guéraud, *Enteuxeis*, 1933.

contain one free-born Macedonian. If Macedonia made the monarchies of the Seleucids and the Ptolemies, Asia and Egypt made them what they were; these kings *were* the State, absolutely and for all purposes, as much as Darius I or Thutmose III; they were not national rulers, and there was no imperial citizenship in their realms, as there was to be in the Roman. One justification of these two dynasties was that only an absolute monarchy, standing above and apart from Greeks and Orientals, had any chance of uniting east and west; this Rome ultimately discovered, for the Republic failed in governing Hellenistic countries. Both Seleucids and Ptolemies often made the crown prince co-ruler with his father in the latter's lifetime; among the Ptolemies dynastic murder was not uncommon, and for over a century prevented civil war.

Every king, however, was affected by Greek ideas, and desired to have some basis for his rule beyond mere conquest, or, as regards the early kings, the fact that they were the most competent men alive and the right people to govern. In Asia and Egypt this basis was ultimately found in the king's divinity,[1] a conception familiar for centuries to many of the subject peoples, and possibly for that very reason valuable to their new rulers. But in considering the history of this idea, the worship of the kings by Greek cities must be distinguished from the official cults instituted by the kings themselves. Alexander's deification[2] during his life was not an official cult; it was a *political* measure only, limited to the cities of the League of Corinth which deified him; he desired it in order to obtain a footing in, and some necessary authority over, the cities of old Greece in whom, as a king, he could otherwise find no place. When the cities began worshipping his Successors, these welcomed the political advantage it was to them, as it had been to him; Antigonus I,[3]

[1] King-worship: E. Kornemann, *Klio* I, 51; Beloch IV, 1, 366; Kaerst II², App. V; A. D. Nock, *J.H.S.* 1928, 21.

[2] Bibliography *C.A.H.* VI, 598; add L. R. Taylor, *J.H.S.* 1927, 53, *C.P.* 1927, 162; Nock *op. c.*; Tarn, *J.H.S.* 1928, 206; *Alexander* II, App. 22

[3] *OGIS* 6, and next note, items starred.

Demetrius I,[1] Lysimachus,[2] Seleucus I,[3] Ptolemy I,[4] even Cassander,[5] were all worshipped in various cities, but none of them officially became gods during life in their kingdoms. Three Greeks in Egypt, saved from some danger, did indeed honour Ptolemy I and his consort Berenice as 'saviour gods',[6] but this need not imply official deification. Alexander, however, was worshipped in Alexandria as the city's founder,[7] as other city founders were often worshipped; after his death Eumenes and his Macedonian army worshipped him,[8] and possibly there was, as the coins suggest, an official worship of him in Lysimachus' kingdom (not in Macedonia); but the worship which gave the precedent to the world was the official worship of the great Macedonian instituted in Egypt by Ptolemy I, probably soon after he took the crown in 305. Soon after 280 Ptolemy II instituted at Alexandria a great festival in worship of his father, Ptolemy I,[9] and Antiochus I followed by deifying Seleucus as Zeus Nikator[10]; and therewith was established the further principle that the kings, like Alexander, officially became gods after death.

Probably it was Ptolemy II who took the final step; his sister and consort Arsinoe II was officially deified before her death as the goddess Philadelphus,[11] and with her Ptolemy II (who was never called Philadelphus) himself officially became a god during his life, being worshipped jointly with her, and also alone.[12] After his death each succeeding Ptolemy officially became a god during life as a matter of course, and took his place in the official worship.

[1] Plut. *Dem.* 10, 12*; Athen. 536 A; Diod. XX, 102, 2; *I.G.* XI, 4, 1036*; XII, 9, 207; *SEG* 1, 362.* Cf. K. Scott, *A.J. Phil.* 1928, 137, 217.

[2] *OGIS* 11; Ditt.[3] 372, 380. [3] *OGIS* 212; Ditt.[3] 412–13; Athen. 255 A.

[4] *OGIS* 16 (emended to make it Ptolemy II, *Philol.* 85, 159; but Sarapis was known to Menander, Weinreich, *Aegyptus* XI, 13); Ditt.[3] 390. Paus. 1, 8, 6.

[5] Ditt.[3] 332 (probably). [6] *Archiv* V, 156 no. 1.

[7] Plaumann, *Archiv* VI, 77; Elizabeth Visser, *Götter und Kulte in ptolemäischen Alexandrien*, 1938.

[8] Diod. XVIII, 61. [9] Ditt.[3] 390. [10] *OGIS* 245, App. *Syr.* 63.

[11] *OGIS* 724; see Beloch, IV, 2, 586 n. 1; Ferguson, *C.A.H.* VII, 17.

[12] *P. Cairo Zen.* 59282 (250 B.C.).

At the head of that worship stood Alexander, whose priesthood was held by the greatest in the land; his name was followed by the list of the deified kings and their consorts under their cult-names—the gods Adelphoi (Ptolemy II and Arsinoe II), the gods Euergetae, the gods Philopatores, and so on; Ptolemy I and Berenice ultimately took their place in the list next after Alexander as the gods Soteres, probably under Ptolemy IV. Arsinoe II had also a separate priestess for her own worship, as had afterwards Berenice, wife of Ptolemy III, and Arsinoe, wife of Ptolemy IV. The Seleucids had an official dynastic cult covering their whole empire[1] with a centre in each satrapy, probably early, but reorganised by Antiochus III or possibly Antiochus II[2]; many cities, too, had their own local worships of the dynasty.[3] Divine pedigrees were invented for both dynasties; the Seleucids descended from Apollo,[4] the Ptolemies from Heracles and Dionysus.[5] The rulers of Pergamum, though after Attalus I took the crown they were worshipped during life in various cities and were officially deified after death, never officially became gods during life, and therefore could never claim divinity as the basis of their rule.[6]

Macedonia was on a different footing. She was a national monarchy, and the Antigonid kings were not conquerors, but national kings constitutionally chosen by the army; there was no question of an official worship of these kings, and no Antigonid was ever a god to Macedonians, though he might be deified in Greek cities or in cities in Macedonia which had retained their Greek character; thus Demetrius I was worshipped in Athens, Euboea, Sicyon, and elsewhere, Antigonus Doson in Sicyon, Histiaea, and Laconia,[7] Philip V in Amphipolis,[8] just as Cassander and Lysimachus had

[1] *OGIS* 224=Welles, *Royal Correspondence* no. 36; Bouché Leclercq, *Hist. d. Sél.* 469; Rostovtzeff, *J.H.S.* LV, 1935, 56; Wilcken, *S. B. Berlin*, 1938 (XXVIII), 317 [22].

[2] Rostovtzeff *ib.* 66 (note).

[3] List, Bikerman, *Inst. d. Sél.*, 243.

[4] *OGIS* 219, 227, 237.

[5] *Ib.* 54; Satyrus, *F.H.G.* III, p. 165.

[6] On *OGIS* 302 see Ferguson *C.P.* 1906, 231.

[7] Plut. *Arat.* 45; Ditt.[3] 493; *I.G.* V, 1, 1122.

[8] *B.C.H.* 1894, 416 no. 1.

been in Cassandreia. One king, Antigonus Gonatas, was an exception even to this, and exhibits the strange phenomenon of a monarch who was apparently never worshipped by anybody anywhere.[1] His Stoic training and sympathies seemingly caused him to regard the thing as a sham, and he may have inherited the feeling of his grandfather Antipater, a Macedonian of the old school who had refused to worship Alexander. Gonatas himself preferred to seek the theoretic basis of his power in satisfying the requirements of philosophy, and his famous definition of his kingship as a 'noble servitude' shows that in his eyes that basis was the duty of service: the king must be the servant of his people.

What now was the meaning of king-worship[2]? Wendland (p. 361) has called it a 'political religion', and this expresses a truth, provided the emphasis be placed on 'political'; for it had nothing to do with religious feeling. To the king, it was a political measure which gave him a footing in Greek cities and ensured the continuing validity of his acts after death; and it was rendered possible by the general disbelief of the educated classes, for the Olympian religion was spiritually dead, and when king-worship was established nothing else had yet taken its place. To talk about the arrogance of these rulers simply misses the point; no king ever thought he *was* a god, or apparently (unless Antiochus Epiphanes) set much store by his own worship. Antipater in an older world had thought king-worship impious[3]; in the third century men would have smiled at such an idea, though Gonatas probably thought it silly. For (as the common man might argue) what was a god? Two prominent gods of the time, Apollo and Dionysus, had had mortal mothers, even as Alexander or Ptolemy; others, like Asclepius, had been men; and Euhemerus' theory that *all* had once been men was widely known. True, they were immortal; but was not Alexander, whose spirit still inspired

[1] For all this, Tarn, *Antigonos Gonatas*, 250, 435. The Epigonos of the Cnidus epigram (Tarn, *J.H.S.* 1910, 214) is now known, *Milet* 1, 3, no. 138 l. 73.

[2] Ferguson, *C.A.H.* VII, 13–22.

[3] Suidas, *s.v.*

the world, by that fact immortal also? The Olympians conferred no personal salvation, no hope of immortality, little spirituality: and as guardians of the higher morality they were mostly sad misfits. And one had to take so much on trust; one might believe in the power and splendour of Zeus, but one could see the power and splendour of Ptolemy. The local god could not feed you in a famine; but the king did. Perhaps the gods saved Themisonium from the Gauls[1]; Antiochus I, for the time, certainly saved all Asia Minor. Apollo could not help the managers of his temple at Delos to get in his debts from the islands; Ptolemy, when appealed to, sent his admiral, who got them in at once.[2] Had not then a king powers denied to a god? So at least men thought. The popular song in which the Athenians invoked Demetrius' protection against Aetolia ran[3]: 'The other gods either are not, or are far away; either they hear not, or they give no heed; but thou art here, and we can see thee, not in wood or stone, but in very truth.'

This was why the common man took to king-worship; and the cult-names of the earlier kings—Soter the Saviour, Euergetes the Benefactor—express the fact that they were worshipped for what they *did*; Athens worshipped Demetrius because he saved her from Cassander, Rhodes and the islands worshipped Ptolemy I because he saved them from Demetrius, Ionia worshipped Antiochus I because he saved her from the Gauls, and Miletus Antiochus II because he put down a tyrant[4]; the typical function of kingship was held to be *philanthropia*, helpfulness to subjects.[5] It must be remembered that such worship was not confined to kings, but was extended to private benefactors,[6] such as Diogenes, who aided Athens to freedom in 229 and was worshipped

[1] Presumably in 278; Paus. X, 32, 4; Wilhelm, *Πρακτικὰ Ἀκαδ. Ἀθηνῶν* VI, 1931, 319 *sqq.*

[2] Tarn, *Ant. Gon.*, 108.

[3] Athen, 253 D.

[4] *OGIS* 219; App. *Syr.* 65.

[5] Suidas, *βασιλεία* 3; Aristeas, ed. Wendland (*Aristeae ad Philocratem epistola*, 1900), 36, 265, 290; Schubart, *Archiv*, XII, 1937, 9–11; cf. Tarn *Alexander* II, 66.

[6] *Ath. Mitt.* 1907, 247 no. 4 l. 39; Hepding, *Klio* XX, 490.

there beside Ptolemy III,[1] and Diodorus, priest of Zeus at Pergamum,[2] to whom in his lifetime a temple was erected and splendidly inaugurated at Philetaireia for the salvation which he had brought to Pergamum in the troubles after 133; he even became eponymous hero of a tribe, an honour otherwise confined to gods or kings. At the same time the Athenian ephebes began to sacrifice to 'the benefactors' of the city generally.[3] In the Achaean League both Aratus and Philopoemen received cults after death[4]; and the cult of men after death as heroes was common, and much older than Hellenism.

Besides Saviour and Benefactor, most of the royal cult-names were drawn from family relationships—Philadelphus, Philopator, Philometor; but there was one which stood on a different footing, Epiphanes,[5] the god manifest. It was first bestowed on Ptolemy V, probably at his coming of age[6] in 197; as he was then only a boy of 12, and was also perhaps the first of his line to be crowned in Egyptian fashion by the priests, the title, whose equivalent in the Egyptian text of the Rosetta Stone is 'He who cometh forth'—an exact representation of Epiphanes—may have been bestowed on him by the Egyptian priests, to whom the boy really was the Sun-god manifest upon earth; the political events of the time will not account for it.[7] But it was in the hands of its second wearer that the title became significant. Antiochus IV Epiphanes was perhaps the one monarch who took his divinity seriously; but whether this was in any sense personal, and whether his brilliance really at times overstepped the line which we call insanity, can hardly be said. But certainly his reasons were mainly political; he saw that, to withstand Rome, his kingdom must become homogeneous in culture and cult,[8] which could both only be Greek; and just

[1] *I.G.* II² 1011 l. 14; A. Wilhelm, *Beiträge* 76 no. 64.

[2] *Ath. Mitt.* 1907, 243 no. 4. [3] Heberdey in Benndorf's *Festschrift*, 114.

[4] Plut. *Arat.* 53; Ditt.³ 624; *I.G.* V, 2, 432.

[5] Pfister, *Epiphanie* in P.W. [6] Nock, *J.H.S.* 1928, 38.

[7] Pfister's theory that it came from the Seleucids breaks down on the dates.

[8] 1 Macc. 1, 41–2.

as he turned native towns into cities with Greek forms on an extensive scale, so he possibly looked to the worship of himself as Zeus manifest for a means of unification; he was the first Seleucid to use his cult-name and divine title on his coinage. In the later period all cult-names lost any particular significance, and even Epiphanes meant no more than The Most Christian King once meant.

As Rome gradually became the dominant factor in Hellenistic politics, the Greek cities began to transfer to her the phenomena of king-worship; the 'goddess Rome'—the sum total of Romans—was worshipped at Smyrna in 195 and Alabanda in 170,[1] in each case as a display of gratitude for 'salvation'—protection against Antiochus III; after the creation of the province of Asia, the same worship is found at Miletus, Elaea, and elsewhere.[2] It gave Rome the same footing in free Greek cities as the deified kings had possessed. It was accompanied by the worship of Roman 'benefactors' —of Flamininus, conqueror of Philip V, at Chalcis,[3] and M'. Aquilius, who settled Asia, at Pergamum.[4] In the first century Roman governors were worshipped indiscriminately, and Cicero had much trouble in preventing it in his own case[5]; and here certainly the servility of fear showed itself, for these people often did little but harm. The culminating point was the worship of Caesar at Ephesus as a god manifest[6]; finally everything passed into the official provincial worships of Rome and Augustus.

As regards marriage, the Successors of the first period were frankly a law to themselves. Antigonus I and Cassander were apparently convinced monogamists; Seleucus, and probably Ptolemy,[7] like Alexander, had two legitimate queens at once; Demetrius and Pyrrhus were free polygamists; Lysimachus always sent the then queen away before marrying her successor. After the first generation, the custom of one wife only at a time became absolute,

[1] Tac. *Ann.* IV, 56; Livy XLIII, 6.
[2] *Milet.* I, 7 no. 203; Ditt.³ 694. [3] *I.G.* XII, 9, 931; Plut. *Flam.* 16.
[4] *Ath. Mitt.* 1907, 247, l. 40; H. Seyrig, *Rev. arch.* 29, 1929, 95, n. 4.
[5] *Ad Quint.* I, 1, 26. [6] Ditt.³ 760. [7] Tarn, *C.Q.* 1929, 138.

though she could be repudiated at will and another taken; some kings kept mistresses, some apparently did not. Queens were generally of some royal house, though the lesser dynasties of Asia Minor counted; Berenice, the ultimate wife of Ptolemy I, may be an exception, but possibly she was related to Antipater[1]; later exceptions were the marriages of Attalus I with the much-praised Apollonis, daughter of a citizen of Cyzicus, and of Antiochus III with a girl of Chalcis. In Egypt, after Arsinoe II Philadelphus set the example, the queen's head always appeared on the coinage with her husband's; and both Arsinoe II and her mother Berenice wore the diadem.[2] From Arsinoe's time onward the queens in Egypt were officially styled 'sister queen',[3] a style which the Seleucids adopted for other reasons[4] (p. 138) and which has led to some misunderstanding; of the first five Ptolemies only two married their sisters. These Macedonian princesses are an interesting study,[5] not merely because of their capabilities, their ambitions, and (often) their loyalties, but because, at least in the third century, there is little even hinted against their morality; no lover is anywhere recorded. It would seem as if, with a woman like Arsinoe II, ambition left no room for anything else; as if she knew her own powers and meant somehow to get free scope for them. She got it after her marriage with Ptolemy II, when she became co-ruler in name and ruler in fact; and the way in which she pulled round the lost war against Antiochus I and turned it into a sweeping Egyptian triumph might rank, if we knew the details, as one of the biggest things a woman ever did. Even when the dynasties were wearing out the women kept their vigour longer than the men; Cleopatra Thea, the only Seleucid queen who coined in her own name, almost made kings at her pleasure, and the last Cleopatra of Egypt was feared by Romans as they had feared no one since Hannibal.

[1] Maas, *Riv. fil.* 1927, 68.

[2] On these coins, Kock, *Z. f. Num.* XXXIV, 67; Robinson, *Cyrenaica*, 75–6.

[3] *OGIS* 60, 65, 84, 99.

[4] *Ib* 219, 224.

[5] G. H. Macurdy, *Hellenistic Queens*, 1932.

Certain features were common to all the kingdoms. The king was the State; ministers and officials were only his men, whom he made or removed at pleasure; his council of 'Friends' was purely advisory.[1] He was the fount of law[2]; and if the officials acted on rules laid down for them in his rescripts, he laid down what rules he chose. He had a secretarial department[3] to draft rescripts, and the Secretary kept an official Journal,[4] checked daily by the king, which recorded military and political events of importance; between Journals and rescripts a secretarial language grew up, whose influence can be seen in Polybius. The provinces, home or foreign, were normally governed by *strategoi*, generals with military powers, though the Antigonids never used the system in Macedonia proper and Thessaly and very sparingly in Greece; the Ptolemies and Seleucids[5] also had a Lord High Admiral (*nauarchos*), the Egyptian nauarch under Ptolemy II being almost a Viceroy of the Sea.[6] But, speaking generally, the system of delegation was inadequate; the work that fell on a conscientious monarch—military, administrative, legal, commercial, even to the mere writing —was overwhelming; the apparent slackness in later life of certain once energetic kings doubtless means that they were worn out.

Since in Macedonia, when the king died, the crown was in the hands of the army till it appointed the new king, it followed that the State was in abeyance with each death, and that all treaties made by or with, and grants made by, the dead king came to an end unless and until his successor renewed them.[7] The new king usually renewed grants on payment of a fine, the 'crown tax'; but the other party to a treaty got a free hand, a bad system whose ill-effects can be seen in the actions of Aetolia when her treaties of neutrality with Gonatas and Doson ended with their respective deaths.

[1] Polyb. V, 41, 6; *OGIS* 315, VI.
[2] E. R. Goodenough, *Yale Class. Studies* 1928, 55.
[3] Collomp *op. c.*; *OGIS* 259; Polyb. IV, 87, 8.
[4] Wilcken, *Phil.* LIII, 80; cf. Aristeas (ed. Wendland) 296 *sqq*.
[5] Polyb. V, 43, 1.
[6] Tarn, *J.H.S.* 1911, 251; 1933, 61.
[7] Rostovtzeff, *Kolonat*, 252.

On the other hand, the acts of a Seleucid or a Ptolemy, once he was a god, must have remained valid after his death; but these kings nevertheless retained the theory that grants ended with the demise of the Crown, for the purpose of imposing the crown tax.

The kings had the ordinary apparatus of a Court,[1] and the military arrangements usual since Alexander—an *agema* or guard, a corps of Royal Pages, boys of good birth training for commissions, and officers called Bodyguards. Alexander's Bodyguards had been his Staff; but by the second century this term, together with Friends and Kinsmen, had merely become Court titles conferred by the king in a definite precedence, Kinsmen being the highest.[2] The outward expression of kingship was the diadem, a band of white linen round the head; kings sometimes granted to others, officials or play-actors, the right to wear the royal purple of Macedonia,[3] now known to have been violet, not crimson.[4] The recognition of the secondary kingdoms of Asia as royal favoured the formation of an international royal caste; a certain amount of royal correspondence remains, and the time-honoured opening 'Hoping this finds you well as it leaves me', now extinct or confined to the uneducated, was then the formula with which the kings of the earth regularly began letters to one another.[5]

The army and navy were the king's. At sea there was a race between Ptolemies and Antigonids in building great warships[6]; it began in 314 with the invention, by or for Demetrius, of the hepteres, a galley of seven men to the oar, whose power-ratio to that of a quinquereme would be expressed by 7 : 5; it proved its value at Salamis (in Cyprus) in 306. Vessels of 8, 9, and 10 men to the oar are often

[1] See G. Corradi, *Studi hellenistici*, 1929, ch. II.

[2] Strack, *Rh. Mus.* LV, 161; Willrich, *Klio* IX, 416.

[3] *Ib.*; also Livy XXX, 42, 6; XXXI, 35, 1; &c.

[4] The Macedonian king of the Villa Boscoreale fresco (p. 322 n. 4).

[5] *OGIS* 168 III, 257, 315 II, IV, V, VI; Jos. *Ant.* XII, 148; XIII, 166; XIV, 306.

[6] Tarn, *Hellenistic military and naval developments*, 1930, 132–41; 'The oarage of Greek warships', *Mariner's Mirror* XIX, 1933, 52, 69 *sqq.* These give references and reasons.

recorded in action; a papyrus has shown that in common speech they were merely known by their numbers, the vessel in question being called 'the nine'.[1] It seems extremely probable that Greeks and Phoenicians, like Venetians later, never put more than ten men to an oar, though more are known later in France; so when Demetrius next built an eleven, it had to embody a new principle; the number must represent two grouped oars of six and five men, echeloned in some way which could now only be ascertained by experiment. By 301 Demetrius had a thirteen, of which Ptolemy II built a whole class; and when in 285 Demetrius lost the sea to Egypt, his two flagships were a fifteen and a sixteen. Ptolemy II secured the fifteen, and must have dedicated it at Delos,[2] for the great dock presumably built for it has been excavated.[3] Lysimachus got the sixteen, a most famous vessel; it led the fleet with which his successor Keraunos defeated Antigonus Gonatas, and was preserved in Macedonia till, after Pydna, Aemilius Paullus took the old ship to Rome and was rowed in her up the Tiber. Another famous vessel was Antigonus Gonatas' later flagship *Isthmia*,[4] an eighteen, in which he defeated Ptolemy's fleet at Cos; after the battle he dedicated her on Delos to Apollo. Ptolemy II then built a twenty and a thirty, and honoured the designer, Pyrgoteles[5]; the thirty must have been a monstrous trireme, with *three* grouped ten-man oars. Finally Ptolemy IV built a forty,[6] a monstrous quadrireme with a double prow and stern, like the old Calais-Douvres; but she was a failure. It cannot be said if any vessel larger than Gonatas' eighteen was ever in action, all accounts of the naval battles between Gonatas and Egypt being lost.

There were two definite theories of sea-fighting throughout the third century; speaking very roughly, the Athenian-

[1] Edgar, *P. Zeno* no. 59036.

[2] Tarn, *B.C.H.* XLVI, 1922, 473; see Couchoud's note p. 476.

[3] Couchoud and Svoronos, *Le monument dit 'des Taureaux' à Délos*, *B.C.H.* XLV, 1921, 270.

[4] Tarn, *The dedicated ship of Antigonus Gonatas*, *J.H.S.* XXX, 1910, 209.

[5] *OGIS* 39.

[6] Athen. 203 E.

Phoenician tradition of swift ships manœuvring for the ram was adopted by Carthage, Rhodes, and probably Egypt (which held Phoenicia), the Corinthian-Syracusan tradition of heavier ships seeking to grapple and board by Macedonia and Rome. In the second century the standard quadriremes and quinqueremes saw their greater sisters die out in the Aegean, possibly a matter of expense and manpower rather than efficiency; while Philip V created a revolution in 201 by successfully putting in line light Illyrian galleys (*lembi*),[1] precursors of the Roman Liburnian. The great Hellenistic ships lingered on in Egypt, and Antony for a moment revived their use; but Rome never adopted them, and the Empire's return to triremes and Liburnians closed a rather extraordinary chapter in naval history.

Land warfare[2] had been transformed by Alexander's use of heavy cavalry; and from Issus in 333 to Sellasia in 222 cavalry was king. Alexander had been a master in the combination of arms—heavy and light infantry of various types, heavy and light cavalry; his successors retained all the types and added war-elephants, which he never used. While his influence lasted, the typical formation of the line was the phalanx of heavy infantry in the centre, light-armed and cavalry on the wings; the cavalry opened, and sometimes ended, the fighting, there being battles where the heavy infantry never engaged at all. For a century after his death war was largely waged by means of mercenaries, drawn from every people of Europe and Asia[3]; after 278 Gallic mercenaries were much in favour, being brave and, at first, cheap. The kings welcomed the use of mercenaries, as they could thus spare their national home-troops who formed the phalanx; also mercenaries rarely fought to the death,[4] and war often meant compelling the enemy's

[1] Polyb. XVI, 2–7.

[2] The latest general work is Kromayer and Veith, *Heerwesen und Kriegsführung der Griechen und Römer*, 1928. See Tarn, *Hellenistic military and naval developments*, 1930, for this and the next section.

[3] G. T. Griffith, *The Mercenaries of the Hellenistic World*, 1935; M. Launey, *Recherches sur les armées hellénistiques*, I, 1949.

[4] A case in Josephus, *Ant.* XIII, 378.

mercenaries to surrender and then enlisting them. But by 222 the mode of warfare was changing, and the phalanx, the national Macedonian arm, coming back into first place; Sellasia in 222 and Raphia in 217 were both decided by the clash of national phalanxes, who fought as men fight when national feeling is involved. It was unfortunate for Macedonia that, when she encountered Rome, Alexander's methods had been forgotten. Alexander's phalanx had been an active and flexible body, organised in numerous battalions, its spears being thirteen to fourteen feet in length[1]; even so, he took enormous care to guard its flanks, and it was more than once in trouble through failure to keep line. But at Cynoscephalae Philip V was using a phalanx which had grown rigid and non-flexible with the weight of the lengthened spears,[2] everything being sacrificed to having as many spearheads as possible projecting before the front rank, while the vital need of very strong flank guards was being neglected. Certainly the phalanx scarcely had a fair chance at either Cynoscephalae or Pydna, as both battles started irregularly; and doubtless *under its own conditions*—level ground and impregnable flank guards—it would have beaten the legions or anything else. But such conditions were rare, and did not in fact happen against Rome; and the ability of the legion to fight well under most conditions was conclusive. The phalanx, like the dinosaurs, perished of over-specialisation.

The age of giant warships at sea was the age of elephant-warfare on land; all Alexander's generals, impressed by the desperate battle with Porus, valued elephants highly, and the arrival of the different batches from India between 324 and 275 can still be traced. By about 275 Ptolemy II was beginning to hunt African elephants[3]; his unique embassy to the Mauryan Vindusara[4] was doubtless sent to obtain Indian trainers and mahouts, and the Ptolemies trained Africans till the second century. But the Seleucids were the true

[1] Theophr. *H. Plant* III, 12, 2, must mean the short Macedonian cubits; Tarn, *Alexander* II, App. 2.

[2] Polyb. XVIII, 29–30.

[3] Date: Tarn, *C.Q.* 1926, 99.

[4] Pliny VI, 58.

'elephant-lords'; it was largely the elephants of Ipsus (p. 11) which gave Seleucus Asia, and when Rome in 163 tried to disarm the dynasty it was the destruction of the elephants which enraged the people most. Elephants were deadly the first time, against troops who had never met them; against experienced infantry they soon lost effectiveness, but were often useful against cavalry. Indians and Africans met once, at Raphia, and on one wing the Africans were beaten; but no deductions can be drawn, as they were heavily outnumbered.[1]

Administration in the kingdoms in Asia and Egypt is dealt with elsewhere; but Macedonia under the Antigonids may be noticed here.[2] This national state retained its vigour to the end; it depended on its national army, mercenaries being used merely to spare the Macedonians where possible. Court life was simpler than in the other kingdoms, the amount of wealth small in comparison—the land tax produced little over 200 talents a year—and the throne, till the later years of Philip V, was occupied by kings of a high type; their family loyalty was proverbial, and the dynasty knew no murders till Philip V, while Gonatas' interest in philosophy and history, and the circle of literary men he collected, were one of the features of his age. Pella was again the capital; no attempt was made to build a rival to Alexandria or Antioch. Probably there was no King's land in Macedonia proper, and the Macedonian peasant owned his farm; but in conquered districts, like Chalcidice and Paeonia, the land passed to the State, *i.e.* the king. The Antigonids treated their King's land much as did the Seleucids (Chap. IV); they gave estates to nobles, and 'lots' of the usual type to military settlers and time-expired mercenaries; but seemingly they never gave the absolute property in the

[1] On the African elephant see Sir William Gowers, *African Affairs* (Journal of the Royal African Society), 1948, 173.

[2] Tarn, *Ant. Gon.* 1913, ch. VII, will give references for this section and the next. See further for Macedonia *C.A.H.* VII, ch. 6, and bibliography p. 880; *ib.* VIII, Holleaux's bibliography to chs. 5–7; W. Fellmann, *Antigonos Gonatas, König der Makedonen, und die griechischen Staaten*, 1930; F. Granier and F. Hampl, *op. c.* on p. 47.

land, as the Seleucids often did, but retained a right of escheat. King's land not in grant was cultivated by tenants, and the kings owned the mines and forests.

Macedonia, or at least its upper classes, became thoroughly hellenised in the third century; the Macedonian dialect was replaced either by Attic Greek or the 'common speech', and the native pantheon[1] by the Olympians. In spite of their mixture of blood the Macedonians were now one people, able to assimilate foreign settlers; and the country had become only one more unit of the Greek circle, more powerful than others, though it never again raised such armies as in the fourth century. Men in the Greek coastal cities were now calling themselves Macedonians.[2] Pella, and doubtless the other old Macedonian towns, had become autonomous cities with Greek city-forms. The Antigonids built a few cities of secondary importance, but the principal new cities in the country were both founded by Cassander: Thessalonica (Salonica), and Cassandreia on the site of Potidea. Both were Greek cities with Greek organisation, and the Cassandreians never called themselves Macedonians. Macedonia seemed strange in Greek eyes because the country had no religious centre and the people were convinced monarchists; the Antigonid house, thanks to Gonatas, so secured the people's affections that the dynasty only fell through the overwhelming power of a foreign enemy. But for all the great men Macedonia produced, perhaps the greatest thing about the little country was the plain Macedonian peasant, free, loyal, and entirely competent in peace and war alike; Macedonia fell before Rome solely because there were so few Macedonians.

For the existing Greek cities, the period bridges the

[1] Given by Tarn, *Ant. Gon.* 177, with references, and more fully in *C.A.H.* VII, 197 *sq.*; see also Lehmann Haupt, *Klio* XXII, 1929, 401, and Costanzi, *Annali Univ. Toscane* XXXIII (1915).

[2] *Ant. Gon.* 185–6; add *'Eφ. 'Aρχ.* 1914, 183 no. 242; *I.G.* XII, 9, 199. At Philippi, however (the Thasian foundation Crenides augmented by Philip II) the inhabitants were still Philippians throughout the Macedonian period: P. Collart, *Philippes ville de Macédoine*, ch. V, contains the little that is known of its history.

transition from free city-states to municipalities of the Roman Empire. It opens with two conflicting theories of the relations of the monarchy and the city. Alexander had treated the Greek cities as free allies,[1] Antipater had desired to treat them as subjects, garrisoning those he chose and maintaining in power oligarchies or tyrants favourable to himself; and the conflict of these rival policies lasted long.[2] Cassander, Lysimachus, the Ptolemies, and the Attalids, all essentially followed Antipater in treating the cities as subjects. Antigonus I, as a political weapon against Cassander, revived Alexander's methods, and for years really treated the cities as free; but later he began to interfere with them, and at the end was garrisoning those he desired. Demetrius followed the same course, beginning with freedom and ending with subjection; he[3] and Lysimachus[4] introduced a new feature, taxation, probably developed out of the nominally voluntary war 'contributions' received by Alexander and Antigonus I from their allied cities. Gonatas employed every system as expediency might dictate; Doson returned frankly to Alexander. Under Seleucus and Antiochus I some cities were free allies, some subject and apparently taxed (chap. IV); the restoration of freedom to Ionia by Antiochus II was a landmark.[5] Perhaps on the whole a tendency to treat the cities as subjects was dominant, varied by strenuous revivals of Alexander's policy of free alliance; but the matter is enormously complicated with every kind of variation and exception, and of course there were cities and (in Greece) countries which never had any connection with any monarchy at all. Free alliance was not unconditioned freedom, for the city's foreign policy was shaped by its more powerful ally; but it was complete internal freedom. As time went on taxation became more and more the sign of subjection, and absence of taxation of freedom; and Antipater's methods

[1] Tarn, *Alexander* II, App. 7, 1.

[2] Traced, *C.A.H.* VI, 362, 418, 438, 485.

[3] Tarn, *Ant. Gon.* 76 n. 15, 113 n. 4.

[4] Beloch IV, 1, 234; cf. Phylarchus, *F.H.G.* I, 350. A. Andréadès, *'Ιστορία τῆς 'Ελληνικῆς δημοσίας οἰκονομίας* II, part 1 (1930), App. B′, p, 94.

[5] *OGIS* 226, cf. 227; Jos. *Ant.* XII, 125 *sqq.*

were replaced by the royal *epistates* or city governor, a system not necessarily oppressive in good hands. Another method occasionally employed was for the king to appoint one or more of the chief magistrates himself, as did the Attalids at Pergamum,[1] Ptolemy I at Cyrene,[2] and probably the later Ptolemies at Ptolemais in Egypt[3]; Gonatas did this at Athens from 262 to 255,[4] perhaps the only instance in Greece itself.

As an example of the complication referred to, Gonatas' reign may be taken. Old Macedonia[5] and Thessaly (p. 70) he governed directly; their cities were under city governors, but their Assemblies were not controlled. Chalcidice he governed through a general; Thessalonica had a city governor who controlled the Assembly,[6] but Cassandreia was probably fully autonomous. In Greece the city Assemblies were never controlled, but Corinth, Chalcis and Piraeus were garrisoned and, with Megara and Euboea, were under generals. Athens was free from 288 onwards, but retained good relations with Gonatas; from 262 to 255 there was a garrison and *epistates*,[7] and Gonatas appointed the magistrates; after 255 Athens was free and ungarrisoned again, but Gonatas was now definitely suzerain.[8] Argos, Megalopolis, and perhaps other Peloponnesian cities were ruled in his interest by partisans of his own who had seized power as tyrants; the rest of Greece had no connection with him and did as it pleased. This kind of thing cannot be summed up under any sweeping phrases about the subjection of Greece. There was much interplay of forces going on, as there always had been; the real difference was that *certain* cities, like Corinth, now got little chance of freedom. But it must be remembered, in talking about freedom, that Greeks too often meant by it

[1] *OGIS* 267 II.

[2] Ferri, *Alcune Iscriz. di Cirene* no. 1=*SEG* IX, 1, which gives the bibliography.

[3] Bevan, *Hist. of Egypt* 106.

[4] Athen. 167 F; *B.C.H.* 1924, 264.

[5] Ditt.[3] 459.

[6] *I.G.* XI, 4, 1053.

[7] Fr. of Philodemos (Jacoby, *Apollodor's Chronik*, 375).

[8] Sacrifices for him, *I.G.* II[2] 775, 776, 780; see Tarn, *Harvard Studies in Class. Philol.*, Suppl. vol. I, 487.

merely freedom to destroy each other, and nothing ever restrained them but a king or a League; when in 217 Agelaus appealed for Greek unity against Rome one of the inducements he offered was retention of the right to fight each other without interference, and even late in the period Byzantium, being independent, practically destroyed Callatis, the most flourishing Greek city of the western Euxine.[1] Indeed even federalism, though it might restrain, could not abolish that spirit of particularism which was the curse of Greece.

Considered from without, the constitution of the self-governing Greek city, in the third century, looked much the same as it had always done; it had its Assembly, Council, and magistrates, its jurisdiction over its citizens, its immature finance, its intestine quarrels. In northern Greece there was even a steady increase in the number of autonomous cities, especially in Aetolia. But in reality modification was going on, due to the root fact that the actual political life of the city, considered as a thing in which all shared, was losing its former importance and interest (Chap. III). By the second quarter of the third century oligarchy and democracy, as political ideologies, were dead; the real line of cleavage took other directions. In Asia it might be pro-Seleucid and pro-Ptolemy, in any city the King's party and the Nationalists; but often it was merely rich and poor, an unhealthy sign, for the old democratic parties had frequently included both. The Assemblies lost ground; power might pass to the Council, but was often exercised by the magistrates as a board; it illustrates their growing importance that a city making an alliance or entering a League often altered its magistracies to conform to those of the League or the ally.[2] Two magistracies steadily grew greater: the *agoranomos*, who saw to the corn supply, and the *gymnasiarchos*, who superintended education. In some cities of

[1] Memnon, 21.

[2] Swoboda, *Klio* XII, 38; *Staatsaltertümer* 414 *sq.*; W. Schönfelder, *Die städtischen und Bundesbeamten des gr. Festlandes*, 50, 53, 107; Plassart and Blum, *B.C.H.* 1914, 472.

Asia the priestly *stephanephoros*, after whom the year was named, became the chief magistrate[1]; only a wealthy man could hold the office, for the duties included entertaining the citizens.[2] It was put up to sale, the city thus doubly benefiting, and it shows the reality of civic patriotism, even in the later period, that men were found to pay for the privilege of paying still further; but in times of trouble there was sometimes no purchaser, and the local god bought in the office and named the year. From the second century priesthoods too were regularly sold,[3] and entailed expenditure, but here the purchaser received some return; he might escape the burden of the gymnasiarchy or trierarchy, or the obligation to provide money or choruses for the festivals, while at Miletus in the first century the priest of the Roman People even received a modest salary.[4] The *gymnasiarchos* and *agoranomos* might also have to spend largely themselves; and the result of the changes above indicated was that ultimately a poor man could no longer hold one of the city offices, unless, as sometimes happened, some king or wealthy citizen had endowed it. When the Roman Republic became dominant these tendencies were carried still further; Rome replaced the democracies by timocracies, new boards of magistrates appeared, like the politarchs in the Macedonian and Thessalian cities,[5] and sometimes a minute oligarchy held power, like the fifty 'Lords of Miletus'.[6] Rome might claim that she was only carrying out to its logical conclusion the powers of the *demiourgoi* and the *apokletoi* in the Achaean and Aetolian Leagues (*post*).

One typical measure, much used by the kings, was synoecism,[7] the making of two or more cities or communities into one; Antigonus I formed Antigoneia Troas out of seven

[1] Priene, *OGIS* 215; Iasos, Michel 462 *sqq.*; Magnesia, *ib.* 914; Miletus, lists in *Milet* I, 3.

[2] *I. Priene* 108, 109, 113.

[3] Ditt.[3] 1002, 1003, 1006, 1009–15; *I. Priene* 174, 201; *Milet* I, 7, 203.

[4] *Milet ib.*

[5] Tarn, *Ant. Gon.* 197; add Ditt.[3] 700. After 168 in Macedonia, because at Phalanna in Thessaly the native ταγοί (*I.G.* IX, 2 1228, 3rd cent., and 'Εφ. 'Αρχ. 1916, 21 no. 274, early 2nd) were then replaced by πτολίαρχοι, *I.G.* IX, 2, 1233.

[6] *Milet* I, 7, 203, l. 39, combined with 208.

[7] The process in detail, Ditt.[3] 344.

cities, and Cassander synoecised twenty-six communities into Thessalonica. The cities synoecised might be obliterated, but often only part of the population was moved, and the old cities survived as 'villages' (*i.e.* demes) of the new great city. The most extraordinary synoecism known was Demetrias,[1] the city on the Gulf of Pagasae which Demetrius founded as his southern capital. It adjoined Pagasae, with a separate wall, making one city with two quarters.[2] Nothing was destroyed to make it, but Pagasae and every city[3] of Magnesia from Cape Sepias to Tempe on the Macedonian frontier became villages of Demetrias, which thus embraced the whole Magnesian territory and formed a projection of Macedonia southwards. When Rome deprived Philip V of Magnesia she broke this synoecism up.

The city was not the only typical Greek state-form; for almost every country of Northern Greece was organised under some traditional form of cantonal commune, called indifferently a *koinon* (Community or League) or a Folk, always with a religious centre. The growing feeling of impotence in the third century among the smaller cities in face of the monarchies led, in Greece itself, to a great extension of the Federal principle, and the big Hellenistic Leagues almost came to constitute a middle term between city and monarchy; they tended to come under single heads, and Aratus enjoyed an authority in the Achaean League very like one-man rule. They rendered much service; they gave greater security and bargaining power as against the monarchies, while they kept their members' disputes within limits and prevented them fighting each other. It is unfortunate that Greeks only possessed one word for almost every form of public and private association; they would have applied *koinon* equally to the League of Nations, the Swiss Republic, a Cambridge College, a Trade Union, and the village cricket club; and it is too late now, in translating it, to avoid various improper uses of the word League.

[1] *I.G.* IX, 2, 1109; Str. 436. [2] Arvanitopoullos, *'Εφ. 'Αρχ.* 1914, 264.
[3] Certain on geographical grounds. On inscriptions, F. Stählin, *Ath. Mitt.* LIV, 201.

Before coming to the Federal State proper (*Bundesstaat*), one body must be noticed which was a confederation of separate sovereign states (*Staatenbund*). The Panhellenic League of Corinth,[1] formed by Philip II, and continued by Alexander under new treaties, was in its way a great conception, and afforded the only chance ever offered of the realisation of that old dream, the unification of the Greek world, if Greeks would have so regarded it. It was an alliance between Alexander and the individual Greek states, Sparta standing out, with a congress of delegates meeting at Corinth; the members remained sovereign states, and their internal affairs were to be free from interference unless there was social revolution in any city (p. 121), but Alexander was President and Commander-in-Chief, and in practice their foreign policy was his. This however was not inevitable; had the greater cities cared to work the League whole-heartedly in unison they were strong enough to prevent any encroachment on their liberties and make their voices heard in foreign politics. The strong point of the League was that it gave the small cities proportionate rights with the large ones, and some cities regarded it as a charter of liberty; but in some cities it was unfortunately based on governments that were unpopular, and to many Greeks it was only a symbol of foreign domination; the moment Alexander died it broke up. Its revival by Demetrius[2] in 303 had a better chance, for his League was based on democratic governments which heartily supported him; but this League also broke up after Ipsus. It was revived a third time by Antigonus Doson, the members now being, not single cities—there were scarcely any single city-states left except Athens and Sparta—but the Leagues of Achaea, Boeotia, Phocis, Thessaly, Epirus, Acarnania, *and* Macedonia; for, as already noticed, the Macedonian king alone was no longer, in form, the Macedonian state. Doson's League had no pretensions to be Panhellenic (p. 21); but the League

[1] Tod. *Gk. Hist. Inscr.* II, 177, with bibliography.

[2] *SEG* I, 75, with Wilcken's new fragment *Berl. S.B.* 1927, 277; literature *C.A.H.* VI, 607; *Woch.* 1928, 700.

states were strong enough to force the Social War upon Philip V against his will, which illustrates what the old League of Corinth might have done had it desired. This League was the last attempt made by Macedonia to unite Greece. But Greece *was* ultimately unified in a single Panhellenic confederation; it was done by the Emperor Hadrian[1] three centuries after it had ceased to have any meaning, an ironical epitaph on the unity which Greece could never achieve for herself.

Turning to Federalism proper,[2] we find three main classes: the League that was created by, or was the instrument of, some king; the League which grew out of a cantonal commune; and the League of cities. Of the first category Thessaly was the principal instance; until Philip V lost the country in 197 each successive Macedonian king from Philip II onwards ruled Thessaly as part of Macedonia by becoming head for life of its League; doubtless the Epirote kings sometimes ruled Acarnania by holding the headship of her League. Epirus itself[3] exhibits a long and complicated conflict between the principles of federalism and monarchy; by about 330–300 its three stems, Molossians, Chaonians, and Thesprotians, had constituted themselves the federal 'Epirote Alliance' under the headship of the Molossian king, whom the Molossians could depose if they desired; in Pyrrhus' hands the monarchy had become practically an autocracy; about 235 the people killed off Pyrrhus' last descendants and became a federal republic. Very peculiar bodies were the Leagues founded by Antigonus I during his struggle for power. He would have liked to have re-formed the League of Corinth, but as until 303 this was impossible, he created three sectional Leagues: the Ionian, a revival of the old League; the Ilian, a League of the Aeolian cities with Ilium as federal centre; and the Islanders, the Ionian Cyclades with their federal centre at Delos. These Leagues were not

[1] Tod, *J.H.S.* 1922, 173.

[2] For what follows see my bibliography of the Leagues, *C.A.H.* VII, 883 *sq.*, especially Swoboda's *Staatsaltertümer*; and *C.A.H.* VIII, Holleaux's bibliography to chs. 5–7.

[3] G. N. Cross, *Epirus*, 1932, who discusses the inscriptions.

sovereign states; they had no Assembly, no civil head, no military or judicial powers, and apparently no coinage; business was transacted by a council of delegates, and extraordinary expenses had to be met by the cities. Their chief business was to conduct their federal festivals and worship Antigonus; they were really channels by which he obtained influence over their constituent free cities.

Of Leagues developed out of the cantonal communes of different Folks there were several in northern Greece; but the principal example was Aetolia, the one country in Greece which from first to last was never conquered by, and never depended on, any king. Aetolia possessed few towns and no capital, the federal centre being the temple of Apollo at Thermum. When her old commune was reorganised, perhaps at the time of the Theban alliance of 370 and under the influence of that great exponent of federalism Epaminondas[1] (or perhaps even earlier), the League units were frequently not towns but country districts grouped round some village or hill fort; but cities continued gradually to develop. All political power belonged to the Assembly, which comprised every free Aetolian; it sprang simply from the army, the people under arms, and was its civil counterpart; it met twice a year, before and after the campaigning season. The head of the League was a general elected annually, who was President and Commander-in-Chief; re-election was only possible after some years' interval. The other officials were a cavalry leader, a secretary, an *agonothetes* to celebrate festivals, and seven stewards of finance. Aetolia was not an instance of constituent states delegating powers to a federal body; the League grew naturally out of the people's war organisation, but the cities had internal autonomy and their own citizenships.

As the Aetolian League expanded, any country that joined was dissolved into, and joined as, separate cities or units. If a new unit adjoined League territory, it entered into sympolity with Aetolia, that is, its people became for all

[1] M. N. Tod, *Gk. Hist. Inscr.*, II, 137, the inscription that provides the earliest evidence (367) for the existence of the League.

purposes Aetolians, and attended the Assembly. But a city at a distance became an ally and entered into isopolity,[1] an exchange of citizenships; its citizens became *potentially* Aetolians, but their potential Aetolian citizenship only became actual if they settled in, and (as they had the right to) became citizens of, some city of the Aetolian sympolity. We shall meet these potential citizenships again in other connections. The Aetolian League had a Council (*boule*) composed of members elected by the League units in proportion to military contingents; but this body had little power, and only decided current matters which could not wait till the next Assembly. As the League expanded, however, government by the Assembly, *i.e.* by mass meeting twice a year, became impossible, and Aetolia never hit on any form of representation; the result was that the Council threw up a small committee called *Apokletoi*,[2] unknown to the constitution, who sat permanently with the General and really governed the country, though the Assembly kept the power of peace and war; between 280 and 220 Aetolia thus passed from being the most democratic to being about the least democratic State in Greece.

Aetolia was the first League to use its federal citizenship to enlarge its territory; Achaea and Boeotia subsequently copied. By 220 the Aetolian sympolity stretched across Greece from sea to sea, embracing Western and Epicnemidian Locris, Malis, Doris, the Aenianes and Dolopes, part of Acarnania, part of Phocis, part of Thessaly, and Achaea Phthiotis; members allied by isopolity were Cephallenia, Ambracia, Ceos, Chios, Vaxos in Crete, Phigaleia, and (in effect) Messenia; later it even took in Lysimacheia, Cius, and Chalcedon. From about 290 to 189 it controlled Delphi, but Delphi never became a member.[3]

Among Leagues of which, though representing some

[1] Its working; Ditt.[3] 622, see A. J. Reinach, *Rev. Arch.* 1908, ii p. 208. The clearest statement is Swoboda's, *Wien S.B.* 1924 Abh. 2 p. 6; cf. L. Robert, *Rev. E.G.* 1927, 214.

[2] W. Schwahn, 'Die Apokleten der Ätoler und die Apoklesia der Lokrer', *Wien. Stud.*, 1930, 141, considers them to be a committee of the principal officials.

[3] Ditt.[3] 480 n. 4 is conclusive.

definite stem, the basis had been a union of cities and not a cantonal commune, Arcadia and Boeotia were old examples; both suffered many vicissitudes of fortune, but the Boeotian League endured permanently and from time to time embraced Opuntian Locris and Megara. Its federal institutions had not changed radically since the fourth century, and the institutions of its separate cities, while they show some uniformity in their main lines, differ considerably in detail: the cities retained a remarkable freedom of action, even (from time to time) in their foreign relations.[1] The Arcadian League,[2] though sometimes mutilated, lasted till its cities joined the Achaean League. The Achaean was originally a League of the 12 Achaean cities, which broke up during the wars of the Successors; it began to re-form in 280, and by 272 embraced the ten surviving Achaean cities, Helice and Bura having been destroyed by natural causes; subsequently Olenus became an eleventh member.[3] Its effective organisation, however, dated from 255, when a single general replaced the former two. The League was a sympolity like the Aetolian, other countries joining being similarly dissolved into their component parts; the cities kept their citizenship, their constitutions (though some assimilated their magistracies to those of the League), their law courts, and so much internal autonomy that, unlike Aetolia, the local mints coined concurrently with the Federal mint; no citizen of any city had private rights in another without a special grant. All foreign policy, however, was the League's, together with the army, the federal taxes, all weights and measures (which were made uniform), and justice for offences against the League. The federal centre was the temple of Zeus Amarios at the capital Aigion. The general, who was President and Commander-in-Chief, could be re-elected every alternate year; and beside the secretary, treasurer, and admiral were ten *demiourgoi*, seemingly

[1] See M. Feyel, *Polybe et l'histoire de la Boeotie au IIIme siècle avant notre ère*, 1942, 206, 252, 266, and especially 270.

[2] Tarn, *C.R.* XXXIX, 1925, 104; de Sanctis, *Riv. fil.* LV, 485.

[3] *SEG* I, 74.

modelled on the Arcadian fifteen[1] and corresponding to the original ten cities (though if each city originally had a right to one demiurge this was soon dropped), who with the general formed a governing board with considerable power.

It seems probable that Achaea had once had, like other small federations, a Council (*boule*) and an Assembly, and that in the revised League the two coalesced to form the Achaean *sunodos*, which after the League expanded was certainly of great size.[2] It held each year a regular number of meetings, most probably four, at one of which the principal business was the election of the League officials for the coming year. The place of meeting in the third century was Aigion, but in 188 Philopoimen introduced a law which extended the meetings to all the cities in turn, though in practice a strict rotation seems not to have been observed. The *sunodos* dealt with all League policy and business except (normally) new treaties and alliances, and peace and war: these had to be referred to a *sunkletos*, a meeting of all citizens over thirty who chose to attend. The *sunkletos*, in effect, was a mass referendum, votes being taken by cities to prevent the meeting being swamped by the people of the city where it met: the *sunodos* voted in the same way. Aigion was the proper home of the *sunkletos* also, but the practice of summoning meetings elsewhere had already begun well before the end of the third century.

Our judgment upon the League's constitution—a constitution which has been highly praised—must largely depend on what the *sunodos* really was, and there is scarcely one of its characteristics which has not been in dispute. The most probable reconstruction makes it a primary assembly open to precisely the same people who were eligible to attend the *sunkletos* (citizens over thirty), but with additional precautions to try to ensure that its voting should genuinely reflect the state of opinion inside the individual cities: in fact it was necessary to make sure that a certain

[1] Tarn, *C.R.* 1925, 107.

[2] On the Achaean constitution, see especially A. Aymard, *Les assemblées de la Confédération achaienne*, 1938 (full discussions and bibliography).

quorum from each city attended at Aigion four times in the year for meetings liable to last for some days. These quorums together made up the so-called council (*boule*), which cannot have been in any sense a separate chamber,[1] whether one with probouleutic functions or one with powers of ratification or veto; these functions or powers quite clearly did not exist. This *boule* was merely *part of* the *sunodos*, that part of it, in fact, which was *obliged* to attend at a particular session (or the sessions of a particular year), and which consequently might perhaps decide by itself the voting at an ill-attended meeting, though it could easily be outvoted at any time if a sufficient number of volunteers chose to go to the *sunodos*. It is not known either how many citizens made up the *boule* or how they were selected; but if, as seems likely, they were paid for their attendance,[2] it may well have been that the companion practice of democracy, election by lot from all the citizens (in this case, all over thirty), was employed too. For the Achaeans certainly thought of their constitution as a democracy.

In practice however this constitution seems to have favoured the well-to-do and the professional politician, partly perhaps owing to a natural conservatism of the citizen-body of 'over-thirties', partly because the poor probably could not afford to attend meetings of the *sunodos* far from their homes and work except when they happened to be *bouleutai* and were paid for it, and not least perhaps because of the personal ascendancy which could be achieved by an Aratus eligible for re-election as sole *strategos* every other year. Another defect was the limitation of the *sunkletos* to citizens over 30, which meant that half the men who would have to fight had no voice in the declaration of war: Aetolia seemingly had no such limitation, and this may help to explain why in war Aetolia was so much more efficient. Strikingly successful in Achaea, on the other hand,

[1] *Pace* M. Cary, *J.H.S.* LIX, 1939, 154 (review of Aymard).

[2] Despite Aymard *op. c.* 331 ff., and others, this seems to follow from Polyb. XXII, 7, 3 ff.; 8, 1–8.

was the balance struck between federal and city interests; for the infrequency of the federal meetings, ordinary (*sunodos*) and extraordinary (*sunkletos*), proves conclusively that there can have been no encroachment by the federal government on the right of the individual cities to manage their private concerns. There simply would not have been time for it to meddle in these things. The *boule*, too, was an interesting if tentative experiment (doubtless by evolution) in the direction of representative government. The Greeks were slow to evolve any true system of representation, but this example of the Achaean League came nearest to it at the date when it came into being.

The later history of the *koinon* type of state, so far as it is not given in Chapter I, may be briefly indicated here. In 189 Rome curtailed the Aetolian League and deprived it of Delphi, and after 168 she broke the League up altogether; all the members,[1] even to little stems like the Oetaeans, became separate Leagues, and these, with the Leagues formed in 196–4 (p. 26), now accounted for the whole of northern Greece. The only feature of note among them is that the Thessalian League possessed, as the Island League had once possessed, the strange power of granting citizenship in its constituent cities,[2] as had the Cretan League.[3] But the principal new feature in federal institutions of the second century is the tendency to dispense with the primary assembly which had been the legacy from the city-state, and to rely instead on an assembly or council of representatives (*sunedrion*), like a modern parliament. This was the case in the four separate republics of Macedonia, set up under Roman supervision in 167 but conforming no doubt to an established Greek practice which happened to suit the Romans best. Other examples known are in Thessaly perhaps, and certainly in Lycia.[4] The arrival of representative government is

[1] For Western Locris, *A.J.A.* XXVI, 445.

[2] *I.G.* IX, 2, 508; XI, 4, 1038–40, 1042, 1046. See however Swoboda *Wien S.B. l.c.* p. 25.

[3] I. *Magnesia*, 20.

[4] J. A. O. Larsen, *Class. Philol.* XL, 1945, 65; XLIV, 1949, 89; XLV, 1950, 180; A. Aymard, *ib.* XLV, 1950, 96. For a contrary view about Macedonia, M. Feyel, *B.C.H.* LXX, 1946, 187.

interesting for two reasons. First, its use in quite small communities (like the Macedonian republics) suggests that it was used not because it was necessary for geographical reasons but because it was expedient, as favouring the well-to-do classes and keeping the masses out of politics as far as possible. Secondly, its existence here and now served as a model for the Romans in Macedonia, and also in Italy if they had cared to use it on themselves, which they did not.

The Achaean League, which had been from 224 to 198 a satellite of Macedonia, became independent again in 197, so far as an ally of Rome could be; but though in 191 it embraced all Peloponnese, it never recovered the position it had held in 228 (p. 20). But the Federal principle still represented a possible element of power which Rome could not tolerate, and after 146 she dissolved the Achaean and its allied Leagues. *Koina* of a kind were subsequently allowed to re-form [1]; beside those of northern Greece, Leagues of Achaea, Arcadia, Argolis,[2] and the Eleutherolacones are known in the Peloponnese; but they were religious bodies, without political significance. Similar non-political *koina* formed, or were formed, in Asia Minor; those of Bithynia and Pontus date from Pompey, that of Asia was possibly in existence under Antony; there were several others later. Their affinities go back to the Leagues created by Antigonus I; they did in one way represent their provinces, for they could complain to Rome of the provincial governor, but their real business was to conduct the official worship of the Emperor. The only *koinon* known which retained true political functions in Augustus' reign was the old League of the 23 towns of Lycia.[3]

Of the contending state-forms of the Hellenistic period it was thus monarchy which survived, though the Macedonian monarchies perished. Caesar possibly contemplated a Graeco-Roman kingdom of the Hellenistic pattern, though

[1] Best in Kornemann, *κοινόν* in P.W.

[2] *B.C.H.* 1909, 175 no. 2; not in Kornemann.

[3] *OGIS* 99, 198; Str. 664 *sq.*; J. A. O. Larsen, *Class. Philol.* XXXVIII, 1943, 177 and 246; XL, 1945, 67.

this is disputed; Antony actually erected one. But the real heir of the Hellenistic kings was Augustus; for, though his principate was in form Roman and not Hellenistic, his empire was joined by many threads to the Macedonian kingdoms. But this subject belongs to the history of Rome.

CHAPTER III

THE GREEK CITIES: SOCIAL-ECONOMIC CONDITIONS[1]

MAN as a political animal, a fraction of the *polis* or self-governing city state, had ended with Aristotle; with Alexander begins man as an individual. This individual needed to consider both the regulation of his own life and also his relations with the other individuals who with him composed the 'inhabited world'; to meet the former need there arose the philosophies of conduct (Chap. X), to meet the latter certain new ideas of human brotherhood. These originated on the day—one of the critical moments of history—when, at a banquet at Opis, Alexander prayed for a union of hearts (*homonoia*) among all peoples and a joint commonwealth of Macedonians and Persians[2]; he was the first to transcend national boundaries and to envisage, however imperfectly, a brotherhood of man in which there should be neither Greek nor barbarian. The Stoic philosophy was quick to grasp the concept, and Zeno, in his Ideal State,[3] exhibited a resplendent hope which has never quite left men since; he dreamt of a world which should no longer be separate states, but one great City under one divine law, where all were citizens and members one of another, bound together, not by human laws, but by their own willing consent, or (as he phrased it) by Love. This is sometimes called cosmopolitanism, a word coined by the Cynics[4] to signify that they belonged to no state; but other Greeks did not use it, and it has acquired

[1] J. A. O. Larsen, *Roman Greece*, esp. 311–435, in *Economic Survey of Ancient Rome*, IV, 1938 (ed. Tenney Frank) collects material for the Hellenistic period.

[2] For all details see now Tarn, *Alexander* II, App. 25 § VI.

[3] Arnim, *S.V.F.* I, nos. 259–271.

[4] Diog. Laert. VI, 2, 63; Tarn, *op. c.*, App. 25 § II.

such unpleasant associations that it is well to avoid it, for it does not at all express what the Stoics meant; it implied a shirking of national duties which no Stoic would have tolerated, for the wise man (they said) would do his duty by his own country,[1] and they seem to have understood that if their brotherhood were ever realised it must be through the national state and not by its denial. Even the practical world was influenced, in spite of itself, by Zeno's dream, through the insistence of Zeno's school on certain notions of equality and brotherhood and by the fact that the 'inhabited world' or *oecumene*[2] now began to be treated as a whole; the stranger could no longer be *ipso facto* an enemy, and Homonoia received perhaps more tributes than any other Hellenistic concept. Certain ideas of the interrelation of states, apart from actual treaties, began to emerge; and the germs of modern international law go back to third-century Stoicism.

Between these ideas of individualism and brotherhood the Greek had to work out his own salvation afresh. The first thing to notice is a certain enlargement of the feeling of humanity. The time was full of extraordinary contradictions—which is perhaps to say that the Greek was human—and this feeling grew up in the midst of interminable dissensions and wars. The Greek was as quarrelsome as ever; the change was, that he began to doubt whether he ought to be. Isocrates in 370 had desired to unite all Greeks for an attack on Persia; Agelaus in 217 desired to unite them for defence against Rome[3]; the difference is eloquent. One result was an enormous growth of arbitration.[4] Arbitration had for long been employed, though sparingly, in Greece, but in and after the third century arbitrations between cities, usually boundary arbitrations,[5] became exceedingly common; generally the arbitrators were a commission from

[1] *S.V.F.* 697.

[2] Kaerst, *Die antike Idee der Oikumene*, 1903.

[3] Polyb. V, 104.

[4] Tod, *International Arbitration among the Greeks*, 1913; *Sidelights on Greek History*, 1932, 39.

[5] Universal. See Arvanitopoullos' list, *Rev. Phil.* 1911, 292.

another city, but Alexander and many of his successors[1] also arbitrated between cities without employing their powers, as did later the Roman Senate. This perpetual boundary litigation, the reason of which was the ever-present dread of starvation and the consequent desire to get a larger share of the limited arable land, was not ideal, but it was better than the alternative; every award was a war strangled, and if awards were not always observed, that only meant more awards; and even cities of no great repute, like some of the Cretan, made permanent treaties of arbitration.

For a while, too, it looked as if war itself might modify its character, for the great Macedonians, notably Alexander, Demetrius, and Antigonus Gonatas, had managed to introduce a little chivalry into the business. It had once been universal custom[2] that you might, on taking a city, kill the men and sell the women and children; by Alexander's time this had been modified into a general sale,[3] and he himself sold the people of four cities—Thebes and Gaza with no excuse save the custom, Tyre and Cyropolis with (as the world went) every excuse as regarded the *men*. But his successors seemingly dropped the horrible practice altogether; you now took a city to make it profitable to yourself,[4] not to make it a desert. It began to look as if the old rule were dead; and when in 279 the Gauls invaded Greece, the Greek cities complained bitterly of the 'cruelty' of the natural man again obtruding itself.[5]

Then came Mantinea: in 223 Antigonus Doson permitted Aratus and the Achaeans to gratify their vengeance on that city by selling the people. There had been great provocation; but we can still hear echoes of the storm of protest[6] which the proceeding evoked. As regarded the rulers of the earth, Mantinea was the end of the hope of better things;

[1] *'Εφ. 'Αρχ.* 1917, 16, no. 308 (Cassander); *OGIS* 13, *I. Priene* 37 l. 131 (Lysimachus); *'Εφ. 'Αρχ.* 1913, 43, nos. 172, 173 (Philip V); *SGDI* 5153–4; Wilhelm, *Jahresh.* 1911, 186.

[2] C. Philippson, *International Law and Custom of Ancient Greece and Rome* II, 251.

[3] Polyb. II, 58, 10.

[4] Polyb. XVIII, 3, 4–9; XXIII, 15.

[5] *OGIS* 765; Ditt.[3] 495 l. 108.

[6] Polyb. II, 56–61.

by the second century, in the hands of the Romans[1] and Philip V, war came back to what it had always been, and the Achaean Philopoemen's treatment of Sparta was little better than Philip's brutality at Cius and Maroneia. But some Greek cities, and many Greeks, held to kindlier courses; when Miletus and Magnesia in the second century ended their struggle with a convention to exchange prisoners head for head, Magnesia returned her surplus prisoners without ransom.[2] Lycurgus had once passed a humane law at Athens[3] forbidding Athenians to purchase free Greek captives; some cities now did better, and undertook by treaty[4] that if one of their citizens purchased a citizen of the other city he should liberate him against repayment of the price. The known cases of individuals who managed, often at personal risk, to release or ransom captives, whether taken in war or by pirates, are very numerous[5]; and though the ransomed captive legally became slave to his ransomer till the ransom was repaid, repayment was often waived. Among instances of altruism may be mentioned the names of two brothers of Aegiale, Hegesippus and Antipappus, who gave themselves as hostages to a pirate crew to save a number of women; for their reward was only a crown of green leaves and the record which by chance has saved their names from oblivion.[6]

There was something too of humanity in the movement for safeguarding certain places against war. A 'holy place'—a temple and its precinct—was immune from war,[7] though the only penalty on the transgressor was the wrath of the gods; the whole island of Delos, Apollo's birthplace, was such a 'holy place', probably from time immemorial. Various cities now sought to get themselves and their territories made 'holy', *i.e.* immune from war, by the consent of the Greek world and the Hellenistic kings[8]; Smyrna[9] came first, about

[1] Cf. Polyb. X, 15, 4–6. [2] Ditt.³ 588.
[3] Plut. *Mor.* 842 A. [4] *Milet* I, 3, no. 140.
[5] *E.g. I.G.* II², 399; IV, 497; XI, 4, 1054*a*, see *SEG* III, 666; XII, 7, 36; 8, 159; 9, 6; Ditt.³ 374, 520, 535; Ἀθηνᾶ 1908, 195 no. 6.
[6] Ditt.³ 521. [7] Tarn, *J.H.S.* 1924, 141.
[8] H. Seyring, 'Les rois séleucides et la concession de l'asylie', *Syria*, 20, 1939, 35. [9] *OGIS* 228, 229.

240, and was followed by Magnesia on the Maeander,[1] Alabanda,[2] Teos,[3] Miletus,[4] Chalcedon,[5] and others; other dedications, never carried out, were recommended by oracles.[6] The influence of Delphi and the Amphictyons counted for much in the movement, and gave it a religious basis.[7] There was a concurrent movement for making places inviolable (*asyla*), *i.e.* immune from reprisals (*syla*) or private war—the right of the claimant, whether individual or city, to carry off persons or goods without a state of war, a right which lay behind much of the privateering of the time.[8] Once every stranger had always been subject to reprisals; but the right had been steadily cut into, partly perhaps for its hampering effect upon trade, and many temples had long been asylums.[9] This quality was conferred on many other temples[10] during the Hellenistic period, but it also became extended to whole cities and their territory; the island of Tenos was first,[11] about 270, and was followed by all the Greek cities which became 'holy' and various others,[12] ultimately by Delphi itself.[13]

To call the title 'holy and inviolable' an empty name is to misunderstand the time. The movement was a serious attempt to limit war; did Seleucus II take the trouble he did to procure an empty name for Smyrna, his most loyal ally? Even in Syria in the first century it retained some significance[14] (p. 154), and only became an empty name in the Roman imperial period. But what *practical* effect holiness had is doubtful, for it did not alter the political quality of a city or circumscribe its political activities. It acted once, however, in a very curious way: Antiochus III, unable to take Xanthus, declared the city 'holy' so as to save his

[1] Ditt.[3] 557 *sqq.* [2] *OGIS* 234. [3] *SGDI* 5165–87, Michel 51–68.
[4] Ditt.[3] 590 (see Wilhelm, *Wien Anz.* XVIII, 19 no. 11).
[5] *SEG* IV, 720. [6] Ditt.[3] 1158, 635 B.
[7] Tarn, *Ant. Gon.* 209 n. 133; Pomtow, *Klio* XIV, 278; XVII, 189.
[8] Dareste, *Rev. E.G.* 1889, 305; Vollgraf, *B.C.H.* 1913, 286; Philippson *op. c.* 353. [9] List: Stengel, *Asylon* in P.W.
[10] Instances: *SGDI* 2532; Ditt.[3] 456, 550, 629, 630, 635 A.
[11] *I.G.* IX, 1, 97, XII, 5, 867, 868 A, B; see Graindor, *Musée Belge* 1911, 254. [12] As Anaphe, *I.G.* XII, 3, 254.
[13] Ditt.[3] 609, 612 B. [14] U. Kahrstedt, *Syr. Terr.*, 76–9.

face when he retired.[1] *Asylia* did produce an effect; it assisted to limit that self-help which was the negation of public order. For it extended far beyond certain cities and temples; the Dionysiac artists were made inviolable[2] so that the public could be sure of its shows, while every proxeny decree conferred *asylia* on the recipient, and the Greek world became a network of people who were inviolable by the subjects of this or that state. One need not suppose that an Aetolian privateersman raided a village with a list of inviolable Aetolian proxeni in his hand; but Aetolia tried to meet that difficulty by giving certificates of exemption[3] to friendly cities and undertaking to make good damage done to individuals. That under the Empire *asylia* became abused, and merely meant that certain cities were crowded with untouchable riff-raff, compelling Rome's interference, has no bearing on its merits as originally instituted.

Quite apart from Federalism, many things were now tending to draw the cities closer together and break down their old isolation. One was the very great number of grants of honorary citizenship to a man and his descendants which now occur; every city came to possess friends in many others who were its citizens. The belief that a man could not be a citizen of two cities requires modification; he could be a citizen of any number,[4] but possibly, in the third and second centuries, he could only at one time be an *active* citizen of one city, his other citizenships being potential only. If Corinth granted honorary citizenship to a citizen of Thebes, the Theban had the right, if he settled in Corinth, to take up that citizenship and become for all purposes a Corinthian; but unless he did so his Corinthian citizenship was potential. What is uncertain is whether, if he took up his Corinthian citizenship, he still remained an *active* citizen of Thebes;

[1] *OGIS* 746. [2] P. 115 n. 3.

[3] Delos, *I.G.* XI, 4, 1050, cf. XI, 2, 287 A l. 80; Tenos, *Musée Belge* 1910, 43, no. 22; Mytilene, *'Εφ. 'Αρχ.*1914, 84; Chios, Ceos, Magnesia, Teos, Ditt.[3] 443, 522, 554, 563; Athens, *Klio* XV, 7 nos. 35, 36; Halicarnassus, *SEG* IV, 182; H. Benecke, *Die Seepolitik der Aitoler*, diss. Hamburg, 1934.

[4] Critodemus, cited by Cumont, *L'Égypte des Astrologues*, 1937, 74, proves the Hellenistic διπολίτης, but does not prove two *active* citizenships.

probably he did not.[1] But in the first century a man could unquestionably exercise two active citizenships—the natural development of events; for in Bithynia Pompey forbade such multiple citizenship, but failed to stop it; Dio was a citizen of Prusa, Nicomedia, and Apamea, and when Trajan desired to abolish multiple citizenship he found it was so common in Bithynia that he could not do so without shattering the whole communal system, and could only prohibit it for the future.[2] Citizenship apart, every city now had many friends elsewhere who, if they visited her, were not mere aliens; they had front seats at the games and dined in the town hall. Inter-city intercourse was taking on a different complexion.

But the matter went much further than individuals; cities had begun to give their citizenship to the whole citizen body of another city, the process known as isopolity (p. 72).[3] Early in the third century Athens gave Priene her citizenship[4] in return for Priene's earlier grant to Athens[5]; later there were mutual grants of citizenship between many cities —Athens and Rhodes,[6] Messene and Phigaleia,[7] Paros and Allaria,[8] Pergamum and Temnos,[9] Miletus and a whole group[10]—Cyzicus, Heraclea-Latmos, Cius, Phygela, Mylasa, Tralles; all Cyreneans were citizens of Tenos,[11] all Theraeans of Cyrene,[12] all Teians of several Cretan cities,[13] all Magnesians of the cities of the Cretan League.[14] This worked as the honorary citizenships worked; it was a potential citizenship, which any grantee could take up as of right if he desired. Beside citizenship, other rights were similarly granted. Athens gave proxeny to whole classes of men in some Thessalian

[1] In *Rev. E.G.* 1911, 378 no. 1, a man has to renounce his old citizenship; this may equally well be the rule or an exception to it.

[2] Brandis, *Bithynia* in P.W.

[3] Early instances: Athens to Samos (405), Tod, *Gk. Hist. Inscr.* I, 96; II, 97; perhaps Corinth and Argos reciprocally (392—389), Griffith, *Historia,* II, 1950; Miletus to Olbia, Cyzicus and Phygela (all about 330), Tod, *op. c.* II, 195; Wiegand, *Milet* I (3), 137; 142.

[4] *I.G.* II² 693.

[5] *I. Priene,* 5; *I.G.* II², 566.

[6] Polyb. XVI, 26, 9; Livy XXXI, 15, 6.

[7] *I.G.* V, 2, 419.

[8] *SGDI* 490.

[9] *OGIS,* 265.

[10] *Milet* I, 3, nos. 136, 141, 143, 146, 150.

[11] *I.G.* XII, 5, 814.

[12] *SEG* IX. 3.

[13] P. 83 n. 3.

[14] *I. Magnesia,* 20.

cities[1]; all Messenians became proxeni of Delphi, all Delphians of Sardes, all Acragantines of the Molossian League.[2] Individual grants of proxeny became so numerous that some cities ceased to set up the decrees; in the third century Epidaurus, a small city, averaged four a year,[3] and merely entered names on a list, as Anaphe was already doing[4]; Delphi did the same from 197[5]; about 264 Histiaea gave 32 in one year.[6] Proxeny was a coveted honour, for it not only conferred immunity from seizure but gave the right to own land in the grantor city; this right was largely exercised, for Rome's first step after the conquest of Achaea, with a view to weakening the Peloponnese, was to forbid ownership of land in two cities,[7] though she subsequently withdrew the prohibition. Whole cities—Messene, Chersonesos, Alexandria, Smyrna, Sardes—were given prior rights of consulting the Delphic oracle[8]; Ithaca gave all Magnesians front seats at her local games, the Odysseia[9]; many cities, to encourage trade, gave freedom from import and export duties to other cities as wholes. All these things tended to bind the cities together; Poseidippus in the third century could say 'There are many cities, but they are one Hellas'.[10] One wonders how far the process might have gone had not Rome intervened.

To what extent honorary citizenships were taken up cannot be said. Few literary men, at any rate, worked in their own cities; they went where work, friends, perhaps libraries, took them. Honours were conferred on many poets and philosophers who gave recitations and lectures in other cities, often of a kind calculated to interest the local patriotism of the city visited, and doubtless this class, when they settled elsewhere, habitually took up their citizenships; Menander of Thyrreion was called a Cassopean,[11] Metrodorus of Scepsis a Chalcedonian[12]; Poseidonius of Apamea, Apollonius of

[1] Ἐφ. Ἀρχ. 1914, 167 no. 232.
[2] Ditt.³ 555, 548, 942.
[3] *I.G.* IV², 96.
[4] *I.G.* XII, 3, 251.
[5] Ditt.³ 585.
[6] Ditt.³ 492.
[7] Brandis, *Achaea* in P.W.; cf. *I.G.* VII, 20 (?).
[8] Ditt.³ 555, 604, 404, 470, 548.
[9] Ditt.³ 558.
[10] Fr. 28, Kock (III, 345).
[11] Ditt.³ 739, see Wilhelm, *Neue Beiträge* IV, 55.
[12] Str. 609.

Alexandria and Deinocrates of Macedonia were called Rhodians, Aristarchus of Samothrace an Alexandrian, Aristobulus of Cos a Cassandreian; many other cases are known.[1] One may probably therefore assume a certain interchange of citizens between the cities. On the other hand, League constitutions were usually so framed that no citizen could acquire personal rights in another city without an express grant.

Another matter which drew the world together was the development of a common language. The educated everywhere began to use Attic; and out of Attic, modified by local usages, arose Hellenistic Greek, the 'common speech', familiar as the Greek of the New Testament. For a while a second 'common speech' began to form out of the Doric dialects, and has left one great monument, Theocritus; but it could not hold its ground. Local dialects persisted in some countries till the first century; but ultimately the 'common speech' conquered every Greek city, for, as it became the general medium of communication between peoples of different dialects, it finally compelled abandonment of the dialect. With the 'common speech' appeared also what lawyers call 'common form'; the decrees of the cities all followed the same lines. In fact, the vast mass of honorary decrees passed during this period also constituted a bond between the cities, for normally, whenever one city honoured a citizen of another, commissioners took a copy of the decree to the city whose member was honoured; there they asked leave to set it up, and were entertained at a dinner and made a speech emphasising the solidarity and good feeling between the two cities.[2] The enormous number of new festivals had the same effect; for, though the performers were only professionals going their round, the games themselves were a religious act and the cities sent religious envoys. The precincts of the city temples were crowded with *stelae* (standing slabs of stone) on which were engraved

[1] See list in Fr. Heichelheim, *Die auswärtige Bevölkerung im Ptolemäerreich*, Klio Beiheft XVIII, 6.

[2] *I. Priene* 47, 50, 53–4, 71; *Milet* I, 3, no. 146.

the city's decrees and records; this was the city's record office (though some also kept records on tablets stored in the Town Hall), and any visitor could there read the honours paid to his own compatriots. In the third century the honorary decree is often a valuable political document or even a political manifesto, but by the first century, when independent politics were passing away, it had degenerated; it grew in prolixity[1] in proportion to the unimportance of its contents, and might record the most trivial details of the man's private life, even the number of guests at his wedding[2]; for he now paid for it himself, and liked value for his money.

Perhaps the most important thing of all was the judicial commissions; not those which arbitrated a political quarrel between two cities, but those which settled lawsuits within the city itself. For before 300 the old system of trying cases by a jury composed of a large body of citizens was fast breaking down, as it deserved; it was about the worst legal system ever invented, for the juries' decisions were habitually influenced by politics, mass passion, and prejudice. It was largely replaced throughout the Hellenistic period by a system under which a commission of one or more judges (dicasts) came from another city and heard all cases entered for trial.[3] It was not an ideal system, for it did not function regularly; seemingly you often asked another city to help you only when things got pretty bad, and it entailed much delay[4] in justice—sometimes when a commission did come it found no cases had been tried for years; and as prompt justice is only less important than impartial justice, this doubtless led to much self-help, with the usual undesirable accompaniments. But when a commission did come, it did well, for it stood outside the passions of local factions; and, judging by the remaining records, commissions may in some

[1] As *I. Priene* 111–114, 117.

[2] *I. Priene* 109 ll. 161–7.

[3] A. Steinwenter, *Die Streitbeendigung* § 11 lists 35 dicast decrees; there are at least twice that number. Typical decrees, mentioning *ὁμόνοια*, are *I.G.* IX, 2, 507, 1230; XII, 5, 870; *SEG* I, 363; *I. Priene* 53, 54, 61.

[4] As *I.G.* VII, 4130; XII, 2, 530; *I. Priene* 59.

places have come often enough to avoid undue delay.[1] Their procedure was uniform; they first settled all cases they could by persuasion or informal arbitration[2]; the residue they either decided in legal form themselves or sent to a jury. In a recorded instance at Calymna[3] the dicasts sent by Iasos found over 350 cases awaiting them, and of these they settled over 340, 10 only being sent to a jury. As the cases which had to be judged strictly were judged by the local law (reinforced by royal rescripts[4] where the city was under some king's suzerainty) and not by that of the commissioners' city,[5] it meant that by the second century there must have grown up in the Greek cities a body of true lawyers, a thing previously unknown—men who had studied the laws of many cities beside their own; Theophrastus' studies in jurisprudence also helped to build up a sounder view of the functions of law. Moreover, as most cases everywhere were settled informally, there must also have grown up a body of rules for doing this, in which we may perhaps see the rudiments of an interstate system of equity; equity in England also began informally enough. It sounds strange to hear judges praised for being 'impartial and just' or for making no distinction between rich and poor,[6] things we take for granted. But impartiality was something quite new in Greece, for the juries had weighted the scales heavily in favour of the poor or of the debtor. Some cities gained a name for impartiality; it seems as if the principal industry of Priene was settling her neighbours' lawsuits.

The kings had an honourable record in the matter, and possibly the first idea of these judicial commissions originated with Antigonus I.[7] Sometimes, where the city was in some king's sphere, a king's governor, instead of appointing a commission, acted as judge himself, thus anticipating the Roman governors of a later period; Cleon,[8] Attalid governor

[1] Pomtow's table, *Klio* 1923, 268, gives 10 known at Delphi in 26 years; a large number from Gonnoi, Arvanitopoullos in *'Εφ. 'Αρχ.* 1911 and 1914.

[2] *SEG* IV, 662.

[3] Michel 417.

[4] Michel 417.

[5] *I.G.* VII, 21; *I. Priene* 59.

[6] *E.g. I.G.* XII, 5, 869.

[7] *OGIS* 7.

[8] *Ib.* 329.

in Aegina, was highly praised by the city for being 'a just judge towards all, shewing no private motives, determined to act neither unfairly nor arbitrarily, but endeavouring in most cases to bring the parties to agree'; that is, he acted precisely as a commission would have acted. Philodemus of Clazomenae was honoured by the Delians for the successful discharge of his mission as arbitrator in suits arising out of contracts, a mission to which he was appointed by an Antigonus, whether Gonatas or Doson.[1] The kings themselves were constantly being called on to settle internal disturbances, which might mean anything from squabbles over mortgages to incipient revolution, and they or their governors frequently sent judicial commissions for the purpose.[2]

Of the cases handled by the dicasts, many arose under a *sumbolon*,[3] *i.e.* a convention between two cities for the settlement of private disputes between their citizens, made to prevent either side being treated as strangers in the courts of the other[4]; though the *sumbolon* long antedates Hellenism, its increasing frequency[5] marks a certain advance, and it has been thought that it, as well as Stoicism, helped to give rise to the latter idea of a Law of Nations. But of all classes of lawsuits, debtor and creditor cases were far the commonest, and were at the bottom of most of the internal dissensions in the cities. The juries had never been honest over cases of debt; and the document from Calymna already referred to explains that dicasts tried to avoid leaving cases to a jury because the decision, taken by vote, of these quasi-political bodies was a fruitful source of new dissensions. And all our information about the judicial commissions emphasises one point: they strove, often successfully, to restore *homonoia*, concord, in the city. Taken in bulk, the surviving dicast decrees are a paean in praise of *homonoia*,

[1] *I.G.* XI, 4, 1052. [2] Ditt.[3] 426, Michel 417, *SEG* 1, 363, *OGIS* 7, 43.

[3] As *I.G.* IX, 2, 1230; *SEG* I, 363; *OGIS* 43.

[4] Arist. *Pol.* 1280 a l. 36; see H. G. Robertson, *The administration of justice in the Athenian Empire*, 1924.

[5] *I.G.* II², 466; V. 2, 419; XII, 5, 829; Ditt.[3] 955 l. 13; Polyb. XXIII, 1, 2; XXXII, 7.

that thing for which men longed but which they could not achieve. It was not lip-service; we know well enough that a State may have trouble when that is the last thing which the bulk of its people desire. Every form of authority—kings,[1] envoys,[2] governors,[3] generals of Leagues[4]—was perpetually urging the people to live in concord; the most praised women of the time, a Phila or an Apollonis, were those who tried to promote it; even the gods intervened, and Apollo exhorts Iasos to *homonoia*.[5] Homonoia herself was worshipped as a goddess at Iasos and Priene,[6] and in Ptolemaic Thera Artemidorus set up an altar to her 'for the city'.[7] She was one of the great conceptions of the Hellenistic age, but she remained a pious aspiration only. Not until Rome had crushed all internal feuds was concord achieved; then, in the Imperial period, cities freely celebrated Homonoia on their coinage, and she was frequently worshipped[8] when all meaning in her worship had for Greeks passed away.

All these things might in time have led to more co-operation among the cities than was ever actually achieved. For in many things which needed common action they failed completely. One was a common calendar. The historian Timaeus introduced the clumsy reckoning by Olympiads (p. 283), but the cities continued each its own dating by its magistrates, and did not even all begin their years at the same time; Athens began about July, Sparta about October, Delos in January, Miletus ultimately about April; the confusion thus caused is terrible. The only city calendars whose translation into Julian years is reasonably certain are the Delian[9] and Milesian[10]; the arrangement of the important third-century Athenian and Delphic calendars is still partly

[1] *I.G.* XI, 4, 1052; XII, 7, 15. [2] P. 87 n. 2.
[3] *I.G.* XII, 5, 1065, *SEG* I, 363, *Klio* XVII, 199, nos. 198–9.
[4] *I.G.* IX, 2, 1100. [5] *OGIS* 237.
[6] Michel 1203; *I. Priene* 111 l. 198. [7] *I.G.* XII, 3 Suppl., 1336, 1341–2.
[8] *I.G.* VII, 2510, 3426; *OGIS* 479; *Hesperia* II, 1933, 507, no. 7, where the restoration 'Ομονοίας seems obvious.
[9] Durrbach, *B.C.H.* 1916, 298, and in *I.G.* XI, 2.
[10] *Milet* I, 3, nos. 122–5, with Rehm's commentary.

conjectural.[1] Worse than this was the failure to provide decent roads and secure communications. Brigandage was common,[2] sometimes organised under an archklepht; when Heracleides toured Greece *c.* 205 he noted that *one* road—that from Oropus to Tanagra—was safe.[3] Piracy[4] was worse than brigandage, and better organised. Here the kings gave no help; Demetrius and Antigonus Gonatas, Ptolemy II and Antiochus III, were all on excellent terms with the pirate captains, whom they found useful allies. Many so-called pirates were privateersmen. The real pirates—exiles, broken men, unemployed mercenaries, escaped slaves—lived in small strongholds round the Aegean; one such band for a time held a stronghold near Phygela[5] in Ephesus' territory. Many attacks on the islands are known, but in the third century these were often only single-ship raids to catch a few slaves; for the pirates had one whole-hearted foe, Rhodes,[6] and so long as Rhodes' power lasted she kept the evil within bounds. Her worst difficulty was Crete. In a Cretan city the old men, grown respectable with years, governed in proper form, while the younger men went out on their lawless occasions under some adventurous leader; Rhodes' efforts were directed to getting

[1] Bibliography, *C.A.H.* VII, p. 886. More recent works on the Athenian calendar include: W. B. Dinsmoor, *The archons of Athens in the Hellenistic Age*, 1931; *The Athenian archon list in the light of recent discoveries*, 1939; S. Dow, 'The list of Athenian *Archontes*', *Hesperia* III, 1934, 140; 'New kinds of evidence for dating Polyeuctus', *A.J.A.* 1936, 57; W. S. Ferguson, *Athenian tribal cycles in the Hellenistic Age*, 1932; 'Polyeuktos and the Soteria', *A.J.P.* 1934, 318; W. Kolbe, 'Randbemerkungen zur Archontenforschung', *Gött. Nachrichten*, 1933, 481. B. D. Meritt, 'Greek Inscriptions', *Hesperia* IV, 1935, 525; *ib.* VII, 1938, 77; W. K. Pritchett and Meritt, *The chronology of Hellenistic Athens*, 1940; Pritchett and O. Neugebauer, *The calendars of Athens*, 1947 (a restatement complete in the light of the evidence available in 1946); W. W. Tarn, 'The new dating of the Chremonidean war', *J.H.S.* LIV, 1934, 26.

On the Delphic calendar: G. Daux, *Delphes au IIme et au Ier siècle*, 1936 (supersedes all former work); R. Flacelière, *Les Aitoliens à Delphes*, 1937 (third century; full bibliography).

[2] Plut. *Arat.* 6; Diog. Laert. II, 136; VI, 47, 52; *SEG* II, 292; Ditt.[3] 405 n. 4; Polyb. IV, 29, 4, XIII, 8, 2.

[3] *F.H.G.* II p. 257.

[4] H. Ormerod, *Piracy in the ancient world*, ch. IV; Tarn, *Ant. Gon.* 85–8.

[5] *I.G.* XII, 3, 171.

[6] Diod. XX, 81, 3; Str. 652.

their city governments to restrain them.[1] That is why, unlike the kings, she seldom interfered in the endless civil wars in the island; from her point of view they were useful, as they kept adventurers at home. But after 168 Rome's policy of weakening all strong states without putting anything in their place bore its fruit; Rhodes became unable to hold the scourge under, while Rome, after annexing Pergamum in 130, allowed the wild country of western Cilicia to become derelict; there the pirates drew together and founded a regular state.[2] Cilicia cost Rome, as Rome deserved, two wars to put down; and even Pompey's great effort only cleared the seas for the moment.

We have now considered the workings of internationalism among the cities; we must turn to certain things which affected the individual, whether as a citizen or simply as a man, conscious (as people have been conscious at each great new advance in civilisation) of the increased importance of his individual life. With the weakening of the city tie came an enormous growth of non-political private associations and clubs.[3] There had been a few such clubs in fourth-century Athens (the fifth-century oligarchic clubs were another matter), but Demetrius of Phalerum (317–307) had forbidden the formation of new ones[4]; and the great outburst of associations all over the Greek world dates from 300 onwards. Most were very small; apart from the Dionysiac artists, a membership of 100 was quite unusual. They were primarily social and religious bodies grouped round the worship of some god; possibly the *thiasoi* were more purely religious, while the *eranoi*, where the subscriptions were of importance—one had an entrance fee of 30 drachmae[5]—were primarily social bodies. About 200, family associations appear, founded by some individual to perpetuate the family memory, the priesthood being hereditary among his descendants. Every club had its temple, however tiny, but

[1] Cf. Ditt.[3] 581.

[2] Ormerod ch. VI.

[3] Fr. Poland, *Gesch. d. griech. Vereinswesens* 1909, is fullest: a good outline in M. N. Tod, *Sidelights on Greek History*, 1932, 71.

[4] Poland 519.

[5] Poland 492.

finance was a perpetual difficulty; many let their temples for secular purposes when not in use, like the Egretes club at Athens, who in leasing theirs reserved one day a year for their annual festival.[1] Epicteta's club at Thera, one of the wealthiest, had an annual revenue from its founder of 210 dr.,[2] and one at Athens once ended a year with 1,770 dr. in hand[3]; but these were exceptions, and the clubs came more and more to depend on some wealthy member who would bear expenses and was honoured with a statue, for which he paid himself—exactly what was happening in the cities (p 109.).

These clubs were in no sense Friendly Societies; they might help a member in trouble, or see to his funeral, probably an excuse for a dinner; but there it ended.[4] Associations of men named from their trades began to appear at Athens[5] and Cos,[6] but the professional trade guild was practically unknown to Hellenism, unless in Egypt[7]; true trade guilds only evolved under the Roman Empire, and finally Justinian's Code took account of their rules, as did English common law of the custom of merchants. Usually a club had no political meaning; but in the last struggle of the Achaean League against Rome clubs of 'patriots' appeared,[8] *i.e.* men united to uphold the constitution of their fathers. The club modelled itself on the city organisation; it had officials with similar names and passed resolutions like city decrees; and it became so much the standard model that the most diverse forms of activity—the philosophic schools, the Museum at Alexandria,[9] the Dionysiac artists,[10] Ptolemy's garrison troops,[11] the poets domiciled at Athens,[12] the physicians trained at Cos or elsewhere,[13] the Old Boys from this or that gymnasium[14]—all adopted the same form

[1] Ditt.[3] 1097. [2] Michel 1001. [3] 'Εφ. 'Αρχ. 1905, 246 no. 11.
[4] Tod, *BSA* XIII, 328. [5] Michel 1045; *I.G.* II, 1332.
[6] *SGDI* 3636, l. 54; 3632, ll. 18, 23; Paton and Hicks no. 129.
[7] M. San Nicolo, *Aegyptisches Vereinswesen* I, 66 *sqq*.
[8] *I.G.* IV, 757, B. 12. [9] Str. 794. [10] Poland 129.
[11] *OGIS* 102, 735, *I.G.* XII, 3, 327, 466, cf. *Archiv* VI, 9.
[12] Ditt.[3] 699. [13] *SGDI* 3636 l. 54; *OGIS* 104; *I.G.* II[2] 772.
[14] Poland 103.

of organisation. The number of clubs was great; in 146 the small city of Troezen[1] possessed 23; obviously they met a want, and prevented the individual feeling lost in a vast new world. That their life seems to us tiresome and unutterably boring is true, but is hardly worth saying; there is no evidence either that the Greek was bored with his life or that the men of 2,000 years hence would not be equally bored with ours. The club's most important function in Greek life was to form the natural avenue for foreigners and foreign worships entering a city; purely Greek clubs[2] occur at Athens and Rhodes, but normally they were either foreign or mixed, the latter assisting to break down racial barriers; thus one at Cnidus, besides Greeks, contained a Thracian, a Phoenician, a Pisidian, a Phrygian, and a Libyan.[3] Slaves were sometimes members, but seemingly the first known slave club occurs only late in the period, in Egypt.[4]

Some advance was made in education during the period[5]; the gymnasiarch,[6] who supervised it, finally became almost the most important magistrate. Some cities, like Miletus,[7] recognised that education should be, as Plato had suggested, the business of the state; but to carry that out they too often depended on donations from kings and wealthy individuals, both for buildings and endowment; even Rhodes accepted a donation in this behalf from Eumenes II.[8] In the more progressive cities elementary schools became well established; in Ionia they included girls as well as boys, and at Teos and Chios the two were educated together,[9] as had long been customary at Sparta. At these schools children, commencing at the age of seven, learned little more than how to read and write: it seems doubtful if even elementary arithmetic, as we understand it, was taught generally.[10] No qualification, seemingly, was required of teachers, but the

[1] *I.G.* IV, 757.
[2] Poland, 305, 318.
[3] *SGDI* 3510.
[4] C. C. Edgar, *Raccolta Lumbroso* 369.
[5] E. Ziebarth, *Aus dem griech. Schulwesen*², 1914; H.-I. Marrou, *Hist. de l'éducation dans l'antiquité*, 1949 (II*me. partie, L'éducation hellénistique*).
[6] His functions: *I. Priene* 112–4, *OGIS* 764, *I.G.* XII, 9, 916.
[7] Ditt.³ 577.
[8] Polyb. XXXI, 31 (25).
[9] Ditt.³ 578; Athen. 566 E.
[10] Marrou *op. c.*, 218.

magistrates tried to get men of character. Girls' education was apparently carried no further[1]; boys passed on, if their fathers cared to pay for it, to a secondary schoolmaster (*grammatikos*), for an elementary literary training in preparation for the study of rhetoric,[2] and ultimately to the ephebate.[3] This had been remodelled at Athens by Lycurgus about 335; it embraced the 19th and 20th years, was compulsory, and though based on military training made some provision for education also; but the names of the instructors, *cosmetes* (teacher of order) and *sophronistes* (teacher of self-control), show that Lycurgus' aim was rather the foundation of moral character. The ephebe system became practically universal in Greek cities, but Athens soon dropped, and other cities never adopted, compulsion; it was voluntary education. Its centre was the gymnasium, which came to play in the Hellenistic city the part played in England by the Public Schools; those who had been through the gymnasium constituted a kind of informal aristocracy. In the new towns of Asia the gymnasium typified Greek life; a place which could set one up was fairly on the road to become a city, and there was even a fair sprinkling of them among the Greek-inhabited villages of Egypt.[4] A well-equipped city, like Pergamum, would have three gymnasia or divisions of the gymnasium, for boys, ephebes, and the 'young men' who had passed through the ephebate. The athletic training was thorough; about the intellectual we are ill informed, but probably it did not go further than grammar, poetry (with music), and some rhetoric. The educational tendency in fact was archaizing and conservative; for its aesthetic and gymnastic content was largely a survival from the age of archaic aristocracy, and even rhetoric was the product of the fifth century. Its growth in the Hellenistic period (see p. 281 *sq.*) was due partly no doubt to the Greek

[1] Ditt.[3] 578.

[2] See, in addition to Marrou, *op. c.*, 223, J. Barns, *C.Q.* XLV, 1951, 8 *sqq.*

[3] A. Brenot, *Recherches sur l'éphébie attique*, 1920; Lofberg, *C.P.* 1925, 330.

[4] Rostovtzeff, *SEH* 324, 1395 n. 121; T. A. Brady, 'The gymnasium in Ptolemaic Egypt', *Univ. Missouri Stud.*, II, 1936, 9.

temperament itself, but partly, too, to the fact that the habits of mind and speech which rhetoric taught still made for worldly success, whether in city politics or at the court of a king; and it will be recalled that the Romans of the Imperial age were not less devoted to it than the Greeks of Hellenistic Alexandria or Pergamum. Anyone who wanted higher education had to go afterwards and work under some recognised teacher for himself. The idea had not yet been born that the average man could hope to profit by advanced studies, in rhetoric or philosophy or one of the sciences. Scholarship was an intellectual adventure for the individual whom it suited and who could afford it. The same perhaps was true of education and training for the medical profession, the only learned profession of the age.[1] The study of Law as a science was still almost unknown, a fact which seems surprising at first, but less so when it is remembered that there was still comparatively little development in the *practice* of Law to raise it from its traditional place (in a Greek community) of servant of the government.

Some gymnasia possessed libraries. The office of gymnasiarch was burdensome; he often spent largely himself, both for necessary outlay and for special prizes or festivals. Indeed much time was wasted by all the scholars marching in procession to the sacrifices, both at the regular city festivals and on special occasions, like kings' visits or birthdays; a Coan calendar[2] gives, in a month, 8 days of festivals and 4 of examinations. Great men would ask for a holiday for the schools, but it generally only meant another procession; one wonders if boys appreciated a holiday chiefly composed of compulsory chapel better than their work of racing and wrestling. In the schoolrooms excavated at Pergamum and Priene the walls are covered from floor to roof with names,[3] as Upper School at Eton used to be. The ephebes, like their elders, formed associations,[4] imitating the city organisation in little; and the Old Boys' association

[1] Marrou, *op. c.*, 264, with references.

[2] Ditt.[3] 1028.

[3] *Ath. Mitt.* 1907, 373; *I. Priene* 313.

[4] Poland 88.

or *gerousia* [1]—those who had passed through the city gymnasium—ultimately under the Roman Empire became a sort of municipal senate. Even the little schoolgirls passed resolutions in proper form in honour of distinguished visitors.[2]

The great Macedonian princesses of the two generations after Alexander (p. 56) exercised much influence on the position of Greek women. If Macedonia produced perhaps the most competent group of men the world had yet seen, the women were in all respects the men's counterparts; they played a large part in affairs, received envoys and obtained concessions for them from their husbands, built temples, founded cities, engaged mercenaries, commanded armies, held fortresses, and acted on occasion as regents or even co-rulers; the influence of a woman like Arsinoe Philadelphus, beautiful, able, masterful, on the men who served her was evidently enormous. These queens had their men's desire for culture; Aratus [3] addressed poems to Phila, Poseidippus of Pella [4] to Arsinoe, Callimachus [5] to Berenice, wife of Ptolemy III; Arsinoe corresponded with the physicist Strato,[6] and Stratonice, the wife of Antiochus I, increased the art-collection at Delos.[7] Hardly less notable were some queens of Greek blood; Apollonis of Cyzicus,[8] who married Attalus I of Pergamum and was the mother of famous sons, was spoken of as Romans spoke of the 'mother of the Gracchi', a model of womanly qualities; Cleomenes' sister Chilonis [9] at Sparta would have honoured any society. One Greek woman, Pythodoris,[10] daughter of a citizen of Tralles, attained to considerable power, and ruled a wild kingdom stretching from Cerasus to Colchis; but she was also Antony's granddaughter.

From the Macedonian courts, (relative) freedom broadened down to the Greek home; and those women who

[1] Poland 102; Levy, *Rev. E.G.* VIII, 203; Judeich in *Altertümer von Hierapolis* on 209.
[2] *C.I.G.* 3185; *I. Pergamon* II, 463.
[3] Suidas, *Aratos.*
[4] Schott, nos. 2, 3 (after her death).
[5] Callimachus, I, fr. 110 (ed. R. Pfeiffer, 1949).
[6] Diog. Laert. V, 60.
[7] Her chief offerings listed, Tarn, *Ant. Gon.* 350.
[8] Polyb. XXII, 20; Plut. *Mor.* 480 C; *OGIS* 307–8.
[9] Plut. *Agis* 17 *sq.*
[10] Str. 499, 555–9, 649; *OGIS* 376–7.

desired emancipation—probably a minority—were able to obtain it in considerable measure. Demetrius of Phalerum had passed laws at Athens to keep woman in her place,[1] but they were repealed when he fell; and though magistrates called *gynaeconomi*—supervisors of women—appear in some cities, the only thing they are known to have supervised was girls' education.[2] Stoicism, which subsequently inspired the better definition of marriage in the Roman jurists, also helped to raise women's status. Women could now get all the education they wanted; many philosophers numbered women among their hearers, like Epicurus' pupil Leontion, who married his friend Metrodorus.[3] Poetesses began to appear again in the third century,[4] and Aristodama of Smyrna[5] toured Greece with her brother as business manager, giving recitals and receiving many honours; a woman scholar, Hestiaea,[6] and at least one painter,[7] are known. Some writers obviously wrote for female readers. Women now received citizenship and proxeny[8] from other cities for the same services as men; and the women magistrates of the Roman period date back at any rate to the first century B.C., when a woman, Phile, held the highest office at Priene and built a new aqueduct and reservoir.[9] The relations between the sexes became less cramped and more natural. Women founded clubs,[10] and took part in club life, though naturally to a less extent than men; there were clubs for women only at Athens[11] and Alexandria.[12] A girl of good family, Hipparchia, a disciple of the Cynic Crates, married him and enthusiastically adopted the life 'according to nature' of a wandering beggar proper to his philosophy; few have carried emancipation further. But most of these things clearly

[1] Ferguson, *Hell. Athens*, 46.
[2] Ziebarth *op. c.* 39.
[3] Seneca fr. 45. Diog. Laert. VI, 23 is the usual scandal.
[4] List in Powell and Barber, *New Chapters in Greek Literature*, II, 43. See Polygnota of Thebes, Ditt.[3] 738; *SEG* II, 322–3; L. Robert, *B.C.H.* LIII, 1929, 34.
[5] Ditt.[3] 532; *SEG* II, 263.
[6] Susemihl, *Gr. Lit.-Gesch.* II, 148.
[7] Wilamowitz, *Hellenistische Dichtung* I, 84; Pliny XXXV, 147.
[8] *SGDI* 2685, 2727, both 2nd century.
[9] *I. Priene* 208.
[10] Michel 1001; cf. *I.G.* XII, 3, 329
[11] *I.G.* II[2], 1346.
[12] Edgar, *J.E.A.* IV, 253

relate only to a minority. Freedom was not automatic, but had to be grasped; education for the mass was rudimentary, and even in the first century there were women, rich enough to own slaves, who could neither read nor write[1]; Greece suffered from the sexes being on different levels of culture. And far beyond these things was that terrible evil in the woman's life, that often she was not allowed to rear the children she bore. To what extent she may have acquiesced in this secular precaution against hunger it is useless to speculate; she has left no record.

For no prosperity among the upper classes could alter the fundamental fact of life in Greece: the country had only a limited amount of arable land, and could not of itself support one man beyond a fixed number, long since reached. Imported food had to be paid for; and as there was no mineral wealth except Laurium, now fast failing, and as every city round the Mediterranean could do its own sea-carriage, food could only be paid for by exporting manufactures or by transit duties. Corinth grew wealthy on its transit trade; but the primitive Greek system of manufacture, though it might enrich a few individuals, was of little account to states as a whole. Consequently the whole of old Greece lived always under the shadow of the fear of too many mouths to feed. In the late fourth and early third centuries this was met by mercenary service and emigration to Asia. Fourth-century writers were still concerned with over-population, and about 300 there was still a considerable surplus; but the surplus gradually vanished. Polybius[2] says that Greeks in the middle of the second century were refusing to rear more than one, or at most two, children; and there is plenty of evidence to bear him out.

The prevalence of infanticide in Greece has been strenuously asserted from the literary texts,[3] and as strenuously denied[4]; but for the late third and the second centuries the

[1] *I.G.* IX, 1, 318, 1066; *B.C.H.* 1898, 89 no. 85, 126 no. 110.
[2] XXXVI, 17, 7.
[3] G. Glotz, *Infanticidium* and *Expositio* in Dar. Sagl.
[4] A. W. Gomme, *The population of Athens*, 1933, 79.

inscriptions are conclusive. The evidence, so far as I have collected it, can only be summarised briefly here. Of some thousand families from Greece who received Milesian citizenship *c.* 228–220, details of 79, with their children, remain[1]; these brought 118 sons and 28 daughters, many being minors; no natural causes can account for those proportions.[2] Similarly Epicteta's relatives, *c.* 200, numbered 25 males to 7 females.[3] Of the Miletus families, 32 had one child and 31 two; and they show a certain striving after two *sons*. The inscriptions at large bear this out. Two sons are fairly common, with a sprinkling of three; at Eretria, third century, certainly two families in 19 had more than one son,[4] which is lower than the Miletus immigrants, but agrees with the evidence from Delphi[5]; at Pharsalus possibly one in seven[6]; and one must allow for some sons having emigrated. But more than one daughter was practically never reared, bearing out Poseidippus' statement that 'even a rich man always exposes a daughter'. Of 600 families from Delphic inscriptions, second century, just 1 per cent. reared 2 daughters[7]; the Miletus evidence agrees, and throughout the whole mass of inscriptions cases of sisters can almost be numbered on one's fingers,[8] with *one* strange local exception: a second-century list of women subscribers from Paros[9] *perhaps* shows 20 sisters (8 families) out of 62 names, but the islands were prosperous and untouched by war, and in population questions must be classed with Asia, not Greece. Some allowance must be made for loss of fertility; thus at Rhodes adoptions were so common that we get (*c.* 100) seven adopted sons in a list of 40 magistrates,[10] and on her deme Telos a case of three in four,[11] while adoption, even of

[1] Collected from *Milet* I, 3, nos. 34–93.

[2] Compare 87 sons to 44 daughters in 61 families from fourth-century Athens (Jardé, *Les céréales dans l'antiquité grecque*, 1925, 137); the disproportion is growing.

[3] Michel 1001.

[4] *I.G.* XII, 9, 249.

[5] Of 600 families of manumittors from *SGDI* II, only 57 show more than one son; but some may be absent.

[6] *I.G.* IX, 2, 234.

[7] See n. 5.

[8] I have only met 3 daughters twice and 2 twelve times; *valeat quantum*.

[9] *I.G.* XII, 5, 186.

[10] *I.G.* XII, 1, 49.

[11] *I.G.* XII, 3, 36.

daughters,[1] was not uncommon elsewhere; people do not kill their own children to adopt others. Telos too boasts a family of seven,[2] perhaps the only known Hellenistic family over five, except the eight children of Cleopatra Thea by three marriages; but the prevalence of artificial restriction is shown by the revival of families of four and five at Athens during her after-bloom of prosperity in the late second century.[3]

The general conclusion from *c.* 230 onwards seems certain: the one child family was commonest, but there was a certain desire for two sons (to allow for a death in war); families of four or five were very rare; more than one daughter was very seldom reared; and infanticide on a considerable scale, particularly of girls, is not in doubt. Now it takes an average of three children per fertile marriage to keep a population stationary; the home-born Greek population *must* therefore have declined considerably by 100 B.C. Greece had overdone the precautions against her secular fear; yet, except among Jews, no voice was raised against infanticide on moral grounds till under the Empire the Stoics Musonius[4] and Epictetus[5] spoke their minds. Philip V after Cynoscephalae, for military reasons, took steps to check it in Macedonia and encourage large families, and raised Macedonia's armed strength nearly 50 per cent. in a generation[6]; and under the Antonines Thebes made the practice illegal,[7] perhaps the only people except the Jews who ever did till Christianity intervened.

Certainly there was no actual depopulation in Greece till the Roman civil wars. Single cities, of course, might fail for many reasons; Larisa under Philip V was half depopulated[8] by war and the exile of Aetolian partisans, and Heraclea-Latmos[9] and Thyrreion[10] in Acarnania contracted their

[1] *E.g. B.C.H.* VI, 265; IX, 331; *J.H.S.* 1890, 120; Wiegand, *Siebenter Milet-Bericht* 67 no. 2; *B.C.H.* LI, 1927, 83 no. 31.

[2] *I.G.* XII, 3, 40.

[3] Ferguson, *Hell. Athens*, 374.

[4] Stob. *Flor.* p. 664, Wachsmuth.

[5] *Diss.* I, ch. 23.

[6] Livy XXXIX, 24; XLII, 11.

[7] Ael. *V.H.* II, 7.

[8] *I.G.* IX, 2, 517.

[9] Krischen, *Milet* III, 2, p. 2.

[10] Noack, *Arch. Anz.* 1916, 215.

ring-walls; but then Thyrrheion, a little city, had been holding a ring-wall larger than the Theban. These things mean nothing; Aristotle quotes temporary cases of the sort as common enough[1]; and in the third century cities who wanted new citizens—Larisa, Dyme,[2] Miletus (to settle Myus)—had no difficulty in getting enough Greeks from other places. But by 100 enfranchisement or incorporation of aliens must have been taking place on a considerable scale in Greece, as it did in Asia (p. 156); no other explanation of the facts seems possible, for the decline of the true Greek population is certain. Evidence is not easy to get, as aliens took Greek names; but Italians were now commonly accepted as ephebes,[3] and if one foreign people was accepted, others were not excluded. It is notable that Pergamum in 133 and Ephesus *c.* 85 gave metic status to the slaves then liberated[4]; and Philip V's idea[5] that the solution of the future might lie in enfranchising freedmen may be correct, for the Greek cities became full of freedmen. Certainly in the first century Greece contained a large alien population, enfranchised or not, and what was happening in Asia and Egypt was happening on a smaller scale in Greece; the Orontes flowed into the Ilissus before it flowed into the Tiber, and Juvenal's esurient Greekling had often little that was Greek about him but his name and speech. This change in the nature of the population can be detected fairly early at Corinth, which in the third century could only muster one quarter the hoplite force of the fifth,[6] though the city had grown; at Delos from 166 onwards it is self-evident. The process can also be seen at work in the breaking down of class and race distinctions. By the first century, when a wealthy man gave a feast to his fellow-citizens, he often invited the metics, the freedmen, and even the slaves[7];

[1] *Pol.* III, 1278 a l. 30. [2] Ditt.[3] 529.

[3] J. Hatzfeld, *Les trafiquants Italiens*, 303; O. W. Reinmuth, 'The foreigners in the Athenian *Ephebia*', *Univ. Nebraska Stud.*, no. 9, 1929.

[4] *OGIS* 338; Ditt.[3] 742. [5] *I.G.* IX, 2, 517.

[6] Beloch, *Klio* VI, 52; cf. Griffith, *Historia* II, 1950, 240, for early 4th century.

[7] *I.G.* V, 2, 22; VII, 190; *I. Priene* 108 l. 259; 109 ll. 179, 194; 113 l. 39; so at religious feasts: slaves, *SEG* IV, 302. 308; slave-girls also, 303.

sacrifices were sometimes now offered for the health, not of the citizens, but of all the inhabitants of the city[1]; and clubs occur like that of (?) Sidectas in Laconia, whose members were the men and women of his family, some city magistrates, many artisans both free and freedmen, and a slave-girl.[2]

One form of slavery in Hellenism stood apart from others, the mines (p. 254); they were a hell on earth which neither Stoicism nor Delphi could touch, and kings and cities were equally guilty. But ordinary domestic slavery was often not unkindly; the slave might be better born and educated than the master, and more than one philosopher who shook the world was, or had been, a slave. Athens, which tolerated the horrors of Laurium, had for long—another strange contradiction—strictly limited the punishments allowable in the case of other slaves,[3] and the Public Health law of Pergamum followed her example.[4] Stoicism worked for a better treatment of slaves, and gradually changed the atmosphere; slaves were to be pitied[5] rather than punished, and all through the third century manumission of slaves by will, especially in philosophic circles, became increasingly common.[6] Some manumission there had always been, but about 200 a great innovation began; under the influence of Delphi, always ready during the Aetolian domination to champion the cause of humanity, it became possible for the slave to *purchase* his freedom through the machinery of a fictitious sale to some god[7]; the movement was aided by the mundane consideration that cheap free labour was rendering industrial slavery unprofitable. Some slaves earned money at their craft, and manumission soon became very common —at Larisa 36 slaves were freed in one year,[8] at Halos, a

[1] As *I.G.* XII, 5, 721.

[2] *I.G.* V, 1, 209.

[3] Glotz, *C.R. Ac. Inscr.* 1908, 571.

[4] *OGIS* 483 ll. 178–183.

[5] Diog. Laert. X, 118; Ditt.[3] 1268 l. 24, where the *v. ll.* show there were *two* maxims, *ἱκέτας αἰδοῦ* and *οἰκέτας ἐλέει*, sometimes confounded.

[6] A regular advance from Plato, 1 in 5, to Lycon, 11 in 12: Diog. Laert. III, 42; V, 1, 13 *sqq.*; 2, 54 *sq.*; 3, 62 *sq.*; 4, 72 *sq.*; Cf. the manumissions *κατὰ διανόησιν*, as *I.G.* IX, 2, 102; 109 b l. 19; 1301.

[7] *One* fourth-century case, *B.C.H.* 1921, 150 no. 3.

[8] *I.G.* IX, 2, 568; for the Thessalian manumissions, see *'Εφ. 'Αρχ.* 1924, 142.

small town, over 40 in two[1]—and freedmen came to constitute a definite class in the cities, differing slightly in status from metics. But even manumission had its shadow side. That the freed slave-woman was often bound to stay on with her mistress during the latter's life, to work off her purchase-money, was not in itself unfair, but she really stayed on under servile conditions[2]; she could be fettered and flogged and even sold,[3] and any children she bore were still slaves[4]—a horrible thing—unless the act of manumission had freed them (sometimes conditionally) in advance.[5] She was sometimes even obliged to provide and even rear one or more children as slaves for her mistress.[6] She might occasionally commute this obligation for a money payment[7]; but her usual course was obvious,[8] and the clause was a compulsion to immorality.

Of the number of slaves in Greece, or their proportion to the free population, nothing is known; but in other respects the manumissions at Delphi and Naupactus have thrown some light on the slave population of Northern Greece.[9] Among purchased slaves the proportions of men and women were equal; but among house-born, judging by those liberated, women so preponderated that seemingly the girl baby born of a slave-mother had a better chance of life than if her mother were free. Purchased slaves were far more numerous than house-born; the commonest nationalities were Greek, Thracian, and Syrian, though every people is represented, from the Bastarnae to Arabia. The standard price of a slave was 3 to 4 minae for either sex; but among

[1] *I.G.* IX, 2, 109.

[2] *B.C.H.* 1898, 1, no. 32; *SEG* II, 307, παραμεινάτω. . ὡς δούλα.

[3] *B.C.H.* 1898, 1, no. 32; *SGDI* 2216 and often.

[4] *B.C.H.* 1898, 1 no. 77.

[5] *Ib.* nos. 47, 53, 62, 74, 88, 97; *SGDI* 1798, 2136, 2171, 2225; *B.C.H.* 1922, 465 no. 10.

[6] *SGDI* 1719; *Ath. Mitt.* 1907, 28 no. 20; *I.G.* IX, 1, 1066; *B.C.H.* 1898, 1, nos. 40, 88, 93, 95–7, 99, 102, 104.

[7] *Ib.* nos. 93, 99.

[8] *Ib.* no. 99 shows plainly that her own child is meant.

[9] This section is taken from the following: *SGDI* II, 1684–2342; *B.C.H.* 1898, 1 *sqq.*; 1922, 453 *sqq.*; *Ath. Mitt.* 1907, 1 *sqq.*; Hatzfeld, *Mélanges Holleaux* 93 (Italians).

purchased slaves some nationalities fetched more. Macedonia easily heads the list with an average of $5\frac{3}{4}$ minae for men and $5\frac{1}{4}$ for women, bearing out what Polybius says of the qualities of that great race.[1] Among men, Thracians with $5\frac{2}{5}$ and Romans and Italians (some of Hannibal's prisoners) with $5\frac{1}{4}$ shew up well, but their women only fetched the standard price; Galatian men with $4\frac{1}{2}$ also stand out, but among women the Greeks with $4\frac{2}{5}$ come next to the Macedonians. There is a curious difference in sex price as well as in sex proportions between house-born and purchased slaves; among purchased, 96 men whose nationalities are known average $3\frac{1}{3}$ minae and 98 women just under 4, but among house-born, while 101 women average just over 4, 47 men average $5\frac{1}{3}$; taken as a whole, the house-born slave, trained from infancy, was the more valuable. The highest recorded price is 25 minae for a Phrygian woman[2]; the few high prices known generally resulted from some special skill.

The most urgent question in Greece was the corn supply. The price of imported wheat at Athens in Demosthenes' time had normally averaged 5 drachmae the *medimnos* (bushel).[3] As Alexander's circulation of the Persian treasure drove down the value of the drachma, wheat naturally rose in price; about 300, with the drachma (6 obols) worth 3 obols, wheat, neglecting the seasonal variation, must have averaged some 10 dr. the bushel; it fell gradually as money rose, but was still $5\frac{1}{3}$ dr. about 200.[4] There was plenty of wheat in the world (p. 254); export of corn was well organised by the Ptolemies, and Athens, Corinth, Delos, many islands, Ionia, and perhaps other cities, relied primarily on imported corn; but usually a city depended on its own harvest, though it might sometimes have to supplement it. A failure of a city's crop meant, therefore, anything from short rations to famine; local famines throughout the period are common,

[1] V, 2, 5, cf. XVI, 22, 5.
[2] *Ath. Mitt.* 1907, 37 no. 29.
[3] Dem, XXXIV, 39.
[4] The wheat curve (see Tarn in *The Hellenistic Age*): *I.G.* XI, 2, 158 A ll. 37–50; 224 A l. 29; 287 A ll. 45, 60–71; Ditt.[3] 976.

land communication being very bad. Normally some magistracy, the *agoranomos* or *sitophylaces*, looked after the corn dealers and saw that the city was fed at a reasonable price. But when prices rose in a shortage this system regularly broke down, unless the *agoranomos*[1] bought corn himself or could persuade some wealthy merchant to sell it under cost price; the great number of men who thus paid the difference themselves furnishes a remarkable testimony to the sound public spirit in the cities.[2] But this was only a palliative; and in the great famine[3] of 329–325, which extended to all Greece and Epirus and was aggravated by the corner in Egyptian wheat engineered by Cleomenes,[4] Alexander's governor in Egypt, the State at Athens stepped in, raised a subscription, and appointed a commission, which bought corn as best it could and retailed it at the normal price, the people also being rationed; bread tickets are not a modern discovery. These special commissions,[5] and the 'measuring out' of corn, became thenceforth a regular system in shortages. But it was an imperfect system; subscription was voluntary, and might be inadequate; and the poor could not always pay for their ration.

It was perhaps Samos—alarmed by her series of famines about 246, when the money raised was twice lost by the merchants employed and the city was only saved by a private citizen, Bulagoras[6]—who took the final step and formed a permanent corn-fund[7]; enough was raised somehow from the rich and invested for the yearly interest to suffice to supply the city with corn. Samos' example was largely followed; a system of state supply obtained at Priene and

[1] *I.G.* IV, 2; XII, 5, 1011; Ditt.[3] 596, 708, 946.

[2] *I.G.* II[2], 398, 400, 401, 408, 416, 903; IV, 932; V, 2, 437; VII, 4132; IX, 2, 1104; XI, 4, 627, 1049; XII, 5, 817; 9, 900[a], 900[c]; *I. Priene* 108; *'Εφ. 'Αρχ.* 1912, 60 no. 89; *'Αθηνᾶ* 1908, 195 no. 6; Ditt.[3] 304, 495; Tod, *B.S.A.* XXIII, 75.

[3] Dem. XXXIV, 37–9; XLII, 20, 31; Köhler, *Ath. Mitt.* 1883, 211; Ferri, *Iscriz. di Cirene* no. 3=*SEG* IX, 1, no. 2.

[4] Van Groningen, *Mnemos.* LIII, 101.

[5] Generally, H. Francotte, *Mélanges Nicole*, 135.

[6] *SEG* I, 366; Ziebarth, *Z. f. Num.* 1924, 356.

[7] Ditt.[3] 976; see Wilhelm, *Mélanges Glotz*, II, 907.

perhaps elsewhere,[1] and permanent corn-funds are known at Miletus,[2] Teos,[3] Demetrias,[4] Delos,[5] Aegina,[6] and Thuria[7]; possibly they became almost universal. Even under rationing these funds meant that the rich (who provided the original capital) were feeding the poor, as the rich at Rhodes were voluntarily doing by their food liturgies, under which each wealthy man looked after a certain number of poor.[8] But Samos and Thuria went beyond this; at Samos the corn was distributed free every year to all citizens, at Thuria (*c.* 100) to the poor only, the rich apparently paying increased prices. As kings and wealthy men often also gave a largesse in corn,[9] and as at Arcesine and Minoa in the second century (and this was hardly unique) wealthy men also began to distribute free tickets of admission to the local festivals,[10] we see that the demoralising *panem et circenses*, free food and free games, were merely copied by Rome from later Hellenism.

In an age full of contradictions, none is more startling than the contrast between the miserable state of wages (p. 120) and the amazing liberality of the wealthy.[11] They would not pay; but they would give. What they gave was, however, invariably given to the State, the citizens (or the inhabitants) treated as a whole. Many a city seemed able to call on some wealthy man to rescue it whenever it chose: to give,[12] or lend without interest,[13] large sums to meet some special expenditure; to go on embassies without pay and champion the city against kings or Roman tax-gatherers[14];

[1] *I. Priene* 82, cf. 108 ll. 42, 68; Ditt.[3] 685 l. 100.

[2] Wiegand, *Siebenter Milet-Bericht* p. 27.

[3] *B.C.H.* 1922, 312 no. 2.

[4] *I.G.* IX, 2, 1104.

[5] Durrbach, *Comptes*, no. 442, Demares (179 B.C.), A ll. 91–4, 107–12, &c.

[6] *SGDI* 3417.

[7] *I.G.* V, 1, 1379.

[8] Str. 653.

[9] Kings: Memnon 25; *I.G.* XI, 4, 1115 n.; Ditt.[3] 374, 671 B; Wiegand *l.c.* 26. Individuals: *I.G.* XII, 5, 863–6; 7, 389; *I. Priene* 108, 109.

[10] *I.G.* XII, 7, 22, 24, 33, 35, 241.

[11] That is, wealthy on Greek standards. Wealth and luxury, in Greek history, are relative terms only.

[12] Ditt.[3] 374, 475, 497; *I. Priene* 109; *SEG* I, 366.

[13] *I.G.* V, 1, 962; XI, 4, 1055; XII, 9, 900 c.; *OGIS* 46; Ditt.[3] 330, 569; *I.G.* IX, 2, 1104.

[14] *SEG* I, 366; *I. Priene* 121, 111 l. 112; Ditt.[3] 330.

to build the bridge,[1] the gymnasium,[2] the temple,[3] if funds ran short; to supply war material,[4] endow a new festival[5] or a new school,[6] fill the burdensome liturgies,[7] provide oil for the athletes,[8] prizes for the school-boys, banquets for the citizens and their wives[9]; finally to be honoured with a statue, for which he himself sometimes paid.[10] Men like Protogenes at Olbia, Menas at Sestos, Moschion at Priene, Polycritus at Erythrae, almost seem to carry the city on their shoulders.[11] This constant reliance on some rich man stepping into the breach seems to indicate that the cities were not on a sound economic basis; but few ages can have shown more public spirit, even if sometimes it was perhaps the equivalent of purchasing a title. 'He impaired his own livelihood for the public good' was Epidaurus' testimony to one Aristobulus,[12] while Pergamum said of Diodorus, 'His care for the common weal prevented him taking thought for his own'.[13] And such public spirit was not confined to the wealthy. Nothing leaves a more pleasing impression than the numerous decrees of thanks passed to physicians.[14] The municipal doctors were not a wealthy class—the one salary known is 1,000 drachmae a year[15]; but often they forwent their salaries during epidemics,[16] and nevertheless, like Damiades of Sparta, 'made no difference between rich and poor, free and slaves'.[17] When all the Coan doctors were down with an epidemic Xenotimus came voluntarily to the city's aid,[18] and Apollonius of Miletus fought the plague in

[1] Ditt.[3] 1048.
[2] Michel 456; Wilhelm, *Jahresh.* 1908, 56.
[3] *I.G.* XII, 3, 248; 7, 388, 433; *SGDI* 3569.
[4] Ditt.[3] 569; *I. Priene* 17.
[5] Ditt.[3] 631; *I.G.* IX, 1, 694; XII, 5, 595; 7, 515.
[6] Ditt.[3] 577–8.
[7] Menas (*post*); cf. *I. Priene* 174.
[8] *I.G.* VII, 190; XII, 9, 236; *I. Priene* 112, ll. 57–66.
[9] *I.G.* VII, 2712 l. 68; *I. Priene* 108 l. 257; 109 ll. 193, 181; 111 l. 238.
[10] *I.G.* VII, 190; *Syria* V, 332 no. 7.
[11] Ditt.[3] 495; *OGIS* 339; *I. Priene* 109; *'Αθηνα* 1908, 195 no. 6; these illustrate most of the foregoing.
[12] *I.G.* IV[2], 65.
[13] *Ath. Mitt.* 1907, 261 l. 12.
[14] A good instance is *Ath. Mitt.* LI, 1926, 26, no. 2.
[15] Wilhelm, *Neue Beiträge* IV, 54 (Annual salary).
[16] *I.G.* XII, 1, 1032; IX, 1, 516; Ditt.[3] 335.
[17] *I.G.* V, 1, 1145.
[18] Ditt.[3] 943.

the islands without reward[1]; there was a high standard of devotion in the profession. Philosophers, too, sometimes remitted the fees for their lectures to those unable to pay.[2] There really seem to have been quite a number of people who thought other things more important than money.

Yet, amid all the philanthropic feeling and public spirit of the time, philanthropy in our sense—the organised aid of the poor by the rich—was almost unknown. Broadly speaking, pity for the poor had little place in the normal Greek character,[3] and consequently for the poor, as such, no provision usually existed; the idea of democracy and equality was so strong that anything done must be done for all alike; there was nothing corresponding to our mass of privately organised charities and hospitals. When we have mentioned the food liturgies at Rhodes, Athens' dole to men crippled,[4] the well-to-do sharing with the poor at Tarentum,[5] Polybius' statement that Opheltas in Boeotia helped the poor from State funds,[6] and Heracleides' that the prosperous people of Tanagra were good to their poor,[7]—'it is easy', he adds drily, 'to be good when you have enough to eat'—we have about exhausted the list, unless we include the cases where organised bodies like demesmen supported the daughter of a deceased member.[8] Distributions of meat from the sacrifices, on which stress has been laid, cannot have been common, unless conceivably at Athens; the priests generally kept their perquisites, for which after all they had often paid, and meat scarcely came within the purview of the poor at all. The Myconos catalogue of *c.* 200[9], supplementary to one lost, mentions one distribution in four months, a dinner to wives of citizens and women initiated only. A Coan list, covering a few days,[10] twice mentions meat which went 'to the city', but it does not follow it was distributed; St. Paul seems clear that much normally found

[1] *I.G.* XII, 5, 824; Ditt.[3] 620.
[2] *SEG* I, 368.
[3] H. Bolkestein, *Wohltatigkeit und Armenpflege im vorchristlichen Altertum*, 1939, 113–150, &c.
[4] Arist. *'Αθ. Πολ.* 49.
[5] Arist. *Pol.* 1320 b, 9.
[6] XX, 6.
[7] *F.H.G.* 11, p. 257. Add Bulagoras' charity, *SEG* I, 366.
[8] As *I.G.* II[2], 1165.
[9] Ditt.[3] 1024.
[10] *Ib.* 1025 ll. 23, 55.

its way into the shops. It might have been expected that the Stoics and Cynics, with their sense of human brotherhood, would have taken up philanthropy; but neither did. To Stoics, poverty, like slavery, affected only the body, and what affected only the body was a matter of indifference; the poorest slave could be a king in his own soul, so they concentrated on the soul and let the body be—the reason why they never advocated abolition. The Cynics glorified the poverty they themselves practised; if absence of possessions did not actually constitute virtue, it was the indispensable condition of acquiring virtue; apparently they did not distinguish between the involuntary poverty of the labourer and the voluntary renunciation of the philosopher. The one expression of philanthropy in literature—Cercidas' poem (p. 279)—was apparently evoked by Cleomenes' revolution.

The prosperity of the Hellenistic age has often been alluded to in this chapter; the matter must now be looked at more closely. Prior to Sulla, and with local fluctuations, it was without question a prosperous time for the upper classes: the enormous expansion of trade (Chap. VII) tells its own story, as does the growth of clubs, of new festivals p. (114), of table luxury with its accompanying literature, of luxury in women's dress, especially silk and gold woven cloth (p. 256), of better-planned cities, improved private houses, and more elaborate furniture (Chap. IX). A distinction must however be drawn between Greece itself and Asia (with the islands). Not all of Greece felt the rising tide; Corinth and Aetolia, Ambracia and Pagasae grew richer (p. 251), but Athens, as regards wealth, fell back till the late second-century revival, as did Sparta for other reasons. Northern Greece was generally prosperous, as is shown by the number of slaves and the manner in which cities hardly heard of before now come into prominence; and the state of things at Messene *c.* 100–91 has been rather a revelation,[1] for Messenia was an agricultural country, unimportant and out

[1] Wilhelm, *Jahresh.* 1914, 1, on *I.G.* V, 1, 1432; cf. Lepsius, *Rh. Mus.* 1916, 161.

of the trade streams. The average fortune of Messenian citizens at the time, according to Professor Wilhelm's calculation, was about one-fifth of a talent, as against one-fourth at Athens in Demosthenes' time, and the 2 per cent. land-tax produced about 2·5 drachmae a head, as against 2·75 fr. in France in 1908, the purchasing power of the drachma being of course far greater than that of the franc; the women often spent over 100 dr. on a dress, and affected the expensive transparent silks[1]; silver plate was common, and fines ran up to 2,000 dr.[2] Another point, easy to follow, is the growth in the scale of penalties for breach of arbitration awards[3]; in the fifth century the highest known is 5 talents, but in the second we get 20 (Cyclades),[4] 30 and 50 (Asia Minor),[5] and 60 (Locris).[6] As to individuals, the richest man in Demosthenes' Greece, the Athenian Diphilos, perhaps possessed 160 talents[7]: the richest c. 200, Alexander the Isian in Aetolia, had 200.[8] We are justified in saying that, while Greece did not grow in prosperity like Asia, it enjoyed a very tolerable measure of it down to Sulla.

For Asia and the islands the evidence, quite apart from the growth of the cities and the expansion of trade, is overwhelming. Athens had drawn 15 talents a year tribute from Byzantium and 1 to 2 talents apiece from her Carian cities; c. 200 Byzantium paid 80 talents a year to the Gauls,[9] and subsequently Rhodes drew 120 talents a year from her Carian possessions, chiefly Caunos and Stratonicea.[10] The scale of girls' dowries at Myconos compared to those in fourth-century Athens,[11] the size of the subscriptions raised at Cos c. 200,[12] the scale of fines in Epicteta's club at Thera compared to Athenian practice,[13] the new custom, originating in the clubs of Cos and Thera, of honouring members with crowns of gold instead of leaves,[14] all tell an

[1] Ditt.³ 736 ll. 18–23. [2] *Ib.* ll. 38, 63. [3] Wilhelm, *Neue Beiträge* VI, 14.
[4] *I.G.* XII, 5, 128 (p. 308). [5] *Milet* I, 3 no. 149; Ditt.³ 633 l. 124.
[6] *Klio* XVI, 170 no. 131. [7] Plut. *Mor.* 843 D (doubtfully).
[8] Polyb. XXI, 26, 9, 14. [9] Polyb. IV, 46, 4. [10] *Ib.* XXX, 31, 7.
[11] *Inscr. Jur. Gr.* I, 48 no. 6 compared with 108 no. 8. [12] Michel 642.
[13] *Ib.* 1001; 150–500 dr. against 50, Poland 449.
[14] Ditt.³ 1107; Michel 1002; cf. *OGIS* 44, 730.

unmistakable story. In Asia Minor, whatever happened politically, prosperity and wealth grew steadily down to 88, perhaps down to the Civil Wars. That kings' ministers should make great fortunes was natural, but by the first century private citizens too were sometimes wealthy out of all proportion to anything known in Greece; one Hieron at Laodicea on the Lycus possessed over 2,000 talents,[1] and at one time Pompey's friend Pythodorus of Tralles was worth over 4,000 talents,[2] including his land. But the best evidence is the amount Rome found to plunder in Asia. In 63 the publican Falcidius,[3] having bought the taxes of Tralles for 900,000 sesterces (say 39 talents), offered a bribe of 50 talents to get them for a second year at the same figure, *i.e.* he had made *at least* 100 talents in one year out of one second-class city—and the whole Macedonian land-tax had only produced some 200 talents annually. This is more eloquent than the vast fortunes extracted from Asia by Pompey and Crassus. In 86 Mithridates took 2,000 talents from Chios[4]; in 70 the Senate demanded 4,000 talents from Crete.[5] Cassius took 500 talents from Rhodes and 8,000 more from individual Rhodians.[6] Sulla in 84 took 20,000 talents from the province of Asia, called 5 years' arrears of taxes[7]; Brutus took 16,000 as a year's tax[8]; and finally Antony demanded 200,000, called nine years' taxes in advance,[9] a greater sum than the treasure amassed by the Persian kings over two centuries from half the continent. One need not elaborate the story; the days when the Hellenistic world was called 'poverty stricken' are, or should be, long past.

This wealth was reflected in people's amusements; not merely the multiplication of games, but the increased cost of celebration, the performers being now professionals. A complete list of the new Hellenistic festivals would fill a page. Between Alexander's death and 189 a great number, with games and sacrifices, entailing corresponding expense,

[1] Str. 578. [2] *Ib.* 649. [3] *Cic. Pro Flacco* 36 (90).
[4] App. *Mith.* 47. [5] Diod. XL, 1. [6] Plut. *Brut.* 32.
[7] Plut. *Sulla* 25; *Lucull.* 20. [8] App. *b.c.* IV, 316.
[9] Plut. *Ant.* 24 combined with App. *b.c.* V, 27.

were founded by the cities everywhere, while five annual festivals, at Thespiae,[1] Cos,[2] Delphi,[3] Magnesia,[4] and Miletus,[5] were turned into 'crowned' games, great quadrennial celebrations. Beside these were the mass of festivals founded by various kings, hardly inferior in number; the greatest of these was the Ptolemaieia at Alexandria, the only festival whose honours ranked equal to those of the Olympia,[6] though several were reckoned equal to the Pythia.[7] In the second century several cities founded festivals called Romaia in honour of Rome [8]—at least 13 are known, that at Delphi in 189 being the first; while even after 146 the Boeotian Ptoia became quadrennial,[9] and Tanagra founded her Serapieia.[10] Then came Sulla; and there were no more foundations till Augustus' peace. Naturally the performers at these festivals, the Dionysiac artists,[11] grew enormously in importance. Their oldest association, the Athenian, dates from soon after Alexander; its privileges were secured to it by the Amphictyons soon after 279. The Isthmian association, with its centre at Corinth and special relations with Thespiae, formed soon afterwards; by the second century it embraced the whole of old Greece except Athens, and had sections in many cities. The destruction of Corinth in 146 hit it hard; internal strife among the sections followed, some joined the Athenian association, and the Isthmian body never recovered. A third association early formed in Asia, with its centre at Teos; it subsequently amalgamated with the players of the Pergamene court theatre, the association of Dionysus Kathegemon, and

[1] Ditt.[3] 457; *I.G.* VII, 1735.

[2] Unpublished; see *Arch. Anz.* 1903, 197; 1905, 11.

[3] Ditt.[3] 402, 408, 424, 489; Roussel, *Rev. E.A.* 1924, 97.

[4] Ditt.[3] 557 *sqq.* [5] Ditt.[3] 590. [6] *Ib.* 390; *G.G.A.* 1913, 170 no. 2.

[7] *E.g.* Thespiae, Magnesia, and two at Pergamum, Ditt.[3] 629 (partly isolympic), *OGIS* 305, *SEG* IV, 502.

[8] Delphi, Ditt.[3] 611 n. 3; Alabanda, Livy XLIII, 6; Euboea, *I.G.* XII, 9, 899; Thespiae, *I.G.* II[2], 1054; Athens, Michel 1539; Miletus, *Milet* I, 7 no. 203; Cos, Ditt.[3] 1066; Magnesia, *ib.* 1079; Rhodes, *ib.* 724; Pergamum, *ib.* 1065; Chalcis, Oropus, Corcyra, *ib.* 1064.

[9] *B.C.H.* 1890, 48 *sqq.*, cf. Holleaux, *ib.* p. 201.

[10] Michel 890. [11] Poland, 129–40.

the whole body became dependent on the Attalids. In their palmy days the Dionysiac artists were almost an independent state, sending and receiving ambassadors[1]; on them were lavished honours, privileges,[2] immunity, safe-conducts[3]; they were subsidised by kings and cities, and the Athenian association had the right to wear the purple; it would seem that it was better to amuse people than to govern them.

The rate of interest[4] is some guide to the capital wealth of a country; but in Greece it is not a certain guide, for there were few of the modern facilities for the circulation of capital. Private banks were normally small, and the chief sources of capital available for traders or farmers to borrow were either some endowment, the capital of which was lent out at interest to obtain an annual revenue for the object of the endowment, or temple funds; but the *liquid* funds of a temple were generally small,[5] and the temple at Delos for centuries lent at 10 per cent. regardless of changes in the value of money. However, the interest curve may be given so far as known. In Alexander's reign the usual rate was 12 per cent., omitting the risky maritime loans, which ran much higher. By about 300 the rate had fallen to 10 per cent., reflecting the fall in the value of the drachma consequent upon the circulation of the Persian treasure, and 10 per cent. remained usual throughout the third century,[6] though $8\frac{1}{3}$ [7] and 6 [8] (this last apparently a political favour) also occur; in the first half of the second century we meet 7 [9] and $6\frac{2}{3}$,[10] both business transactions. After the middle of the century the rate rises again and by Sulla's time it has got back to the old 12 per cent. After Sulla, interest is an index of nothing but

[1] *I. Pergamon* 163, *I. Magnesia* 54, 89, 90, Michel 1009, 1012, 1014.

[2] *B.C.H.* 1911, 168; 1922, 312 no. 2; Ditt.[3] 460; *SEG* II, 580.

[3] *I.G.* II[2], 1132; XI, 4, 1061; XII, 9, 207; Ditt.[3] 399, 507, 563, 692.

[4] G. Billeter, *Gesch. des Zinsfusses*, 1898.

[5] Estimated at Delos to be 50,000 dr. out of a capital value of $5\frac{1}{2}$ million: Homolle, *B.C.H.* 1891, 164–8.

[6] Ditt.[3] 544, 546 B l. 22, 955, 1200; *C.I.G.* 3599.

[7] Ditt.[3] 364 l. 74; possibly *I.G.* XII, 7, 67 (fraction uncertain).

[8] *Milet* 1, 3 no. 138.

[9] Michel 1001, I l. 24, II l. 7.

[10] Ditt.[3] 672 l. 23.

Roman rapacity; Lucullus stemmed the rise in Asia for a time by fixing 12 per cent. as a maximum,[1] but in the Civil Wars extraordinary rates, up to 48 per cent.,[2] were extorted by Romans. So far as it goes, interest indicates continuous prosperity down to 146 anyhow, with money (as the world went) plentiful and cheap. The drachma had become stable again before 200, for the farm tenants at Thespiae have apparently the option then of renewing at the same rent,[3] while at Delos *c.* 300 they could only renew at a rent 10 per cent. higher; but whether it ever quite got back to the value of Alexander's time—wheat at 5 drachmae—is uncertain; there are indications that down to *c.* 100 wheat remained at somewhat over 5 drachmae.

A certain development in banking[4] took place, but too much must not be made of Greek banking, which never attained the importance of the Roman. Private banks, beside money-changing, took money on deposit and made loans. The so-called 'state' banks in some Greek cities, were not a mere monopoly of money-changing farmed out to some individual, were really an adjunct of the Treasury; they received and paid out the revenue, kept the city accounts, and might advance money for an unforeseen disbursement, recouping themselves later; they did thus save the city the trouble of borrowing abroad, which otherwise it often had to do.

For most of the city borrowing met with was mere machinery; it had no more to do with poverty than municipal borrowing to-day. The reason was simple. A city had no budget[5]; certain receipts were merely earmarked to certain expenses; an unforeseen expense, however small,

[1] Plut. *Luc.* 20, App. *Mith.* 83.

[2] Ditt.[3] 748 l. 36; Cic. *ad. Att.* V, 21.

[3] *B.C.H.* 1897, 565.

[4] Th. Reinach. *B.C.H.* 1896, 531; Ziebarth, *Z. f. Num.* 1923, 26; Laum, *Banken* in P.W.; Glotz, *Ancient Greece at Work*, 365; Heichelheim, *Wirtschaftsgesch.*, 550 *sqq.*, 1090 n. 32 (bibliography); Cary, *A History of the Greek World*, 300–1.

[5] Francotte, *Les finances des cités grecques*, 133 *sqq.* The 'city accounts' mentioned at Miletus (*Milet* I, 3 no. 147 l. 16) and Halicarnassus (Michel 456 l. 17) are hardly budgets.

meant a new tax or a subscription,[1] which took time, and the city borrowed the amount for convenience[2] and repaid at leisure. There was sometimes deliberate procrastination over repayment,[3] but again this had nothing to do with poverty. One instance may be given. About 220–200, says Polybius,[4] there was plenty of money in Boeotia; but Heracleides says debts were almost irrecoverable.[5] Now during this period Orchomenus borrowed twice; over Nicareta's loan the city procrastinated to the utmost,[6] while Eubulus' was paid off before the appointed day[7]; obviously the governing considerations were personal or political, not economic. The city of Delos understood systematic borrowing, and was regularly financed from the temple funds, perpetually borrowing and repaying.[8] Officially, of course, almost every city was poor, for the city Treasury rarely had any reserves; but that did not mean that the citizens were poor—Cambridge men are not necessarily poor because the University is. It meant however that one city could seldom lend to another[9]; but its *citizens* could and did, by a subscription in the city's name.[10] The cities really lived from hand to mouth. For this reason Ephesus once raised money to arm some friends by selling a dozen citizenships as a favour[11]; Thasos *c.* 285 sold four or five at a great price, 2000 drachmae apiece[12]; in the Social War Tritaea sold some to raise mercenaries[13]; these things had no more to do with poverty than the sale of memberships by the

[1] Delos sometimes had a fund, ἀδιάτακτα, for unforeseen expenses; Durrbach, *Comptes* no. 442 (Demares, 179 B.C.), A ll. 95–6 &c.

[2] Even Delos would borrow for a crown, *ib.* ll. 25, 43, 61, 66; *id.* no. 449 (175 B.C.) ll. 14, 18, 22.

[3] As *Inscr. Jur. Gr.* I, 158 no. 10. [4] XX, 6. [5] *F.H.G.* II, 258.

[6] *I.G.* VII, 3172 (literature, Tod, *J.H.S.* 1927, 195). [7] *I.G.* VII, 3171.

[8] *I.G.* XI, 2, 147 B l. 7; 158 B; 161 A l. 25; 203 A l. 73; 287 A l. 122; &c. Conceivably too Carthaea, *I.G.* XII, 5, 544.

[9] But see *Αρχ. Δελτ.* 8 (1923), 182 (Boeotian Thisbe to Chorsiae), and *Mnemos*, 1916, 219 (Rhodes to Argos).

[10] *I.G.* VII, 1737–8, 2405–6; XII, 9, 7; *SEG* 3, 342. *Milet* I, 3 no. 318 shows the practice.

[11] *I. Priene* 494; Roussel, *Rev. Phil.* 1913, 334; Holleaux, *Rev. E.G.* 1916, 29.

[12] *B.C.H.* 1921, 153 no. 6. [13] Wilhelm, *Neue Beiträge* I, 38.

Marylebone Cricket Club to build its present pavilion. A particular city of course might lose credit; Oropus once had to entice lenders by the promise of civic honours.[1] And the wealthiest might be thrown out of gear by war; thus in 201 the actions of Philip V in Caria prevented Miletus getting in her revenue, and she had to borrow from her citizens in order to carry on, repaying by means of life annuities.[2] But cities thus damaged soon recovered, as simple economic forms do.

The worst trouble of this immature financial system was the difficulty of carrying out public works. Co-operative works—even decent roads—were almost impossible unless kings took the lead, as they did when the world co-operated to restore Thebes in 316[3] and Rhodes after the earthquake of 225[4]; and even city works were difficult unless a city had some special resource. Eretria did get a marsh drained by giving the contractor substantial privileges[5]; but Delos paid for her new harbour from the new trade Rome presented to her, and Miletus' superb market-places, where not built for her by the Seleucids, must have been made possible by the fact that the city itself owned wool factories, like a king (p. 250).

It was not that the cities did not tax themselves. Direct taxes were repugnant to Greeks; the traditional 10 per cent. of the harvest was Asiatic. Still, necessity sometimes compelled them to overcome their repugnance: Athens had long had a tax, the *eisphora*, on the sum total of a man's property, and in the Hellenistic period this was adopted by some cities, notably Miletus.[6] Others, as Crannon[7] and Delos,[8] did take 10 per cent. of the harvest, or, as Delos[8] and Cos,[9] 10 per cent. of house rents. But generally money was raised indirectly, and very many indirect taxes are known. A tax of 2 per cent. on all exports and imports (p. 175 n. 4), a pasture tax on the number of animals reared, harbour

[1] Ditt.³ 544. [2] *Milet* I, 3 no. 147; life annuities also *I.G.* VII, 3054.
[3] Ditt.³ 337. [4] Polyb. V, 88. [5] *I.G.* XII, 9, 191.
[6] P. Guiraud, *Études économiques sur l'antiquité*, 83–112; Francotte *op. c.* 53. [7] Polyaen. II, 34. [8] *I.G.* XI, 2, 161 A ll. 26, 27; &c.
[9] Michel 720.

dues, and taxes on stalls in the market, were general; Cos had a special export duty on its wine, and taxed bread, flour, vegetables, salt fish, and many other things [1]; Teos in the third century [2] taxed ploughing oxen, timber mules, timber cutting, sheep and pigs, garments woven from Milesian wool (possibly the raw material also), purple dyeing, gardens, and bees. In some cases such taxation was perhaps partly due to the city having to raise taxes (tribute) for some king [3]; the city did not get the whole benefit. But, even if it did, there was, throughout the whole vexatious system, no proper means of making private wealth available to the state except where the *eisphora* obtained, and even the *eisphora* was imperfect, for men were taxed on a simple declaration of their property, and often under-declared. Farming-out of taxes was known, but was unimportant till the coming of the Roman tax-farmer, the hated publican.

We have sketched the prosperity of the Greek world; we must now turn to the reverse side, the condition of the small man and the working class. Apart from some Asiatic cities like Miletus, industry in Greece had not kept pace with trade; and the little man who employed a dozen hands could not compete with the great serf and slave factories of Alexandria and Pergamum. As to farming, it has been thought that the real fall in farm rents at Delos after 250 means that agriculture was failing [4]; but it only means that *on Delos* men found transit trade more lucrative, for the perpetual desire of men throughout the third and second centuries for a division of land suggests that farming was much as usual, though in several countries—Laconia, Aetolia, Thessaly [5]—land at different times became overburdened with debt. The great cities naturally tended to form a proletariat class, but of *consumers*; the few industries of Hellenism were small and scattered, and there was no class-conscious proletariat of *producers*. But evidence on the whole subject is lamentably defective, except in one

[1] Michel 720. [2] *SEG* II, 579. [3] Cf. *I.G.* XII, 5, 570; *C.I.G.* 2673.
[4] See now J. H. Kent, 'The temple estates of Delos', *Hesperia*, XVII 1948, 243. [5] Livy XLII, 5.

quarter[1]; we do know the condition of the working man on Delos *c.* 300–250, and where a particular trade like cutting inscriptions can be traced later, conditions do not improve; and as men came to Delos from other islands, one must suppose the outlook in the other islands, prosperous as they were, was worse.

The depreciation of money about 300 led to a corresponding rise in prices[2]; wheat about doubled, oil rose 3½ times, common wine 2½ times.[3] The average rent of a house at Delos, under 20 drachmae in the fourth century, was 100 dr. by the second,[4] though here local overcrowding[5] played a part; but food prices everywhere had not got back to the level of Demosthenes' time by 250, and possibly not by 200. Against this, wages at Delos had actually fallen compared with Demosthenes' Athens,[6] probably the result of untempered competition. The line of bare subsistence, the pauper and slave rate, with wheat at 5 drachmae, was 2 obols a day per year for one man[7] and a drachma (6 obols) for a family[8]; but at Delos a skilled artisan was only making, *at best*, 4 obols a day per year, and the unskilled 2 obols, sometimes less,[9] even while wheat might be anything up to 10 dr.; that is, unskilled free labour, which could be replaced by slaves, could not rise above the slave rate and occasionally fell below it. Consequently, as compared with the fourth century, the gap between rich and poor grew wider; and that was the most unhealthy phenomenon in Hellenism. The bearing of this on the population question is obvious; for the poor, rearing children was most difficult. That the year

[1] This and the next section are largely abridged from Tarn's *Social Question* in *The Hellenistic Age, q.v.*

[2] See Glotz' tables, *J. des Savants* 1913, 15 *sqq.*, and Heichelheim's tables in his *Wirtschaftliche Schwankungen*, with Tarn's criticisms, *Economica* 1930, 315–18; also Rostovtzeff, *SEH* 230 *sqq.*, with his notes. The basis of everything is the temple accounts.

[3] Oil (45 dr.) compares with 12 dr., Michel 673; wine (10–11½) with 4, Dem. XLII, 20.

[4] S. Molonier, *Les 'maisons sacrées' de Délos*, 75.

[5] Homolle, *B.C.H.* 1890, 441.

[6] Cf. Glotz *l.c.* 206.

[7] Arist. *'Αθ. Πολ.* 49; Dem. *Phil.* I, 28; Michel 642 D ll. 65 *sqq.* (so many men for 10 months).

[8] *OGIS* 218 l. 36.

[9] 'Less': *I.G.* XI, 2, 146 A l. 75 (Tlesis' labourers); 158 A ll. 38–47 (Artemisia).

included many non-working (festival) days is immaterial; men must eat on Sundays. These wages may explain why some cities were driven to free corn, *i.e.* pauperisation.

Of course there was social unrest. There were no trade organisations, and in a slave society strikes were almost impossible. (The strikes in Egypt, p. 199, are not in point.) The bakers at Paros once came out because their wages were withheld—apparently no uncommon event; the *agoranomos* promptly intervened, saw that they were paid, and got them back.[1] No other strike is recorded till those in Roman Asia in the second century A.D.,[2] when trade guilds were beginning to form, while the first recorded strike for better conditions was not till the fifth century A.D. If things became quite unbearable, the only known resource was a rising or a revolution.[3]

The fourth century was already obsessed by the fear of social revolution[4]—one reason why the well-to-do turned to Macedonia as champion of the existing order. In the treaties between Alexander and the cities of the League of Corinth it was provided that Macedonia and the League should repress, in any League city, any movement for abolition of debt, division of land, confiscation of personal property, or liberation of slaves to assist the revolution[5]; the constitution of Demetrius' revived League of 303 contained similar provisions.[6] The revolution therefore had now a general programme under four heads. The poor desired the land, but with the small men of every type the driving force was debt; simple communities may be patient of rude conditions of life, but they always hate the creditor. The temple accounts of Delos, which show many very small loans and many bad debts, throw some light on the debt question.[7]

[1] *I.G.* XII, 5, 129. [2] W. H. Buckler in *Anatolian Studies* 27.

[3] From here onward see R. von Pöhlmann, *Gesch. d. sozialen Frage und des Sozialismus in der antiken Welt*, 3rd ed. by F. Oertel, 1925.

[4] Dem. XXIV, 149; Isocr. *Archidamos* 50, 64 *sqq.*; Aeneas Tacticus 14, 1 and *passim*. [5] [Dem.] XVII, 15. [6] *SEG* I, 75, col. 1 l. 28.

[7] Schulhof's tables, *B.C.H.* 1908, 459–72, show that the temple between 279 and 179 perhaps lost a talent, *i.e.* ⅛th of its liquid capital.

From quite another angle, philosophy made its contribution to the subject; the Stoic insistence on equality and brotherhood sank into men's souls, and inspired visions of something better than the existing order. Some took refuge from civilisation in drawing fancy pictures of virtuous barbarians living according to Nature, prototypes of Tacitus' *Germania*; and Utopias began to appear. Plato and Aristotle had indeed drawn Ideal States, but not states of much use to working men; and the first Utopia, Zeno's (p. 79), was too splendid and too remote for human nature to grasp. But Euhemerus (*c.* 300)[1] and Iambulus (third century)[2] created true modern Utopias, located on islands in the Indian Ocean; and in Iambulus' great Sun-state[3] Communism appears full-grown. The people were equal in all respects, even in wisdom; they lived in social bodies or 'systems' in which all worked equally and equally shared the produce; they escaped 'slavery to the means of production' because the island fortunately bore crops, partly by itself, all the year round; each in turn filled every duty from servant to governor, the governor of each system being the oldest member, who had to die at a certain age (a provision taken from a tradition at Ceos)[4]; there was thus no place for wealth, ambition, or learning, the foes of equality, or for class war, because there were no classes; above all things the people prized Homonoia and were united in concord and love. What Iambulus and his fellows really aimed at was the abolition of that class war whose horrors many Greeks had seen; and indeed, even while revolutionary philosophers and conservative governments were alike honouring Concord, some practical devotees of that goddess were always ready to massacre their fellows in her name.

Except possibly for a slave rising in Chios,[5] the first outbreak recorded in the third century was a proletarian revolt at Cassandreia in 279, engineered by one Apollodorus, who

[1] *F. Gr. Hist.* I, 300; Jacoby, *Euemeros* 3 in P.W.; Tarn, *Proc. Brit. Acad.*, 1933, 163 [43]; H. F. van der Meer, *Euhemeros van Messene*, 1949.

[2] Diod. II, 55–60; Tarn, *C.Q.* XXXIII, 1939, 193.

[3] *Not* Stoic: Tarn, *Alex.* II, App. 25 § 3; Rostovtzeff, *SEH* 1523 n. 81.

[4] Str. 486.

[5] Athen. 265 C; date, Susemihl I, 475 n. 70.

made himself tyrant, tortured the wealthy, and gave part of their property to his followers; he showed that a mercenary force made this easy of accomplishment, and had a powerful career till Antigonus Gonatas suppressed him.[1] Four disturbances in the islands followed, one certainly between rich and poor, which the kings got settled without open revolt.[2] But the great revolutions of the third century were the two at Sparta,[3] which was in an unhealthy state because a few had monopolised all the land. Agis IV (*acc.* 244) attempted to cancel debts and divide up the land by peaceful reform, and failed; his stronger successor Cleomenes III, aided by the Stoic Sphaerus, Zeno's pupil, carried the reform through by force, abolished debts, and nationalised the land, which he divided into 4,000 lots for Spartiates and 15,000 for Perioeci, filling up the Spartiate body from Perioeci and metics. Neither king touched the Helot question, for both believed that, far from being revolutionaries, they were restoring the old Sparta of Lycurgus; but Greece thought that Cleomenes was carrying out the programme of the revolution, and in his ensuing war with the Achaean League he had the poor in every city on his side; at one city, Cynaetha, the revolution went through and the land was divided.[4] Had he forgone his military ambitions, which aimed at the headship of the Peloponnese, he could have made his reform at Sparta a permanent success; but the well-to-do rulers of the League in desperation called on Macedonia for help, and Antigonus Doson took Sparta (222) and restored the old state of things. Revolution broke out again at Sparta in 207 under the lead of Nabis (p. 23); he carried out all the four points of the revolutionary programme,[5] freeing many Helots, though he too never dealt radically with the Helot question; every Greek revolution, except perhaps the Pergamene, conveys a sense of unreality, as it never included slaves. Nabis plundered the wealthy,

[1] Diod. XXII, 5; Polyaen. VI, 7; Plut. *Mor.* 555 B.

[2] *I.G.* XI, 4, 1052; XII, 5, 1065; 7, 221; *OGIS* 43.

[3] Tarn, *C.A.H.* VII ch. 23; cf. (a different interpretation), K. M. T. Chrimes, *Ancient Sparta*, 1949, ch. 1.

[4] Polyb. IV, 17, 4; 20 *sq.*

[5] Polyb. XIII, 6 *sq.*; Livy XXXIV, 30–32.

but—so he said—solely for the State; perhaps the State now paid for the common meals (this, if many Helots were freed, would have been unavoidable), and there are indications that Nabis was not as cruel as his enemies have drawn him.[1] Rome, having overthrown Macedonia, ultimately intervened in Macedonia's stead and clipped Nabis' wings; and though she did not interfere with the revolution in Sparta itself, the wealthy in Greece were henceforth ready to welcome her as their champion.

About 200 there was trouble between debtors and creditors in the Aetolian League; the successful general Scopas tried to cancel debts, failed before the opposition of the wealthy, and went into exile to Egypt, the trouble continuing for years.[2] There was also chronic trouble in Thessaly,[3] and in Boeotia in the last quarter of the third century and later[4]; and Eumenes II accused Perseus before the Senate of intending to use the Thessalian debtors to murder Rome's wealthy friends—in fact of favouring social revolution—a changed rôle indeed for a Macedonian king. But no great outbreak is known between 200 and 132, whether from lack of information or because prices had reached a better relation to wages. Certainly in 146, in the last struggle with Rome, the Achaean League decreed a moratorium and the freeing and arming of 12,000 slaves[5] (though the number of men the League put into the field, 14,700, shows that this was not carried out); but this was hardly revolution, though the debtors' rising in Dyme after the Roman conquest, when the town archives were burnt, may have been.[6] Mithridates however did attempt later to use social revolution as a weapon against Rome[7] (p. 42), while Ephesus employed much the same weapon to counter him.[8] The great slave rising in Sicily affected the Aegean; the slaves rose on Delos (130), but were suppressed; they rose in the mines of Macedonia; they rose at Laurium, captured Sunium, and for some

[1] Polyb. XXIV, 7, 3 must mean Nabis.
[2] Polyb. XIII, 1 *sq.*, XXX, 11; Livy XLII, 4 *sq.*
[3] Livy XLII, 5.
[4] Polyb. XX, 6, 1–3; Heraclides in *G.G.M.* I, pp. 102–3; M. Feyel, *Polybe* etc., 277, cf. 262.
[5] Polyb. XXXVIII, 11, 10; 15, 3.
[6] Ditt.³ 684.
[7] App. *Mith.* 48.
[8] Ditt.³ 742.

time ravaged Attica[1]; they apparently rose at Pergamum. Professor Kahrstedt has argued that there was a sort of Red International *c.* 130–63, and that Sulla and Pompey delivered the world from Bolshevism[2]; but Bolshevism was a very strict social-economic theory, and these slave-risings, as I see them, were a blind product of the misery of mass slavery in mines or royal factories or (in Italy) on the great estates. Slaves rose to get liberty, debtors to get property; as to Mithridates, he would have utilised anything that promised vengeance on Rome. There was only one movement, apart from those at Sparta, which was working on a theory or which can be called socialistic; and the Pergamene, if we had details, might be more interesting than the Spartan, since for the first time a new constructive idea emerged. When Aristonicus in 132 raised the banner of revolt against Rome (p. 41),[3] he threw in his lot with the slave rising, and was joined by the Stoic Blossius of Cumae, the outspoken friend of Tiberius Gracchus, who played the part of Sphaerus at Sparta; and the two proposed to set up something resembling Iambulus' Sun-State upon earth. The effect on their mixed following—Asiatic mercenaries, city volunteers, Mysian highlanders, broken men and slaves—was such that they destroyed a Roman consul and a consular army, which even Macedonia had never done. It was indeed a great dream. But Rome finally conquered Aristonicus and shattered the hope of a Sun-State; and under Roman rule there was no further place for dreams.

[1] Beside Pöhlmann, see Ferguson, *Hell. Athens* 379. 428; K. Bücher, *Die Aufstände der unfreien Arbeiter*, 1874; and next note.

[2] *G.G.A.* 1926, 97; 1928, 484. *Contra*, Oertel, *N.J. Kl. Alt.* 1927, 1.

[3] G. Cardinali in Beloch's *Saggi*, 269.

CHAPTER IV

ASIA

THE interest of Seleucid history[1] lies in the attempt made by the early kings of the dynasty to colonise most of western Asia with Greek cities and settlements, one of the most amazing works of the ancient world. The material for this history has long been imperfect and often controversial; and though excavation has helped, the bulk of recent work, putting aside the old Greek cities of Asia Minor, has illumined the later Parthian and Roman periods rather than the constructive reigns of Seleucus and his son. A brief summary of this work, omitting Palestine, may be given. After a generation of excavation of the old Elamite city of Susa, the French mission came on the now famous pocket of Greek inscriptions[2] whose value to the historian is out of all proportion to their bulk. An American expedition has excavated a large block of houses in Seleuceia and secured many small articles of historical value—coins,[3] bullae (seals)[4] and clay figures.[5] Uruk has produced a large crop of bullae[6] and has shown the care of the Seleucids for the native

[1] Generally (besides the general histories): Ed. Meyer, *Blüte und Niedergang des Hellenismus in Asien*, 1925; Kahrstedt, *Syr. Terr.* 1926; W. Otto, *Beiträge zur Seleukidengeschichte*, 1928; Rostovtzeff in *C.A.H.* VII, ch. V; the works by Kugler and Kolbe, ch. VI n. 1 (*post*); Rostovtzeff, *Seleucid Babylonia*: *Bullae and seals of clay with Greek inscriptions*, Yale Class. Stud. III, 1932, 1; Tarn, *Bactria*, Part I, 1938; E. Bikerman, *Institutions des Séleucides*, 1938; Heichelheim, *Wirtschaftgesch.* 1938 ch. VII; Rostovtzeff, *SEH* 422–552, 695–705, 841–70, with copious bibliographical and critical notes, 1941 (much the best thing). 'Seleuceia' through this book means Seleuceia on the Tigris unless otherwise specified.

[2] *SEG* VII, 1–34; see Fr. Cumont in *C.R.Ac.I.* 1930–33, and in *Mém. de la mission archéol. de Perse* XX, 1928.

[3] R. H. Macdowell, *Coins from Seleucia on the Tigris*, 1935.

[4] Same, *Stamped and inscribed objects from Seleucia on the Tigris*, 1935.

[5] W. van Ingen, *Figurines from Seleucia on the Tigris*, 1939.

[6] Rostovtzeff, *Seleucid Babylonia.*

temples and religion, while Babylonian commercial documents have given help over dating, commerce, and economics generally.[1] A French mission is now attempting to locate Bactra in the vast desolated plain of Balkh, once a garden of the earth, and have found the first Greek inscription from Bactria,[2] the letters *ατρος* on a potsherd. Doura-Europus on the Euphrates has been most thoroughly worked out, first by French and then by American scholars,[3] and a wonderful picture has been obtained of later times; but, except for the Succession Law (p. 149 *post*) and some details of building, it has added little to our knowledge of a Hellenistic city in its bloom, and the very excellence of the excavations may have tended to make the place seem more important than it really was. The results obtained at Antioch belong to Roman times.

The Seleucid realm itself fluctuated greatly. Seleucus, from 312 ruler of Babylon, conquered the east and lost India before 303, but gained Northern Syria and Mesopotamia in 301, Cilicia in 296, and all Asia Minor but the native kingdoms and certain cities in 281; his son and grandson ruled an empire stretching from the Aegean and the Mediterranean to Turkestan and Afghanistan. Between 250 and 277, with the gradual establishment of the Graeco-Bactrian and Parthian kingdoms, everything east of Media–Susiana–Persis–Carmania was lost; but in 198 Antiochus III took the rest of Syria from Egypt. In 189, following his defeat by Rome, this king lost Asia Minor, except Cilicia; but the Seleucids still ruled a great empire, till the death of Antiochus Sidetes in 129 entailed the final loss of Babylonia and Judaea and reduced them to a local dynasty in Northern Syria. Unfortunately we know all too little about Northern Syria, the real homeland of the dynasty; much of our information about the west has to be drawn from Asia Minor.

The Seleucid empire possessed three separate nerve-

[1] Dating: Tarn, *C.A.H.* IX, 950. Business documents: Rostovtzeff, *SEH* 1423 n. 220.

[2] D. Schlumberger, *C.R.Ac.I.* 1947, 119, 241 *sq.*

[3] French results summarised: Cumont, *Doura*, 1926; American, the annual *Preliminary Reports*, 1929–39.

centres, Ionia with its capital at Sardes, Northern Syria, and Babylonia; all else was secondary, and if Antioch, the North Syrian capital, stood in the best position for reaching the other centres, Seleuceia on the Tigris was also a capital little inferior in importance. Many waves of conquerors had passed over Western Asia, all leaving some deposit behind; beside the cultures of Babylon and Persia there stood races of primitive barbarism, while the coast was in the hands of the Greek cities of Asia Minor and the great mercantile towns of Phoenicia. Persia had imposed some semblance of unity on the country, outside the Greek cities, and in some respects the Seleucid administration was rooted in the Achaemenid, as that had perhaps been in the Assyrian; there is a sort of historical continuity, though the rulers and the dominant culture might change. One feature of Seleucid rule was the resurrection of Babylonia,[1] whose ancient culture was to the Seleucids what that of Egypt was to the Ptolemies. Cuneiform literature revived; besides scientific astronomical work (Chap. IX) and business documents, chronicles of current events were written, and myths were versified; one carries on Marduk's story from the end of the Creation Epic. Rituals, incantations, and omen literature, especially the latter, were frequently copied and studied, as were Sumerian hymns and their Babylonian translations; many commentaries and syllabaries are known, with a new form of the latter, apparently for Greek use; the last cuneiform document extant dates from 7 B.C.[2] This activity points to a religious revival, which was fostered by the early kings; Antiochus I carried to completion Alexander's project of restoring E-Sagila,[3] Bel's temple at Babylon which Xerxes had destroyed, and re-founded Nebo's temple at Borsippa, while Bel's priest Berossus dedicated to him his work on Babylonian history; under Seleucus a priest of Uruk, possibly at his request, found at Susa and copied the old

[1] Largely communicated by Mr. Sidney Smith in 1927. Cf. R. Campbell Thompson, *C.A.H.* III, 246; and Tarn, *Bactria*, 56–60.

[2] P. Schnabel, *Z. Assyr.* 1925, 66.

[3] Schnabel, *Berossos*, 6. On the temples generally, see Rostovtzeff, *SEH* 1384, 1427 n. 234, and literature cited.

ritual of the gods of Uruk, whose worship was re-established[1]; the temple of Anu at Uruk was restored in 110 Sel. (201), under Antiochus III[2]; and the Seleucids did, or encouraged the people to do, much building in that town.[3] The priests of Uruk also collected a temple library.[4] Mr. Sidney Smith suggested to me that the Seleucids favoured Babylonian religion as a bulwark against Zoroastrianism, the creed of Persian nationalism; and indeed the principal weakness which broke up the empire was its failure to secure the co-operation of the Iranian element, which Alexander had recognised as vital. The Oriental reaction, when it came, was partly a revolt of the countryside and its creed against the Greek and Babylonian townsman.

The Seleucids themselves, like the Achaemenids, regarded their empire as embracing the four categories of subject kings, dynasts, peoples, and cities[5]; and a survey of that empire at its fullest extent, omitting the farther east, may be briefly given. The Seleucid satrapies in Asia Minor, which were governed by generals in the usual form, were Hellespontine Phrygia, Phrygia, Lydia, Caria, Cilicia, and southern Cappadocia (Cappadocia Seleucis) with Cataonia; Lycia was Egyptian, and the coasts of southern Ionia, Caria, Pamphylia, and western Cilicia were taken by Egypt before 272; Egypt's hold fluctuated, but the Seleucids were never fully masters of the coast-line till 197. From the Black Sea the empire was cut off entirely by three states: the native kingdoms of Pontus or northern Cappadocia (including much of Paphlagonia) and Bithynia, and between them the powerful Greek city of Heraclea, whose territory included several other towns—Tios, Cierus, Amastris. Bithynia and Pontus were penetrating northern Phrygia, and soon after 275 they settled their allies,[6] the invading Gauls, in that

[1] Thureau-Dangin, *Rituels accadiens*, 86.

[2] J. Jordan, *Uruk-Warka*, 1928, 41, but the date has now been re-read; see Rostovtzeff in Tarn, *Bactria* 26 n. 1, and in *SEH* 1428 n. 235.

[3] *id. SEH* 435–7, 513, 1424 n. 226, 1437 nn. 234, 235, 1441 nn. 290 *sqq* with copious refs.

[4] Weidner, *Studia Orientalia* I, 347.

[5] *OGIS* 229 l. 12; cf. Diod. XIX, 57, 3; Ditt.[3] 590 l. 11.

[6] Ed. Meyer, *B. Ph. W.* 1897, 1584.

country (Galatia); later in the century southern Cappadocia made itself a native kingdom under Ariarathes. From 262 the Pergamene dynasts began to carve out a little principality in Aeolis. Pisidia—the table-land of the Taurus—was unsubdued; it was ruled by petty dynasts, but the semi-Greek city of Selge was strong enough to resist all attempts, Seleucid or other, on its independence. Later in the century dynasts are found established outside Pisidia, as Olympichus in Caria, the Macedonian house of Lysias about Philomelium in Phrygia, and (from 189) the native line of Moagetes in populous Cibyra.[1] All that the Seleucids were ever sure of in Asia Minor was Hellespontine Phrygia, Lydia, inner Caria, southern Phrygia, eastern Cilicia, and the Royal Road, the great through route from Sardes to Antioch; and after Seleucus' death they never pressed their power upon the smaller native dynasties, their aim rather being good relations secured by treaties and intermarriage. Beside the Gauls, their one consistent enemy was Pergamum. In Syria they generally held the country north of the Lebanon, with Aradus in Phoenicia and, from time to time, Damascus, though the boundary between Seleucid and Ptolemaic Syria fluctuated[2]; northward of Syria and Mesopotamia their only permanent province was probably Commagene, though rulers in Armenia were intermittently tributary.

The Seleucids, like Alexander, retained the great Persian satrapies, with names usually ending in -ια, but in the lands east of the Euphrates they had a threefold division into satrapy, eparchy,[3] hyparchy, corresponding to the threefold division in Egypt into nome, topos, village; but as their

[1] Dynasts: Holleaux, *Rev. E.A.* 1915, 237; Wilhelm, *Neue Beiträge* I, 48.

[2] Tscherikower, *Mizraim* 1937, 32 *sqq.*, minimises the fluctuations, perhaps rightly; see *ib.* 34, for the evidence about Damascus.

[3] Tarn, *Seleucid-Parthian Studies* § IV (Proc. Brit. Ac. 1930, 105); *id.*, *Bactria* p. 2 (with *Addendum*) and App. 2; M. Cary, *A history of the Greek world* 1932, 256; Rostovtzeff and C. B. Welles, *Yale Class. Stud.* II, 1931, 48 n. 66. A recent attempt by H. Bengtson (*Die Strategie in der hellenistischen Zeit*, II, 1944, 30 *sqq.*, 152, 188), to disprove the existence of eparchies, cannot be supported; see Tarn, *Bactria* 2nd ed., Addendum to pp. 1–4.

empire was vastly more extensive than Egypt, and as the hyparchy might contain a considerable number of villages, their organisation was of necessity much looser than that of the Ptolemies (the subdivision of some hyparchies into *stathmoi*, known from Isidore of Charax, was Parthian). This threefold division in the two countries may have had a common source, but, if so, what it was is unknown; the eparchy might equally well be something old or a Seleucid innovation. The typical eparchy name ended in -ηνη, though -ιανη, -ια, and -ῖτις all occur; it was the mass of -ηνη names in Asia which enabled the eparchy to be identified. It became the most important Seleucid subdivision; when the empire began to break up, the Succession States, led by the Graeco-Bactrians and the Parthians, all turned their eparchies into satrapies, *i.e.* primary divisions; and as each Seleucid eparchy had had its own organisation, with a governor (under the general of the satrapy) who had his own staff and official residence (βασίλειον),[1] some eparchy governors, as Hyspaosines of Mesene,[2] were able to turn their eparchies by themselves into independent kingdoms, with fresh -ηνη subdivisions. By the first century the one-time Seleucid Asia beyond the Euphrates had become a complex of -ηνη names, mostly now primary divisions, and the word ἐπαρχία had become the usual translation of the Latin *provincia*; and literary men confused eparchies with the old Seleucid satrapies because *in their own day* the -ηνη divisions *were* satrapies; Appian's 72 Seleucid satrapies, for example, doubtless mean eparchies. The eparchy system, at first confined to the satrapies east of the Euphrates, may perhaps subsequently have extended west of that river into Cappadocia-Pontus[3] and certainly extended northward into Armenia, neither properly Succession States; that Armenia was copying a known system is shown by her creation of

[1] Tarn, *Bactria*, 4 n. 1 (three instances). The βασίλειον at Doura cannot be discussed here.

[2] G. F. Hill, *B.M. Coins, Arabia &c.* CXCVI; E. T. Newell, *Num. Notes* XXVI, 1925; Tarn, *C.A.H.* IX, 578, 584; N. C. Debevoise, *Political History of Parthia*, 1938, 38; A. R. Bellinger, *Yale Class. Stud.* VIII, 1942, 53.

[3] Str. XII, 580; Rostovtzeff, *C.A.H.* IX, 215 n. 2.

fancy names in -ηνη, like Xerxene, Cambysene, for new territorial divisions.[1] Two districts stood apart: Asia Minor west of the Halys, where, save for the old satrapy names, the organisation is unknown, and Syria, where it is obscure.[2] Seleucus' four great cities in northern Syria (p. 154) were called satrapies by Poseidonius,[3] but this probably refers only to a subdivision of the Seleucis when Seleucid rule was breaking up; and whether the Seleucids ever made satrapies of southern Syria with Judaea, which were Ptolemaic till 200, may be doubtful[4]; divisions called *merides* appear, apparently unknown elsewhere in Asia except in Greek India when under Saca rule,[5] and Judaea itself became a tributary priest-state under Seleucid suzerainty. Too much weight has often been laid on information professedly derived from Judaea, merely because it exists; Jewish writers indeed had plenty to say, but they cannot be trusted blindly, and anyhow the peculiar circumstances of that province do not necessarily throw light on the empire at large.

In theory, the Seleucid kings were autocrats. But in actual fact their autocracy was limited by the necessity of respecting the rights which they themselves had bestowed on the numerous cities and colonies they founded; that they did respect them is shown by their popularity. Little is known of the officials[6] who managed the empire. It was once the common opinion that each satrapy was governed not by a satrap but by a general (*strategos*); he had military powers, for most satrapies included hill-tribes or other unconquered elements. But recently another view has been strongly put forward, that each satrapy contained both a satrap and a *strategos*[7]; the subject and the evidence are alike obscure, and cannot be argued here. Over the empire was a minister 'for affairs', ὁ ἐπὶ τῶν πραγμάτων, apparently

[1] Str. 528.
[2] Kahrstedt, *Syr. Terr.*
[3] Str. 750 (from Poseidonius).
[4] Str. 750. It is largely guesswork.
[5] *Merides* appear also in the four Macedonian republics after 167: J. A. O. Larsen, *Class. Phil.* XL, 1945, 67 n. 13 (an inscription).
[6] Bikerman, *Inst. d. Sél.* 127–30; Rostovtzeff, *SEH* 440–6.
[7] H. Bengtson, *op. c.*, 64–142.

corresponding to the Persian vizier; but he is not heard of much before Antiochus III.[1] Another minister called 'over the revenues', ὁ ἐπὶ τῶν προσόδων, may have been the head of the imperial financial administration, but the name sometimes seems to indicate a subordinate. What office corresponded to the titles *oikonomos* and *dioiketes* is obscure. Like Antigonus I, the Seleucids imitated, though sparingly, Alexander's use of Persians as provincial governors[2]; they maintained the Persian postal service,[3] and perhaps did something to improve the Persian road system.[4]

There was a land register in each hyparchy,[5] which gave the boundaries of villages and properties; from these were compiled the register of the satrapy, which was kept at the capital of the satrapy by a registrar in a bureau called 'the royal records'; from the satrapal registers were compiled the central register which the king used. As an eparchy had a governor's seat, βασίλειον, it must, it would seem, have had a land register also intermediate between those of the hyparchies and the satrapy; otherwise it is difficult to see what happened when later the eparchy became a satrapy itself. The central and satrapal registers did not give the detailed boundaries, and the central register, in view of the distances involved, was not always up to date. It was the same system as the Egyptian, with the hyparchy as the unit instead of the village; it seems obvious that, considering the scale, the Seleucids could never have drawn the taxation net so close as did the Ptolemies. The administration introduced the Greek system of leases and sometimes leased King's land[6]; and in some Seleucid cities, possibly in all, deeds of sale were registered.[7]

[1] Polyb. V, 41, 1; *OGIS* 247 (Seleucus IV).

[2] Wilcken, *Chrestomathie* no. 1, col. II l. 6; Polyaen. 7, 40; Hyspaosines.

[3] Rostovtzeff, *Klio* VI, 249.

[4] Rostovtzeff, *SEH* 1433. But the 'royal roads' mentioned could have been Persian.

[5] *OGIS* 225 l. 24; Wiegand, *Sechster Milet-Bericht* p. 36; Westermann, *Class. Phil.* 1921, 12, 391.

[6] Ditt.[3] 302.

[7] Driver, *J.H.S.* 1923, 55; Cumont, *Doura* 281, 296, 487, *Mém. Délégation en Perse* XX, 1928, 84 no. 4; *C.R.Ac.I.* 1937, 313; Jordan, *Uruk-Warka*, 32.

The relation of the Seleucid kings to the land,[1] in Asia Minor and northern Syria, was rooted far back in history. Possibly all or most of the land had originally been owned by a number of priest-states,[2] and prior to Alexander the history of the country had consisted in a steady encroachment upon these states by the various conquerors, who brought their own religions. Omitting independent hill-folk, such as the Pisidians, the land as Alexander found it fell into three categories, King's land, Temple land, and city land, the land of the established Greek cities; but the Seleucids claimed the temple lands as over-lords, and in the Seleucid period the real distinction was between King's land and city land; the King's land must have included the bulk of the country and certainly all mines and forests not on city land. Of the King's land, part was in hand and part had been granted out to large landowners, natives and Persians. Some of these landed families might long antedate Persian rule, just as some lasted into Roman times; but the king was their feudal superior, and the actual property in the land was in him. These landowners, like mediaeval barons, lived in castles on their estates—fortified quadrangles built round a courtyard[3]—kept a body of retainers, collected the taxes from their land, and remitted them to the Treasury.

The actual inhabitants of the agricultural land everywhere were the native peasantry living in villages,[4] a class which rarely changes, whatever conquerors may come and go. Where the King's land was in hand, the peasantry, the 'king's people', cultivated it and paid their taxes to the officials. Where the land was in grant to a landowner, the peasants of the villages on the estate, though they paid their taxes through him, were still officially the king's people, not his. The peasants were not quasi-serfs, as in Egypt, but full serfs,[5] bought and sold with the land; they could not

[1] Generally, Rostovtzeff, *Kolonat*, esp. 240–68, 305–309; Kornemann, *Domänen* in P.W.

[2] Sir W. M. Ramsay, *J.R.S.* 1917, 267.

[3] Xen. *Anab.* VII, 8, 13; Plut. *Eum.* 8; *OGIS* 225, IV, l. 36=Welles, *Royal Correspondence* no. 18 n. 2; Jos. *Ant.* XIII, 36.

[4] Add Kornemann, *Bauernstand* in P.W.

[5] *OGIS* 225.

leave their 'own place' and they had no village organisation; their taxes were paid individually[1] and not through their villages, but as between the king and the landowner it was doubtless better for the peasant when his taxes were collected by a responsible official. But when a Greek city had acquired land and with it peasantry, conditions had often been modified, whether by deliberate freeing of serfs or by natural evolution is uncertain; the peasants *might* sometimes still be serfs, as in Alexander's time at Zelea,[2] but generally they became free hereditary 'settlers' (*katoikoi*),[3] paying taxes to the city, and their villages sometimes began to acquire a kind of corporate life[4]; they were in a different category from the slave-cultivators in *e.g.* Laconia. The Greek city then was a boon to the Asiatic peasant and tended to raise his status.

The Seleucids did not free the serfs; but they possibly had special judges for the king's peasants,[5] thus wisely keeping law and administration separate, and they initiated three schemes which progressively diminished the area of serfdom and might in time have abolished it altogether. First came the Greek cities they founded, which turned King's land into city-land on a great scale. Secondly, they were ready, unlike the Ptolemies, to give or sell King's land out and out,[6] on condition that the grantee joined his land to some city and made of it city-land; naturally the cities were willing enough to increase their territories. Thirdly, they set to work to abolish the feudal landowners, which entailed the abolition of what had practically been private ownership of serfs. Eumenes of Cardia and Antigonus I had begun to transfer feudal estates to Greeks or Macedonians,[7] and under the Seleucids, who were whole-heartedly on the side of the cities, feudal estates, transferred to new owners, also tended to become city-land; it seems to have been mainly outside their sphere, in Pisidia, Cappadocia, Pontus, that the great

[1] *OGIS* 1.
[2] Ditt.[3] 279; *SGDI* 5533e.
[3] *I. Priene* I l. 2.
[4] *J.H.S.* 1904, 21, and see *post*.
[5] Athen. 697 D (doubtless Seleucid). But there are other interpretations.
[6] *OGIS* 221, 225, 335 l. 133.
[7] Plut. *Eum.* 8; *A.J.A.* 1912, 11 (date, H. C. Butler, *Sardis* I, i, 52 n. 2).

BLACK
MEDITERRANEAN
SEA
Amastris
Tios
PAPHLA
Heraclea
Lysimacheia
Byzantium
Chalcedon
Nicomedia
Cierus-Prusias
BITHYNIA
Cyzicus
Cius
Nicea
Lampsacus
Abydus
Phrygia
Prusa
Apollonia
R. Sangarius
R. Halys
MYSIA
Dorylaeum
Ancyra
GALATIA
Lesbos
Pessinus
PHRYGIA
Magnesia
R. Hermus
Docimeum
Sardes
LYDIA
Smyrna
Synnada
Ipsus
L. Tatta
Teos
Philadelphia
Apollonia
Philomelium
LYCAONIA
Ephesus
Magnesia
Nysa
Apamea Celaenae
Antioch
Laodicea Katakekaumene
Miletus
R. Meander
Laodicea
Iconium
Alabanda
Seleuceia the Iron
CARIA
Stratonicea
PISIDIA
Selge
Halicarnassus
Cibyra
Attaleia
R. Calycadnus
Cos
Aspendus
Cnidus
Ptolemais
Philadelphia
Olba
LYCIA
Xanthus
Rhodes
Arsinoe
Seleuceia
Salamis
CYPRUS
Azotus (Ashdod)
Ascalon
Gaza
Raphia
Alexandria
Naucratis
Pelusium
28
32
40
36
R.C.

40
44
Phasis
COLCHIS
S E A
Trapezus
Pharnacia-Cerasus
Cabeira
N T U S
40
A R M E N I A
Melitene
O C I A
Tigranocerta
Commagene
Samosata
Antioch-Edessa (Orrhoë)
Antioch-Nisibis
Mygdonia
Apamea
Zeugma
Carrhae (Harran)
Hierapolis-Bambyce
Ichnae
M E S O P O T A M I A
Singara
36
Beroea
Nicephorium
Thapsacus (Amphipolis)
R. Euphrates
R. Tigris
Hamath (Epiphaneia)
Doura (Europus)
Palmyra
SYRIAN
DESERT
Akkad
Seleuceia
Babylon
Borsippa
32
English Miles
0 20 40 60 80 100 120 140 160
40
44

feudal estates lasted into Roman times. Wherever land became city-land, the peasant might, and doubtless generally did, cease to be a serf. This must have also affected the peasants on the remaining King's land, for under the earlier Roman Empire these peasants were approximating to settlers with corporate organisation; indeed a group of villages in Syria (the Hauran) had acquired an organisation which closely imitated that of a Greek city.[1] Possibly for a time they were even better off economically than those on city-land. But under the later Roman Empire they fell back, and by Justinian's time even private ownership of serfs had again appeared in Asia.

The ancient temple states,[2] great and small, were extremely numerous, and some still possessed a large amount of land. They dated back to a pre-Aryan social system based on matriarchy, utterly foreign to Greek or Persian ideas; originally they probably all worshipped the great fertility goddess of Asia and the companion god who was alike her son and consort. Probably to this ancient religion belongs the custom of the marriage of a full brother and sister[3] which has been traced in so many ruling families of western Asia—the house of Maussollus in Caria is a well-known instance—and which even led to the Seleucid, and later the Nabataean,[4] queens being officially styled 'sister' (p. 56); another trace of it, which lasted long, is that in Greek inscriptions from Phrygia the mother alone is sometimes named,[5] or the wife's name precedes her husband's.[6] Some of these sanctuaries had been invaded by alien deities, who nevertheless succumbed to the old organisation; and by

[1] G. McL. Harper, Jr., in *Yale Class. Stud.* I, 1929, 105–168, with bibliography; A. H. M. Jones, *J.R.S.* XXI, 1931, 270; Rost., *SEH* 512, 1441 n. 288.

[2] Generally: Ramsay, *Cities and Bishoprics of Phrygia*, and in *C.R.* 1905, 417, *J.R.S.* VIII, 107, XII, 147, *J.H.S.* 1918, 130–168; and see ch. X.

[3] Kornemann, *Klio* XIX, 355.

[4] Hill, *B.M. Coins, Arabia* &c., 11, 12, but see XVII; Head, *Hist. Num.*^{2}, 811.

[5] Ramsay, *C. and B.*, I, 95, 116; W. M. Calder, *C.R.* XXIV, 79.

[6] *J.H.S.* 1911, 210 no. LXIV (bilingual); Ramsay, *C. and B.* I, 77 no. 11; II, 658 no. 610.

Hellenistic times the accumulated influence of Indo-European ideas—Phrygian, Persian, Greek—had sometimes raised the god to the first place at the expense of the goddess, and some names had been hellenised (p. 344). The ruler of the temple state, an hereditary high priest, had often learnt to trace his descent from some hero of the Greek mythological cycle. But the *system* had never changed; the priest ruled the lands of the temple state and the peasantry on them, the 'god's peasants', and to him they paid their taxes. The temple village itself contained a number of men devoted to the god, sometimes eunuchs; but the feature that so struck Greeks was the crowd of female temple slaves, many of them sacred prostitutes who ministered to the fertility worship of the goddess. They were usually the daughters of the god's peasants, who served awhile in the temple before becoming peasants' wives; for land and people lived by the power of the goddess, and to give a daughter to assist to spread her influence was only an act of right feeling towards society; women boasted their descent from a line of temple prostitutes.[1] The temple often acted as the local bank, and its village was the scene of a great annual fair.[2]

The best known temple states and their deities may be noticed,[3] though most of the greater ones lay outside the Seleucid bounds. In Cappadocia, Ma of Comana (the 'place of hymns')[4] with 6,000 temple slaves, men and women; Zeus of Venasa with 3,000; and Artemis Perasia of Castabala—Hieropolis,[5] whose priestesses could walk barefoot over hot charcoal. In Pontus, Ma of Comana Pontica, with 6,000 temple slaves and a strict taboo on pigs and pigs' flesh; Anaïtis of Zela; and Mēn Pharnakou (with Selene) of Cabeira, by whom the Pontic kings officially swore. In Phrygia, Cybele-Agdistis and Attis at Pessinus,[6] Leto and Lairbenos near Dionysopolis,[7] Mēn Karou near Attoudda,[8] the Dindymene Mother near Pessinus and in Cyzicus' territory,[9]

1 Ramsay, *C. and B.* I, 115 no. 18; L. Robert, *Ét. Anatol.* 406.

2 Str. 559, 567.

3 Most of this is from Str. XII.

4 Ramsay, *J.R.S.* VII, 270.

5 *OGIS* 752, 754.

6 *OGIS* 315.

7 Ramsay, *C. and B.* I, 130; *SEG* VI, 253.

8 Ramsay, *ib.* 167.

9 Str. 567, 575.

and Zeus of Aizani.[1] Also the two temples of Mēn Askaenos (Mannes of Ouramna)[2] and Selene near Pisidian Antioch; the Zizimene Mother in Lycaonia[3]; Mēn Tiamou or Tyrannus and Mother Anaïtis in Lydia[4]; Zeus of Olba in Cilicia[5]; and a number of others known from inscriptions, including the various places called Hieropolis, 'city of the temple', which if Greek influence was strong became Hierapolis, 'sacred city'—a fundamental distinction. Artemis of Ephesus herself was only the fertility goddess whose old temple had been annexed to a Greek city; for long that temple, with its high priest, the Megabyzus or King Bee, and its swarm of consecrated girls, who at Ephesus were virgins and were possibly known as 'bees', remained a state within the state till Lysimachus gave the temple administration to a Greek board, and removed the bee from Ephesus' coinage.[6] Similar priest-states existed in Northern Syria, as at Bambyce, Baetocaece,[7] and Emesa, and extended into Albania and Iberia under the Caucasus,[8] home of so many broken fragments of older races.

Though the earlier Seleucids were ready to respect the religious feelings of their subjects,[9] and besides the temples which they rebuilt in Babylonia also rebuilt temples at Bambyce[10] and Olba,[11] they fought the temporal power of the priest-kings as they fought feudalism. Their policy aimed at leaving undisturbed to the temple state its priest, temple, and temple village, with enough land for the temple's service, and secularising the rest of the temple estate[12]; Antioch towards Pisidia, for example, was probably carved out of the once vast estate of Mēn Askaenos. The priest-states, however, were able to prevent the policy being fully

[1] A. B. Cook, *Zeus* II, 964. [2] Ramsay, *J.H.S.* 1918, 148. See ch. X.
[3] Robinson, *A.J.A.* 1927, 27; *SEG* VI, 391, 404.
[4] J. G. C. Anderson, *J.R.S.* III, 272; Ditt.[3] 1042; Ramsay, *B.S.A.* XVIII, 56; *SEG* IV, 647–652. [5] Str. 672; Hill, *B.M. Coins, Lycaonia &c.* LII.
[6] Str. 640–1; *B.M. Inscr.* III pp. 76 *sqq.*; Ch. Picard, *Ephèse et Claros*, 92.
[7] *OGIS* 262, II. [8] Str. 503.
[9] Antiochus III at Ecbatana and Elymais was plundering enemy territory.
[10] Lucian, *de dea Syria* 17, 19.
[11] Heberdey and Wilhelm, *Denkschriften Akad. Wien* 1896, VI, p. 85 no. 166. [12] *OGIS* 502, Str. 559, Rostovtzeff, *Kolonat* 270.

carried out, and in the days of their decline the Seleucids again enlarged the territories of some Syrian temples and gave them the right of asylum,[1] a parallel to what happened in Egypt. In the troubled period before Augustus some of the hereditary priesthoods vanished, and a Pompey or an Antony made priests at his pleasure; at Olba Antony gave the priest-state to a woman[2]; Zela, Cabeira, and later Comana Pontica became Graeco-Roman cities,[3] and the Roman Empire continued to cut down temple lands to the minimum necessary. But some of the great priestly families[4] lasted into Christian times, and gave distinguished bishops to the Church.

The treasure amassed by the Achaemenids shows that western Asia was already passing from economy in kind to a money basis, and the Seleucid cities must have quickened the process, though probably it proceeded more slowly than in Egypt, and in many rural districts economy in kind must have remained the rule. Taxation[5] in the Seleucid empire is an obscure subject. From an extant list of taxes presumably Seleucid,[6] and from the seals (*bullae*) recovered in such numbers from Uruk and Seleuceia, it has been possible to compile a list, though the meaning of the separate items is not always clear; it includes import duties (customs) and harbour dues, octroi duties, and taxes on markets, sales, cattle, salt, the carrying on of certain businesses, the registration of documents; the crown tax; a tax on slaves, the nature of which is unknown; possibly a poll-tax, which can only have been levied on the King's peasants, but this is very uncertain; last and most important, the land tax on the King's land. In addition, the kings drew revenue from their personal possessions, such as mines, quarries, and forests, and from the tribute paid by such cities as were subject to it. It is more than possible that taxation was not the same in every satrapy of the vast empire; Babylonia may well

[1] Kahrstedt, *Syr. Terr.* 73. [2] Str. 672.
[3] Str. 557, 560; Brandis, *Bithynia* in P.W., 530.
[4] Ramsay, *J.H.S.* 1918, 146; *C.R.* 1919, 1.
[5] Bikerman, *Inst. d. Sél.* 110–19; Rostovtzeff, *SEH* 444, 464, 469.
[6] [Arist.] *Oeconomica* II, 1345 b.

have differed from the norm, and Jewish writers give some details of taxation in Judaea which, if true, would make it extraordinarily heavy; but, though several theories have been put forward to account for this, the figures should be treated with reserve, as Jewish writers were ready enough to represent the Seleucids as tyrants. The Seleucid system was certainly 'less elaborate and more flexible' than the Ptolemaic[1]; and indeed, so far as our scanty knowledge goes, the differences from the Egyptian system were great. No royal monopolies of commerce or manufacture are known; none of the perpetual discontent which characterised the Egyptian peasantry and workers is heard of; and the all-important land-tax on the King's land was raised quite differently. For while the Egyptian peasant under the Ptolemies paid a fixed annual sum, the Seleucids continued the practice, which was immemorial in Asia and had also obtained in Egypt under the Pharaohs and the Persians, of taking a tenth of the harvest[2]; they were thus true partners with the peasantry, sharing losses in a bad year, a matter of which Antony boasted when he stressed the beneficence of Rome in following the Seleucid system of taking a tenth.[3] Possibly part of the land-tax was paid in money[4]; but enough was rendered in kind to make the king a great corn merchant.[5] How the corn was dealt with is unknown, except that the taxes of each satrapy flowed into its capital[6]; the money would be remitted to the central Treasury (*Basilikon*), but distance and transport would prevent the corn being so treated; there must have been several centres. The peasantry had to perform some forced labour.

The coinage[7] the Seleucids kept in their own hands, and made it the basic coinage of the East; they generally, like

[1] Rostovtzeff's phrase, *SEH* 472.

[2] On this custom see E. Cavaignac, *Population et Capital* 1923, chs. I–IV; cf. Jos. *Ant.* XIII, 51; XIV, 210.

[3] Appian *b.c.* V, 4, 18.

[4] *OGIS* 225.

[5] Ditt.³ 344 ll. 81–101.

[6] Str. 752; Pliny VI, 119; cf. Isidore of Charax, *Mansiones Parth.* § 6.

[7] Rostovtzeff, *SEH* 446, 1428 n. 243, which gives bibliographies. Add to McDowell's bibliography in *Coins of Seleucia*, E. T. Newell, *The coinage of the Eastern Seleucid Mints from Seleucus I to Antiochus III*, 1938.

Alexander, used the Attic standard, and carefully excluded from their empire the money of their enemies the Ptolemies, who used the Phoenician standard, though they did occasionally use that standard themselves; these two standards now shared the world between them (p. 251). No new Seleucid city was allowed to coin for itself, not even copper for small change[1]; and about the middle of the third century these kings ceased coining gold, presumably owing to the disturbance of the 'gold route' from Siberia.[2] All estimates of Seleucid revenue are conjectural. The value of the land-tax varied with the price of corn, and there are no recorded corn-prices for the country districts and few for the coastal cities (just a few from Uruk[3]); also corn was not necessarily the same price in Syria or Babylonia as in Miletus or Samos. Judging by what happened elsewhere, there must have been a great rise in price culminating about 300, followed by a long decline. The first two Seleucid kings, who were generous givers and must have spent masses of money on the settlement of Asia, seem often to have been short of available funds, though some of their officials, judging by rather later examples, may have made great fortunes; and though the inland provinces must have prospered under the (for them) long Seleucid peace, the coastal cities of Asia Minor and northern Syria must have suffered from the interminable 'Syrian Wars' between Seleucids and Ptolemies (273–200). But after Antiochus III in 200 secured the whole of Syria, including all the outlets of the overland trade from the East, money must have poured in from that trade; and though he was straitened at the end by the loss of western Asia Minor and by the indemnity exacted by Rome, Antiochus IV later was certainly richer than any Seleucid king before him.[4] But even so the Seleucids, speaking generally, never acquired such wealth as the Ptolemies drew from Egypt, and, as they never amassed a treasure, they must have spent much more

[1] Rostovtzeff, *SEH* 448. [2] Tarn, *Bactria*, 104–8.

[3] Heichelheim, *Wirtschaft. Schwankungen.*

[4] Cf. Rostovtzeff, *SEH* 703, 860; Tarn, *Bactria*, 194 (Daphne); see Athen. V, 194 c *sqq.*

on the country in proportion to their income; Antiochus IV used his wealth, as Seleucus I had done, to found or hellenise a new and considerable number of cities.[1]

Before coming to the Seleucid settlement, the disputed question of the relation of the earlier Seleucid kings to such of the old Greek cities of Asia Minor as were from time to time within the geographical limits of their empire must be noticed. The dominant view, no doubt, is that these cities were subjects; but it is not quite so simple as that. All had been Alexander's free allies[2]; in the wars of the Successors, some had become subject to this or that one; Antigonus I had 'freed' them all, but some may have become subject again, to Lysimachus or some other ruler. Of Seleucus' own reign hardly anything seems known, but some cities were united to his son, Antiochus I, by an alliance, *symmachia*,[3] while others, as Teos[4] and Bargylia,[5] were subject towns. The view that *all* the cities were subject towns seems now based on a belief that the *symmachia* included all relevant Seleucid territory and thus acquired a territorial meaning,[6] and that therefore, as some cities *were* subject, all must have been[7]; but *symmachia* can only mean a free alliance, and the words 'whatever city he may desire of those in the *symmachia*' cannot imply that *all* cities were necessarily in the *symmachia*; besides, there were cities like Erythrae which had never been anything but 'free',[8] in the meaning which freedom was beginning to take: 'own laws, no garrison, no tribute.' The third Seleucid, Antiochus II, a king on whom an inscription has thrown a favourable light,[9] purported to restore complete freedom to all the Ionian cities, an act to which they long looked back as a charter,[10] and some cities appear, for the last time, to

[1] Tarn, *Bactria*, 186.
[2] Tarn, *Alexander* II App. 7.
[3] *OGIS* 221 ll. 59, 73.
[4] Ditt.[3] 426.
[5] *Ib.*
[6] But *OGIS ib.* l. 49 distinguishes the συμμαχία from the χώρα.
[7] Bikerman, *Inst. d. Sél.* 136 *sqq.*, 144 *sqq.*; Rostovtzeff, *SEH* 525–6.
[8] *OGIS* 223=Welles, *Royal Correspondence* 78 no. 15; Tarn, *Alexander* II, 211.
[9] *SEG* I, 366.
[10] Nicolaus of Damascus, *F. Gr. Hist.* II A no. 90 fr. 81=Jos. *Ant.* XII, 125.

exercise their own foreign policy again; no one can question that under Seleucus II Smyrna was an absolutely independent State,[1] as were Miletus and Magnesia-on-the-Maeander when in 196, in the heyday of the power of Antiochus III, they went to war with each other and were reconciled by some other Greek cities,[2] precisely as if Antiochus did not exist. Subsequently Antiochus III claimed that all Greek cities were, notionally, his subjects and freedom an act of grace on his part,[3] a view that can perhaps be traced earlier; but after he lost western Asia Minor in 189, the position of the cities depended on Pergamum and on Rome. Probably the cities all through had a good juridical claim to freedom, as Alexander had recognised[4]; but they could not in the long run stand up against the encroachments of the kings, and the time was to come when freedom would mean little but freedom from tribute.

To turn now to the Seleucid settlement of Asia. Its basis was the military colony,[5] and not, as was once believed, the Greek city, the *polis*; the kings did indeed ultimately fill much of their empire with Greek cities, but it was largely done indirectly. For only the king could found a *polis*; and though the tradition remembered that Seleucus was a hard worker,[6] as was his son, to found even one *polis* meant for the king hard work.[7] He had to find land and settlers for it, build the wall, supply food, seed-corn, cattle, and tools to give the people a start, remit taxation till the city found its feet, decide personally innumerable housing, economic, and social questions, give a constitution and get political life started, and settle the city law, though here he could order

[1] *OGIS* 229, III; see Tarn, *Alexander* II, 206. [2] Ditt.[3] 588.

[3] Polyb. XVIII, 51, 9; Livy XXXIII, 38, 6.

[4] Tarn, *Alexander* II, App. 7, 1.

[5] First brought out by V. Tscherikower, *Die hellenistischen Städtegründungen*, 1927, 121. On the military colony see Oertel, *Katoikoi* in P.W.; G. T. Griffith, *The mercenaries of the Hellenistic world*, 1935, 147 *sqq.*; Tarn, *Bactria* 6; Rostovtzeff, *C.A.H.* VII, 180, cf. *SEH* 492, 499.

[6] Plut. *Mor.* 790 A.

[7] Ditt.[3] 344 (many details); •Holleaux, *B.C.H.* XLVIII, 1924, 1 on *SEG* II, 663; Buckler and Robinson, *Sardis* VII, 1 no. 2; Rostovtzeff, *C.A.H.* VII, 178.

the adoption of some well-known Greek city code, with or without modifications.[1] But as regards the military colony, though he still had to find land and money, he could and almost always did delegate the actual work to a subordinate, usually the local governor.[2] Though the military colony soon became the main army reserve, its primary object was defence; Alexander had founded some in Bactria-Sogdiana for defence against the Saca nomads, and in Media to bridle the tribes of the Elburz; and the Seleucid chain which stretched across Asia Minor from the Caïcus to the Maeander —Nacrasa, Thyateira, Hyrcanis, Cadoi, Blaundos, the Myso-Macedonians, Pella—was clearly intended to protect the coastal district from the Galatians. Some of the early colonies may have been purely Macedonian, but the bulk of those in the west were Greek; the settlers were time-expired troops, mercenaries, men able and willing to serve. Each colonist was given a parcel of land to cultivate for his livelihood, called a *kleros* (a 'lot'); the tenure was military, the life-holder having to serve in the army when called upon; the *kleros* was heritable, but could be sold or willed, though only subject to the obligation to serve; it seems that once a *kleros* always a *kleros*, the obligation to serve (or else presumably to provide a substitute) running with the land for ever.[3] There may have been, as Professor Rostovtzeff thinks, more than one type of military colony, though a pattern to copy would have facilitated the work of settlement so greatly that probably such patterns existed[4]; but however that may be, it was the men of the *kleroi*, the cleruchs, who formed the backbone of the Seleucid armies, the Graeco-Macedonian phalanx; their loyalty to the reigning Seleucid was proverbial, and argued good conditions. A military colony usually stood at or beside some native village or town; it often had no name but that of the village, but the colony

[1] As Doura-Europus had Athenian law, modified; see p. 149 n. 1 *post*.

[2] Shown by the names; Tarn, *Bactria* 10–11.

[3] This follows from the kleroi at Susa (*post*).

[4] The so-called charter at Avroman (*Perg*. 1, ἐν τῇ παλαιᾷ συγγραφῇ: E. H. Minns, *J.H.S.* XXXV, 1915, 52; L. Mitteis, *Z. Savigny-Stiftung, Röm. Abt.* XXXVI, 1915, 428) might be such a pattern.

sometimes named itself after the official who founded it or after the Greek city or district from which most of the colonists happened to come.[1] The Seleucid cleruch system was far more successful than the Ptolemaic.[2]

The difference between the military colony and the city is not too easy to define; Greek writers give little help, for most of them will call anything a *polis* and some of them will call a military colony a village because at first it often bore the name of a village. Greeks before Alexander had known only the city, *polis*, and the village, *kome*. To be a city, a place had to possess self-government and certain organs of corporate life. The indispensable minimum was a division of the citizens into tribes, a Council chosen from these tribes, responsible magistrates elected or chosen by lot, and its own city-land, laws, and finances; generally, though not necessarily, there was also a city wall, a primary Assembly, and local subdivisions of the city territory (*demes*). A collection of houses without these marks was a village; size had nothing to do with it, and to Greeks Babylon, Memphis, Jerusalem, were properly speaking villages, though they made one exception among barbarians: they recognised the highly organised Phoenician towns as cities,[3] and Aristotle included among his Greek city-constitutions that of Carthage. But after Alexander the old antithesis 'either city or village' no longer applied; one shaded off into the other; new and intermediate forms grew up, and new forms are found, such as *politeuma*[4] (corporation) and *katoikia*[5] (settlement), to describe communities with some quasi-autonomous organisation falling short of that of the city, the members of the latter organisation being called *katoikoi*, settlers. The *politeuma*, like the city, had a religious centre, might possess a council and magistrates, and supplied a means of incorporating in the city a body of aliens without making them citizens. Great native centres, too, began to

[1] Names: Tarn, *Bactria*, 10–11. [2] Griffith, *op. c.* 162–3.

[3] Tyre called a *polis*, *SEG* IV, 601 (2nd cent.).

[4] Ruppel, *Phil.* 1927, 268; Gr. Halensis, *Dikaiomata* (*P. Hal. I*).

[5] *OGIS* 238; *Inscr. Hierapolis* no. 212; Str. 625; Oertel, *Katoikoi*, and Swoboda, κώμη, in P.W.

be called cities,[1] though careful writers, like Isidore and sometimes Strabo, use *komopolis*, village-city, for a native town with no organisation a Greek could understand; what a native subject town was like before it became hellenised is usually unknown.

It is generally believed that the settlers in a military colony were called *katoikoi*, a useful word which had more than one meaning. Alexander's cities themselves, the Alexandrias, had not been ordinary Greek *poleis*, though they became such under the Seleucids, but a new form designed to accommodate people of more than one race, perhaps a collection of *politeumata* with the Greek as the most important[2]; they were subject to royal governors,[3] and the Greeks settled in them refused to regard the system as 'Hellenic life and training'.[4] The Seleucid military colonies had some form of self-government by their own officials, and were fortified; as they grew, they approximated more and more to the *polis* form, and many of them finally achieved their ambition and became full-blown cities. This would require, at the least, the king's consent, and probably some remodelling on his part; for example, when the military colony at Susa became Seleuceia-on-the-Eulaeus, the new name, being dynastic, can only have been given by the reigning monarch. But the military colony which became a city still retained its *kleroi*, as shown by Doura (*post*), while a place directly founded as a city had none; this meant that those citizens who occupied *kleroi* could still be called up for military service, while the citizens of a city which started full-blown could not.[5] For example, when the Greek inscriptions from Susa showed that the place was a Greek *polis* but that it had *kleroi*, it could be seen that it had once been a military colony but had been turned into a *polis* and renamed by some king. Now a Greek city, old or new, was absolute owner of its own land, but a military colony was not; the

[1] Jos. c. Ap. I, 197, 209 (quotations).

[2] For an attempted sketch see Tarn, *Alexander* I, 135.

[3] Arr. IV, 22, 4, cf. VII, 6, 1.

[4] Diod. XVIII, 7, 1.

[5] Agreeing with Bikerman, *op. c.* 73 *sqq.* Rostovtzeff, *SEH* 500–1, seems to differ.

Succession Law of Doura-Europus,[1] which is probably very early though the actual copy we have is later, shows that though the settler had perpetual user of his *kleros* and could sell or bequeath that user, the king was still the ultimate owner, for in an intestacy he retained the right of escheat in case of a failure of heirs. So it may well be, though it cannot at present be definitely stated, that the bedrock difference between the city and the military colony was not so much size or degree of self-government as whether or not it owned its land.

Putting the old Greek cities aside, the new cities in Seleucid Asia which had the Greek *polis*-form of organisation fell into two classes, those that were essentially Greek and those that were essentially native; the latter will be considered presently. The sole writer whose use of the word *polis* can be trusted is Isidore of Charax, as he is reproducing the official Parthian survey; Strabo is often careful, but by no means always so. It may be taken that every place in the empire with a Greek or Macedonian place-name (with the possible but unlikely exception of Europus, Seleucus' birthplace) was, or had been, either a military colony which had named itself or a *polis* which had grown out of a military colony; and that every city which had *kleroi*, like Susa (Seleuceia-on-the-Eulaeus) or Doura-Europus, had first been a military colony. But it may also be taken that every place with one of the four dynastic names—Seleuceia, Antioch (named from Seleucus' father), Laodicea (from his mother), and Apamea (from his Iranian wife)—was a Greek *polis*, either the primary foundation of a king or a place renamed by a king, as Susa had been; the cities with divine names, like Artemita, Heracleia, *may* have been royal foundations also. But nomenclature soon became a difficulty with this great mass of dynastic names, as it had already become with Alexander's seventeen Alexandrias. Certainly, as

[1] *D. Perg.* I, see Cumont, *Doura* 286; P. Koschaker, *Z. f. Sav. Stift. rom. Abt.* XLVI, 1926, 207; D. Pappulias, Ἀκαδ. Ἀθηνῶν 28 Nov. 1929, given by L. Wenger, *Arch.* X, 1932, 131; Tarn, *Bactria*, 7; Rostovtzeff, *SEH* 488.

regards Seleucid cities, the *official* name included in each case some geographical addition,[1] just as we know that, *officially*, a Greek of Seleuceia–Susa called himself, not a Seleuceian, but a Seleuceian-of-those-on-the-Eulaeus[2]; but for everyday use the position was impossible, and many, perhaps nearly all, of the Seleucid cities acquired nicknames (popular names),[3] as many of the Alexandrias had done; very many of these nicknames, of many types, are now known, and in our literary sources they have often ousted the official name altogether, a cause of endless confusion to modern writers before the system was recognised.

The work of the individual Seleucids cannot always be distinguished; but, roughly, the city organisation in Northern Syria, Babylonia, and about the Persian Gulf was primarily due to Seleucus, that in Iran to Antiochus I, and that in Asia Minor to Antiochus I and Antiochus II, with a noteworthy extension in Cilicia and the East due to Antiochus IV Epiphanes, his cities being often distinguished by the name Epiphaneia. A brief list of the principal Seleucid cities may be given.[4] Northern Syria, already full of Antigonus' veterans, became under Seleucus a second Macedonia; here was a new Pieria and Cyrrhestice, and across the Euphrates a new Mygdonia; and here were Seleucus' four great name-cities. Antioch, the capital of the empire, on the then navigable Orontes, had ultimately four quarters, each with its own wall, within the city wall; Seleucus built the first quarter, Seleucus II the third, Antiochus IV the fourth. Antioch was never a centre of learning; though a great trade emporium, its repute was always that of a pleasure city, and its park, Daphne, became notorious; Poseidonius, himself a native of the neighbouring Apamea, castigates the luxury of the Syrian Greeks.[5] Near the mouth of the Orontes

[1] *OGIS* 233, Antioch in Persis; *ib.* l. 100, several cities; Seleuceia on the Tigris, *ib.*, and the coins (McDowell, *Coins from Seleucia*, 94 *sqq.*); a number of cities on coins of Antiochus IV, *B.M. Coin Cat.* Seleucids, 40–2.

[2] *SEG* VII, 1, last line; *ib.* no. 14, where the acrostic shows it is part of Herodorus' name.

[3] Tarn, *Bactria*, 12–16.

[4] Usual references in V. Tscherikower, *Die hellenistischen Städtegründungen*, 1927.

[5] *F. Gr. Hist.* II A no. 87, fr. 10.

was the harbour city, the strong Seleuceia in Pieria, burial-place of the dynasty, rising gloriously from the sea in terrace after terrace up its great cliff, and worshipping a conical stone come down from an older world. Farther south lay Laodicea on the Sea (Latakiyeh), and on the middle Orontes, in a steaming plain, Apamea, the Seleucid arsenal, which replaced Antigonus' Pella; here were the quarters of the elephants, and great studs of horses. Besides these four, the country became thick with settlement down to Laodicea of the Lebanon and Heliopolis (Baalbek), near the Orontes' source; thicker still were the cities to the eastward, grouped about Beroea (Aleppo) on the Chalus, on the road from Antioch to Hierapolis-Bambyce, and about Chalcis farther south; northward an Antioch in Cyrrhestice. A long line of cities fringed the Euphrates; among them, Doura was re-founded as Europus, Thapsacus as Amphipolis; farther north an Apamea guarded the boat-bridge at Zeugma, which superseded Thapsacus as the usual crossing. In northern Mesopotamia, among others, were two famous cities, Antioch-Nisibis in Mygdonia and Antioch-Edessa in the Urfa valley. In the second century Hamath became Epiphaneia, Berytus Laodicea,[1] and an Antioch appears on the Sea of Galilee; and for a moment Jerusalem was named Antioch (p. 214).

In Babylonia and Susiana Seleucus was working on Alexander's ideas with regard to the Persian Gulf, as Lysimachus perhaps did for the Black Sea. The greatest city here was Seleucus' first foundation, Seleuceia on the Tigris,[2] some distance below Baghdad, which took the place of Babylon. Susa became Seleuceia on the Eulaeus (*ante*); there was another Seleuceia in Susiana on the Hedyphon,[3] and a third 'on the Erythrean Sea' (*i.e.* the Persian Gulf), home of the astronomer Seleucus (p. 158 n. 7). There was an Apamea in Mesene; above Baghdad another Apamea, an Antioch, another Doura; toward the Susian hills, where the main road

[1] Both names used: Picard, *Ann. Univ. Grenoble* 1925, 136, 9; *SEG* III, 676.

[2] Description in Tarn, *Bactria*, 60–2.

[3] Str. 744.

eastward from Seleuceia bifurcated, stood the important Artemita. Alexandria at the Tigris mouth, the later Charax Spasinu, was refounded as an Antioch by Antiochus IV, but the three places known on the Arabian side of the Gulf, Larisa, Chalcis, Arethusa, must have been military colonies[1]; other colonies on the Gulf are known. Babylon itself was ruined by Antigonus I, and in 275 Antiochus I moved the remaining civil population, leaving merely the temple[2]; its resurrection later as a Greek city (p. 157) was probably due to Epiphanes. Uruk (Warka) also became partially hellenised as Orchoi[3]; but in spite of its large Greek population it was governed by its own native magistrates and apparently never had Greek city forms.[4]

In Iran there was a large group of foundations in Media, partly to bridle the hill tribes, among them Europus–Rhagae near Teheran and Apamea at the Caspian Gates; in Parthia, Hecatompylos and four other towns; in Persis, Antioch on the Persian Gulf (probably Bushire) and perhaps a Laodicea, though native feeling was strong and the native priest-kings, ancestors of the Sassanian dynasty, still ruled at Persepolis. The great Saca invasion of *c.* 293, which was probably the cause of Seleucus sending his son Antiochus (I) to govern the East, destroyed at least three Alexandrias, Chodjend, Merv, and Tarmita (Termez) on the Oxus[5]; all were refounded as Antiochs by Antiochus, who possibly did other building also, but here the texts defy interpretation. Finally Susa was turned into Seleuceia on the Eulaeus by (apparently) Antiochus III,[6] and Ecbatana was refounded as Epiphaneia by Epiphanes.

In Asia Minor the through route between Syria and Ionia

[1] Pliny VI, 160; Tarn, *Bactria*, 66 n. 2.

[2] S. Smith, *Babylonian Historical Texts* nos. 5, 6, and *Rev. d'Assyr.* 1925, 196; cf. Oppert, *C.R.Ac.I.* 1901, 830.

[3] Cumont, *Doura* 281, 487, and Rostovtzeff, *Seleucid Babylonia* (the seals), Jordan, *Uruk-Warka*; see p. 129 *ante*.

[4] Rostovtzeff, *SEH* 514, not a *polis*; see p. 154 n. 3 *post*.

[5] Tarn, *Tarmita*, *J.H.S.* LX, 1940, 89; *Alex* II, 235. But the idea that later it became a Demetrias is a mistake.

[6] No Greek inscriptions before his reign. Sketch of Greek Susa: Tarn, *Bactria*, 27–30, 39.

was well cared for. Where the roads[1] from Melitene through the Cappadocian Mazaka and from Tarsus through Iconium joined rose Laodicea 'the Burnt', so called from the furnaces of the quicksilver mines at Zizima; westward stood the great Apamea–Celaenae, called 'the Ark', a name of unknown meaning which led it later to put Noah's Ark on its coins; farther westward on the Lycus, where the roads to Ephesus and Sardes diverged, another Laodicea. These were the main knots of traffic. From Laodicea the Burnt a road ran south which reached the sea at Seleuceia (Selefkia) on the Calycadnus, and another north by Philomelium and Synnada to Nicea and Nicomedia in Bithynia. From Apamea–Celaenae roads ran to Antioch, Apollonia, and Seleuceia 'the iron', outpost cities towards independent Pisidia; from Laodicea on the Lycus a road went south through native Cibyra to the Pamphylian coast. At this Laodicea the main road branched; one road went to Sardes and continued northward to Seleucid Thyateira, whence one road ran to Pergamum and another north by Stratonicea on the Caïcus to Cyzicus; the other road went to Ephesus, passing through Antioch on the Maeander, Antioch-Nysa, and Seleuceia-Tralles, whence a branch ran southward by Antioch-Alabanda to Stratonicea in Caria. Under Epiphanes many Cilician towns were remodelled, though the statement that 50 Greek cities were known there later must be an exaggeration; Mallos and Adana became Antiochs and Mopsuestia a Seleuceia. Tarsus, already an Antioch in the third century,[2] became later an important university town.[3]

The new Seleucid cities certainly paid taxes, for so much King's land went to supply them with city-land that the Treasury could never have stood the loss of land-tax involved had it not received an equivalent. Some of these cities were under governors (*epistatai*) responsible to the king, who are however only actually mentioned twice, in

[1] For these roads generally: Ramsay, *Historical Geography of Asia Minor.*

[2] *Fouilles de Delphes* III, 2 no. 208; see Roussel on *I.G.* XI, 4, 822. Stephanus is therefore wrong.

[3] Ramsay, *Cities of St. Paul,* 232.

Seleuceia in Pieria[1] and in Seleuceia on the Tigris,[2] putting aside the Babylonian 'city-lord' at Uruk.[3] Obviously, wherever there was a large native population, some authority beyond the city magistrates was desirable; but at Antioch in Persis, if there was an *epistates*, he did not control the Assembly, and the city dated by the priest of the Seleucid worship and not by the Seleucid era.[4] But when the dynasty began to decline, the Syrian cities gradually succeeded in securing a large measure of independence.[5] By 148/7 the four great North Syrian cities had autonomy enough to form the coinage alliance of the 'sister peoples'.[6] In the civil wars of the dynasty, the Syrian cities figure as political factors, supporting this or that contestant; and as the price of help very many from 140 onwards secured from some king the title 'holy and inviolable' (p. 83), which meant immunity from attacks by him and the right to shelter offenders against him, and began to coin, often using eras from which they dated their freedom.

Besides cities and military colonies, there may have been some civilian settlements in Asia Minor,[7] though they are not mentioned till Roman times and are not easily distinguished from the development of the native village, which tended steadily towards acquiring some corporate form; in this the villagers would no longer be called *laoi*, semi-serfs, but would be designated by that useful word *katoikoi*, settlers. Here the old Greek cities helped, for the peasants in their territories tended to become *katoikoi* (p. 135), which implied some sort of local government in the villages, however rudimentary at first; doubtless the same thing took place in the territories of the new Greek cities. This was a step upward for the peasantry, as is shown by Eumenes II of Pergamum once degrading some *katoikoi* into *laoi* again[8];

[1] *SEG* VII, 62. [2] Polyb. V, 48, 12.

[3] Jordan, *Uruk-Warka* 41. If Uruk were not a *polis* (p. 152), the difficulty about the city-lord Kephalon (Tarn, *Bactria*, 26 n. 1) vanishes.

[4] *OGIS* 233. [5] Kahrstedt, *op. c.* 73; cf. Rostovtzeff, *SEH* 856.

[6] Head[2] 778. [7] Oertel, *Katoikoi* in P.W.

[8] Letter of Eumenes II: M. Segre, *Clara Rhodos* IX, 1938, 190. See Rostovtzeff, *SEH* 648.

the growth of local government in some villages in northern Syria has already been noticed (p. 138 n. 1). Indeed one of the most characteristic features of the Seleucid period was the steady upward growth of the various political forms,[1] which went on without interruption far into Roman times, the amorphous native village tending to become a settlement, which might in turn become a hellenised city. The organised villages ultimately grouped themselves, probably with some imitations of Greek forms, into associations or Leagues, whose roots go back to Seleucid times; such associations were the Caystriani, Hyrgaleis, Heptakometai, Pentedemiti, and many others, some of which ultimately coined, a right usually confined to cities. Of course the development of the village into the hellenised city was not absolutely new, and the process was at work in Greece also, *e.g.* in Aetolia; but an Aetolian village differed considerably from one of Phrygian serfs, and what was unparalleled under the Seleucids was the scale of operations. Given time enough, the final result, in Asia Minor and northern Syria, would have been a kingdom composed entirely of cities with contiguous territories and enjoying domestic autonomy, the whole under the suzerainty of a god-king who saw to security and managed policy. Whether the early Seleucids actually envisaged this is unknown; but certainly Rome did, and the way Rome at the start tried to rush matters suggests that the idea was Hellenistic. For when Pompey, having struck down Mithridates, found himself able to make what settlement he chose, he tried in some places to carry through this idea by one stroke of the pen[2]; thus he divided Pontus into eleven city districts, and of the eleven cities only three, Sinope, Amisus, and Amaseia were Greek, the rest being native towns or villages turned into Graeco-Roman cities, like Eupatoria-Magnopolis or Cabeira-Diospolis; similarly he made twelve city districts of Bithynia. But the Roman Empire was content with a slower and more natural growth, which was not uniform; for a city might decay and become a village again.

[1] Oertel, *op. c.*; Swoboda, *κώμη* in P.W.

[2] Brandis, *Bithynia* in P.W.

One instance may be given of the complexity which Hellenistic state-forms might assume in Asia. In Caria was an old religious League of native villages who worshipped Zeus Chrysaoreus.[1] One village, Alabanda, was refounded as an Antioch,[2] and, though now a Greek city, remained a member of this Carian League. An important new city, Stratonicea, had some of these villages assigned to it as city-land; they became its demes, and through them it also became a member of the League. One of these demes, Panamara, which itself worshipped Zeus Panamaros,[3] became far enough advanced in organisation to pass decrees and confer its 'citizenship', *i.e.* demesmanship, on strangers[4]; among others, it conferred citizenship on certain citizens of Stratonicea, the city of which, in Greek eyes, it formed part. No wonder Strabo abandoned the attempt to find a name in Greek phraseology for this old Carian League as he knew it, and took refuge in calling it a 'system'.

Turning now to the part played by Asiatics in the Seleucid settlement, one has first to distinguish the *polis* which was mainly Greek from that which was mainly Asiatic. Some new cities, like Antioch in Persis (Bushire), which was settled for some Seleucid by Magnesia on the Maeander,[5] appear to be purely Greek; but Greek names mean little, for Phoenicians were adopting such soon after 300,[6] and many Asiatics did the same. Then some Greek cities, old and new, admitted selected Asiatics to citizenship even in the third century (there were old precedents, for there was much Carian and Libyan blood in the citizen bodies of Miletus and Cyrene); thus Aspendus enrolled some mixed Asiatic mercenaries in her tribes,[7] Smyrna enfranchised a body of Persian troops,[8] Stratonicea had Carian demes (*ante*). Sardes, which in the fourth century had only its native

[1] Str. 660; Swoboda, *op. c.*

[2] L. Robert, *B.C.H.* 1925, 228 on this controversy.

[3] The inscriptions from this god's temple are *SEG* IV. 243–91.

[4] Holleaux, *B.C.H.* 1904, 353.

[5] *OGIS* 233.

[6] As 'Philocles', king of Sidon; Tarn, *Ant. Gon.* 104.

[7] Decree of Aspendus: Wilhelm, *Neue Beiträge* IV, 61; M. Segre, *Aegyptus* XIV, 1934, 253.

[8] *OGIS* 229 l. 105.

organisation, was in the second a *polis*[1]; it seems inconceivable that it had not a number of Lydian citizens, just as Selge, which invented for itself a Greek foundation legend, certainly had many Pisidian,[2] and the hellenised Lycian towns many Lycian; Antioch-Tarsus too must have had many native citizens, while Pergamum in 133 enfranchised Asiatics wholesale (p. 170).

But actual enfranchisement of Asiatics was not, it would seem, the usual form. In all probability the usual form for the admission of Asiatics into a Greek city was the *politeuma*, in Asia apparently also known as a *katoikia* (p. 147); this implied an organised body of foreigners, like the Syrian *politeuma* at Seleuceia[3] or the Jewish in many cities, who had definite political rights short of citizenship, with their own organisation, their own (equivalent of) magistrates, but were not part of the city; the Greeks alone were the citizens, the 'Antiochenes' or 'Seleuceians' or what not, and the Greek magistrates looked after *all* the inhabitants in matters like food or public health.[4]

But where there was a great body of natives, the native problem might be solved on many lines besides citizenship or *politeumata*. The refounded Babylon had a Greek theatre, gymnasium, and city organisation[5]; but the religious and scientific activity of the Babylonians continued, notwithstanding Greek forms, just as it did at Uruk, which was seemingly not a Greek *polis* (p. 152). Seleuceia kept its Hellenic character to the end,[6] but also drained Babylon's native population; it replaced Opis,[7] a large native town,

[1] Cf. Ditt.[3] 273, 4th cent., with *ib.* 548 and *OGIS* 305, 2nd cent.

[2] Polyb. V, 74, 4 *sqq.*

[3] Jos. *Ant.* XVIII, 372, cf. 378; ἐμπολιτευόμενον is the verb of *politeuma*, not of *polites*.

[4] *Dikaiomata* (*P. Hal.* I).

[5] Koldewey, *Das wiedererstehende Babylon*, 293; Haussoullier, *Klio* IX, 352 *sqq.*; E. Schmidt, *Arch. Anz.* 1941, 786.

[6] The older literature in Strack, *Seleukeia am Tigris* in P.W.

[7] Opis: Watermann, *Preliminary Reports upon the excavations at Tel Umar.* But N. C. Debevoise (*Class. Weekly*, 5 Feb. 1939) has pointed out that the reading and value of the numerous Ak-sak inscriptions, on which this view is based, are uncertain, and that other views could be, and are, held.

and as its total population, ultimately, is given as 600,000,[1] there must anyhow have been a great native population outside the wall; but Opis continued to have a separate existence and to be an important centre of commerce in itself[2] just as at Apollonia towards Pisidia the Thracian and Lycian towns remained distinct.[3] Opis may have been Seleuceia's 'village'[4]; but in some sense Seleuceia became a double city, for on some of its coins two turreted city-goddesses clasp hands; the second goddess is usually taken to represent Old Ctesiphon,[5] but it might perhaps be Opis as representing Seleuceia's Babylonian population; that is, the coin might, in a wider sense, stand for friendship between the Greek and the Babylonian. This native population may be one of the reasons (the traditional reasons are, same country and neighbourhood) why Seleuceians, more often than not, are called Babylonians,[6] confusing the modern scholar; in the same way the Greek astronomer Seleucus, of Seleuceia on the Persian Gulf, was called a Chaldean.[7] Antioch (the capital) again differed; Seleucus' city was purely Graeco-Macedonian, but in Antioch later there was a large Syrian element, and this may be the explanation of the mysterious second quarter, which had no royal founder[8]: Syrians settled outside the wall, and were subsequently taken in and enclosed by the second wall; possibly they formed a *politeuma*, like the Syrian *politeuma* at Seleuceia, but one cannot say. Antioch-Edessa, called 'semi-barbarian',[9] may have been of this type, and so may Antioch toward Pisidia; though a Greek city, it required the foundation

[1] Pliny VI, 22; this may be exaggerated.

[2] Str. 739, ἐμπόριον τῶν κύκλῳ τόπων.

[3] Ramsay, *J.R.S.* XII, 184–6.

[4] Str. 739, κώμη.

[5] Hill, *B.M. Coins, Arabia &c.* XCV; Allotte de la Fuye, *Mém. Dél. en Perse*, XX, 1928, 39 no. 24; McDowell, *Coins from Seleucia*, 100, 177–9. Other suggestions are the Semitic 'double Fortune' (Cumont, *Ét. syr.* 263 doubtfully); astral goddesses (S. Smith, *Babyl. Hist. Texts* 66).

[6] Str. 743; Diog. Laert. VI, 81.

[7] Susemihl 1, 763; Cumont, *Syria* 1927, 83 (quite certain); J. Bidez, *Les écoles chaldéennes sous Alexandre et les Séleucides*, Mélanges Capart, 1935, 81; cf. pp. 297, n. 5, 305 *post*, and Tarn, *Bactria*, 43.

[8] Str. 750, founded by τοῦ πλήθους τῶν οἰκητόρων.

[9] Malalas XVII, 418.

near it of a separate sanctuary of Mēn Askaenos (p. 345), which points to a large native quarter from the start. One old native city, the Phoenician Aradus, received very exceptional privileges from Seleucus II, including the right to harbour political refugees.[1]

But, beside these phenomena, there were also new cities which had only native names; Isidore of Charax gives a number, largely in eastern Iran, and as he is reproducing the Parthian official survey of somewhere about 100 B.C., if he calls a place a *polis*, a *polis* it was. East of the Euphrates there must have been military colonies either mixed or entirely Asiatic (for the Seleucids used some Asiatic troops), like the one at Avroman in Kurdistan (p. 146 n. 4), where the official language was Greek but all the persons mentioned were Asiatics, and from these military colonies some of the *poleis* with native names must have developed; what Greeks there were in such cities, if any, must have lived under the local government of the Asiatic citizens, like the Greeks in Syrinx[2] in Hyrcania or in the Greek quarter of an unnamed Syrian town.[3] A first century inscription from Anisa in Cappadocia[4] may illustrate the start of such a city, in this case perhaps by order of the Cappadocian monarch; it had the full Greek *polis* organisation, with Greek as the official language, but all the men mentioned either had Cappadocian names or had fathers with Cappadocian names, and the record office was the temple of a native goddess. What these cities do show is the great attraction for Asiatics of Greek city-forms.

Although the Seleucids had no definite purpose of hellenising Asia, mere contiguity naturally produced some effect, and there were two other forces at work besides the political. One was law. Greek law made its way, aided probably by the policy, doubtless originally Alexander's,

[1] Str. 754. [2] Polyb. X, 31, 6 *sqq.*; Tarn, *Bactria*, 15–16, 20.

[3] *P. Cairo Zen.* 59034, ἐν τῆι Ἑλληνικῆι (*sc.* μερίδι). So at Memphis, *P. Lond.* I, 50, ἐν τῶι Ἑλληνιῶι; see Schubart, *Klio* X, 1910, p. 63 n. 2, and Wilcken, *Grundzüge* I, p. 18.

[4] Michel 546; Cumont, *R.É.A.* XXXIV, 1932, 135; Rostovtzeff, *SEH* 840, 1533 n. 120.

which placed under that law foreign *politeumata* in the cities[1]; a Graeco-Syrian law developed of which Rome had to take account and whose history in Asia has been traced for many centuries; and Greek legal forms penetrated far. As the city-law of Alexandria, though Greek, is not apparently Greek of any one city,[2] so the Succession Law recovered from Doura (p. 149 n. 1) is Athenian with other elements; but most striking are the first-century documents —Greek leases, written in Greek, made between men with Iranian names—found at Avroman,[3] for these came, not from any city, but from a remote village in Persian Kurdistan. The other force was the Greek language, which was a conquering speech wherever it went. It was used by very many Asiatics, and had a footing even in polyglot Cibyra[4]; some Asiatics wrote books in Greek.[5] Probably, Babylonia apart, it became a *lingua franca* for merchants everywhere[6]; and even in Babylonia some priests in the first century B.C. wrote a dedication in Greek letters.[7] A little later, Nabataean epitaphs were translating Greek forms[8]; Greek documents have even come from Georgia, which hardly a Greek can ever have visited.[9] There are many Greek loan words in Syriac and Aramaic,[10] and Greek expelled the native languages entirely from Lydia and western Phrygia.[11] But powerful instrument as Greek was, its success had its limits; eastern Phrygia, Lycia, Lycaonia, Syria, retained their own languages in the country districts, as naturally did inner Asia; even at Byblos[12] and Tyre[13] on the sea-coast Phoenician was still spoken at the Christian era. But one result of the contiguity of races in life and trade was the emergence of the so-called 'culture-Greek',

[1] *Dikaiomata* 38; but see Schubart, *Einführung* 280.

[2] *Dikaiomata*. [3] Tarn, *Bactria*, 9 n. 1. [4] Str. 631.

[5] Tarn, *Bactria*, 56–9; F. Altheim, *Weltgeschichte Asiens im griechischen Zeitalter* II, 1948, part IV, ch. 2. [6] Rostovtzeff, *SEH* 522.

[7] Schilieco, *Arch. f. Orientforschung* 1928, 11.

[8] Bruno Keil, *Hermes* XLIII, 587.

[9] Tarn, *Alexander* II, 226 n. 4 (refs.). [10] W. Otto, *Kulturgeschichte* 99.

[11] Calder, *J.R.S.* II, 249; last dated Lydian inscriptions are 4th cent. B.C., Buckler, *Sardis* VI, ii, nos. 3, 50; Str. 631.

[12] Dussaud, *Syria* VI, 269. [13] *Ib.* 270; cf. *B.C.H.* 1925, 470.

an Asiatic who 'went Greek', so to speak, and adopted a Greek name and Greek speech and culture; the 'Greek woman, a Syro-Phoenician by race' of Mark vii, 26 was such a one. Instances can be collected of various small borrowings both ways, which cannot be treated here.

One of the greatest things which the Seleucids did was the introduction of a true calendar.[1] It was not quite the first, for some Phoenician cities had already begun to use a fixed era[2]; but it was the first comprehensive one, and marked a great advance on reckoning by eponymous magistrates or the years of a king's reign—a barbarism still employed in the *official* dating of the Statutes of Great Britain. Dates were reckoned in plain figures from the Seleucid era, but there were two versions of that era; in Babylonia the year One began with 1 Nisan (March-April) 311, Seleucus' first New Year festival after he recovered Babylon, but in Syria it began with the first day of the then current Macedonian year, 1 Dios (October) 312. There was thus some 5 months difference between the two eras. The Seleucid calendar, often with Babylonian or Persian months instead of Macedonian, was widely adopted in Asia,[3] even by Jews, and lasted long; it was used throughout the Parthian empire and its sub-kingdoms, reached India, and was (it is said) still surviving in parts of Syria in the present century.

Looking at the great scale of the Seleucid settlement of Asia, it seems hard to believe that it should have failed; but fail it did, except in those parts of Asia Minor and Syria where Rome salved it. But it did *not* fail because, as was once believed, mixed marriages had, before the end of the third century, turned the Greeks into half-caste Levantines.[4] Nothing of the sort took place. Greeks could take in much foreign blood and remain Greeks, as witness Miletus and Cyrene, or half-breeds like Themistocles and Cimon; but in fact, down to about the Christian era, the Greeks in Asia

[1] Ginzel, *Handbuch der Chronologie* I, 1906, 137; later literature, Tarn, *Bactria*, 64, and add Bikerman, *Inst. d. Sél.* 205 and *Chronologie* in Gercke-Norden III, 5, 1933.

[2] Hill, *B.M. Coins, Phoenicia*.

[3] List of countries, with the months used, in Tarn, *Bactria*, 64.

[4] Discussed, Tarn, *Bactria*, 34–8.

took much trouble to keep their blood racially pure, and the outburst of Greek literature[1] after the Parthian conquest was simply an assertion of their Greek blood. In northern Mesopotamia, about 50 B.C., half-breeds formed a caste apart, regarded as nearer to the 'barbarian' than to the Greek, and with a special and derogatory name of their own[2]; and even at Doura-Europus in the first century A.D. there were *genearchs*, one of whose functions was to keep pure the blood of the Greek families.[3] Of course Doura has been quoted for free mixture of blood, but that is all later than the Christian era; the Doura of the inscriptions was not, as it has been called, a Greek city in decay, but a city changing to a new life in Parthian and later in Roman hands; the Parthians, a tolerant aristocracy, normally treated their Greek cities well, but Doura on their frontier they had occupied and partly rebuilt. Certainly *then* the nomenclature became eloquent enough. There was an extraordinary mixture of forms, Babylonian, Persian, Syrian; men's names like Samisilabos (Shamash is my father), Baphaladados and Zebidadados (compounds of Adad), Rhagaibelos (the repose of Bel), Daniel and Barnabas, and women's names formed from Asiatic deities, preferably from Nanaia, the Babylonian goddess of the city, as Maththanath (gift of Anaïtis), Bathnanaia (daughter of Nanaia), Mekatnanaia, Baribonnaia, Rhigoutai (the name of Esther's Sabbath handmaid), and the goddess-name of Flaubert's heroine Salammbo, who has now appeared as a woman, Salamboua, both at Doura[4] and Gaza.[5] Free admixture of blood *had* taken place, and the Greek used was becoming ungrammatical and losing its inflections, like that on the late Parthian, and Kushan, coins.

There were several reasons for the Seleucid failure. There were not enough Greeks in the world to colonise Asia; they never went on the land, but congregated in the cities, and the

[1] *Bactria*, 42 *sqq*

[2] *Bactria*, 38, cf. 51 (Plutarch's eastern Greek source in *Crassus*).

[3] *Ib.* 37.

[4] *SEG* II, 822.

[5] Fr. Hommel, *Ethnologie und Geographie des alten Orients*, 603 n.5 (a Minaean inscription).

land ultimately belongs to those who till it. Some districts were unsuited to the Greek way of life, and many had no access to the sea, the reason why the Seleucids, following Alexander's lead, tried to colonise round the Persian Gulf. Again, these kings, unlike the Euthydemids, never managed to reconcile the great Iranian peoples to their rule; and this probably counted for more than the influence of Oriental religions, sometimes overstressed. The Greek, as a polytheist, naturally in a strange country worshipped the god who knew the way of the land; but it is instructive to see the Greeks of Susa compelling the great goddess Nanaia to serve their purposes to her own detriment,[1] or the Greek merchants of Seleuceia putting for choice on their signets Athena,[2] the one Greek deity who (Nabataeans apart) was never equated with anything Asiatic. But possibly the chief reason was that what the Asiatic was willing to take from the Greek was form only, never the informing spirit; in matters of the spirit Asia knew that she could outstay the Greek, as she did. The Greeks made a good fight, though the end must have come by one place after another being swamped by the Asiatic flood; but, even so, some cities—Susa and Seleuceia are known—were still Greek cities in the second century A.D., and the virtual destruction of Seleuceia in A.D. 163, though she opened her gates, was due, not to anything Asiatic, but to a Roman emperor. The plague which forthwith swept the Roman Empire from Syria to the Rhine was looked on by many as the vengeance of heaven for Seleuceia.

* * * * *

To turn to Pergamum.[3] Starting from humble beginnings as dynasts of a hill fortress (p. 18), the Attalids soon mastered Aeolis, and then, after Attalus I had taken the

[1] Tarn, *Bactria*, 68–9.

[2] Macdowell, *Stamped objects from Seleucia* 226, and Table p. 224.

[3] Rostovtzeff, *C.A.H.* VIII ch. XIX, with bibliography, and *SEH* 553–65, 637–65, 799 *sqq*; G. Cardinali, *Il regno di Pergamo*, 1906; E. V. Hansen, *The Attalids of Pergamum*, 1946 (very full). The basis is the German excavations; references, *C.A.H.* VIII, 787 A, 4.

royal title, ruled Asia Minor within the Taurus from 228 to 223 and from 188 to 133; but indications point to a kingdom of the Ptolemaic pattern, an organised machine for the accumulation of wealth, which from the point of view of Hellenism stood on a lower level than the Seleucid. The political position made of the Attalids consistent enemies of the Seleucids and friends of Egypt; Egypt therefore they naturally imitated, but, as they could not claim divinity as the basis of their rule (p. 51) and were not national kings, they posed instead as democratic rulers; they never used the royal 'We', and they sometimes called themselves citizens of Pergamum.[1] Possibly their idea was to be First Citizen, a sort of anticipation of Augustus. But the fact that the Attalids made a business-like and competent affair of their dominion, and that Romans and pro-Roman Greeks speak well of Rome's loyal supporters, cannot conceal the real undercurrent of Greek feeling about them; to nationally-minded Greeks Eumenes II was Judas, the arch-traitor to Hellenism, the man who instigated Rome to break the Seleucid dynasty, which stood for Hellenistic evolution. The people of Antioch might laugh at their Antiochus, and he might demean himself to play practical jokes upon them; but the grammarian Daphitas in bitter earnest likened the upstart Attalids, lording it over Greek cities in their purple, to the purple weals on the back of a whipped slave, and was crucified accordingly.[2] No Greek ever spoke thus of the Seleucids.

Where Pergamum ruled, the Seleucid policy of steadily diminishing King's land and the area of serfdom was abolished; the Attalids seemingly not only conserved their King's land but extended it[3] by appropriating the temple estates and making the temples dependent on some city; they were aided in this by the fact that, while there were many old temple states in Aeolis, none were really powerful.[4] Like the Ptolemies, they must have gifted the (revocable)

[1] *OGIS* 310, 311, 749 *sq.*, with the *Addenda* 1, 655.
[2] Str. 647.
[3] Rostovtzeff, *Kolonat* 280.
[4] List, Rostovtzeff in *Anatolian Studies* 370.

user of estates on King's land to officials, for Attalus III found many such estates to confiscate, or rather resume. They made a number of foundations,[1] however, of which two were certainly full cities: Attaleia in Pamphylia, their seaport toward Egypt, where the Laodicea–Cibyra road reached the sea, and Philadelphia in the volcanic district of Lydia, which became a considerable place later; it was called 'Little Athens', and was built with a view to resisting the earthquakes which often shook it.[2] They enlarged Elaea as Pergamum's port, and built another harbour, Hellenopolis, on the Propontis. They founded some military colonies of the usual type, the first two being Philetaireia under Mount Ida and Attaleia on the Hermus; several other names of Attalid foundations are known, but whether cities or military colonies cannot be said. The Attalids depended on a mercenary army, though they utilised the Mysian highlanders[3] both for war and colonies. In their enlarged kingdom they governed the satrapies by generals in the usual form,[4] and had a minister 'for affairs' or vizier like the Seleucids.[5]

Their relations to the Greek cities in their kingdom were clearly exposed at the peace conference after the defeat of Antiochus III, when Rome gave to Eumenes II Seleucid Asia Minor[6]: while Rhodes pleaded for the freedom of the Greek cities, Eumenes asked for them as his subjects. Rome compromised and gave him as subjects[7] all those that had been tributary to Attalus I or had aided Antiochus, and declared the rest free; among those subject were Ephesus, Teos, and Tralles, while some of the cities declared free—Samos, Priene, Magnesia, Lampsacus are known—afterwards entered into 'friendship and alliance' with Rome, which circumscribed their actions in another direction. But a considerable number of cities, including Miletus and Smyrna, were really free; and Apollonia towards Pisidia

[1] Tscherikower *op. c.*; A. J. Reinach, *Rev. Arch.* II, 1908, 190; E. V Hansen *op. c.* ch. VII.
[2] Str. 579, 628; Steph, *s.v.*
[3] *OGIS* 338; Polyb. V, 77, 7.
[4] *SEG* II, 663.
[5] *OGIS* 291–6.
[6] Polyb. XXI, 18–23; Livy XXXVII, 52.
[7] Their position: Brandis, *Asia* in P.W.; *Milet.* I, 7, Rehm on no. 203.

dated an era from 189.[1] Naturally there was discontent among the subject cities, and it is known how Eumenes dealt with one Greek city, possibly Apollonia on the Rhyndacus in Hellespontine Phrygia[2]: he abolished autonomy, confiscated its temples, and placed it under the general of the satrapy. Later on he restored its domestic autonomy and temples, but the city remained tributary and subject to the general; Teos was also tributary,[3] and doubtless therefore, as later writers state, all the non-free Greek cities, for Teos had the advantage of being the headquarters in Asia of the Dionysiac artists, whom the Attalids favoured. Some cities—Ephesus and Amblada are named [4]—were apparently taxed at a lump sum, assessed on a property valuation, which they raised from their citizens as they chose. But at Apollonia the citizens were taxed directly and not through the city; there seem to have been many taxes, and perhaps the long list which Teos herself imposed on her citizens (p. 119), though much earlier (*c.* 300), may give some idea of the later Attalid taxation.[5] Certainly, as against this, the kings gave from the Treasury subventions to some cities, as Teos and Apollonia, which were paid annually to the city stewards and could be used both for the civil and religious expenses of the city, but their general system, as regarded their Greek cities, was clear enough; they exacted from the cities in taxes and tribute more than the cities could raise and then made up the deficit themselves,[6] thus getting the cities into their power by financial means no less potent than political ones.

The non-free Greek cities, then, under the Attalids had little of autonomy but the form, and even that was precarious and could be withdrawn at the king's pleasure; the city was subject in some way to the provincial general, and was taxed, while its acceptance of royal subsidies gave the

[1] Ramsay, *J.R.S.* XII, 182.

[2] *SEG* II, 663; see for this paragraph Holleaux *B.C.H.* 1924, 1; De Sanctis, *Riv. fil.* 1925, 68.

[3] *B.C.H.* 1922, 312 no. 2; *SEG* II, 580.

[4] App. *b.c.* V, 15, 17; *OGIS* 751.

[5] Rostovtzeff, *C.A.H.* VIII, 605.

[6] Rostovtzeff *ib.*; E. V. Hansen, 191.

king the right to interfere in its internal financial administration. There were other arbitrary interferences. Some Attalid confiscated the revenues produced by the fisheries in the sacred lakes of Artemis at Ephesus, a thing Ephesus never forgave[1]; and the kings claimed the right, as Antigonus I at the end and Lysimachus had done, to shift populations about as seemed to them expedient; part of Priapus' territory was given to Parium, Dardanus was joined to Abydus, Gargara was half-swamped by a forced influx of barbarian tribesmen, the village of Gergitha was moved from the Troad to the Caïcus.[2] At Nacrasa and Aegina, and doubtless elsewhere, there was an *epistates* (city governor),[3] at Pergamum an inspector of the temple revenues.[4] Pergamum itself, though it had the forms of a Greek city, was controlled by the king through his appointment of the principal magistrates, the five city generals, who were nominated by and took orders from him[5]; probably they alone could bring matters before the Assembly and Council. This enabled the Attalids to control the city's finances, as the Ptolemies did with their cities in Asia Minor, though on different lines.

Pergamene finance flourished[6] and enabled the kings to employ large armies; they were proverbially the wealthiest rulers in Asia. Their King's land, other than that in gift to officials or used for military settlements (cleruch land), they managed themselves, as was usual, but probably they employed the Egyptian system of taking a calculated amount from the peasants and not, as did the Seleucids, a proportion of the harvest; for the general of Hellespontine Phrygia is found assuming that, if seed corn be needed, application must be made to the king, who therefore controlled all surplus wheat outside the cities.[7] The favoured cleruchs in the military colonies, however, paid a tenth of the produce as taxes.[8] Aeolis and the Troad were good agricultural and

[1] Str. 642.

[2] Str. 588–9, 595, 611, 616.

[3] *OGIS* 268, 329, 483 l. 56.

[4] *OGIS* 483 l. 165.

[5] *OGIS* 267 II.

[6] For this paragraph, Rostovtzeff in *Anatolian Studies* 359.

[7] *SEG* II, 663 l. 17.

[8] *I. Pergamon* 158.

cattle-raising districts; the royal studs of horses were probably kept near Mount Ida, and Ida itself supplied timber and pitch. It was partly the need of Idaean pitch which held Egypt to the Attalids, while their cattle and the hides they imported from the Euxine through Cyzicus supplied the world with parchment. Their economic system is unknown, but doubtless it was highly developed, especially as regards natural products; the kings were as interested in scientific agriculture as the early Ptolemies, and Attalus I wrote on Mount Ida[1] and Attalus III on gardens.[2] It is noteworthy that, to describe the king's treasure, the Ptolemaic term *rhiscus* was used[3] and not *gaza*, which was used by the Macedonian kings in Asia—Antigonus I, Lysimachus, and the Seleucids. No royal monopolies are heard of, but presumably parchment and pitch, at any rate, must have been such. One feature of their system, however, differed from that of any other kingdom: their extended use of slave labour. All, kings and cities alike, used slave labour in mines. But whereas in Egypt the monopoly manufactures were carried on by quasi-serfs, the royal factories in Pergamum, which turned out parchment, textiles, and the famous 'Attalid brocade' interwoven with gold thread, employed masses of slaves, largely women, under a 'superintendent of the royal factories'[4]; and the Attalid state must really have been based, not on cities and settlements like the Seleucid, but on wealth produced by serf and slave labour. But it did render two services to the world; it shielded a large number of cities from the Galatians, and it assembled at Pergamum a library second only to the Alexandrian.

The Attalid kings, notably Eumenes II and Attalus II, gradually transformed the old hill-fortress of Pergamum on its crescent ridge into a magnificent capital,[5] not laid out on the usual rectangular plan, but picturesque in a way that

[1] Str. 603. [2] Susemihl I, 845.
[3] Rostovtzeff *op. c.* 386 (inscr.); Cumont, *Syria* V, 349.
[4] *SGDI* 2001; *OGIS* 338.
[5] *Altertümer von Pergamon,* 1885–; M. Collignon and E. Pontremoli, *Pergame,* 1900; D. M. Robinson, *Art and Archaeology* 1920, 157; Hansen *op. c.* 219–62.

perhaps Seleuceia in Pieria alone could approach. At its foot the houses of the common people were crowded together; the Greek city climbed the flanks of the hill, and along the summit towered the splendid buildings of the kings. The main approach road led to the propylaea which formed the entrance to the three gymnasia, rising one above the other in terraces buttressed by great retaining walls; the theatre opened on the upper terrace, and above it the citadel wall enclosed part of the ridge. Within this wall along the ridge from north to south stood the palace, the library, and Athena's temple; next to this, but outside the wall, rose the huge altar of Zeus Soter (p. 319), surrounded by a tiled court which served as a market-place; beyond this were Dionysus' temple and a lower market-place, where stood a clock, Hermes with a cornucopia from which water flowed at intervals. The Public Health law of the city, given by some Attalid, is partially known.[1] It provided for house-owners scavenging the streets and repairing houses ruinous or likely to become so; if the owner did not do his duty, the *astynomi* could fine him and do the work at his expense, and if they neglected to do so the city generals could do it; as the generals took orders from the king, the king was the ultimate health authority. There was provision for keeping the roads in good order; all cisterns were registered, and the penalties for fouling the town water supply by washing clothes or watering animals were severe. But for all its grandeur and its Greek city forms, Pergamum was a semi-Asiatic town; in Athena's temple there was worshipped beside her Zeus Sabazios,[2] a form of the universal deity of Asia Minor whom Stratonice, the wife of Eumenes II, had brought with her from her Cappadocian home; and the lower city was crowded with foreign traders, corporations of mercenaries, freedmen, and the great mass of slave workers in the Crown factories. Attalus III, by the will which bequeathed his kingdom to Rome, also made Pergamum a free city; and the citizens, to

[1] *OGIS* 483; W. Kolbe, *Ath. Mitt.* 1902, 48; Hitzig, *Z. f. Savigny-Stiftung, Röm. Abt.*, 1905, 432.

[2] *OGIS* 331.

forestall a slave revolt in imitation of the Sicilian, enfranchised all metics and mercenaries, including the Mysians and Paphlagonians settled in the city's territory, and raised freedmen and slaves, except some of the women, to the status of metics—a revolution in itself, and the most wholesale enfranchisement of Asiatics actually recorded.[1]

* * * * *

The native kingdoms of Asia Minor were only superficially hellenised. Cappadocia, Pontus, Armenia retained their old feudal systems; and though Cappadocia, in imitation of the Seleucids, was divided into ten satrapies or generalships,[2] she dated by a Persian calendar.[3] These Asiatic kings took Greek cult-names, used Greek speech and titles at their courts and cultivated the Dionysiac artists; they employed Greek experts of every kind where they could, and built towns with their own names—Ariarathea in Cappadocia, Eupatoria in Pontus, Arsamosata and later Tigranocerta in Armenia; but these were generally only king's towns,[4] and the kingdoms remained essentially Asiatic; Cappadocia and Pontus were strongholds of Mazdaism, and Mithridates Eupator himself was only a barbarian varnished. The Greek inscription on the tomb on Nimrud-dagh of Pompey's friend Antiochus I of Commagene illustrates this mixed Hellenism.[5] It is written in very florid Greek of poor quality by one who did not understand the use of the Greek article. The king, who was really half a Seleucid, traces his descent from Darius I and Alexander[6] (the latter through Seleucus' wife Apama as Alexander's supposed daughter), and treats Persia and Macedonia as the two 'roots' of his kingship; he uses the Macedonian calendar, but attributes his successes to piety and holiness, and the gods he worships are the Persian Ahura-mazda and Mithras with Greek names attached. He makes a foundation to secure for ever their

[1] *OGIS* 337–8; P. Foucart, *Mém. Ac. Inscr.* XXXVII, 1904, 297; Cardinali in Beloch's *Saggi*, 269. [2] Str. 533–4.

[3] Discussed, J. H. Moulton, *Early Zoroastrianism*, 431.

[4] For an attempt to hellenise a Cappadocian town (Anisa) see p. 159 *ante*.

[5] *OGIS* 383. [6] *Ib.* 388–402; Tarn, *C.Q.* 1929, 141; *Bactria*, App. 3.

worship at his tomb, with worship of himself as a hero—a Greek form—but the foundation resembles nothing Greek; a number of villages were consecrated to the service and also a body of hierodules (temple slaves) whose descendants should minister to the cult for ever—the old Asiatic forms of the priest-state revived.

In Bithynia alone Hellenism possibly went deeper; the native dynasty regarded itself as a rival and counterpoise to the Attalids, and founded many towns.[1] Nicomedia 'the beautiful' replaced the Greek Astacus, destroyed by Lysimachus, and became an important city in Roman times; Prusias I built Prusias on the Sea, which had the right of coining, to replace Cius, a once Greek city destroyed by Philip V, and refounded Cierus as Prusias on the Hypius; he also on Hannibal's advice founded Prusa (Broussa)—possibly to replace another lost Greek city, Atussa—whose port Myrleia later became hellenised as Apamea; the kingdom also included Lysimachus' Nicea. Nicea and Prusias must have had some autonomy, and the other towns may have possessed at least Greek city-forms, for it is noteworthy that all replaced older Greek cities.

One people in Asia Minor remained practically untouched by Hellenism till the Roman period, the Galatians.[2] They were a foreign body camped in a strange land, living in strongholds whence they raided and plundered, and ruling over the native peasantry who cultivated their fields; they perhaps received accessions from Europe, and kept their language, tribal organisation, customs, and virtues—the bravery of the men, the fierce chastity of the women. As finally constituted,[3] their three tribes fell each into four divisions or tetrarchies, each division governed by a tetrarch with a judge under him; the judges tried civil cases, but criminal jurisdiction, and perhaps policy, was in the hands of a council of 300 elders, who met at their holy place Drynemetos,[4] perhaps a circular moot in a grove; from the

[1] Tscherikower *op. c.*; Sölch, *Klio* XIX, 140.
[2] Bibliography *C.A.H.* VII, 883. [3] Str. 567.
[4] Unidentified. Ruge, *Drynemeton* in P.W.; Loth, *Rev. E.A.* 1915, 193.

tetrarchs were chosen those war-leaders who appear in Greek and Roman literature as 'kings'. With the temple-state of Pessinus, which lay within their territory, they did not interfere till after 166, when they occupied Pessinus and their religion gradually became Phrygianised. The correspondence of Eumenes II, when suzerain of Galatia (183–166), with the priest-king of Pessinus, Attis,[1] is illuminating; Eumenes wrote to him as one king to another, and Attis' friendship supported his influence in Galatia, while Attis' brother had gone over to the Gauls, taken a Galatian name, and was striving to win the priesthood for himself, doubtless in Galatian interest and with Galatian support. Eumenes II built a temple and porticoes at Pessinus and finally broke what remained of Galatian power, and after the massacre of their aristocracy by Mithridates the Gauls began to adopt the general civilisation of the country; but even in the third century A.D. their language was not yet extinct and they still worshipped a Celtic god as Zeus Boussourigios.[2]

* * * * *

This chapter may properly conclude with some indication of the importance of the old Greek cities of Asia,[3] cities which with their ancient traditions, large populations, compact and busy life, growing wealth, magnificent public buildings, and vast walls, scarcely felt themselves inferior to a kingdom. Though none of these cities ever rivalled fourth-century Athens in size, much less Syracuse, Miletus in the second century, with her territory, perhaps had a population of nearly 100,000, including slaves,[4] while Ephesus was larger and Rhodes cannot have been much smaller. About 300 Miletus was still the greatest of the Ionian cities, firmly based on her wool trade and building the largest Greek temple in Asia; but subsequently Ephesus and Smyrna passed her. After 250 Smyrna[5] was in the

[1] *OGIS* 315. [2] Anderson, *J.H.S.* 1910, 163.

[3] Cf. J. S. Reid, *The Municipalities of the Roman Empire*, 1913; A. H. M. Jones, *The cities of the eastern Roman provinces*, 1937.

[4] Wiegand, *Siebenter Milet-Bericht* 26. Beloch IV, 1, 275 makes it much less. [5] Str. 646.

ascendant; her independence was complete, and a striking account remains of her relations with and hearty support of Seleucus II; when in 244 he crossed the Taurus Smyrna almost acted as his viceroy, for in his name she confirmed grants of land made by his father, engaged him to make new grants, and engaged his Treasury to make payments to mercenaries.[1] At Ephesus[2] the concentration of the eastern trade along the Apamea–Ephesus route, conjoined with Lysimachus' removal of the city to the sea after the old harbour silted up, brought about a great development; possibly Ephesus originated the cistophori[3] which became the typical coinage of the Pergamene kingdom, and spread throughout Asia Minor. In the second century the Attalids began to make her the port of their kingdom, but she never forgave their confiscations, and in 132 she seized her chance of revenge; her fleet defeated Aristonicus at sea, and cleared Rome's way into Asia. Thereon, though Pergamum was the formal capital of the Roman province of Asia, Ephesus became in fact the chief city, with the governor's seat and the provincial treasury. She was the natural gateway of the land, for she was more than a Greek city; her far-famed temple of the Asiatic fertility goddess, with its eunuchs and its consecrated girls, its prehistoric asylum and its sacred fish, belonged to an older world.

Passing northward, Magnesia on the Maeander could stretch her arms from Ithaca[4] to the Oxus; she helped to defend Delphi against the Gauls,[5] she gave to Bactrian Hellenism its most powerful dynasty[6] and thereby invaded India, and she helped the Seleucid to create Antioch towards Pisidia,[7] Antioch in Persis,[8] and doubtless, if we knew, other cities; there was not much infanticide in third-century Magnesia. Her great temple of Artemis Leukophryene, successor of the Dindymene Mother, was inferior in size only to those at Ephesus and Didyma (p. 314), and was said to be

[1] *OGIS* 229. [2] Str. 640 *sqq.* [3] Head[2] 575.
[4] Ditt.[3] 558. [5] *Ib.* 560.
[6] Euthydemus. Which Magnesia is disputed (*Camb. Hist. India* I. 440); but Polybius (XI, 34, 1) could hardly call the Lydian city 'Magnesia' *alone.* [7] Str. 577. [8] *OGIS* 233.

more beautiful than either. In actual strength, Heraclea Pontica about 280 probably surpassed any mainland city; she ruled a great territory, including other cities, and once boasted herself stronger than Seleucus[1]; but she could not hold her position in the later period. This applies also to Sinope; it had looked for a moment as if Lysimachus would make the Black Sea his lake and Sinope would queen it over a vast new trade[2]; but Lysimachus left no successor, and Sinope fell back to become the capital of the Pontic kings. But independent Cyzicus, with her wonderful double harbour and competent fleet, more than held her place; she had a good road up the Macestus valley to Sardes, and through her passed the trade between the Pergamene kingdom and the Black Sea[3]; Strabo ranks her with Rhodes, Carthage, and Marseilles.[4] Her policy was consistent friendship, possibly alliance, with Pergamum[5]; her relations with that monarchy resembled those of Rhodes with Egypt, and she gave to the dynasty its best queen, Apollonis (p. 98), whom she subsequently deified. Princes of many lines were sent to Cyzicus for their education.[6] In 277 she was already strong enough to fight the Galatian Trocmi single-handed[7]; but two centuries later she could face and almost capture Mithridates at the height of his power. Under Augustus she ruled an extensive territory, including old cities like Zelea, and performed a more dangerous feat than fighting Mithridates: she flogged some Romans.[8] She had good reason; but she was lucky to escape with nothing worse than five years of taxation.

But no other city—so Strabo says—was the equal of Rhodes.[9] In the historic siege of 304 she had successfully resisted the full power of Demetrius, and down to 166 she

[1] Memnon 11. [2] Newell, *A.J. Num.* 1918, 117
[3] F. W. Hasluck, *Cyzicus*, 171. [4] Str. 575 *sq.*
[5] *OGIS* 748. [6] App. *b.c.* IV, 320; Hasluck 177; Wilhelm, *Klio* V, 293.
[7] *OGIS* 748 l. 17 (dates are a year out). [8] Dio Cass. LIV, 7 and 23.
[9] Str. 652–5; Beloch IV, 1, 290; H. van Gelder, *Gesch. d. alten Rhodier*, 1900; E. Ziebarth in *Mélanges Glotz* II, 1932, 909; Rostovtzeff, *C.A.H.* VIII ch. XIX and bibliography, 790; *SEH* 677–91, 771–7, and notes, esp. 1485–7; P. Fraser, *Studies in the history and epigraphy of Hellenistic Rhodes* (forthcoming).

grew steadily in strength and resources; her merchants and bankers desired peace, but she stood for two things, a balance of power and a free sea, and for these she would always fight the aggressor; she helped Macedonia to pull down the overwhelming sea-power of Ptolemy II, Pergamum to check Philip V, Rome to defeat Antiochus III. Her government was a limited democracy,[1] or perhaps rather an aristocracy, under which, as in eighteenth-century England, power rested with the leading families; but they did their duty by the poor, and in spite of her cosmopolitan harbour population Rhodes never had internal troubles,[2] and could in an emergency arm her slaves. The surrounding islands were her demes, and she claimed the strange power of vetoing honours they might grant.[3] Magnificently situated, the trade between Egypt and the north, between Syria and the west, passed through her port; in 170 her 2 per cent. import and export duty produced a million drachmae,[4] and the mass of Rhodian amphorae handles found all over the world attest her trade. She was the centre of international banking and exchange, a key city of Hellenistic commerce; when in 225 she was shattered by an earthquake and a commercial crisis threatened, the Hellenistic world demonstrated its commercial solidarity by the lavish help in money and kind sent to her by every Greek-speaking king and many cities.[5]

By 200, when the Macedonian fleet had decayed, Rhodes ruled the Aegean, re-formed the Island League under her presidency like a king,[6] and kept piracy under; after 188 she ruled most of Caria and Lycia. When in 220 Byzantium put a toll on shipping passing the Bosphorus, Rhodes at once took measures to free the Straits.[7] Her fleet probably never exceeded some fifty ships at sea at once, but its quality

[1] Cic. *de Rep.* I, 31; III, 35.

[2] Dio Chrys. XXXI, 70.

[3] Ditt.[3] 570, 931; Ditt.[2] 491.

[4] Polyb. XXX, 31, 12. Two per cent. (a deduction) was the usual Greek figure: *I.G.* II[2], 1128; V, 1, 1421; Ditt.[3] 229; Michel 595; Delos, accounts *passim*.

[5] Polyb. V, 88–90; Diod. XXVI fr. 8.

[6] Demoulin, *B.C.H.* 1903, 233; Roussel, *ib.* 1907, 359; W. König, *Der Bund der Nesioten*, 1911.

[7] Polyb. IV, 38–49.

was the best in the world[1]; she had defeated Egyptian and Syrian fleets single-handed, and her boast ran that every Rhodian was worth a warship.[2] At Myonnesus, where the Roman fleet encountered that of Antiochus III, it was the Rhodian squadron which pulled Rome through; had the day gone otherwise it was still Rhodes' victory, for a Rhodian exile commanded for Antiochus. Entry to some of her arsenals was forbidden to the public under pain of death. The city was adorned with works of art, including many paintings by Protogenes and Parrhasius, the well-known Colossus (p. 318), and many other colossal statues, and in the second century was a centre of Greek learning, a home of philosophy and rhetoric, rendered illustrious by the names of Panaetius and Poseidonius; she long remained a considerable University. Her code of maritime law was famous, and was adopted by the Antonines; possibly fragments of it are imbedded in the Byzantine compilation called the *Rhodian Sea Law*,[3] and thence passed to Venice, the only Greek law which may thus in living form have reached the modern world.

[1] Polyb. XVI, 14, 4.

[2] Diogenianos, παροιμίαι V, 19.

[3] Dareste, *Rev. Phil.* 1905, 1; W. Ashburner, *The Rhodian Sea Law*, 1909; S. Runciman, *Byzantine Civilisation*, 1932, 77 and 174; Rostovtzeff, *SEH* 688.

CHAPTER V

EGYPT[1]

THE papyri which, during the last half-century or more, have been recovered from Egypt give a picture of that country under the Ptolemies far more detailed in some respects than anything else in Greek antiquity and, within its limitations, comparable in some ways to the picture which is made possible by the documents of modern history. But these limitations are very severe, because the survival of the

[1] Generally: besides the general histories (see p. 361), see, on the papyri, L. Mitteis and U. Wilcken, *Grundzüge und Chrestomathie der Papyruskunde*, 1912; Schubart, *Einführung*, 1918; K. Preisendanz, *Papyrusfunde und Papyrusforschung*, 1933; J. G. Winter, *Life and letters in the papyri*, 1933.

Fundamentally important are the works of M. Rostovtzeff, *C.A.H.* VII, ch. 4; *SEH* (with full notes and bibliography); and numerous special studies: and of Claire Préaux, *L'économie royale des Lagides*, 1939; and numerous studies mostly in *Chronique d'Égypte* (*C.d'É.*).

Useful surveys are those by W. Schubart, *Die Griechen in Ägypten*, 1927; P. Jouguet, *L'Égypte ptolémaique*, 1933 (in G. Hanoteaux, *Hist. de la nation égyptienne* III); and H. I. Bell, *Egypt from Alexander the Great to the Arab conquest*, 1948 (with bibliography of the papyri).

On the army, and the foreign populations: J. Lesquier, *Les institutions militaires de l'Égypte sous les Lagides*, 1911; Fr. Heichelheim, *Die auswärtige Bevölkerung im Ptolemäerreich*, and *Nachträge* in *Archiv* IX, 47 and XII, 54; W. Peremans, *Vreemdelingen en Egyptenaren in Vroeg-Ptolemaisch Egypte*, 1937 (with a summary in French); M. Launey, *Recherches sur les armées hellénistiques* I, 1949; II, 1950.

On the administration and law, besides the works of Rostovtzeff and Préaux cited above, *passim*, see: W. Schubart, *Verfassung und Verwaltung des Ptolemaerreichs*; V. Martin, 'Les papyrus et l'histoire administrative de l'Égypte gréco-romaine', *Münch. Beiträge z. Papyrusf.* 19, 1934, 102; P. Collart, 'La papyrologie et l'histoire du droit', *ib.* 186; R. Taubenschlag, *The law of Greco-Roman Egypt in the light of the papyri* I, 1944 M. T. Lenger, 'Les lois et ordonnances des Lagides', *C.d'É.* XXXVII, 1944, 108; E. Seidl, *Ptolemaische Rechtsgeschichte*, 1947; C. B. Welles, 'The Ptolemaic administration in Egypt , *Journ. Jurist. Pap.* III, 1949, 21.

For (especially) the Pharaonic background, see S. R. K. Glanville (ed.). *The Legacy of Egypt*.

papyri has been fortuitous and because their provenance (the country districts of Egypt and not the capital itself) ensures that local interests predominate and that it is only occasionally and incidentally that the high policies of the central government stand revealed in them.[1] Moreover Egypt is a world in itself, whose interest lies primarily in its economic system, a legacy (in its main principles) from the Egypt of the Pharaohs,[2] which became elaborated into the most thorough-going system of State nationalisation known prior to the twentieth century, unless conceivably the Peruvian; on Hellenism in general Egypt throws comparatively little light, and but for the Museum and Library at Alexandria would hardly have affected the development of Greek civilisation. For the Greek in Egypt remained a stranger amid the dense mass of natives, who would ultimately have absorbed him but for Rome's intervention. The country was not indeed peopled up to the limit under Ptolemy I, as there was still uncultivated land; tradition makes the population 7 or 7½ millions (excluding Alexandria) in the Hellenistic period, but some scholars have argued for higher figures.[3] Some Macedonians came with Ptolemy I and always held a privileged position, but were too few to matter; and the rule of the early Ptolemies reposed on Greeks, who flooded into the country down to the middle of the third century, whether as mercenaries or settlers. With them came Thracians and western Asiatics, most of whom, except the Jews, soon became hellenised[4]; in 252 there was a Roman in Ptolemy's army.[5]

For a time the Greeks ruled Egypt like a conquered country. This was not what Alexander had meant; in his system, while Europeans managed finance and the army of occupation, the civil government (under himself) was

[1] Cf. A. H. M. Jones, *Ancient economic history*, 1948, 2 (inaugural lecture).

[2] On the extent of that legacy opinion is divided: see Andreades, *Mélanges Maspéro* II, 1934–7, 289 *sqq.*; Préaux, *C.d'É.*, 1943, 148; Welles, *op. c. supra*, p. 177 n. 1.

[3] Discussed by Rostovtzeff, *SEH* 1137–8, 1605.

[4] Fr. Heichelheim, *op. c. supra*, p. 177 n. 1; Wilcken, *Archiv* VI, 385 (Thracians); Launey, *op. c. supra*, I, 87 *sqq.*

[5] H. I. Bell, *J.E.A.* 1922, 141. Cf. *Rev. E.G.* 1911, 400 no. 3.

entrusted to Egyptians; the nomes (divisions of the country) remained under native nomarchs, and he appointed native governors instead of a Macedonian satrap. Even Ptolemy I, while satrap, did not entirely discard Alexander's idea,[1] and gave more place to natives than they subsequently possessed; the change came when he initiated a policy of over-sea conquest. His immediate successors aimed at the empire of the Aegean and its coasts, and treated Egypt as a money-making machine; and under the first three Ptolemies no native, after 312, ever bore arms. But by the end of the third century the position had altered. In 217 the newly enrolled native troops won the battle of Raphia for Ptolemy IV, and learnt their importance; and, Greek immigration having ceased, the Greek element thenceforth lost ground to the Egyptian. It will be best to give a sketch of Ptolemaic Egypt and its system as it existed in the third century, and then notice the later changes, particularly as revealed by the great series of ordinances of Ptolemy Euergetes II.

The resemblances and divergences in the political, administrative, and economic systems of the Ptolemaic and Seleucid empires show that both systems derived from common sources but did not develop in the same way; the main differences lay in their economic policies and their attitudes toward Greek city-life. The Ptolemies were certain from the first that they could not found a strong state in Egypt, as the Seleucids were doing in Asia, on the basis of the Greek city; and though Ptolemy I would have been no Successor of Alexander's had he not founded some city, in Egypt he only founded one, Ptolemais in Upper Egypt, doubtless to counterbalance the centre of priestly influence at Thebes. Ptolemais[2] was in form an autonomous Greek city, but its autonomy was presently limited by the general of the Thebaid becoming its chief magistrate,[3] a measure which recalls the limited autonomy of Pergamum or Thessalonica. Naucratis continued to exist, but lost all

[1] Kornemann, *Raccolta Lumbroso* 235; cf. Tarn *C.Q.* 1929, 138.
[2] G. Plaumann, *Ptolemais in Oberägypten*, 1910.
[3] Plaumann, *op. c.* 29; cf. *OGIS* 51, 728.

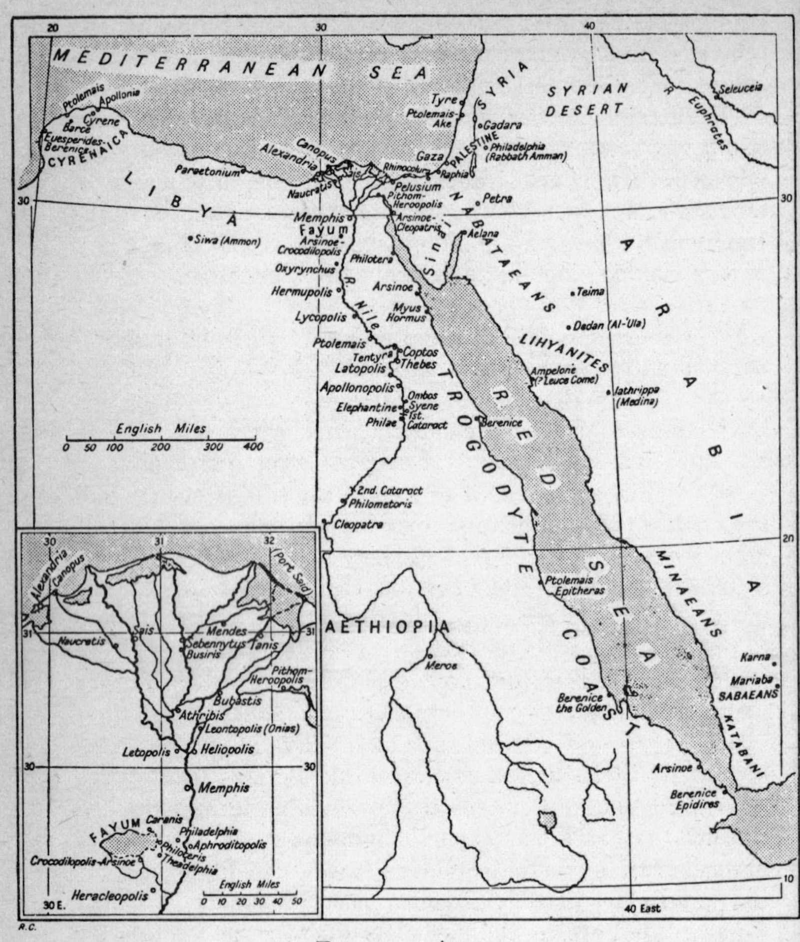

EGYPT AND ARABIA
(inset: The Delta and the Fayum)

importance in face of Alexandria[1]; and, Alexandria apart, the only activity shown by the Ptolemies in regard to cities was in their foreign possessions. These possessions were once very extensive, though they fluctuated from time to time.[2] The Ptolemies held or controlled the Cyclades, with some intermission, from 285 to 245; Samos from 281 to 201[3]; most of the coast of Asia Minor from the Calycadnus in Cilicia to Ephesus from *c.* 273 (or earlier) intermittently to 197, though many cities and districts often changed hands in their wars with the Seleucids; much of the Hellespontine and Thracian coasts with Lesbos and Samothrace from *c.* 241 to *c.* 202, including even Abdera in Macedonia's sphere; Southern Syria up to the Lebanon and much of Phoenicia, with a fluctuating boundary, till 200; Thera,[4] Methana in the Argolid,[5] and Itanos in Crete,[6] till 146; the Cyrenaica (except for its brief independence *c.* 258–246) till 96; and Cyprus, their last foreign possession, till 58.[7] They renamed many cities; Methana,[8] Patara in Lycia, some city in Ceos, all became Arsinoe.[9] But Arsinoe and Philadelphia in Cilicia[10] may be new foundations, and there were such in Syria, as Philoteria on Lake Gennesareth; while other native towns were refounded as Greek cities, Ake (Acre) becoming Ptolemais and Rabbath-Amman Philadelphia. Whether the foreign policy of the first three Ptolemies was defensive or aggressive has been much argued; one may suppose that they held southern Syria and Cyprus (with its ship-timber) for defensive purposes, but that everything beyond that was aggression.

[1] E. Marion Smith, 'Naucratis', in *Journ. Soc. Or. Res.* X, 1926, 147.

[2] Ernst Meyer, *Die Grenzen der hell. Staaten in Kleinasien*; Kahrstedt, *Syrische Territorien*; Otto, *Beiträge zur Seleukidengeschichte*; Tarn, *C.A.H.* VII, ch. 22; F. M. Abel, 'Les confins de la Palestine et de l'Égypte sous les Ptolemées', *Rev. bibl.*, 1939, 207 and 531; 1940, 55 and 224.

[3] For inscriptions of the Ptolemaic period, L. Robert, *Études epigraphiques et philologiques*, 1938, 113.

[4] *I.G.* XII, 3, Index IV.

[5] *OGIS* 102, 115.

[6] Ditt.[3] 685 l. 42.

[7] Sir George Hill, *Hist. of. Cyprus*, I (1940), esp. 173 *sqq.*

[8] Hiller, *'Εφ. 'Αρχ.* 1925–6, 68.

[9] Str. 666; Ditt.[3] 562. See Tscherikower *op. c.*, index *s.v.* Arsinoe.

[10] Tscherikower 39 makes Philadelphia much later. I doubt this.

The Greek cities in their foreign possessions were frankly subject towns and, as such, taxed, and the form of government was connected with the Egyptian form. One innovation of the Ptolemies in Egypt had been to abolish the native nomarchs and govern the nomes by Greek or Macedonian generals, as though they were satrapies; the foreign possessions were also governed by generals, as was usual in all Macedonian kingdoms, with *epistatai* (city governors) over the cities.[1] But the important thing was that the internal affairs of these Greek cities were under the control, not only of Ptolemy through the general and *epistates*, but of the finance minister (*dioiketes*) at Alexandria; for just as in each nome there stood beside the general a subordinate of the finance minister, an *oikonomos*, so there was an *oikonomos* as well as a general in provinces like Caria, exercising authority in the Greek cities.[2] No other monarchy went to this length, and it suggests an attempt to introduce the Egyptian economic system into the Greek world. How far this was really done is unfortunately unknown; but the Greek Lesbos, besides money taxes, paid a tax in corn,[3] which means that its city-land was treated as though it were King's land; at Halicarnassus there was seemingly a trierarchy to help maintain Egypt's navy[4]; and Ptolemy II attempted to replace the city-coinages in Asia by his own.[5] Syria was doubtless organised somewhat on the Egyptian model, but not nearly so thoroughly; beside the priest-state of Judaea, native chiefs like the Tobiads in Ammon (p. 212) still existed under Ptolemaic suzerainty, and perhaps even owned the lands which they administered.[6]

As regards public works in Egypt, Ptolemy I founded the Library and Museum (p. 269), while Ptolemy II completed the Library, restored the canal which Darius I had con-

[1] *OGIS* 44, 113, 134; Tscherikower however (*Mizraim* 1937, 38) doubts the existence of a *strategos* in South Syria.

[2] *P. Cairo Zen.* 59036–7. Fully in Rostovtzeff, *C.A.H.* VII.

[3] Wilcken, *Chrestomathie* no. 2.

[4] *P. Cairo Zen.* 59036; see Wilcken, *Raccolta Lumbroso*, 93.

[5] *P. Cairo Zen.* 59021; Schubart, *Z. f. Num.* 1921, 68.

[6] Tscherikower, *loc. c.*

structed to connect the Red Sea with the Nile by way of the Bitter Lakes, and early in his reign began to drain Lake Moeris to create the Arsinoïte nome, the Fayum, thus recovering much fertile land which he made a centre of Greek settlement[1]; the original swamp was ultimately reduced to a lake about the size of Lake Karun to-day. The caravan route from Coptos on the Nile to Berenice on the Red Sea was equipped with wells and block-houses[2]; there was a swift official post modelled on the Persian, and a slower method of forwarding heavy parcels and persons, based on a system of requisitioning draught animals along the route[3]; Ptolemy II introduced the camel,[4] and later a camel post ran from the south to Alexandria. The notable series of explorations along the Red Sea coast are mentioned elsewhere (Chap. VII). But the greatest achievement was probably the completion of Alexandria.

Alexandria,[5] called Alexandria *by* Egypt and distinguished from the rest of Egypt as 'the city', stood on the neck of land between the sea and Lake Mareotis, with harbours on both. Deinocrates had laid it out on the rectangular plan usual in Hellenistic cities (p. 310) and found even in Greek villages in the Fayum; but the roads actually uncovered are Roman, and the Hellenistic city is known principally from Strabo, who describes a great street 100 feet wide running east and west, and crossed at right angles by a second. Several streets bore the cult-names of Arsinoe II.[6] Alexander had joined the island of Pharos to the mainland by a mole seven furlongs long called Heptastadion, which formed

[1] Topography: *P. Tebt.* II App. II; cf. Rostovtzeff, *SEH* I, 420, for Philadelphia the new settlement (not a city in the Greek sense).

[2] *OGIS* 132.

[3] Rostovtzeff, *Klio* VI, 249; Preisigke, *ib.* VII, 241.

[4] Athen. 200 F; *P. Cairo Zen.* 59008, 59010, 59143, 59207; *P.S.I.* VI, 562.

[5] Str. 791–5, 801; Diod. XVII, 52; Ausfeld, *Rh. Mus.* 1900, 348; E. Breccia, *Alexandrea ad Aegyptum*, Eng. ed. 1922; Schubart, *Ägypten von Alexander d. Gr. bis auf Mohamed*, 1922; Bell, *J.E.A.* 1927, 171; E. Leider, *Der Handel von Alexandria*, 1935; Bell, *J.R.S.* XXXVI, 1946, 130: see most recently, on the site of the harbour, Sir Halliday Savile, *Antiquity*, 1941, 209; cf. G. Jondet, *Atlas historique de la ville et les ports d'Alexandrie*, 1921, Pl. LII.

[6] Bell, *Archiv* VII, 17.

a double harbour, a type known at Syracuse, Sinope, and Cyzicus; to the east of the mole was a natural basin, now neglected, to the west an artificial port, Eunostos, formed by breakwaters, and connected with Lake Mareotis by a canal. Each had a small closed inner harbour opening from it—from the eastern harbour Ptolemy's private port, and from Eunostos the war harbour, Kibotos. The harbour on Lake Mareotis took the Nile traffic and was said to clear a bigger tonnage even than the sea-harbours; there lay the gorgeous pleasure fleet of Ptolemy II, and later the splendid villa mounted on a barge built for Ptolemy IV. On the eastern harbour lay the Royal quarter, Brucheion, where amid temples and spacious gardens stood the Palace, the Museum and Library, the quarters of the Guard, the tombs of the Ptolemies, and the wonderful tomb built for Alexander's body by Ptolemy II when he brought it from Memphis, a tomb still regarded as holy by the Roman Emperors and to which Caracalla made a pilgrimage. Over the whole kept watch the Pharos, the lighthouse erected on the island by Sostratus of Cnidus for the safety of mariners (p. 313).

Within the city were the buildings which housed the central bureaux of the whole administration, the central stores for corn, oil, and other products, the Hall of Justice, and the Gymnasium; beyond the east gate lay the stadium, and the hippodrome for chariot races; in the west, near the native quarter, stood the great temple of Sarapis[1]; an artificial hill dedicated to Pan gave a view of the whole city. Shops and bazaars lined the central thoroughfare, and by 100 the houses were probably several storeys high; lodging houses were known, managed by the owner's slaves. A canal brought Nile water to the city, distributed through conduits to fill a system of underground cisterns,[2] from which

[1] Wilcken, *Archiv* VII, 78. See now A. Rowe, 'Discovery of the famous temple and enclosure of Serapis at Alexandria', (*Suppl. des Annales du Service*, 1946); reviewed by C. Préaux, *C.d'É.* 48, 1949, 362. The question whether the temple, built by Ptolemy III, of which the foundations have now been discovered, can be that of Parmeniscus is still unresolved; cf. P. Jouguet, *Hommages à Joseph Bidez et à Franz Cumont*, 1949, 159.

[2] Hirtius, *Bell. Alex.* 5.

the inhabitants drew; later on some houses apparently could get their water by pumping. The city overflowed its wall on both sides; on the west lay the native Egyptian quarter, on the east, beyond the suburb of Eleusis, the gardens of the wealthy extended to Canopus, Alexandria's playground. By 200 Alexandria was the greatest city of the known world, though Rome passed her later; by Augustus' time the total population was perhaps a million.[1] In a recently discovered dialogue an enthusiast claims that Alexandria *is* the world: the whole earth is her city-land, and other cities only her villages.[2] Something of her wealth and magnificence under Ptolemy II can be gathered from Callixenus' account, preserved by Athenaeus, of that king's festival procession.

That this vast agglomeration of humanity could ever be a 'city' in the strict Greek sense was a physical impossibility.[3] Alexandria was a collection of *politeumata* (p. 147), based on nationalities, the Greek *politeuma* being much the most important; outside these stood a few privileged Macedonians at one end and the mass of Egyptians at the other. It had not even a city Council (though some think otherwise)[4]; and Wilcken's argument[5] that Alexander could not have founded a city without a Council presupposes that what he founded was a 'city', a *polis*, whereas his foundations were probably of a new mixed type. The Greek *politeuma* of Alexandria, however, approximated more closely to the *polis* type than any other actually known; the Greeks were called 'the citizens', 'the Alexandrians', and were divided into tribes[6]; they supplied the magistrates, of Greek type, who looked after building, public health, and so on, and also

[1] Beloch IV, 1, 287, makes it too small. *SEG* III, 378 B l. 9, speaks of the king who ruled in Alexandria and Egypt.

[2] *P. Berl.* 13045 l. 28, in *B.G.U.* VII, 13; cf. Lumbroso in *Archiv* VIII, 60.

[3] On this section: *Dikaiomata*; Schubart, *Klio* X, 41, and *Einführung* 245, 280, 284; Plaumann, *Archiv* VI, 77, *Klio* XIII, 485. On politeumata, besides p. 147 n. 4, see Rostovtzeff, *SEH* 1401 n. 137.

[4] Bell, *Jews and Christians in Egypt*, 1924 (Claudius' letter); see *J.E.A.* XI, 95; XIII, 98, 106; XIV, 146; XV, 123; XVII, 128; and especially *Aegyptus* XII, 1932, 173, 'The problem of the Alexandrian senate'.

[5] *Archiv* VII, 308, 310.

[6] Perdrizet, *Rev. E.A.* 1910, 217

Greek courts which administered a law compounded of the 'city law'—the law of the Greek citizens—and royal rescripts, and which seemingly had jurisdiction over all the inhabitants except (after the third century)[1] the Jewish *politeuma*; the land attached to Alexandria was the land 'of the Alexandrians', *i.e.* of the Greek *politeuma*, and if a Council be ever discovered it is probable that it will be that *politeuma*'s governing council, which must have existed. There were, however, many Greek inhabitants not members of the Greek *politeuma*, and the whole population was subject to Ptolemy's governor,[2] who in the later period had military power; there were other royal officials, like the prefect of police, the *exegetes* (who wore the purple), and the *eutheniarch*; one of the two latter may have managed the food supply,[3] but the king himself saw to it that the great city was fed.[4] The interesting thing about the constitution is to see the personal 'city law' of the Greeks, by its extension to non-Greeks, well on its way to become a true territorial law; this may have been part of Alexander's scheme for fusing different races, and certainly, after Graeco-Egyptian intermarriage began in the second century, Alexandria, apart from the Jews and a minority of Greeks, did ultimately fuse into a more or less homogeneous mass, turbulent, crazy for shows, sarcastic and sometimes hostile towards the dynasty, for which at the end it nevertheless fought and which it long regretted.

To describe the Ptolemaic system is to describe a body without a head, for all threads ran to Alexandria, and of the central bureaux there nothing is known; the extant information comes from the country. Already under the Persians payment in money was displacing payment in kind, and the process gained momentum under the Ptolemies; but the latter form of economy still persisted, and capital was always relatively scarce in the country, interest being 24 per cent.

[1] Because of Mitteis, *Chrestomathie* no. 21.
[2] Polyb. V, 39; *OGIS* 743; Schubart, *Klio* X, 68.
[3] Cf. Wilcken, *Grundzüge* 365 n. 5; Bell, *J.E.A.* XIII, 174.
[4] Kunkel, *Archiv* VIII, 212 no. 15; Wilcken, *Hermes* LXIII, 48.

to 26 per cent.,[1] rates unknown in Greece except upon maritime loans. As regards the fellahin, the basis of the system was that each man had his 'own place', which he could not leave except by official order or permission.[2] The germs of the monopoly system have been traced in the old temple monopolies of Pharaonic times and in the famous corner in wheat brought off by Alexander's financial superintendent Cleomenes[3] when he was virtually in control of the country; but the system as we know it appears as the creation of Ptolemy II, though conceivably his father originated it.

The king was the State; and Ptolemy I after Perdiccas' death had claimed Egypt as 'spear-won' territory,[4] which by Macedonian custom passed to the king. He therefore claimed to own the entire soil of Egypt, except the lands of Naucratis, Alexandria, and Ptolemais: not only the old royal domains, but also the temple lands and the lands of the feudal nobility, whom the Ptolemies abolished. The entire land[5] was divided into two categories only: King's land in the narrower sense, *i.e.* land in hand, and land in grant. King's land was farmed for Ptolemy by the 'royal peasants', the 'king's people'. These formed a substantial part of the fellahin population of the villages, and their ancestors had cultivated King's land for untold centuries; many were small peasants, but among them were farmers of some substance. Their customary tenure became partly translated into Greek forms: they were registered as lessees. But they had no written leases and the king did not undertake the corresponding duties of a lessor; and as they could not leave their villages, were compelled to cultivate their land and could be compelled to cultivate more if ground fell vacant (for the State was built up on the maxim that the king's cultivation must be carried on), could have their animals

[1] Beloch IV, 1, 323.

[2] Rostovtzeff, *Kolonat* 305–8; Wilcken, *Grundzüge* 26.

[3] Ehrenberg, *Alexander und Ägypten*, 50; Tarn, *Alex.* II, 303–5, and notes.

[4] Diod. XVIII, 39, 5.

[5] Land: to general works cited add Rostovtzeff, *Kolonat* ch. 1 and in *J.E.A.* VI, 165; Kornemann, *Bauernstand* in P.W.

requisitioned, gave compulsory labour on the dykes and canals, and could be turned out at any time, they differed little in fact from serfs. How much of Egypt was King's land is unknown; certainly a very substantial part, and in the Fayum and the Delta perhaps the larger part.

Land in grant fell into four classes: (*a*) temple lands, (*b*) cleruch land, (*c*) gift land, and (*d*) the so-called private land. (*a*) The king, who was also an Egyptian god, cultivated the former temple lands himself, allotted what produce was required to the temple, and kept the rest. Probably extensive lands in the Thebaid belonged to this class. (*b*) The cleruchs (holders of a *kleros* or military allotment) were military settlers, originally mercenaries of many nationalities, Greeks predominating, grouped in settlements; to place them on the land ensured a supply of soldiers. In the third century they received good land; but subsequently they were settled on waste or uncultivated ground, the user being sold to them at a low price on terms that they should reclaim their lots; they could make it corn-land or garden-land as they wished (vineyards being reckoned with garden-land), and paid rent accordingly, for corn-land in corn, for garden-land in money; their rents were not heavy, as part of their rent was their obligation to military service. If a cleruch died, or failed to render his rent or military service, the king could resume the land; but by 218 the 'lot' had become heritable and passed to the cleruch's son, and later it became alienable.[1] (*c*) Gift land meant an extensive estate, comprising one or more villages with their lands, conferred on some official, who became the superior of the village authorities; the object was to get the land fully developed through his agency, but the king could resume the estate. The Zeno papyri have supplied much information about the estate in the Fayum bestowed by Ptolemy II on his finance minister Apollonius.[2] (*d*) Private land originally meant house, garden, and vineyard; even the house and

[1] Préaux, *Écon. royale*, 463–77.

[2] *P. Cairo Zen.* and *P.S.I.*; Rostovtzeff, *A large estate in Egypt*, 1922; F. Zucker, *Hist. Zeits.* 1924, 69.

garden of a royal peasant were 'private'. Greeks sometimes called it property, but it was, like every other Ptolemaic form, not property but user; apart from the Greek cities, the property or legal estate in any land in Egypt never left the king. But the kings presently began to give to civilians the perpetual user of land other than house and garden—waste land, or cleruch land that had escheated, or even King's land that had become unoccupied; and this land also was reckoned 'private'. It grew greatly in importance by the first century, and even more under Roman rule; as the cleruchs furnished the military element of the State, so the 'private' occupiers probably staffed the smaller offices of the bureaucracy. One may compare the parallel forms in Seleucid Asia, where civil colonies are perhaps found alongside the military ones (p. 154).

We pass to the economic system itself.[1] The main Egyptian staple was wheat. All corn-land, in whatsoever hand, paid a tax in corn direct to the king[2]; and on the King's land no part of the crop belonged to the peasant till he had taken out the king's quota, which was the larger share, and transported this to the king's barn in his village. While in Asia the Seleucids were partners with the peasantry and must have shared losses in a bad year (p. 142), in Egypt every parcel of ground cultivated by the native peasantry contributed its allotted amount to the king as a first charge, loss falling on the cultivator alone[3]; this was one of the sources of Ptolemy's great wealth. The royal peasants had not more than enough left to live on; the king supplied next year's seed corn. From the village barns the wheat passed to the central barn of the nome, and was thence taken down the Nile and stored in the King's Barn in Alexandria; the wheat was a second Nile, a vast river fed by a thousand rills

[1] Cf. the works cited p. 177, see especially, for this section, Rostovtzeff, *SEH* 300 *sqq.*, Préaux, *Écon. royale*, 61 *sqq.*, Heichelheim, P.W., *s.v. Monopole.*

[2] Cf. A. H. Gardiner, *P. Wilbour* II and III, 1948, for the same principle, it seems, in Ramesid land assessments.

[3] Wilcken, *Grundzüge* 171. Seemingly this may not apply to large holdings, Greek or otherwise.

pouring down to the capital.[1] Ptolemy was the greatest corn merchant the world had seen.

For the staples which were royal monopolies or contained some element of monopoly, like textiles and oil,[2] the treatment differed, as was dictated for textiles by the raw materials themselves. Although the king could decide each year how much flax should be sown in the country, he could not decide with any precision how many sheep could be reared: the most he could do here was to impose a 20 per cent. import duty on foreign wool,[3] which led to Apollonius experimenting with Milesian sheep (the merino of Greece) within the tariff wall.[4] For wool and linen alike no attempt seems to have been made to 'corner' the raw material by enforcing its sale to the king only. The royal workshops took what was needed probably to supply the court, the army and (in the case of linen) the export trade; but in the wool-weaving industry much seems to have been left to private enterprise as well. The weaving of linen was more closely controlled, though it was not a complete monopoly. Although each nome, and each weaver, was under orders to produce for the State goods of a certain quantity and quality, and the individual was liable to make good in money any deficiency, it seems that there was no ban on production over and above the quota for the State. The temples, for example, were still allowed to produce for themselves, provided that they produced their quota. As to the marketing of textile products, it is still uncertain to what extent prices and quantities were regulated by the government.

But the great royal monopoly was oil.[5] The olive, though long since introduced into Egypt, was scarce; the trees were planted for ornament, and the olives were only used as

[1] On the transport of grain from the nomes to Alexandria, see *P. Tebt.* III, 703 ll. 70–87; Rostovtzeff, *SEH* 1391 n. 115; E. Börner, *Der staatl. Korntransport in gr.-röm. Ägypten*, Diss. Hamburg, 1939.

[2] For textiles, see especially in addition to the works cited, p. 177 n. 1; *P. Tebt.* III, i, 703.

[3] *P. Cairo Zen.* 59012.

[4] *Ib.* 59195.

[5] B. P. Grenfell and J. P. Mahaffy, *The revenue laws of Ptolemy Philadelphus* (Revenue papyrus).

fruit,[1] and oil was derived from sesame (the best), croton, linseed, safflower, and colocynth (gourd seeds). The king decided each year how much land should be planted with oil-producing plants; planting was compulsory, and the king took the whole produce at a fixed price; the oil was made in the state factories, the workers being serfs, compelled to work and tied to their 'own place' unless shifted elsewhere by official orders; finally the oil was distributed through retailers at a fixed price. To prevent competition, there was a heavy import duty on foreign oil[2]; in 259 Ptolemy II sold his oil in Egypt at 52 drachmae the metretes, and the import duty was 50 per cent., with a regulation that oil imported must be sold to himself at 46 drachmae. It worked thus. The shipper of Greek oil had to pay 26 Ptolemaic drachmae duty and also the Alexandrian harbour and other dues, about 2 drachmae, and sell at 46 Ptolemaic drachmae; that left him some 18 Ptolemaic drachmae the metretes to cover the cost price of the oil, the 2 per cent. export duty of the city he shipped from, the cost of the voyage, and his own profit; he therefore could not ship oil to Egypt unless its cost price were very far below 18 Ptolemaic drachmae, which was equivalent to about 15 Attic (Alexander) drachmae. But about 259 the retail price of free oil at Delos ranged from 21 to 17 Attic drachmae; that is, the Egyptian duty was calculated to prevent import altogether, and if nevertheless Apollonius did import olive oil, using his own ships, the great *dioiketes* could afford to pay for his fancies. But Ptolemy took no chances; if anyone, despite the duty, *did* take foreign oil up the Nile for his own use he paid another 12 per cent., and if he tried to sell it it was confiscated and he was fined 100 drachmae the metretes. Oil was a cast-iron monopoly, in which everything was nationalised—production, fabrication, distribution;

[1] *P. Cairo Zen.* 59159, 59184; Str. 809; Ch. Dubois, *Rev. Phil.* 1925, 60; 1927, 7.

[2] These figures, from *P. Cairo Zen.* 59012, 59015 (*recto*), and the Revenue papyrus, are given by me in rather more detail, with the Delos references, *J.E.A.* XIV, 257. Mlle. Préaux' calculations, *Écon. royale* 85, differ slightly from mine.

and Ptolemy's profits ranged from 70 per cent. on sesame oil to 300 per cent. or more on colocynth.[1]

Of many other things the king had either a monopoly[2] or a share in the business.[3] The manufacture of papyrus, the world's writing material, perhaps became a monopoly under Ptolemy II. In 333 a roll of papyrus cost in Greece 2 drachmae; in 296, with Egypt opened up, a drachma bought several rolls; but after 279 (under the monopoly?) a roll averaged nearly 2 drachmae again.[4] Further monopolies were mines, quarries, saltworks, and natron pits (carbonate of soda, used as soap); possibly too the business of fulling cloth. Hemp was treated like flax. All imported spices had to be sold to the king at his own price. He had a 25 per cent. share in all fisheries and all honey, with corresponding 25 per cent. import duties to protect his interests.[5] He owned part of the merchant fleet on the Nile, and perhaps leather factories; Cleopatra ran a wool mill, possibly with her own maids.[6] Banking was really a monopoly; there was a State bank in Alexandria, and banks in the nome capitals and the villages, let out to private individuals, which beside banking and moneychanging acted as branches of the State bank (if indeed they were not really branches under officials),[7] receiving the money taxes and making payments on Treasury account like the so-called State banks in Greek cities (p. 116). Many businesses beside banking, *e.g.* brewing, bee-keeping, and breeding pigs, could only be carried on by purchasing an annual licence from the Treasury; conceivably this applied to all businesses not monopolised. The king owned all pasture land, and had large herds of cattle; the royal peasants, after reaping their corn, had to grow a green crop

[1] Deduced from *Rev. P.* p. 151.

[2] Fullest list, Wilcken, *Grundzüge* 239–57.

[3] Generally: Wilcken, *Schmoller's Jahrb.* XLV, 49; Rostovtzeff, *J.E.A.* 1920, 161; N. Lewis, *L'industrie du papyrus dans l'Égypte gréco-romaine*, 1934, 125.

[4] Refs. Glotz, *J. d. Savants* 1913, 28; *Bull. soc. arch. Alex.* XXV, 1930, 83; Lewis, *op. c.* 152; Rostovtzeff, *SEH* 1391 n. 111. We cannot be sure, however, that the roll was always of the same length or quality.

[5] *P. Cairo Zen.* 59012; Wilcken, *Chrest.* no. 167.

[6] Oros. VI, 19, 20.

[7] So Wilcken, *Schmoller's J.* XLV, 85; Préaux, *Écon. royale* 280.

on which they fed the royal cattle. He also owned large flocks of pigs and geese, which were let out; no tree could be cut in Egypt but by his leave, for it was rooted in his soil.

Last came the *apomoira*,[1] a tax of one-sixth of the produce of vineyards, paid in kind, and of orchards and gardens, paid in money. The *apomoira* had belonged to the temples, but in 266/5 Ptolemy II diverted it to the cult of the deified Arsinoe Philadelphus, which probably meant that part went to the Treasury. As in addition to the *apomoira* Ptolemy II took a 33⅓ per cent. tax[2] on the produce of vineyards, orchards, and gardens, based on a three years' average, a large part of the year's vintage was his, even though wine delivered in kind at once passed into trade through the financial officials; the 33⅓ per cent. import duty[3] on fine Greek wines corresponded to the tax, nicely calculated so as not to spoil Ptolemy's wine-business and yet admit those Ionian wines which Alexandria could not do without. The form of the tax on vineyards made Ptolemy a partner with the vine-growers, who were often Greeks—a sort of racial discrimination, as he was not a partner with the Egyptian corn-growers; though generally speaking the kings had little race-prejudice as such.[4] What happened to the natural monopolies in the countries which Egypt ruled—the silphium of Cyrene, the balsam of Jericho, the bitumen of the Dead Sea—is unknown.

These measures meant that, just as all the land in Egypt belonged to Ptolemy, so in a sense did all business, for those businesses which were not royal monopolies could, it seems, only be carried on upon terms either of purchasing a licence to do so or rendering to the king part of the product.

In addition there was a formidable list of money taxes and duties. A succession duty on estates; a house duty of

[1] Fully in Bevan 183.

[2] *P. Cairo Zen.* 59170, 59012, with Edgar's commentary, *Ann. Serv.* XIX, 23, 85, XXIII, 73; Rostovtzeff, *Large Estate*, 99; Westermann, *J.E.A* XII, 38.

[3] *P. Cairo Zen.* 59012.

[4] Préaux, *Écon. royale* 451 n. 3; Westermann, *American. Hist. Rev.* XLIII, 1937-8, 270-2, with good notes.

5 per cent. on the rent; a 10 per cent. tax on sales; 2 per cent. on sales in a market; $33\frac{1}{3}$ per cent. on dovecots[1]; taxes on cattle and slaves; a poll tax, though apparently at differential rates, on the whole country except the priests and some privileged bodies—an economic measure and not, as was once believed, 'a political impost intended to mark the inferior status of the Egyptians"[2] There was an octroi on goods passing from Upper to Lower Egypt, and from the country into the towns; a 2 per cent. import and export duty at the Nile harbours; and import and export duties, some very heavy, at Alexandria and the other seaports. There were taxes for a gold crown on the king's accession, taxes to maintain the fleet and the lighthouse, and taxes for local objects, as police, doctors, baths. The reform was introduced of separating the Treasury from the king's privy purse, the latter being under an official called the *Idios Logos*[3] ('private account'), subordinate to the *dioiketes*; among other things (judging from the regulations of Augustus' time) all exposed babies were Ptolemy's perquisite and were collected by the *Idios Logos* as saleable articles.[4] The care taken over trifles was astounding; the great Apollonius makes a few shillings by selling his roses,[5] and re-uses Milesian oil jars.[6] Unhappily the income of the Ptolemies is unknown[7]; but the dynasty was generally regarded as much the richest thing in the world, and accumulated that 'Treasure of the Ptolemies' which so excited Roman covetousness.

To run a State on these lines full statistics were necessary; and the system of registration was very thorough. Every village had its land register, kept up to date, which described every parcel of land in the village territory; the capital of the

[1] A. Hunt, *J.E.A.* XII, 113.

[2] H. I. Bell, *J.E.A.* XXIII, 1937, 135; Préaux, *Écon. royale*, 382; Rostovtzeff, *SEH* 1392 n. 117; Bell, *J.R.S.* XXXVII, 1947, 17.

[3] Str. 797; *OGIS* 188.

[4] *BGU* V, 1, *Der Gnomon des Idios Logos*, § § 41, 107.

[5] *P. Cairo Zen.* 59269.

[6] *Ib.* 59015 (*recto*) (259 B.C., Miletus was in revolt).

[7] Jerome's figure (on Daniel xi, 5), 14,800 talents under Ptolemy II is worth little.

nome had a register for the nome, compiled from the village registers; at Alexandria there must have been a register for the whole country, compiled from the nome registers. There must have been a register of houses; all draught oxen and working animals were registered; if a man bought a licence to go fishing an agent followed him to register his catch. The official land register sufficed for the taxation of real property; taxation of movables was based on a system of declarations by the owners combined with official inspection. A form of census of the population was probably taken annually.[1] Supervision was as thorough as registration; everything was inspected, and Ptolemy knew each day what each of his subjects was worth and what most of them were doing. There was probably no such thing as independent trade in the home market, unless in the Greek cities; retail traders were only State agents for distribution, with their profits fixed. Even when the taxes collected in money were farmed out it was not a free operation, unless in the foreign possessions; the tax-farmer was controlled by the State[2]—about the best thing the Ptolemies did—and was only a piece of machinery for collecting the taxes; but care was taken that he did collect them, for, if he did not pay the calculated amount, his property and that of his sureties could be confiscated. Not only the royal peasants but other farmers were ordered what crops to sow; even Apollonius once received such an order, which could only have been given by Ptolemy II personally.[3] All the ploughing oxen of the royal peasants were at the State's disposal, and at seed time and harvest were so distributed as to get the land cultivated to the best advantage. A good deal was done to improve agriculture[4]; beside the stricter organisation, new seeds were experimented with[5] and Arabian sheep were introduced[6]; Apollonius too imported Milesian sheep for his estate,[7] and planted fir-trees to see if Egypt's dearth of

[1] Wilcken, *Grundzüge* 173.
[2] *Rev. P.* A col. 1 *sqq.*
[3] *P. Cairo Zen.* 59155.
[4] R. Johannsen, *C.P.* 1923, 156; *P. Cairo Zen.* 59033, 59156–7, 59159; Pliny XII, 56, 76.
[5] Athen. 369 F.
[6] *P. Cairo Zen.* 59430.
[7] *Ib.* 59195.

timber were curable[1]; by Augustus' time olives were plentiful in the Fayum.[2] The planting and care of trees native to the country was not neglected.[3]

The system necessitated a whole army of officials, administrative and financial. For administration, each nome was divided into *topoi* and each *topos* comprised so many villages; over each village and each *topos* were two native officials, and, theoretically, two in each nome, the nomarch and his scribe. But the general was really head of the nome, his functions being chiefly civil and legal, though his name remained a symbol of conquest. The *dioiketes* or finance minister, the second man in the kingdom, was head of the financial side, and appointed the smaller financial officials; from his bureau in Alexandria he exercised control over the two great centres there, the King's Barn for the corn and natural produce, the State Bank for the taxes in money. In the nome capitals and the villages were the nome and village barns in which the corn was collected on its way to Alexandria, with their appropriate officials, and the nome and village banks, through which the money taxes passed; these were looked after by the subordinate of the *dioiketes* in each nome, the *oikonomos*, but later this office was doubled, one *oikonomos* for the produce and one for the money. No trust was placed in the honesty of the financial officials; they not only had to find sureties, but to each was assigned a 'counter-scribe' or checker; when a peasant brought his corn to the barn he got no receipt till the checker had verified the barn-master's weighing. If enough men did not volunteer, the smaller offices were filled compulsorily.

Ptolemy, as absolute monarch, was the fount of law,[4] and his rescripts had legal force. But the ordinary administration of law[5] had to take account of two different systems, the Greek and the Egyptian; for though Greeks had come from many cities, their law had to be treated as a whole, and in fact the 'city law' of Alexandria shows a mixture of

[1] *P. Cairo Zen.* 59157.
[2] Str. 809.
[3] *P. Tebt.* III, 1, 703 l. 191.
[4] P. 57 n. 2.
[5] Rostovtzeff, *C.A.H.* VII, 894 (bibliography).

elements from Athens and (possibly) Asia Minor.[1] The Ptolemies recognised the Greek principle that law was personal, not territorial, and that the Egyptians must live under their own law; they had their old native judges, the Laocritae, their native land-law was translated into Greek, and later in the third century a special tribunal was erected to judge disputes between Greeks and Egyptians, taking account of both laws. For judging Greeks, panels of judges called Chrematistae, usually three in a panel, were created, each panel going circuit in its own district; appeals lay to the Chief Justice in Alexandria. Egyptian law could be pleaded before the Chrematistae, and they tended in time to oust the Laocritae. Naturally the two laws began to influence each other, but on the whole the Greek grew at the expense of the Egyptian. But much more important was the encroachment of the administration upon the law. A judge is actually found taking orders from Apollonius,[2] and even Greeks, if in conflict with the Treasury, were not allowed to employ advocates.[3] Also a habit grew up of taking to the administrative officials all small matters (magistrate's cases) instead of waiting for assizes, and in the second century the officials were fast cutting into the judges' powers, apparently in every sort of civil case; their decisions were apparently informal, not judicial, but people were content with the speedier and easier way. The same thing then was happening in Egypt as with the judicial commissions in Greece (p. 89): informal jurisdiction gained ground on the regular jurisdiction. Finally in Egypt the whole vast class of royal peasants and monopoly workers were withdrawn from the sphere of the regular courts and placed under the jurisdiction of the financial officials and the *dioiketes*, who gave severe sentences; administration and law had become confounded, normally a very bad thing, and administration had usurped the law's powers.

Egyptian society in the third century was sharply divided;

[1] *Dikaiomata*. [2] *P. Cairo Zen.* 59202–3.
[3] Letter of Ptolemy II, *P. Amherst* II, 33.

the upper stratum, which supplied the bureaucracy, comprised the Egyptian priestly caste, the cleruchs (who were tending to form a military aristocracy), the civilian occupiers of 'private' land, and the Greeks of the three cities; the lower consisted of the vast mass of fellahin. The fellahin had no education, and orders, especially those relating to taxes, were often issued in demotic,[1] the late-Egyptian speech of the time. They suffered from the very efficiency of the system under which they lived; it had been tightened up till there were none of those loopholes for evasion which have so often tempered rigorous conditions in the East. Poor as their life was, they knew nothing better; but it is obvious, from the numerous risings from 216 onwards, that there was much discontent. For wages, an artisan got 2–3 obols a day, a labourer (in 254) one obol for heavy work, less for light.[2] Even on the wretched Greek standard (p. 120) such wages seem impossible; but bread was so cheap that it has been said that real wages, if the price of foodstuffs be taken into account, were higher than in Greece.[3] There was, however, except in the mines, no slavery in Egypt, apart from the household slaves of the Greeks; native labour was too cheap and too thoroughly controlled for slavery to be worth while.[4]

It has been noticed (pp. 187 *sq.*) that the Ptolemaic system was based on two principles, that each man had his 'own place' which he could not leave without official orders or permission, and that the king's cultivation must be carried on. The system may not have been too difficult to work under Ptolemy II, with a strong king who could manage his officials; it was a *dioiketes* who said of the system, 'No one has a right to do what he wishes; all is ordered for the best.'[5] But from the start the native Egyptians disliked

[1] Schubart, *Einführung* 307.

[2] Oertel, *N.J. Kl. Alt.* XLV, 364; Westermann and Laird, *J.E.A.* IX, 81; Beloch IV, 1, 321.

[3] Rostovtzeff, *SEH* 412 and 1420 n. 209.

[4] For slavery, see W. L. Westermann, *Slavery in Ptolemaic Egypt*, 1929, and *s.v. Sklaverei* in P.W.; Rostovtzeff, *SEH* 1393 n. 119.

[5] C. Préaux, *Écon. royale*, 566.

this system, stricter than anything they had ever known, and even in the third century, as well as later, strikes,[1] an old Egyptian custom, were numerous; not merely riots in which the manager got beaten, but regular withdrawals of labour; strikes are known of miners, quarry-men, boatmen, workers of all sorts, royal peasants, retailers, police, even officials. Workmen's strikes were not strikes for better wages or conditions, for there were none to be got; they were the product of blank despair, aggravated perhaps by some accident, as delay in sending seed-corn. The men had one weapon which officialdom feared; they could throw the machine out of gear by leaving their 'own place'. A strike notice reads: 'We are worn out; we will run away'[2]; and they usually took refuge in some temple with the right of asylum.[3] Asylum has been called the Egyptians' *Habeas Corpus*[4]; Ptolemy's power ended at the precinct wall, and the worried officials had no weapon but persuasion or some little concession with which to get the men back to their 'own place'. The first three Ptolemies reduced the number of temples that could give asylum; to abolish or violate the right even they did not dare. It is the more noteworthy, and evidence of the hatred felt in Egypt for Persian rule, that the Egyptian priests, with the sanction of Ptolemy I, themselves denied the right to one class, the descendants of Persians settled in Egypt. These cannot have been numerous, but their exclusion gave rise later to a strange legal fiction: creditors bringing actions would describe the debtor, whatever he was, as 'descendant of a Persian', to prevent him taking sanctuary.[5]

But by the second century things were changing, especially as regarded the peasantry. The country population was falling,[6] partly because of civil wars and revolutions, but

[1] Bouché-Leclercq, *Rev. E.G.* 1908, 140; Rostovtzeff, *J.E.A.* 1920, 178.

[2] *P.S.I.* IV, 421.

[3] Fr. von Woess, *Das Asylwesen Ägyptens*, 1923, and in *Z. d. Savigny-Stiftung, Röm. Abt.* 1926, 32.

[4] Woess, *Asylwesen*, 3.

[5] Following Tait, *Archiv* VII, 175; see Bell, *J.E.A.* XI, 98; F. Zucker, *s.v.* *Πέρσαι*, in P.W. XIX, col. 917 *sqq*.

[6] C. Préaux, *op. c.* 492.

partly also through poverty and its consequence, more frequent exposure of children; there were fewer cultivators, and land began to go out of cultivation. When this happened, the officials would order someone else to cultivate the vacant farm in addition to his own; this was most unpopular, and that in turn reacted on the tempers of the smaller officials, who were personally liable for the State receiving its due; as full cultivation became more and more difficult to maintain,[1] they became more exacting and brutal; men not ready with their taxes were freely thrown into prison, and an Egyptian prison was a horror.[2] For a time, it would seem, some of the higher officials tried to behave honestly; they would make adjustments in difficult times,[3] or attempt to keep their subordinates in order; we possess an admonition[4] by a *dioiketes* to his *oikonomoi* to treat the people kindly and honestly, which shows it was not being done. But something happened more important than strikes, for a strike by its nature envisaged a final return to work. Peasants, unable to pay their taxes and dreading official brutality, would abandon their land altogether and try to escape (*anachoresis*)[5]; the man might get no further than sanctuary, but, if he had luck, he might get right away and join some native prince in revolt or the brigands in the marshes. This ended in the officials making the whole village responsible for the defaulter; the village had to pay his taxes and cultivate his land, the system of 'collective responsibility' which was to play such a part in ruining the Roman Empire.[6] But even so, whether a man escaped or was imprisoned, the State was short of one man's labour; and a system was invented—it had to be—whereby a prisoner was given a safe-conduct (*pistis*)[7] which released him from

[1] C. Préaux, *C.d'É.* 1935, 343.

[2] Cumont, *L'Égypte des Astrologues*, 192.

[3] C. Préaux, *op. c.* p. 504.

[4] *P. Tebt.* III, 703; see Rostovtzeff, *SEH* 1421 n. 212.

[5] *Anachoresis*, see C. Préaux, *Écon. royale*, 500 *sqq.*, and in *C.d'É.* 1935, 343; cf. M. N. Lewis, *J.E.A.* XXIII, 1937, fasc. 1 (see *C.d'É.* 1938, 176).

[6] C. Préaux, *Écon. royale* p. 509.

[7] *Pistis*, C. Préaux, *ib.* 533–44, and in *C.d'É.* 1935, 109 *sqq.* See also the refs in n. 5 (above).

prison for a limited time (say for the harvest) so that his labour might not be lost altogether. This had nothing to do with the liberty of the subject, but only with the man's work. Finally the whole bureaucratic system began to break down, and the brutality and greed of the officials passed all bounds; what the condition of the country became under their rule, with the kings little but ciphers (p. 208) can be seen in the great series of decrees issued by Ptolemy Euergetes II (p. 204).

The power of the priestly caste, the only remains of the old native aristocracy, was early broken; the king took the temple lands, the peasants on which became indistinguishable from the royal peasants, caused all priests to come to Alexandria to celebrate his birthday, and deprived them of their lucrative monopolies of oil and flax; he did, however, allow the temples—and this was the most important breach in the State monopolies—to manufacture sufficient linen and oil for their own use. The priestly caste had also to help to fill the smaller administrative offices, service in which was compulsory; the priests could hold meetings (synods),[1] but only apparently to regulate religious matters, and to confer honours on the king. But the kings at the same time took care not to offend the strong religious susceptibilities of the natives; they distinguished gods from priests, honoured and fostered the Egyptian religion, provided endowments, and built native temples at Dendera, Edfu, Kom Ombo, and Philae; for Ptolemy, like Pharaoh, was himself an Egyptian god, the Sun-god's son.

The Greeks[2] came to Egypt to grow rich; so far as they could they transported to Egypt their own life, and for a century did not mix freely with the Egyptians. They brought their own gods, read Homer and Euripides, and formed endless clubs. Their elementary education was neither compulsory nor run by the State, one of the few things in Egypt which was not; we have school books and

[1] Spiegelberg and Otto, *Bay. S.B.* 1926, Abh. 4.

[2] Generally: Bell, *J.E.A.* 1922, 142; Schubart, *Die Griechen in Ägypten*, 1927.

school exercises in plenty, the subjects being reading and writing, some grammar and mathematics, and Homer; but illiteracy was not uncommon. Gymnasia were founded in all the nome capitals (*metropoleis*) and even in villages where Greeks were numerous, like Philadelphia in the Fayum; later one is found at Thebes[1] and even as far south as Ombi near the First Cataract.[2] With the gymnasium came the ephebe system. As to secondary education, many authors were apparently read, but rhetoric was the principal subject, for it led to the higher offices; mathematics were studied for land surveying and for working the complicated equations between the Egyptian and Macedonian calendars, so complicated that Apollonius' steward Zeno sometimes gave up trying to guess *what* day it was by Macedonian reckoning.[3] The formation of private associations extended to the native Egyptians; a long list of trade associations is known,[4] but it is not certain if they were more than religious and social centres. The mercenaries formed numerous clubs, some local, as the mercenaries in Cyprus,[5] others on an ethnic basis which called themselves *politeumata*[6] as though they were part of the state—those of the Cretans,[7] Idumaeans,[8] Cilicians,[9] Boeotians,[10] are known; their nationality of course soon became only a name. But the Greeks themselves, scattered about Egypt and unable to form cities, formed themselves into true *politeumata*; each might cover a considerable district—we get 'the Greeks in the Delta', 'in the Thebaid', 'in the Arsinoite nome',[11]—but the members imitated what of autonomous Greek organisation they could. Private life is illustrated by masses of extant correspondence, sometimes quite interesting; the letter[12] written to Cleon, the hydraulic engineer who drained

[1] *Rev. E.G.* 1924, 359.
[2] Wilcken, *Archiv* V, 410.
[3] Edgar, *Ann. Serv.* XIX p. 32, XXIV p. 29.
[4] San Nicolo, *Äg. Vereinswesen*, I, 66; and in *Epit. Swoboda* 1927, 255.
[5] *OGIS* 143, 145–8, &c.
[6] Discussed fully by M. Launey, *op. c.* II 1064 with references.
[7] *P. Tebt.* 1 no. 32.
[8] *OGIS* 737.
[9] *SEG* VIII 573.
[10] *SEG* II 871.
[11] *OGIS* 709; Plaumann, *Archiv* VI, 176; Schubart, *Einführung* 247.
[12] Witkowski, *Epist. priv. graecae* no. 6.

Lake Moeris,[1] by his wife Metrodora after his disgrace and fall is a credit to human nature. The letters show a much greater degree of freedom among women than was expected, and they also show one of those strange contradictions of which Hellenism is full—a large measure of family affection and frequent exposure of children[2] (see p. 101).

But the Ptolemies, for all their early successes, failed to build a permanently powerful state on the exploitation of a people. And the economy of the kingdom itself, for all its wealth, was not so stable as it may have seemed. External shocks and internal stresses took effect. Ptolemy I had introduced a silver coinage, strange to most Egyptians, the mass of whom had not previously outgrown barter. But the Ptolemaic copper coinage was the one most used by the common people, the ratio of copper to silver being 60 : 1 (not very different from the ratio at Delos in the third century); some taxes, however, could be paid only in silver and others in silver or in copper with an agio. After 220 the ratio of 60 : 1 became disturbed, owing apparently to a scarcity of silver (though the symptom was not as yet widespread elsewhere in the Mediterranean). Although the consequent rise in prices (in terms of copper) was checked by the Government's decision in 211 to accept payment of taxes in copper, the balance was upset again in the 180's consequent on an approximate doubling of the Mediterranean ratio of copper to silver. In 174–3 the ratio 480 : 1 (the free market rate in Egypt by this time) was officially accepted for the conversion of tax-payments in copper, and the rise in prices was not immediately compensated by corresponding increases in wages, presumably for fear of an uncontrolled inflation. Altogether this copper inflation, the fluctuations of which cannot have failed to undermine confidence in the currency and to have caused hardship particularly to the poorest people, must be counted as a contributory cause of the native unrest in the period after

[1] Bouche-Leclercq, *Rev. E.G.* 1908, 121.
[2] Schubart, *Einführung*, 467.

Raphia.[1] The leading cause was Raphia itself (see pp. 22, 61), coming at the end of a century during which the Egyptians, though not positively oppressed, had been systematically exploited by foreigners who took their own superiority for granted.

But once the influx of Greeks ceased, even the military power of the Ptolemies soon decayed, and in 168 only Rome's intervention saved Egypt from conquest by Antiochus Epiphanes. The Ptolemaic system depended absolutely on the competence and honesty of the officials; it may have worked well in the strong hands of Ptolemy II, but under the weaker kings of the second century abuses began to multiply, till in the long civil war between Euergetes II and his sister Cleopatra II officialdom finally broke down. Euergetes' great series of decrees[2] about 118 give a vivid picture of the disorganisation: officials were collecting or extorting money for their own ends, and had seized the best of the King's land; they forced the people to work for them without payment, quartered troops on those exempt, cheated the taxpayer with false weights and measures, and seized even royal peasants for debt, with their cattle and implements; Egyptians were dragged before the Greek courts, and, worst of all, were imprisoned without trial by the officials themselves. Was the fault in the officials or in the system? Probably both; the system could only work decently if administered by men superior to the common failings of humanity. Doubtless the long civil war aggravated the mischief; but, whatever the faults of Euergetes II, once that war was over he met the evil vigorously, even to the imposition of the death penalty, stopped imprisonment

[1] A. Segrè in *A.J.Ph.* 1942, 174; G. Mickwitz in P.W., *s.v. Inflation*; Tony Reekmans, 'Economic and social repercussions of the Ptolemaic copper inflation', in *C.d'É.*, 48, 1949, 324. See also Rostovtzeff, *SEH* 710, who attributes the unrest mainly to high taxation, which amounts to the same thing, in the years (before 211) when taxes had to be paid in silver. On the coinage generally, see the full references in Rostovtzeff, *ib.* 1416 n. 201.

[2] *P. Tebt.* I, 5, with the commentary; summary, Bevan, 315; Preisigke, *Archiv* V, 301. Fully discussed, Rostovtzeff, *SEH* 878–96; and see Préaux, 'La signification de l'épôque d'Euergète II', *Actes Ve Congr. Pap.*, 1938, 345.

without proper trial, and re-established the power of the native judges, the Laocritae, on the basis that in contractual cases between Greek and Egyptian the forum should depend on the language of the contract, but that all suits between Egyptians should go before the Laocritae. He also introduced a number of measures for protecting the person and property of the taxpayer, and for repairing the damages of the war; for equity and fair-mindedness his regulations stand high above most things of the second century. He had little success, though the dynasty lasted another century, and in spite of a succession of poor rulers remained strong enough to conduct further exploration southward and to make a tolerable fight against Caesar. But the economic system itself Euergetes did not question; his aim was to restore its efficiency and to get it justly administered.

Raphia had aroused the national consciousness of the Egyptians, and in the second century the Greeks were on the defensive.[1] The priestly decrees for Ptolemy IV after Raphia[2] and for Ptolemy V (the Rosetta stone)[3] show strong Egyptian colouring and give to the kings the titles of a native Pharaoh; Ptolemy V was crowned in Egyptian fashion at Memphis, which became a second royal residence; the native risings which began in 216 culminated in the great revolt under Ptolemy V, and continued spasmodically throughout the century. Euergetes II greatly extended the powers, privileges, and possessions of the priesthood in an attempt to conciliate the natives. This strange man was hated by the Greeks—by the literary men because he temporarily broke up the Museum, by the Alexandrians because in the civil war he had let his troops loose on the hostile mob, by all because, as they thought, he favoured the Egyptians; and they have blackened his memory accordingly. But he partially understood the position, realised the

[1] On the Egyptians see in general Préaux, 'Esquisses d'une histoire des révolutions sous les Lagides', *C. d'É.*, 1936, 530; and 'Les Égyptiens dans la civilisation hellénistique', *ib.*, 1942, 148.

[2] Gautier and Sottas, *Un décret trilingue en l'honneur de Ptolémée IV*, 1925; Spiegelberg, *Bay. S.B.* 1925, Abh. 4; translation in Bevan, 388.

[3] *OGIS* 90.

ambitions of Rome, and entertained the great idea of constructing a national Graeco-Egyptian monarchy; beside his other reforms he remodelled the native army organisation, and made an Egyptian, Paōs, his 'kinsman' and governor of the Thebaid.[1] His aim, like that of Antiochus Epiphanes, was to strengthen his kingdom as against Rome on a new basis; and by admitting Egyptians to participation he hoped to avoid the difficulties which had wrecked Antiochus' purely hellenising policy. But he in turn failed to create a national monarchy because it was incompatible with the economic system of Ptolemy II, and he did not attempt to revise that too lucrative system; hence he was unable to win over the Egyptians, and revolts continued till in 85 Ptolemy Lathyros suppressed the last and partly destroyed Thebes.

Many things illustrate the native revival[2] after 200, and the Egyptianising policy of the kings. No more great estates were conferred on Greek officials. Many new asylums were made or old ones restored; between 93 and 57 four were created in one village, Theadelphia,[3] and the right became so abused that Rome curtailed it drastically, though possibly it lasted till the Christian Church took it over. Under Euergetes II the long struggle between the calendars ended in the Macedonian having to conform to the Egyptian. After Raphia the Egyptian warrior-class, the *machimoi*, was revived; they were made cleruchs with smaller lots, and the Greek cleruchs began to be called *katoikoi* for distinction; later *katoikoi* came to mean cleruchs of Greek *culture*; finally *katoikoi* and *machimoi* lost all racial meaning, and only meant men who held larger or smaller lots.[4] In 215 a Greek and an Egyptian were joint tenants in a lease,[5] and after 200 mixture of blood began; names ceased to be any criterion of race,[6] as some natives rose in the scale and took Greek names, and some Greeks sank; Greek and native names occur in the same family. Some Greeks kept them-

[1] *OGIS* 132.

[2] Generally: Oertel, *N.J. Kl. Alt.* XLV, 361; Bell, *J.E.A.* 1922, 139; Schubart 307.

[3] Lefebvre, *Ann. Serv.* XIX, 37.

[4] *OGIS* 731; Oertel, *Katoikoi* in P.W.

[5] *P. Frankf.* 2.

[6] Earliest case, Wilcken, *Chrest.* no. 51 (Ptol. III).

selves aloof; but a new mixed race formed intermediate between Greeks and fellahin, and Hellene came to mean a man with some Greek *culture*.[1] The dynasty came to rely, too, on many who were not even called Greek, like the bilingual non-Greek soldier Horus, or Hor, of the Adler papyri, who, whatever his race of origin, was called 'descendant of a Persian', and who may be taken as typical of his period: he was on active service in the Thebaid for about thirty years beginning in 124, on guard with others like him in a district which certainly needed watching.[2] The living Greek language of the third-century papyri was replaced by the barbarous Greek of the natives; some Greeks too learnt Egyptian.[3] The Egyptianised Greek adopted native religion[4] and customs, even to embalming his dead; in the first century brother and sister marriage appeared among Greeks,[5] and became so common that Rome subsequently had to stop it; even those who had passed through the gymnasium made offerings to Egyptian gods.[6] Popular literature began to prophesy the downfall of the hated Alexandria.[7] What the Ptolemies had brought to Egypt was not the spirit of Greece, but only external forms; by the first century Egypt was fast absorbing the foreign element in her body, and Augustus, to save what remained of Hellenism, had to return to Ptolemy I, nurse the Greek element, foster the gymnasia, and again break the re-acquired power of the priests.

Egypt was Ptolemy's estate. It enables us to study a thorough-going system of nationalisation, so thorough that

[1] Bell, *op. c.* 146; Otto, *Phil. Woch.* 1926, 39. Perhaps the weakening of Greek family organisation is illustrated by the appearance of marriages without ἔκδοσις of the bride (συγγραφὴ ὁμολογίας): so H. J. Wolff, *Written and unwritten marriages in Hellenistic and postclassical Roman Law*, 1939, esp. ch. I.

[2] *P. Adler, passim.* On the comprehensive term Πέρσης τῆς Ἐπιγονῆς, cf. p. 199 n. 5 *ante*, and see *P. Adler*, p. 3 n. 1 (bibliography), and M. Launey, *op. c.* I, 569.

[3] Wilcken, *Chrest.* no. 136.

[4] As *OGIS* 111, 130, 175; cf. Bell, 'Popular religion in Graeco-Roman Egypt', *J.E.A.* XXXIV, 1948, 82.

[5] Bell, *op. c.* 146.

[6] *OGIS* 176, 178.

[7] *Potter's Oracle* col. II l. 2 (see p. 228).

an unknown writer of the third century, who has left an invaluable fragment on the theory of the Hellenistic monarchy, condemned some king—he certainly meant the reigning Ptolemy—who treated his people's possessions as his own[1]; and also enables us to study, both in its earlier efficiency and its later brutality and decay, the great bureaucracy which largely supplied the model for that of Imperial Rome. The widespread belief that the earlier Ptolemies were the fathers of their people, ready to fulfil the dictates of philosophy,[2] rests on scarcely any evidence except some exhortations to the officials to behave properly, even when, contrary to the custom elsewhere, the whole loss of a bad crop was being thrown on the peasantry; and we know too well the value of good and noble sentiments unaccompanied by action. Action did, no doubt, occasionally take place: Ptolemy III did remit some taxes in a year of a low Nile and famine,[3] and Ptolemy V is said in a priestly decree to have remitted a number after his accession,[4] but as he was only a child, whatever was done was done, not by that cruel ruler, but by his Greek minister Aristomenes of Acarnania. Certainly the later Ptolemies strove, *so far as they could*,[5] to protect their subjects against the monster which their fathers had created and which they continued to employ; but they were no longer strong enough to do more than issue edicts of which the bureaucracy took no notice.[6] These kings were not unpopular with the people; they were merely something remote, having little connection with the bureaucracy which governed that people's daily lives.

Doubtless the early Ptolemies desired to acquire money as an aid to the construction of a strong state; their condemnation is that the money they acquired was in no sense used for the benefit of those who made it. They improved

[1] Suidas, *βασιλεία* 3.

[2] See in the last place Rostovtzeff, *SEH* 911, 1379 n. 83, 1552 n. 191. Schubart's interesting article in *Archiv* XII (1936) p. 1 deals, not with what was, but with what ought to have been.

[3] *OGIS* 56 l. 18.

[4] *OGIS* 90 ll. 13 *sqq.*

[5] Rostovtzeff's phrase, 911.

[6] C. Preaux, *Un problème de la politique des Lagides; la faiblesse des édits*; Atti IV Congr. Pap. 153 *sqq.*, cf. *C.d'É.* 1937, 292, and *ib.* 1935, 343.

the land; they did not improve the condition of the people. There was no desire to oppress the Egyptians; but there was no desire to help them, beyond keeping them fit to work, a thing done by every business-like slave-owner. Even that failed at the end; and though the political history shows that there was still plenty of wealth in Egypt at the top,[1] many of the common people, under the rule of 'corrupt, greedy, and lawless officials', became sunk in poverty and apathy. If the Library and the Museum glorify the Ptolemies in the eyes of world-history, that did not help their subjects; and material wealth and wealth of material need not blind us to the fact that their government, ethically considered, stood well below that of the other two Macedonian dynasties. The Antigonids, with small resources, but national rulers of a free people, were the shield of the Greek world against northern barbarism and enabled the growth of the rather wonderful culture of the third century; the Seleucids, overweighted and overworked, nevertheless strove, not without success, to raise the civilisation level of half a continent. But the Ptolemies farmed their estate and filled their Treasury.

[1] Isidorus' Hymns to Isis, *SEG* VIII, 548 *sqq.*, esp. 550, 551 (Fayum, early 1st century B.C.), may suggest the same.

CHAPTER VI

HELLENISM AND THE JEWS[1]

THE aim of this chapter is to sketch the workings of Hellenism on the Jews, the rise and the fortunes of a movement which brought the Greek world into contact with the one race strong enough to resist the impact of its victorious culture.

Few Greeks in the Hellenistic period ever managed to learn very much about the Jews. Alexander, who had seen the civilisation of Egypt and Babylon, conversed with Indian ascetics, and brought to Europe the first knowledge of the Iranian Avesta, never visited Jerusalem[2]; his Staff probably thought it another priest-state of the type familiar to them in Asia Minor and Syria, and Theophrastus[3] only

[1] Generally: E. Schürer, *Gesch. d. jüdischen Volkes im Zeitalter Jesu Christi*, III⁴, 1909; P. Wendland, *Die hell.-röm. Kultur*, 1912, ch. IX; E. R. Bevan, *Jerusalem under the High Priests*⁵, 1924, and in *C.A.H.* IX ch. IX; Ed. Meyer, *Ursprung und Anfänge des Christentums* II, 1921; Beer, *Israel und Juda* in P.W.; F. X. Kugler, *Von Moses bis Paulus*, 1922; W. Kolbe, *Beiträge zur syrischen und jüdischen Geschichte*, 1926; N. H. Baynes, *Israel amongst the Nations*, 1927; J. W. Hunkin in *Palestine in General History*, 1929 (Schweich Lectures 1926); G. F. Moore, *Judaism in the first centuries of the Christian era*, I, 1927; S. A. Cook, *The religion of ancient Palestine in the light of archaeology*, 1930; E. Bickerman, 'La charte séleucide de Jerusalem', *Rev. ét juives*, 1935, 4; *id.*, *Der Gott der Makkabäer*, 1937; *id.*, 'Un document relatif à la persecution d'Antiochos IV Epiphane', *Rev. d'hist. des religions*, 1937, 188; R. Marcus (ed.), Josephus, *Ant.* (Loeb Class. Library, vol. VII), Appendices and bibliographies, 1942. Literature: R. H. Charles, *The Apocrypha and Pseudepigrapha of the Old Testament*, 1913, and *Religious Development between the Old and New Testaments*, 1914; W. O. E. Oesterley, *The Books of the Apocrypha*, 1915; R. Laqueur, 'Griechische Urkunden in der jüdisch-hellenistischen Literatur', *Hist. Zeits.* 1927, 229. See in particular Baynes' bibliographical notes.

[2] On this legend see Fr. Pfister, *Eine jüdische Gründungsgeschichte* App., 1914.

[3] Th. Reinach, *Textes relatifs à Judaisme* p. 7.

knew of the Jews as philosophic star-gazers who had invented human sacrifice. A little knowledge began under Ptolemy I, whose contemporary Hecataeus of Abdera,[1] in a rather mixed account, did seize on two salient facts: the Jew made no images of the gods, and by command of his lawgiver Moses did not practise infanticide. From the start the Greek felt that the Jew differed from other men. But no Jew made his history available to Greeks before Josephus, late in the first century A.D., and when the Greek Alexander Polyhistor (*c.* 50 B.C.) attempted the task he could only produce a burlesque; even Strabo, who knew so much, was utterly at sea over Jewish history and had obviously never even heard of a Jewish literature.[2] In some sense the Jews always formed a world apart.

The little hill-state of Judaea, where Ezra had originated modern Judaism, contained only part of the race when Ptolemy I acquired it in 301. Gaza and the coastal plain were not Jewish, and the Philistine towns became hellenised; the land of Samaria was inhabited by a mixed race, who worshipped Yahweh at Shechem; in Galilee and the Peraea Antigonus I had already made Greek settlements, to be reinforced, especially east of the Jordan, by those of the Ptolemies (p. 181). The fighting Idumaeans (Edomites), important to Egypt as mercenaries, occupied southern Judaea as well as the land south of the Dead Sea. Judaea had no outlet to the great world. But many of Jewish race still lived east of the Euphrates, chiefly in Babylonia; *Jonah* about 300 represents the point of view of a Jew from Assyria, while the scene in *Tobit* is laid among the colony in Media. In Jewish tradition these eastern Jews were the Ten Tribes, those in Judaea being Judah, Benjamin, and Levi; but probably the tribal system, whatever it originally represented, had lost all local meaning, and a Jew of Judaea might belong by descent to any tribe; Anna the prophetess was of Asher, and the Aristeas-letter makes the High Priest send representatives of all the twelve to Ptolemy II, which

[1] *F.H.G.* II p. 392 §§ 4, 8; cf. Jos. *c. Ap.* I, 199; II, 202.
[2] XVI, 760–1; perhaps from Poseidonius, *F. Gr. Hist.* II A no. 87 fr. 70.

the author could hardly have done had this been a known impossibility.

Down to 200 Judaea was under Ptolemaic rule, and little is heard of its history except stories of quarrels between two leading families, the Oniads, who held the High Priesthood, and the Tobiads,[1] whose stronghold was near Heshbon in Ammon and who may or may not have been partly of Ammonite blood. As regards literature, the third century seems a blank. The *Epistle of Jeremy* may date from 306, and *Jonah* about 300; part of *Zechariah*, chaps. ix–xiv, may possibly be later than Alexander; then there seems nothing else till *Ecclesiastes*, *c.* 200. The revival of literature took place in the subsequent troubles of the Seleucid period; and if absence of history and literature be a test of happiness, Judaea may have been fairly happy under the Ptolemies, though obviously by 200 the wealthy class were discontented, largely perhaps under the burden of the heavy Egyptian taxation. A certain expansion of the people was inevitably taking place, for as Jews reared all their children they increased faster than other races, and Jewish communities formed in Transjordania and subsequently in Galilee. Doubtless the Ptolemies would try to direct emigration to their own possessions; but how far the Egyptian Jews came from Judaea cannot be said.

The first three Ptolemies seemingly followed the usual Hellenistic practice of not interfering with the religion of their subjects; but Ptolemy IV, an enthusiastic worshipper of Dionysus, was perhaps deceived by the supposed equation of Sabazios and Sabaoth into believing that the Jews merely worshipped Dionysus under another name and form, and as Dionysus was also equated with Sarapis through the Osiris element in the latter, he possibly dreamt of establishing one religion in his empire, that of Dionysus, which should unify its principal racial elements.[2] What attempt, if any, he actually made to introduce Dionysus-worship into Judaea

[1] Büchler, *Tobiaden und Oniaden*, 1899; Gressmann, *Berl. S.B.* 1921, 663; Willrich, *Archiv* VII, 61; *P. Cairo Zen.* 59003, 59075–6.

[2] Perdrizet, *Rev. E.A.* 1910, 234.

is quite uncertain; but he did incur the hostility of a section, who worked hard to blacken his memory, as can be seen in *III Maccabees*. *Ecclesiastes*[1] gives a lamentable account, from the aristocratic side, of the state of Judaea at the end of his reign: the land was full of the tears of the oppressed, and the dead happier than the living; his spies were so ubiquitous that a bird of the air would carry the matter. The Preacher himself was evidently prepared to welcome Antiochus III, the 'king well-born'. But Polybius[2] says the common people favoured Egypt; it means therefore that before 200—how long before cannot be said—an aristocratic party had fallen out with Ptolemy and were turning to his rival. That party must now be considered.

Egyptian rule, and the neighbouring Hellenistic cities, had accustomed the Jews to the Greek language and nomenclature and other external phenomena of Greek civilisation, and though Ezra's influence remained strong in Judaea, elements of the governing class, those about the High Priest, were favourable to Hellenism; they claimed to be as good Jews as their fellows, but were willing to adopt the outward forms of the dominant civilisation. This was the party which supported the Seleucids, the strict Jews usually looking to Egypt; with reason *Ecclesiastes* has been the hunting-ground of those scholars who have sought in Jewish literature traces of the Greek spirit. These hellenising Jews provoked bitter enmity among the pious; they are 'the ungodly' so often referred to in subsequent Jewish writings, and Jewish Hellenism may be the 'strange woman' of *Proverbs*, 'which flattereth with her lips', but whose 'house inclineth unto death'. They were accused of neglecting circumcision and of exhibiting all the moral shortcomings commonly attributed in the Old Testament to backsliders; it comes as an anti-climax when in 169 the two definite charges[3] made against them were that they favoured Greek athletic exercises (which involved nudity) and wore Greek hats. In 200 Judaea changed masters; Antiochus III wrested all southern Syria from Egypt, and, as was customary with new

[1] G. A. Barton, *Ecclesiastes*. [2] V, 86, 10. [3] II Macc. 4, 12.

acquisitions, temporarily remitted various taxes. But the country did not settle down well under Seleucid rule, though it adopted, and retained, the Seleucid calendar; the parties tended to try and play off Syria and Egypt against one another, and matters were not improved by the attempt of Heliodorus, minister of Seleucus IV, to seize the Temple treasure. A party of strict Jews, who tried and failed to reform some irregularities connected with the Temple, left Judaea under the leadership of one called 'the Star' and went to Damascus, where they established a 'New Covenant' of repentance.[1] This was the general position when Antiochus Epiphanes turned his attention to Judaea.

Pious Jews could not speak too much evil of Antiochus, 'the man clad in purple, fierce, unjust, fiery, lightning-born' of the Sibylline books,[2] who persecuted their worship and drenched the land in blood; *Daniel* shows how the 'Little Horn' was hated, and he became the prototype of Antichrist. But it was the Jewish Hellenisers, not Antiochus, who began the trouble, and his first interference was in a domestic quarrel, though doubtless he would have done better to have stood aloof. The High Priest, Onias III, had gone to Antioch before Antiochus' accession to gain the king's ear over some matter in the unending feud with the Tobiad faction; his brother Jason, a leader of the hellenising party, intrigued against him and persuaded Antiochus by promise of higher tribute to depose Onias and make him High Priest; he also obtained leave for the Jews to set up a gymnasium in Jerusalem and call themselves Antiochenes, *i.e.* Jerusalem was renamed Antioch.[3] But in 170 Antiochus, being dissatisfied, expelled Jason and gave the High Priesthood to Menelaus of the Tobiad faction, possibly himself a Tobiad, who offered yet higher tribute. Both Oniads and Tobiads were Hellenisers, and their quarrel had no religious import. In 169, while Antiochus was invading Egypt, Jason returned, took all Jerusalem but the citadel, where

[1] Charles, *Apocrypha* II, 785; Ed. Meyer, *Berl. Abh.* 1919; Oesterley, 138. Some now date this *c.* 80 B.C.

[2] III, 389.

[3] II Macc. 4, 9.

Menelaus found refuge, and slaughtered Menelaus' partisans. Clearly Jason had considerable support, and to Antiochus it looked as if, at a critical moment, Jerusalem had risen in his rear. On his way back from Egypt he entered the city; Jason fled, his partisans were slaughtered by the Syrian troops, and Menelaus, restored to power, conducted Antiochus into the Temple and put part of the treasure into his hands. Antiochus entered the Holy of Holies, and strange stories were told later of what he saw there (p. 233).

So far Antiochus had not touched the Jewish religion, and it must be remembered that, though he was important to the Jews, they were not equally important to him; he was concerned at first with conquering Egypt, and subsequently with his plan to reconquer Bactria and crush Parthia (p. 34); Judaea to him was only one small vassal-state among others, whose affairs one generally left to one's provincial governors. But in 168 Rome warned him off Egypt in a manner which violated every decency of international intercourse and outraged the whole of Hellenism in his person; and the friend of Rome saw what he had to expect from her. He decided that his best chance was to make of his empire a united people in culture and religion, which could alike only be Greek; Judaea must bow to the common need, like other places. Menelaus may have told him there would be no difficulty, and, as E. R. Bevan once pointed out, the earlier tradition (*Maccabees* I and II) does not represent Antiochus as hostile to the Jews themselves[1]; there is no evidence indeed that he ever suppressed Jewish practices in Babylonia. But what he had in mind at this time was liberty to turn eastward. In 167 his general Apollonius occupied Jerusalem, levelled the wall, and built and garrisoned a new citadel in the 'city of David'; he was followed by a commissioner with an order prohibiting the Jewish religion. A Greek altar, the 'Abomination of Desolation',[2] was placed upon the Jewish altar in the Temple court, on which doubtless pigs *were* sacrificed for the monthly purification; and the

[1] *House of Seleucus* II, 171. Jos. *Ant.* XII, 296 is very different.

[2] 'Desolation' is generally recognised as Baal-Shamem; S. A. Cook, 189.

Temple became a temple of Zeus Olympius, whose manifestation on earth was Antiochus himself. Yahweh's temple in Shechem similarly became a temple of Zeus Xenios, by request (so the Jews said) of the Samaritans.[1]

Many conformed, for the hellenising party supported Antiochus, but many offered passive resistance; that some met death heroically as martyrs is certain, though the highly coloured details are untrustworthy. Active resistance was, in the tradition, started at Modin by Mattathiah of the Hasmonaean family; he died in 166–5, and his son Judas, called Maccabaeus (the Hammer), collected a band of men like-minded, waged guerilla war, and in 164 defeated 6,000 troops under Gorgias, sent by the governor of Syria. To Antiochus, Judas was merely an unimportant rebel against lawful authority; he had already crossed the Euphrates to attack Parthia, and in 163 he died. Judas took the Temple, but not the citadel, and restored the worship of Yahweh; and in December 164 a great thanksgiving festival was held in Jerusalem. In 162 Lysias, regent for the infant Antiochus V, came in person, mastered the country, and besieged Jerusalem, but the advance on Antioch of his rival Philippus, Epiphanes' minister for affairs,[2] recalled him, and to win the Jews he gave them back their religion, preserving only the Seleucid suzerainty; he also executed Menelaus. This was the end of the war of religion, for Antiochus' attempt at uniformity did not survive his death; but though Judas played the part of a patriot, what saved the worship of Yahweh was not his sword but Seleucid dissension.

The same dissension enabled the Maccabees to set up an independent state. The Roman Senate, always ready to damage the Seleucids, accepted Judas as an ally; but when Demetrius I secured the Seleucid throne he reconquered Judaea. After Judas on the 15th of Adar (March) 160 had defeated and killed his general Nicanor—a day long kept as a festival—Nicanor's successor Bacchides, with whom was the new High Priest Alcimus, of the priestly house, defeated

[1] But see now E. Bikerman, *Rev. de l'hist. des religions*, 1937, 188.
[2] II Macc. 13, 23.

and killed Judas, garrisoned the country, and installed Alcimus, but did not meddle with religion; Judas' brother Jonathan and his guerillas made peace, and all seemed settled. Then the pretender Alexander Balas attacked Demetrius. Both bid for Jonathan's help, but Balas won him by offering him the High Priesthood; and when in 150 Balas conquered Demetrius, Jonathan the High Priest, clever and unscrupulous, became nominally the Seleucid military governor of Judaea, but really an independent prince. In 147 he took Joppa and gave Judaea an outlet to the sea. After his death his brother Simon, favoured by fresh conflicts in Syria, expelled the garrison from the citadel of Jerusalem and in 142 made a peace with Demetrius II which was reckoned the beginning of freedom; the Jews made Simon hereditary High Priest and Governor, and Rome recognised him as such.

We must now turn to the history of the *Diaspora* (Dispersion); the Jews outside Judaea. In Egypt there had for long been Jewish settlements.[1] From the seventh to the fifth century a body, originally mercenaries settled by some king, existed at Elephantine on the upper Nile[2]; they had a temple of Yahweh, whom they worshipped beside the goddesses Aschima and Anat (Anaïtis), were under an Egyptian governor, swore by Egyptian gods, and in the fifth century spoke Aramaic, the *lingua franca* of the Persian empire, and had an Aramaic folkbook which contained the story of Achikar the Wise. Other Jews settled in Egypt in Jeremiah's time, and there was an old colony at Memphis.[3] Subsequently Ptolemy I brought a number to Alexandria, and perhaps gave their upper class the same position of privilege as Macedonians.[4] All through the third century Jews came to Egypt, generally settling in Alexandria, but

[1] See also the works on Egypt in ch. V; add L. Fuchs, *Die Juden Ägyptens*, 1924; H. I. Bell, *Juden und Griechen in röm. Alexandreia*, 1926, with bibliography; M. Launey *Recherches sur les armées hellénistiques*, I 543, II 1232 (prosopography).

[2] Ed. Meyer, *Die Papyrusfund von Elephantine*, 1912; Schubart, *Einführung* 329.

[3] Jer. 42–4.

[4] Jos. *Ant.* XII, 8; see Bell *op. c.* 12.

sometimes in the country, where under Ptolemy III they already had three synagogues; two were dedicated for the king, the queen and their children,[1] while to the third, at Leontopolis, Ptolemy III gave the right of asylum.[2] They took up land,[3] and were often employed as tax-collectors, but seldom did banking or money-lending and hardly ever occur as traders[4] (p. 261). They mainly occupied one quarter in Alexandria, and, as their numbers increased, were organised separately (p. 220), and ceased to be 'Macedonians'; the Jew who under Augustus *called* himself a Macedonian was a proselyte or an antiquary.[5]

In the second century their settlements in Egypt were numerous; synagogues were built in several places, and the village authorities distinguished sharply between Jews and Greeks; one Jewish-Egyptian marriage is known.[6] Under Ptolemy VI, Onias, son of the High Priest Onias III, came to Egypt and was presented with a ruined temple in Leontopolis, where about 160 he built a smaller model of the Temple in Jerusalem as a religious centre for the Jews of Egypt, and copied the Temple service; it lasted till A.D. 73, but the more pious Jews still looked to Jerusalem.[7] It is related that both Ptolemy VI and subsequently Cleopatra III employed Jewish generals; and a Jewish mercenary, Abram, appears as a member of a Graeco-Egyptian military association.[8] In the civil war between Cleopatra III and her son Ptolemy Lathyros the Jews supported her, the beginning of tension in Alexandria between Jew and Greek, for the Greeks favoured the victorious Lathyros; but the tension, which was primarily political, only showed itself in words; anti-Semitism accompanied by violence was unknown in Egypt before the Roman Empire. In the first century the Jews in Alexandria were the largest body outside Judaea; after the

[1] *OGIS* 726; Vogliano, *Riv. di fil.* LXVII, 247 (at Crocodilopolis).
[2] *OGIS* 129, and Add., II p. 544.
[3] Fuchs 52; add *P. Cairo Zen.* 59377.
[4] Occupations, Fuchs § V.
[5] *B.G.U.* 1132 + 1151.
[6] Schubart, *Einführung* 330, citing *P. Berl.* 11641.
[7] Jos. *Ant.* XIII, 62–73; *B.J.* VII, 422; Kahrstedt, *Syr. Terr.*, App. II.
[8] Lefebvre, *Ann. Serv.* XIII, 217 no. 28.

Christian era their number in Egypt is given as a million, and they largely filled two of the five quarters of Alexandria within the wall[1]; but there was no Ghetto, and some lived scattered throughout the other quarters.

The course of Jewish settlement in Asia is less easy to trace. Certain religious phenomena (p. 225) make it probable that much of the immigration into Asia Minor came from Babylonia; if so, the immigration doubtless started before the Seleucids lost Asia Minor in 188, for seemingly at first they, like the Ptolemies, favoured the Jews as good settlers,[2] and there is no reason for rejecting the story that Antiochus III settled 2,000 Jewish families in Lydia and Phrygia, even if his letter has been doctored for propaganda purposes.[3] We must suppose a parallel phenomenon to the settlements in Egypt, though actual knowledge of the great Jewish communities in many cities of Asia Minor only dates from the first century[4]; but by 140 the Sibylline books could claim that every land was full of Jews.[5] At Sardes, and possibly in other cities, a special quarter of the city was allotted to them.[6] There was a community of Jews on Delos before 100, and their handsome synagogue had been built before 88[7]; the settlements known later in Greece and Macedonia can hardly have been made before Macedonia became a Roman province in 148. By the Christian era Jews had become very numerous in Damascus and Syria generally, including Antioch; when the large settlement at Antioch began to form cannot be said. In this sphere also, as in Egypt, it is generally supposed that there was no active anti-Semitism before the Roman Empire. Certainly the Jews of Delos once invoked curses on some persons unknown who had shed the innocent blood of two Jewish women[8]; but this need not indicate an outbreak against Jews as such.

As Jews filtered into a Greek city, their position was at

[1] Philo *in Flacc.* 6, 8.

[2] Jos. *Ant.* XII, 119, 134, 148; XIV, 186.

[3] Jos. *Ant.* XII, 148.

[4] *Ib.* XIV, 213–64; *B.M. Inscr.* 676–7; *Inscr. Hierapolis* 69, 212, 242, *Acts passim*; other refs. in Schürer.

[5] III, 271.

[6] Jos. *Ant.* XIV, 260–1.

[7] A. Plassart, *Mélanges Holleaux*, 201.

[8] Ditt.[3] 1181.

first merely that of metics; but as soon as they were numerous enough, they set up a synagogue, and probably formed a private association for worship, as was the custom of other metics (p. 338).[1] Such an association would have its officials—the 'ruler of the synagogue' and others—to whom the Jews submitted their disputes according to Jewish law, in preference to going to the Greek courts; this would be informal at first, but as all rulers were ready to favour the Jews, the privilege of judging themselves by their own law became in many places a right formally granted. In Rome the Jewish community had no organisation beyond these synagogue associations; and when the Jewish prisoners whom Pompey took to Rome were freed and returned, they set up even in Jerusalem their own synagogue, built by one Theodotus, with a hostel, living-rooms, and baths.[2] But in Greek cities this form of synagogue community, where it existed, ultimately passed from private law into public, and became the political form under which the Jewish body acted; though this cannot be traced before the Christian era, it certainly antedates the destruction of Jerusalem.

In many cities, however, including the new Hellenistic foundations, the Jewish organisation went much beyond this; the Jews, as they grew numerous, were allowed, or directed, to form a *politeuma* (p. 147), which made them quasi-autonomous 'settlers' with rights greater than those of metics. Jewish *politeumata*, like others, managed their own internal and religious affairs, but in one respect they were privileged beyond any other: they ultimately acquired (at Alexandria not until after the third century)[3] the right of being judged by their own magistrates according to their own law, which *probably* means that they were excepted from the jurisdiction of the Greek Courts; perhaps this, rather than religious exclusiveness, was the origin of the discontent Greeks began to feel later, seeing that Hellenistic Greeks held firmly to the principle that no man's religion

[1] Schürer II³, 430 *sqq.*

[2] Vincent, *Rev. Biblique* 1921, 247; literature, Tod, *J.H.S.* 1923, 37; 1925, 198.

[3] P. 186 n. 1.

was anyone else's business. The existence of these Jewish *politeumata* is explicitly attested for Alexandria[1] and Berenice in the Cyrenaica,[2] and seems certain in many cities, notably Hierapolis in Asia Minor.[3] That in Alexandria was by Augustus' time governed by an ethnarch, who judged the people by Jewish law, but took into account Ptolemy's rescripts; Augustus added a Council of Elders. At Berenice in 13 B.C. a board of nine archons governed the *politeuma*, and archons are referred to elsewhere[4]; probably after Augustus this became the usual form.

Many scholars have believed, following Josephus, that Jews as a body were full citizens in Alexandria, Antioch, and the cities of Ionia. This was always impossible, for full citizenship, *i.e.* participation in government and legal administration, entailed worship of the city gods, which to a Jew meant apostasy; and though individuals might bow down in the house of Rimmon, like that Nicetas of Jerusalem who at Iasos contributed to the Dionysia,[5] or the two Jews who gave thanks in Pan's temple at Edfu,[6] Jews as a rule, Hellenisers or otherwise, held fast to their religion. In fact, Jews in a city call themselves a racial unit only (*laos*),[7] and never (apparently) an enfranchised people (*demos*); and the letter of the Emperor Claudius is to me conclusive that at Alexandria the Jews as a body never were citizens.[8] Now Josephus is sometimes untrustworthy over Hellenistic matters, and even uses falsified documents for propaganda purposes[9]; but in this case, though his

[1] Jos. *Ant.* XII, 108; XIV, 117; Aristeas, ed. Wendland, 310. See Engers, *Klio* XVIII, 79; Bell, *op. c.*

[2] *C.I.G.* 5361; Str. *ap.* Jos. *Ant.* XIV, 115–18.

[3] *Inscr. Hierapolis* 212, called κατοικία (see *ante* p. 147 n. 5); κατοικεῖν often, Jos. *c. Ap.* II, 33, 39, 44; *Ant.* XIV, 113, 117 *sqq.*, XIX, 281, &c.

[4] As Tlos; Hula, *Eranos Vindobonensis*, 77.

[5] Le Bas and Waddington III, 294.

[6] *OGIS* 73–4.

[7] *I. Hierapolis* 69; III Macc. 2, 28; Jos. *Ant.* XII, 158, 161, 224, 228, 240, 285, 363 and universally.

[8] Bell, *Jews and Christians in Egypt*, see *ante* p. 185 n. 4. For another reason, see Wilcken, *Hermes* LXIII, 48.

[9] *E.g.* the decree of Sardes, *Ant.* XIV, 259, where οἱ κατοικοῦντες ἐν τῇ πόλει Ἰουδαῖοι πολῖται is a contradiction in terms; the interpolation of πολῖται is self-evident.

terminology is confused, I rather doubt if he meant to claim full citizenship for the Jews, and I see no ground for doubting either his statements that at Antioch and Alexandria the Jews called themselves Antiochenes and Alexandrians,[1] or his account of the 'Ephesian process', when the Greeks of Ephesus petitioned M. Agrippa not to let Jews participate in their citizenship.[2] Moreover, Josephus apart, St. Paul's much-canvassed claim to be a citizen of Tarsus has to be considered. The explanation is really very simple. Where the kings had power, as they had in new foundations like Alexandria or Antioch or in cities where, like Ephesus, the Seleucids restored democracy and could make terms, they gave the Jewish settlers isopolity, *potential* citizenship (p. 72)[3]; that is, a Jew could become a citizen on demand, provided of course that he apostatised by worshipping the city gods. This would explain, not only the Ephesian process, but also the 'Antiochenes' and 'Alexandrians': when Aetolia, for example, gave Ceos isopolity the Ceans called themselves Aetolians.[4] It would, literally, account for the insistence of Josephus and Jerome on the 'equal honour' of the Jews. And there really seems no serious explanation of Paul's claim but potential citizenship, whether because the Jews of Antioch-Tarsus had isopolity or because he (or his father) had been given an honorary citizenship[5] which of course had not been taken up; the only alternative is that he worshipped the city gods, which need not be considered. A potential citizen might in an emergency appeal to his citizenship, and there is a parallel to Paul's case: when Alexander's treasurer Harpalus, who was an honorary citizen of Athens, revolted and was refused admission to

[1] *c. Ap.* II, 33, 39.

[2] *Ant.* XII, 125–6; XVI, 27 (probably from Nicolaos of Damascus).

[3] Isopolity explicitly mentioned: Antioch, Jos. *B.J.* VII, 44; Alexandria, 3 Macc. II, 30; Jos. *Ant.* XII, 8; and Claudius' edict, *ib.* XIX, 281, which also rightly calls the Jews συγκατοικισθέντας Ἀλεξανδρεῦσιν, *i.e.* a *politeuma* beside the Greek *politeuma*. De Sanctis, *Riv. fil.* 1924, 473, saw that isopolity was the key. For a rather different view, H. Stuart Jones, *J.R.S.* XVI, 17.

[4] Ditt.[3] 522, I.

[5] Sometimes treated as a grant of isopolity to an individual; Ditt.[3] 501; Memnon 9; *SEG* IV, 183, 238.

Athens as a rebel, he sent away his army, appealed personally to his (potential) citizenship, and was received.[1]

The great monument of the Hellenism of the Jewish Dispersion is the Septuagint or 'Book of the Seventy', the translation of the Old Testament into Greek, the Bible of Paul and of Philo; but it is a monument entirely of form, not of substance. The Jewish tradition[2] that Ptolemy II called seventy Jewish elders together and requested them to translate their Scriptures into Greek, the seventy translations being found to agree exactly, is legend; but it shows the Jewish belief that by the second generation the Jews of Alexandria had adopted Greek speech and lost their own, and also their belief that Ptolemy II was sufficiently their friend for such action to be attributed to him. The translation was really spread over a long period; the *Pentateuch* was completed in the third century, *Isaiah* and *Jeremiah* between 170 and 132, the prophets and *Psalms* generally by 132, the last book, *Ecclesiastes*, not till about A.D. 100. The translation, apart from variations due to the use of a much older Hebrew text than ours, occasionally introduces contemporary history; thus Greeks sometimes replace Philistines as the oppressors,[3] and Ezechiel alludes to the wool-trade of Miletus.[4]

Taken as a whole, the Jews of the Dispersion continued to worship Yahweh, looked to Jerusalem as the Holy City, and paid the half-shekel annual tribute for the Temple service; the arrest of this tribute by a Roman governor in 61 revealed the great number of Jews in the province of Asia.[5] But within these limits were many diversities, for the Dispersion was spiritually, even if not racially, the heir of the Northern Kingdom, and had some sympathy with the religions of those around them and a tendency to universalism; some were willing to believe that their religion might save Gentiles as well as Jews, and *Jonah* is an appeal to Jews to spread

[1] *C.A.H.* VI. 450,

[2] Jos. *Ant.* XII, 103 *sqq.*, and more fully in Aristeas.

[3] As Isaiah ix, 12; Jer. xxvi, 16, LXX (=xlvi, 16).

[4] xxvii, 18.

[5] Cic. *pro Flacco* 66–9.

that religion throughout the Hellenistic world. Doubtless the Dispersion in general conformed to the Law; but while there were Jews in Judaea whose minds were receptive of Greek thought, such receptivity must have been much more common in the Dispersion, which on the whole was open to Hellenistic influences. The fact that many Jews lost Hebrew and spoke Aramaic rendered it easier to adopt yet another language, and many Jews everywhere began to speak Greek and take Greek names, preferably those compounded with *Theos*, God, like Theodotus, Theophilus, Dorothea; even in the third century the Hebrew Scriptures were useless to many Alexandrian Jews. The services in many synagogues were conducted in Greek, and a long list of Greek words hebraised has been compiled, ranging from political terms to articles of domestic use.[1] With Greek speech came Greek customs. Jewish settlers imitated their Greek neighbours; they formed trade associations, like the purple-dippers and carpet-makers of Hierapolis,[2] passed decrees in Greek form, set them up on steles before their synagogues, conferred the usual honours, like crowns, and instead of front seats at the games gave chief seats in the synagogue[3]; like Greeks they gave titles and honours to women; they copied Greek forms of manumission and Greek grave inscriptions. Some Jews in Asia Minor tolerated mixed marriages and dropped circumcision; and, corresponding to this, beside the strict proselytes there were sympathisers who were not compelled to be circumcised or to keep the whole Law, but who kept only the Sabbath and the food ordinances and worshipped Yahweh; the Sabbatistai of Cilicia[4] were probably a Gentile association who kept the Sabbath and worshipped Yahweh as Sabbatistes. These proselytes show that Jewish propaganda had some effect on Gentiles; occasionally too Greeks adopted Jewish forms, like those Greek associations in Egypt and Chios whose head was called *archisynagogus*, 'ruler of the synagogue'.[5]

[1] Much of this section from Schürer.
[2] *I. Hierapolis* 342; Ziebarth, *Gr. Vereinswesen* 127.
[3] *C.I.G.* 5361; *B.C.H.* X, 328. [4] *OGIS* 573. [5] Poland 356.

But in Asia Minor and Syria some Jews went far beyond the imitation of Greek *forms*; they adopted Graeco-Oriental cults. It may be evidence that they came from Babylonia (p. 219), for the eastern Jews had long been receptive in this respect; women had learnt to wail for Tammuz and make cakes for the Queen of Heaven, Jews had taken Babylonian names, which 'implied at all events an identification of Yahweh with Bel-Merodach and Nebo',[1] and a Persian demon figures in *Tobit*. In Asia Minor Yahweh himself took a Greek name as *Theos Hypsistos*,[2] God the Highest, a name used later even by Philo; the inscriptions from the synagogue at Delos[3] are conclusive that Hypsistos often meant Yahweh. But when in Egypt the synagogue at Athribis was dedicated to Hypsistos by the local Jews, jointly with the prefect of police on behalf of Ptolemy V and his queen,[4] possibly the Jews meant one thing and the prefect another; for Hypsistos could mean other deities beside Yahweh, notably Zeus,[5] and in Syria the term was applied to Zeus (Baal) of Heliopolis and other gods. The 'synagogues of Satan' at Smyrna and Philadelphia, 'which say they are Jews but are not', may point to some blended worship of the kind, seeing that the altar of Zeus at Pergamum figures in the *Revelation* as 'Satan's seat'. Sabazios too was equated with the god of the Jews, from a fancied identity of Lord Sabazios with Lord Sabaoth[6]; his mysteries, which purified men from ancestral sin, could be fitted to a religion which believed in the original sin of Adam. A society of Sabazios-worshippers is known who also worshipped Hypsistos, and in 139 some Jews were expelled from Rome ostensibly for introducing the worship of Zeus Sabazios.[7] Lastly, the name Sambathaios, Sabbath-born,

[1] Charles, *Religious Development*, 213.

[2] Cumont, *C.R. Ac. Inscr.* 1906, 63, and *Hypsistos* in P.W.; Roberts, Skeat and Nock, *The Gild of Zeus Hypsistos*, in *Harvard Theol. Rev.* XXIX, 1936, 55. For the identification of Yahweh with Zeus, as early as the fourth century, see S. A. Cook, 179, 186, 212.

[3] Plassart, *Mélanges Holleaux* 201.

[4] *OGIS* 96, cf. 101.

[5] A. B. Cook, *Zeus, passim.*

[6] Cumont, *C.R.Ac.I.* 1906, 76.

[7] Val. Max. I, 3, 2.

common among Egyptian Jews,[1] may really be derived, not from Sabbath, but from Sambethe, the Chaldean Sibyl who had a shrine, Sambatheion, at Thyateira[2]; probably her name was identified with Sabbath. Doubtless the Jewish devotees of these Judaeo-Pagan cults believed they were still worshipping the God of their fathers; but they were influenced by Hellenistic syncretism, the belief that different peoples really worshipped the same god under different names, and that names and cults could therefore be united. These cults may conceivably have been sufficiently important to make Antiochus IV think that there would be no insuperable difficulty in introducing, even in Judaea, the worship of Zeus.

Apart from these cults, anything Jews took from Hellenism was only outward forms; few learnt anything of its spirit. Whether a Jew adopted or rejected Greek forms he remained a Jew, a man whose ideals were not those of the Greek, even if expressed in the same words. Both desired political freedom; but, to the Greek, freedom was an end, expressed in the free self-governing community, making its own laws and worshipping what gods it pleased, while to the Jew it was a means, preventing interference with his devotion to a Law divinely given and unalterable by man, and to a God beside Whom there could be no other object of worship. Both praised Wisdom; but, to the Greek, wisdom was a thing which grew with the toil of many brains, while to the Jew it was the fear of the Lord, unchangeable for ever. Judaism by the first century was offering the strange spectacle of a system which refused to accept Greek thought while it opened its doors wide to the infinitely lower influences of the east—astrology, demonology, magic; because of these it hoped to make handmaids for its own spirit, while the Greek spirit could be no handmaid. But if the ideals of the Jew and the Greek conflicted, the world was to need both; and it was therefore to the good that, when Greek thought was overrunning the east, the Jew should stand out against it.

[1] Fuchs *op. c.*, Index p. 140 *sq.*; San Nicolo, *Äg. Vereinswesen*, 22.

[2] *C.I.G.* 3509; Beer, *Sambethe*, and Gressmann, *Sabbatistai*, and Rzach, *Sibyllen (die einzelnen)*, no. 18, in P.W.

But in one respect the Jew and the Greek had a parallel experience. As the political decline of the self-governing city state after Alexander made individualism inevitable for the Greek, so the destruction of the old national State and of the Temple had made it inevitable for the Jew; the idea of a blessed future for Israel was ultimately replaced by that of a blessed future for the Israelite. And as the Greek had his problems of individualism and universalism, so, on other lines, had the Jew: would Yahweh extend the hope of that blessed future to all mankind? Were men indeed to be brothers, not (as the Stoics hoped) in this world, but nevertheless at the end? In the second century the idea of personal immortality, or rather of resurrection from the dead, became firmly established in certain Jewish circles. It is strange that some should have believed that the Jew took his belief in immortality from the Greek, seeing that the Hellenistic Greek had no such belief: certain people might attain to immortality, but certain people only; the normal reward of a good man was only everlasting remembrance.[1] The vexed question of what, if anything, the Jews borrowed from Persia cannot be discussed here. More probably they evolved this belief for themselves, though opinions have differed as to their reasons. It has been attributed to Antiochus' persecution (for unless the dead lived again, the upholder of the Law who suffered martyrdom was worse off than the ungodly who conformed),[2] to the growing consciousness that the Messianic kingdom could not be realised in this world,[3] and to the growing experience of personal communion with God.[4] *All* these reasons may well have contributed to the new belief.

We must return to Judaea, where other things beside the belief in immortality developed amid the ferment of Antiochus' persecution and the rise of the Maccabees: a fresh outburst of literary activity, the formation of the Jewish

[1] *Ath. Mitt.* 1907, 261 l. 16.

[2] Bevan, *High Priests*[5], 84; Ed. Meyer, *Ursprung* II, 183.

[3] Oesterley 109; S. R. Driver, *Daniel*, 90.

[4] Charles, *Religious Development* 102; cf. Moulton, *Early Zoroastrianism* 331.

sects, the growth and modification of the Messianic hope. The sects are too well known to require much notice here. Since Ezra there had been a strong body, the Chasidim or 'Pious Ones', who stood for the whole Law; naturally they opposed Hellenism, and from them in Maccabean times there developed the Pharisees, first actually mentioned in 120, who observed oral tradition as well as the written Law, and their allies the Scribes; the name Pharisees is usually explained as 'Expounders' of the Scriptures, but some take it to mean 'Those set apart'. The Sadducees, 'followers of Zadok'—perhaps not David's priest, but some unknown founder—developed out of the well-to-do governing class about the High Priest; they were strict Jews, who rejected oral tradition and the new belief in immortality, unknown to the Old Testament, and had no connection with the Hellenisers; they supported the Maccabee State, to which the Pharisees were sometimes in opposition after Jonathan became High Priest. There were smaller sects, like the ascetic Essenes, and the already noticed 'Covenanters' of Damascus, who held themselves to be a remnant to whom God had revealed the hidden things in which all Israel, notably the Pharisees, erred, and who perhaps under the Maccabees returned to Judaea. Behind all the sects came the mass of the people; they supported the Maccabees down to the reign of Jannaeus, and their prophets were the Apocalyptic writers.

It must now be asked whether any and what Greek influence can be traced in the Jewish literature of this period. There was no reverse influence; seemingly no Greek throughout these centuries so much as suspected[1] that the Jews possessed a literature, still living and growing, which might rival his own. Except for the Babylonian revival (p. 128), other Oriental literatures were almost dead; the Egyptians, for instance, seemingly produced only the *Potter's Oracle*,[2]

[1] Cf. Jos. c. *Ap.* 1, 217.

[2] Wilcken, *Hermes* XL, 544; W. Struve, *Raccolta Lumbroso*, 273; latest text, R. Reitzenstein and H. H. Schaeder, *Studien zum antiken Synkretismus*, 1926, 39.

foretelling the downfall of Alexandria, and the queer jumble of prophecies called the *Demotic Chronicle*,[1] a vague yearning for one of their own race who should come out of Ethiopia and deliver them from the Ptolemies. But from 200 onwards the Jews produced an enormous literature, in which three languages, Hebrew, Aramaic, and Greek, bore their part; among it were portions of the Old Testament canon—*Ecclesiastes*, *Daniel* (a vivid monument of Antiochus' persecution), part of *Proverbs*, perhaps some *Psalms*[2]—and most of the *Apocrypha*. This literature included hymns and wisdom-literature, some of the highest merit; the new religious orientation of the Apocalyptic writers; history, true and false; stories and proverbs, propaganda, magical books, and forgeries—a literature of many complicated currents, testifying to the vitality of the people who produced it. Except for *Ecclesiasticus*, *II Maccabees*, and some of the propaganda writings, the names of the authors are in every case unknown; unlike the Greek, the Jew had no personal pride in authorship, probably because he so often felt himself the vehicle of something before which his own personality sank into insignificance.

Scholars have differed as to Hellenistic influences on this literature; some have traced such influence on a considerable scale, others have denied it altogether. Certain general considerations are of importance here. Both Jews and Greeks during the Hellenistic period were fond of attributing new works to great names of an older day, but as both peoples had begun the practice before they came into contact we have here merely a naïve tendency of the human mind; but if in one undoubted case the Greek and the Jewish mind ran parallel, the same phenomenon may occur elsewhere. For instance, *I* and *II Maccabees* quote state documents, true or forged, like Greek historians; but the model of the writers was the books of *Kings*, and it does not follow that they borrowed this obvious practice from Greeks, though the possibility is not excluded. Again, the mere resemblance

[1] Ed. Spiegelberg, 1914.

[2] On the question of Maccabean Psalms see refs. in Baynes, *op. c.*, 303 *sq.*

of two passages in two writers means nothing unless the matter is such that two men would hardly think of it independently. Few would maintain that Ben Sira, when he wrote the famous praise of his forefathers in *Ecclesiasticus*, was thinking of the equally famous panegyric on the same theme in Aristophanes' *Wasps*, or that when Theocritus alludes to the foxes in the vineyards he was copying from the *Song of Songs*; for many people might praise their fathers or observe the habits of foxes. But when the author of *Daniel* says that Nebuchadnezzar ate grass like an ox he is certainly drawing upon the lament of Shubsi-meshrā-Nergal, the so-called 'Babylonian *Job*'[1]; for men do not eat grass, and this allegorical figure seemingly never occurs elsewhere. If these tests be applied, most of the supposed Greek influence vanishes at once. Perhaps in the higher literature of the time, *Ecclesiastes* apart, the one thing definite is that the learned Alexandrian Jew who at the end of the first century wrote the beautiful first part of *Wisdom* had *probably* read Plato; God is to him transcendent, without immediate contact with the world, and immortality is a purely spiritual survival; and it has been suggested that Plato may have inspired the passage beginning 'The souls of the righteous are in the hand of God'. Nevertheless the author definitely writes as a Jew, and holds to rewards and punishments after death, though spiritual ones; to read a thing is not necessarily to be influenced by it.

Ecclesiastes is rather different. The aristocratic author of this fascinating book lived in Palestine *c.* 200; his inclusion among 'the ungodly' in *Wisdom* (ch. II) shows that he was considered a Helleniser, and his language is said to be slightly affected by Greek; one feels that in his time he had somewhere breathed Greek air. Many different views of his relationship to Greek thought have found advocates[2]; but, despite Dr. Ranston's interesting *parallels* with Theognis, one cannot find any evidence of direct borrowing, not

[1] Translation in C. J. Ball, *The Book of Job*, 12.

[2] List in H. Ranston, *Ecclesiastes and the early Greek Wisdom literature*, 1925, 11.

even in the famous passage IX, 7 *sqq.*, which Jerome first suggested was taken from Epicurus. For just as clear a parallel has been adduced with a passage in the Babylonian Gilgamesh epic[1]; and, while Greeks believed that the thought 'Let us eat and drink, for to-morrow we die' was older than Epicurus and first enunciated by an Assyrian king,[2] *Daniel* shows that some Jews of the time knew Babylonian literature. But it is quite unnecessary to suppose that *Ecclesiastes* borrowed from either source; for the thought is as old as humanity, and must have been, as it still is, acted on by many in many places who had never read *Ecclesiastes* or Epicurus or Babylonian poetry.

I feel much diffidence in expressing opinions on Jewish literature, but *Ecclesiastes* illustrates what seems to me the true view.[3] Greeks and Jews were developing in the same world, and some developed in the same way; just as to-day, there was a body of thought in the air, call it the spirit of the age or what you will, which unconsciously affected men. *Ecclesiastes* could not have been written in Isaiah's time, but there is no need to seek definite borrowing; the Preacher lived in a world which was what it was, and he felt it. But, if a certain Hellenistic atmosphere may be traced in this or that Jewish writer, nowhere is there any proof of a real penetration by Greek ideas.

Much the most important thing in the Jewish world of the time was the Apocalyptic literature; for the mass of the people it replaced the prophets, whose roll was closed, and its two greatest works—the collection of writings called *Enoch*, and the *Testaments of the Twelve Patriarchs*—considerably influenced the New Testament writers. It dealt with the future, which Yahweh was supposed to have revealed to some sage of olden time, like Enoch or Moses; and its central thought was the Messiah, 'the hope of those who are troubled at heart',[4] the Saviour who should come and who is sometimes called 'The Son of Man' and 'The

[1] Barton, *Ecclesiastes*, 39.
[2] Diod. II, 23, 3; Arr. II, 5, 4; Str. 672; Athen. 530 A; Maass, *Orpheus*, 211.
[3] Compare Baynes *op. c.* 142.
[4] I Enoch XXXVIII, 4.

Christ'. The teaching concerning the Messiah varied greatly: sometimes he was divine and existent before the world, sometimes human and subject to death; but thought steadily moved from a Messianic kingdom on earth, with resurrection of the body, to one eternal in heaven, with spiritual immortality. Usually immortality was for righteous Jews only, but occasionally—the greatest thought of the time—it was extended to all men. This doctrine, and the parallel one of rewards and punishments after death, which seems first expressed in the earliest section of *Enoch* (*c*. 200–170), have influenced the world ever since. Both were connected with a problem which greatly exercised Greeks as well as Jews, the problem of the unrighteous flourishing; its handling illustrates the two mentalities. The philosopher Carneades (p. 336) considered it,[1] and argued that if there were gods who cared for the world they would never allow it; therefore, even if there *were* gods, they did not care. The Jewish writers, certain that there was a God who cared, concluded that we could not be seeing the whole process; there must be another life in which the balance would be redressed, the righteous rewarded and the wicked punished. It had nothing to do with the modern hope that some day we may reach true values; for the writers were good Jews, to whom righteousness meant the fulfilment of the Law. They themselves simply stated the reward of righteousness as a fact; but the doctrine led, soon enough, to that abuse of it which has played such a part in the world: 'Be virtuous in order that you may be rewarded'. Mankind was to travel far from the virile Stoic teaching: 'Be virtuous because it is your duty.'

One book that stands apart must be noticed here: *Susannah*. About 95–80 the Pharisees were attempting to reform legal procedure,[2] and *Susannah* is an extremely effective argument in favour of cross-examination as a means of eliciting the truth in legal processes. It is interesting to find a purely mundane matter in which Jews were in advance of

[1] Cic. *De Nat. Deorum* III, 32; Arnim, *Karneades* in P.W., 1972.

[2] Charles, *Religious Development*, 196; Oesterley 393.

Greeks; for apparently this powerful instrument of justice was unknown to Hellenism. An interesting suggestion, however, has been put forward of the influence exerted by Hellenistic rhetorical technique upon the Rabbinic methods of interpreting the Scriptures.[1]

Besides the great Jewish literature was a group of propaganda writers, who wrote in Greek; these borrowed freely enough from Hellenism, but what they borrowed from was not philosophy or history, but that pseudo-history which always so attracts the half-educated. Manetho (*c.* 280) had early voiced a dislike of Jews,[2] but he was an Egyptian priest; however before 100 some Greek writers, of whom Apollonius,[3] a rhetorician living at Rhodes, was the most notorious, were attacking the Jews, and even Poseidonius[4] deigned to spread the story—whether the origin of or an outcome of the scandal that in the Holy of Holies was an ass's head—that Antiochus IV had found there a statue of a man (? Moses) riding on an ass. Naturally the Jews replied; which side began cannot now be said, but the war of words was to culminate in the first century A.D. in Apion's attack and Josephus' answer. The accusations brought against the Jews were, that their culture was merely borrowed from others; that they did not share any feeling of human brotherhood, but kept to themselves; and that they were in fact atheists, because they said no god except Yahweh really existed at all, a charge they themselves did something to provoke by insisting that what other people worshipped was the actual image, and not (as the fact was) the god of whom the image was but a symbol.

Alexander Polyhistor[5] has preserved the attempts of various hellenised Jews to show that Jewish culture was the oldest in the world and that Jews really taught other peoples. The first writer, Demetrius, gives Jewish history fairly correctly, but is interested in such trifles as proving that

[1] D. Daube, 'Rabbinic methods of interpretation and Hellenistic rhetoric', *Hebr. Union Coll. Annual*, XXII, 1949, 239.

[2] Jos. *c. Ap.* I, 228–287.

[3] Jos. *c. Ap.* II, *passim.*

[4] *F. Gr. Hist.* II, A no. 87, fr. 69. Seemingly first told by Mnaseas, *c.* 200 B.C.; *c. Ap.* II, 80, 114.

[5] *F.H.G.* III, 206 *sqq.*

Jacob's 13 children could have been born within 7 years; Leah becomes a mathematical scheme. To Eupolemus, history has no meaning at all: Abraham was one of the giants who survived the Flood and built Babylon; he rediscovered astrology, originally discovered by Enoch who was Atlas, and taught the Egyptians, while Moses, the first philosopher, invented letters and taught the Greeks; Hiram and Solomon correspond in the style of Hellenistic courts, and Solomon outdoes Alexander by spending 160,000 talents on the Temple in wages alone. Artapanus is not ashamed to quote *adespota,* the anonymous flotsam of Hellenistic writing: Joseph becomes the (Ptolemaic) *dioiketes* of Egypt and brings waste land into cultivation; Moses invents almost everything—weapons, machines, ships, philosophy—teaches the Egyptians to worship animals, and is deified after death in good Hellenistic phraseology. Cleodemus, less ambitious, merely made Abraham's sons outrival the Ptolemies by conquering, not only the Trogodytes, but the whole Spice-land of Arabia and Africa; and Polyhistor himself was so confused by the nonsense he had collected that he made of Moses a woman, Moso. Probably allied to this literature was a group of Jewish poets; Philo and Theodotus versified Jewish history in Greek hexameters, and Ezechiel wrote a tragedy on the Exodus, in which the catastrophe of the Red Sea was narrated by a messenger after the best Greek models.

Naturally Jews could write better propaganda than this.[1] The letter attributed to Aristeas is a serious panegyric on Jewish law and Jewish sacred books put into the mouth of a heathen, who argues that all peoples worship Yahweh though they do not know it; and the third book of the Sibylline oracles (the rest is post-Christian) makes a heathen prophetess witness, in Greek hexameters, to the superiority of the Jewish religion over all others. More important, if genuine, would be the work professedly written by the Jew Aristobulus under Ptolemy VI; the author, a Peripatetic, knew Greek philosophy, and undertook to show that the Jewish Law already contained all that was best in that

[1] See further Baynes *op. c.* 166.

philosophy, and that Pythagoras and Plato had learnt from Moses. But some hold that the work is a late forgery.

The distance between the highest and the lowest thought was thus as great among Jews as among Greeks; and when in the later Hellenistic period the hand of the conquering Greek began to slacken and the east came flooding back on the west in one great stream of astrology and magic, the Jew played a conspicuous part; Jewish magicians were reckoned second to none, and the Jewish exorcist was a familiar figure for centuries. The Jews had their own books of magic formulae, like those of which St. Paul's influence made a bonfire at Ephesus; the most famous was the collection attributed to Solomon, of which, legend said, Hezekiah had once prohibited the use, since it seduced men from Yahweh's ordinances.

The fortunes of Hellenism in Judaea itself, after the country attained independence in 142 (p. 217), must now be followed. In 135 Simon was succeeded by his son John Hyrcanus, but his rule began unhappily, for in 134 the last strong Seleucid, Antiochus VII Sidetes, took Jerusalem and razed the walls. Sidetes could not carry out Epiphanes' policy, for he had no longer a party of hellenising Jews to support him; Jonathan and Simon had almost wiped that party out. His Council advised him to exterminate the Jews and have done with trouble, but he followed the moderate course of leaving the High Priesthood to Hyrcanus and refusing to interfere with religious questions, merely making Hyrcanus a tributary vassal. But his death in 129 was the end of Seleucid power and authority, and Hyrcanus had a free hand. The rest of his reign was the golden age of the Maccabee dynasty. He set to work to restore the kingdom of David; he refortified Jerusalem, conquered Edom and parts of Transjordania, secured Rome's alliance, took Shechem, and finally, after stubborn resistance, took and destroyed Samaria. The rise of the Maccabees, who were Levites, had had the consequence that the Apocalyptists now looked for a Messiah, not from Judah and the house of David, but from Levi and the house of Aaron; and to the Galilean author of the chief monument of Hyrcanus' reign, the already mentioned *Testaments of the Twelve Patriarchs*, with its lofty anticipations of the Sermon on the Mount,[1] Hyrcanus himself, prophet, priest, and king[2]—king in fact though not in name—seemed the realisation of the Messianic hope; to him the writer addresses two Messianic hymns.[3]

But the glory soon faded. Hyrcanus' eldest son Aristobulus (105–104) murdered his mother, and his second son Alexander Jannaeus (104–76), who took the royal title, was about as bad as a man could be. A large section of the people, with the sympathy of the Pharisees, revolted against the brutal soldier; after six years of civil war and much misery he mastered the revolt, and the final picture is of Jannaeus reclining at dinner among his harem and watching the crucifixion of the last 600 rebels. There was no more question of a Messianic kingdom of Levi; the Messiah was again to be of Judah, and the Messianic hope was transferred to some unknown future on earth, or sometimes even to a spiritual kingdom in heaven. One thing, however, the Maccabees, from Jonathan to Jannaeus, had achieved. As their forefathers had smitten the Canaanite and the Amalekite, so they had smitten the Helleniser and those neighbouring Syrian cities where Greek culture ruled; a long list has been compiled of cities destroyed or ruined by them, largely by Jannaeus.[4] The twenty years after Jannaeus' death were merely years of war between his sons Hyrcanus II, the High Priest, and Aristobulus II; and it was well when in 63 Pompey appeared, took Jerusalem, abolished the monarchy, carried off Aristobulus, placed Hyrcanus under the Roman governor of Syria, and began to restore the towns the Maccabees had destroyed.

The attempt to hellenise Judaea had gone down in blood; yet for a short time it was to be accomplished from the outside, when few remained in the country who desired it.

[1] Notably *Gad* VI, 3–7; *Dan* V, 3. See Charles, *Testaments of the Twelve Patriarchs*, LXXVIII. [2] *Levi* VIII, 14–15; Jos. *Ant.* XIII, 299.

[3] *Levi* XVIII, 2 *sqq*; *Judah* XXIV, 1–2; (from Charles).

[4] Meyer, *Ursprung* II, 280. The list Jos. *Ant.* XIII, 395–7 were not necessarily all ruined.

The real power in Judaea under the weak Hyrcanus II was his minister, the Idumaean Antipater; after Antipater's murder his son Herod[1] persuaded the triumvirs to make him king of Judaea, and in 37 he took Jerusalem and established the authority which, by grace of Rome, he was to wield for 43 years. Among the Roman client-kings of the transition period he is the outstanding personality; able, cruel, and utterly unscrupulous—the nature of the man is shown in the recipe for success, as correct as abominable, which he gave to Antony: 'Kill Cleopatra'[2]—he succeeded where the far greater Antiochus Epiphanes had failed, and forcibly made of Judaea a very passable imitation of a Hellenistic kingdom. He was not a Hellenistic king, but an Idumaean barbarian moderately well varnished; but Hellenism was the only system he could apply to his mixed realm, stretching from the Lebanon to Egypt. His governors and officials reproduced the usual Seleucid forms; but his numerous Greek cities were only subject towns, and petitioned Rome to transfer them to her province of Syria. As regards the Jews, it seems he never could make up his mind. He tried to conciliate the Pharisees, but butchered the Sadducees; he forbore to build Caesar-temples in Judaea itself, but built a hippodrome in Jerusalem and a theatre and amphitheatre outside the wall; he tried to win the people by rebuilding the Temple with considerable magnificence, while he perhaps hankered after being a god himself,[3] and ultimately expressed his desire by putting on the Temple an eagle, the bird of Zeus,[4] the worst provocation Jews could receive. He built important cities—Sebaste to replace Samaria, Caesarea on the coast with a harbour larger than Piraeus—and helped to adorn Antioch and many other cities; but the Jews disliked his Greek building, for the money was wrung from themselves. He needed masses of money; he confiscated much land, and his private domains

[1] All the facts are in Otto's *Herodes* in P.W. See also *C.A.H.* X (1934), ch. XI; A. H. M. Jones, *The Herods of Judaea*, 1938.
[2] Jos. *Ant.* XV, 191.
[3] Jos. *Ant.* XVI, 157; Otto, *Herodes,* 112 *sq.*
[4] For eagles on unorthodox synagogues, see S. A.Cook, 201.

and their revenue must have been large; his taxation was heavy, and was a perpetual source of discontent. He did give peace and prosperity, but he really ruled by fear and held Judaea down by fortresses; he made and removed High Priests at his pleasure, and the Jews hated him principally for the danger they saw in him to their religion. They rose repeatedly till he became too strong; his last years were a reign of terror, and they rose again the moment he was dead; and they took a belated revenge by ascribing to him a death too horrible to repeat (it was probably cancer of the bowels). His attempted Hellenisation of Judaea did not outlive him, for it was imposed by force from without on an unwilling people. He died in 4 B.C., and in A.D. 6 Judaea became a Roman province, and a new chapter of her history opened. It can only be said here that in the future, as in the past, the devotion of the Jew to his nationality and his religion was to prove a stronger force than any pressure from Graeco-Roman civilisation, and that what survived at the end was the full rigour of the Law.

CHAPTER VII

TRADE[1] AND EXPLORATION

ALEXANDER had opened to Greek influence a world which stretched from the Aegean to the Hindu Kush, from the Jaxartes to the Cataracts. Had he lived he would have enlarged it further, for at his death he had in hand the exploration of the Caspian and an attempt to complete the sea-route from India to Egypt (of which he had explored the section from India to Babylonia) by circumnavigating Arabia; his ships had already reached Bahrein and Ras Mussendam on one side, Yemen on the other.[2] Though abandoned at his death, these plans were again taken up by his successors; but, except for the Graeco-Bactrians, the only plans carried out in Hellenistic times other than his were the Arabian expedition of Ptolemy II (p. 245) and the

[1] The principal work is now Rostovtzeff, *SEH*, which covers the whole field. See also Rostovtzeff, *C.A.H.* VIII, ch. XX, with bibliography; Fr. Heichelheim, *Wirtschaftsgeschichte*, ch. VII, with full bibliographical notes. M. P. Charlesworth, *Trade routes and commerce of the Roman Empire*, 1924, and E. H. Warmington, *The commerce between the Roman Empire and India*, 1928, still have some use for the Hellenistic period. Among a mass of special studies, largely concerned with Egypt (see ch. V), may be mentioned Heichelheim, *Wirtschaftliche Schwankungen* (Egypt, Uruk, and Delos); Rostovtzeff, 'Foreign commerce of Ptolemaic Egypt', *J. Econ. & Business Hist.* IV, 1932, 725; E. Leider, *Der Handel von Alexandria*, 1933; and G. Glotz' articles on Delos (many listed, Heichelheim, *Wirtschaftsg.* 1065 n. 5). For the Eastern trade: H. Kortenbeutel, *Der ägyptische Sud- und Osthandel in der Politik der Ptolemäer und römischen Kaiser*, 1931, and the works mentioned by Heichelheim, *Wirtschaftsg.* 1084 nn. 25, 26, and Rostovtzeff, *SEH* 1414 n. 185. For the sea-route to India, in the last place, Tarn, *Bactria*, ch. IX; Otto-Bengtson, *Zur Gesch. d. Niederganges des Ptolemäerreiches*, Bayer Abh. 17, 1938, pp. 194 *sqq.*, and Tarn's review, *J.H.S.* LIX, 1939, 324. For exploration generally: M. Cary and E. H. Warmington, *The Ancient Explorers*, 1929; W. W. Hyde, *Ancient Greek Mariners*, 1947; J. O. Thomson, *History of Ancient Geography*, 1948, ch. IV, and ch. VI, § 1.

[2] Tarn, *J.E.A.* XV, 1929, 13.

African exploration of the later Ptolemies. In particular, the wonderful voyage made up the coast of Britain to Norway or Jutland by Alexander's contemporary, Pytheas of Marseilles, the first Greek to hear of the Arctic Sea, remained fruitless; the empiric geographers even discredited its truth, though the mathematicians Eratosthenes and Hipparchus, with greater knowledge, wisely accepted it.[1]

The Seleucids were too busy in other directions to give much thought to exploration. Seleucus, in accordance with Alexander's scheme to utilise the Persian Gulf, maintained a fleet there,[2] colonised along the lower Tigris and round the head of the Gulf, and had good relations with the Gerrhaeans[3] of the Arabian coast, who supplied Seleuceia with spices; but naturally he made no attempt to circumnavigate Arabia and divert the Indian trade from Seleuceia to the Red Sea for Ptolemy's benefit. In the north-east his general Demodamas again crossed the Jaxartes,[4] and his son Antiochus I sent Patrocles, distinguished both as general and geographer, to explore the Caspian.[5] Aristotle and Alexander had known that there were two lakes, called the Hyrcanian Sea (our Caspian) and the Caspian Sea (our Aral)[6]; subsequently, however, Alexander had wondered whether an old view, rejected by Aristotle, that the Hyrcanian Sea was not a lake but a gulf of ocean, might not after all be true, while knowledge of the Aral was lost for good within a generation after his death. Patrocles started from the Kizil Usen in Atropatene (Azerbaijan), and explored the south coast and parts of the east and west coasts, but his conclusion that the Hyrcanian Sea *was* a gulf of ocean was possibly due to some native story, badly interpreted; for 150 years later the Chinese Chang-k'ien heard much the same story, in the form that the Aral *was* the Northern Sea.[7] Nothing more was done in the north-east till the Graeco-

[1] Str. 104, 75. [2] Follows from Polyb. XIII, 9, 5; Pliny VI, 152.

[3] Tkač, *Gerrha* in P.W.

[4] Pliny VI, 49; Tarn, *Tarmita*, *J.H.S.* LX, 1940, 89.

[5] Str. 507–8; Tarn, *Alexander* II, 5 *sqq.* But see now L. Pearson C. Q. 1951, 80.

[6] Arist. *Meteor.* II, 1, 10; Tarn, *Alexander* II, pt. 1, § B, p. 6.

[7] Ssu-ma-ch'ien, *Shi-ki*, ch. 123 § 28, tr. Hirth, *JAOS* 1917, 89.

Bactrian kings[1] colonised Ferghana and secured touch with Chinese Turkestan; they began to pave the way for the ultimate extension eastward of Graeco-Persian artistic influences.

From India Seleucus was debarred by the Mauryan empire, and no Greek in arms again penetrated that country till that empire came to an end in 184; but Megasthenes,[2] whom Seleucus sent as envoy to Chandragupta at his capital Pātaliputra near Patna on the Ganges, now partly excavated,[3] greatly enlarged Greek *knowledge* of India. He told some traveller's tales; but he gave the west its first knowledge of the Ganges and of the great kingdom of Magadha, and his account of the organisation of the country under Chandragupta's government, which can now be compared with the *Artha-śastra,* is first-rate.[4] His book remained the basis of all knowledge of Northern India till about 180 the Euthydemid Demetrius of Bactria conquered or annexed the derelict country and for a few years ruled from Pātaliputra to Kathiawar.[5]

Seleucid activity was connected with the question of the Indian or eastern trade, a dominant factor throughout the period. Our tradition assigns to this trade three main routes, northern, central, and southern, this last bound up with the history of the Ptolemies. Of the northern route[6] little need be said. It was supposed to run by Bactra (Balkh) down the Oxus, across the Caspian, and along the Kur and Phasis to the Black Sea; but it is quite certain that it never existed.[7] In Seleucus' time it was still believed that ocean washed the northern base of the Himalaya and was near the Jaxartes (Syr-Daria),[8] and undoubtedly part of Patrocles' business was to ascertain if a northern *sea-route* were possible; later legends even made him partially explore that

[1] Tarn, *Bactria,* ch. IV.
[2] *F.H.G.* II, 397.
[3] D. B. Spooner, *Arch. Survey Ind.* 1912–13, 53; *JRAS* 1915, 63.
[4] *Camb. Hist. India* I, bibliog. to chs. XVIII, XIX.
[5] Tarn, *Bactria,* ch. IV.
[6] Str. 71, 73, 498, 509; Pliny VI, 52.
[7] Tarn, *Bactria,* App. 14.
[8] Arist. *Meteor.* I, 350 a ll. 18–22; Str. 519 (probably Patrocles, cf. 491, 518).

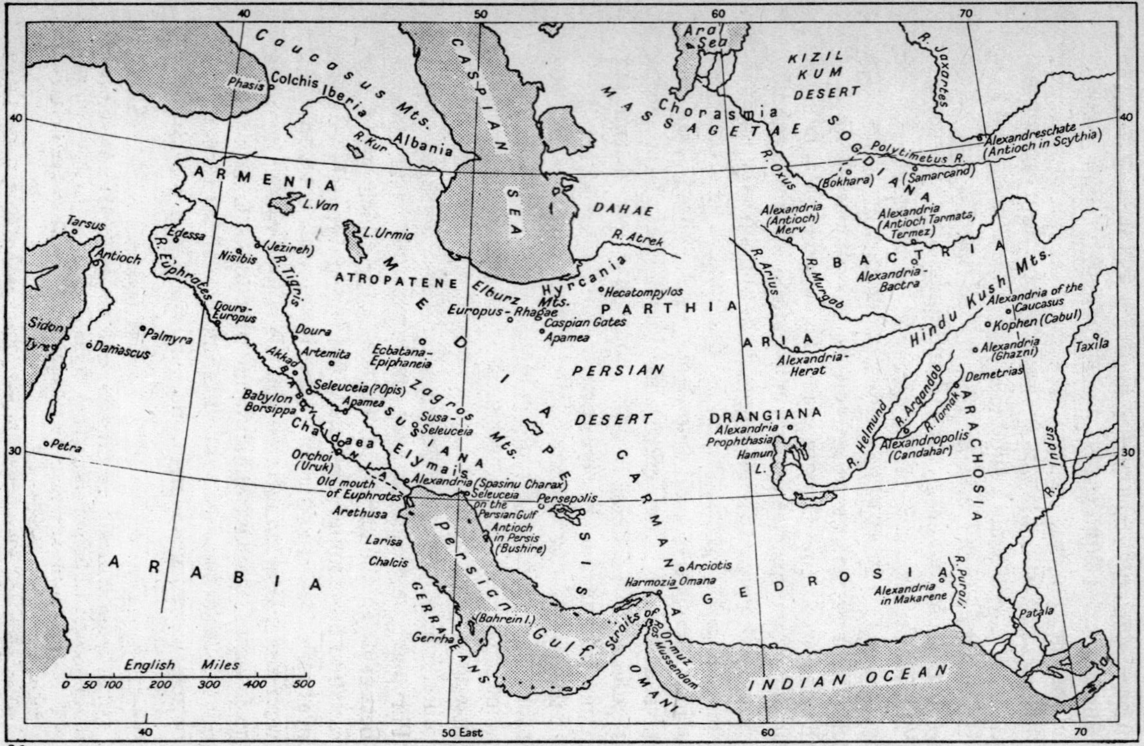

THE MIDDLE EAST

sea-route,[1] and brought Indians by it to the German coast.[2] After Seleucus' death the Seleucids were cut off from the Black Sea and had no further interest in any northern route.

During the third century the important route was the central. This came by sea from India to the Persian Gulf and up the Tigris to Seleuceia, and was supplemented by the overland caravan-trade which Seleuceia gathered in; one route came thither from India by Persepolis and Susa,[3] but its importance is doubtful. The great main road, attested by Greek and Chinese evidence, started from Pātaliputra and ran Taxila–Alexandria of the Caucasus–Bactra–Hecatompylus–Ecbatana–Seleuceia; it was joined by a loop road starting from Alexandria of the Caucasus and running Cabul–Ghazni–Alexandria Prophthasia (on the Seistan lake)–Herat–Hecatompylus.[4] From Seleuceia the accumulated trade passed westward, either by the new Seleucid route[5] up the Euphrates to Antioch, or by the old road east of the Tigris which crossed the river at Jezireh or Libba (Ashur), swept northwards by Nisibis, where it collected the Armenian trade, and so to Edessa, whence part took the traditional road to Damascus and Tyre, while part went to Antioch, crossing the Euphrates at Zeugma, which now superseded Thapsacus.[6] From Antioch a great through route, the old Royal Road, ran by Tarsus and Apamea in Phrygia to the sea at Ephesus (p. 130).[7] The struggles between the Seleucids and the Ptolemies, which lasted from *c.* 280 to 198, though primarily due to the dynastic ambition of the Ptolemies and their desire for empire in the Aegean, were also partly connected with this trade route; its outlet at Ephesus changed hands more than once, and the Ptolemies, by their possession of Phoenicia and the Marsyas valley between Damascus and Antioch, were probably able to

[1] Str. 74, 518. [2] Pliny II, 170.

[3] The route followed by Craterus and Antiochus III. But Strabo thrice gives it as from Persepolis to Carmania, and no farther: 79, 727, 744. [4] For the loop road, Str. 514, 723, and Isidore of Charax *passim*.

[5] Given minutely, Isidore § 1.

[6] Xenophon and Alexander. Jezireh, Xen. *Anab.* III, 5, 7–12; Libba, Polyb. V, 51, 1–2. [7] Xenophon and Alexander; Calder, *C.R.* 1925, 7.

exercise pressure on Seleucid Damascus. In 198–7 the struggle ended with the expulsion of Egypt from Syria and Asia Minor; and the main lines of trade stood till the Seleucids lost Babylonia, and the central route, in Parthian hands, began to give ground to the southern. Various changes occurred after this; in the first century the route Edessa–Mazaca (Caesarea)–Apamea came into use,[1] cutting out Antioch, and by 100 the short cut from Babylonia to Damascus across the desert by Palmyra[2] was probably becoming frequented; finally Rome, following in Pompey's steps, and reaching out from Pontus towards Armenia and the Caucasus for unexploited minerals, brought into some prominence the Caspian–Black Sea route along the Kur.[3]

We turn to the southern route and the Ptolemaic exploration of Africa. This route came from India by sea to depôts in south or south-eastern Arabia, where the Indian shippers landed their goods, and they became part of the Arabian trade; the route was so entirely in Indian and Arabian hands[4] that its very existence in the third century is only certain because Eratosthenes chanced to remark that cinnamon (which grew only in India) came from Arabia east of the Hadramaut.[5] The Arabs guarded their monopoly so jealously that no Indian vessel was allowed inside Bab-el-Mandeb, and the early Ptolemies learnt little about southern Arabia; Eratosthenes knew nothing east of the Hadramaut, which Alexander's expedition had already heard of. The history of South Arabia[6] is one of wars and combinations among its various peoples to control the Indian and incense trades; Solomon's Ophir was probably a name applied to whatever locality was at the time the Indian depôt. In the third and second centuries the dominant power was an

[1] Str. 539.

[2] Pedigree on tomb of Iamblichus; S. B. Murray, *A.J.A.* 1915, 268; Cumont, *Doura* XXXII.

[3] Pliny VI, 52; Solinus, 19, 4.

[4] Str. 780–1; cf. Diod. III, 47, 9. Minaean shipping, refs. Tarn, *J.E.A.* XV, 1929, 17 n. 1; Gerrhaean, Str. 766; Arabs generally, *σχεδίαι* (merchantmen), Agatharchides *passim*; Str. 780–1 *μήτι γε κατὰ θάλασσαν* is wrong.

[5] Str. 769, where *τὴν σμυρνοφόρον* (see 768)=Hadramaut.

[6] Tkač, *Saba* in P.W.; D. Nielsen, *Handbuch der altarabischen Altertumskunde* 1927.

alliance of the Habashat of Mahra and the Sabaeans of southern Yemen, the chief Indian emporium being the Sabaean Adana (Aden), and the accumulated trade being brought north to Petra by the caravans of the Sabaeans and Minaeans over the traditional 'incense route'[1] by Iathrib (Medina) and Dedan (Al-'ula). About 280 Ptolemy II sent Ariston to explore the Arabian coast, and seemingly followed this up by an expedition designed to secure influence at Dedan and get astride the incense route south of the unfriendly Nabataeans.[2] Of the trade which reached Petra, part came to the sea either at Gaza[3] or at Arsinoe (Suez) and so to Alexandria; part may have crossed the desert to Seleuccia[4]; and the rest went north. Normally this last would go by Damascus to Antioch, as it did after 200, when the importance of the Seleucid acquisition of Syria is shown by the display of gold, ivory, and Indian spices made by Antiochus Epiphanes in the great triumph which he celebrated at Daphne[5]; but while the Ptolemies held Syria it also took a route they made by Philadelphia (Rabbath-Amman) and Gerasa (Jerash) across Galilee to Ptolemais (Acre) and so to Phoenicia[6]; the importance of Ptolemais is shown by the town retaining that name under the Seleucids.[7] The fall of the Sabaean kingdom in 115[8] perhaps gave the Ptolemies an opening; but the movement which ultimately led to Egypt sharing the southern route to India started in a side-issue, the desire of Ptolemy II for elephants.[9]

Ptolemy I had begun to explore the Red Sea,[10] and his admiral Philo[11] had discovered the 'Topaz Island',[12] which

[1] Tkač *op. c.* [2] Tarn, *J.E.A.* 1929, 9.

[3] Benzinger, *Gaza* in P.W.; cf. Str. 781.

[4] Route Petra-Babylon: Str. 767 (Eratosthenes); cf. Arr. *Ind.* 43, 4–5.

[5] Polyb. XXXI, 3–4; Diod. XXXI, 16; Athen. X, 439 B.

[6] Polyb. V, 68–71; cf. R. Dussaud, *Topographie historique de la Syrie,* 1927, 44. [7] Hill, *B.M. Coins, Phoenicia,* 128. [8] Tkač, *op. c.*, 1378.

[9] Diod. III, 36, 3; Str. 769, 789; Agatharch., *G.G.M.* 1, p. 111; App. *Prooim.* 10; *OGIS* 54 l. 12.

[10] Generally: Agatharchides in *G.G.M.* 1 and in Str. 769–76 (through Artemidorus); Rostovtzeff, *Archiv* IV, 298; Tscherikower *op. c.* (foundations). [11] Str. 77; *Milet* 1, 7 no. 244.

[12] Diod. III, 39, 4; Pliny XXXVII, 108; Agatharch. *G.G.M.* 1, 170.

some Ptolemy cleared of snakes. Early in the reign of Ptolemy II his general Satyrus founded Philotera on the Gulf of Suez[1]; Arsinoe at its head must also belong to this reign, and probably Berenice on the Gulf of Elath.[2] Ptolemy II then pushed steadily southward; his generals in succession founded Myos Hormos (Mussel Harbour) at Kosseir, Berenice of the Trogodytes on the 'Foul' gulf (*i.e.* full of reefs), whose ruins (latitude of Assouan) remain, and Ptolemais of the Elephant-hunts near Suakim; Ptolemy III founded Berenice the Golden (perhaps Adulis) near Massowah, and possibly Koloë (Kohaito) in Ethiopia, whose ruins are said to be Ptolemaic; later it was a depôt for ivory, which came to sea at Adulis. Many of these settlements became towns,[3] though probably they began as fortified trading posts, for the primary business of this exploration was to collect ivory and capture elephants for war; Ptolemy III organised the hunts on a military basis under a general.[4] Expeditions fitted out at the northern Berenice, whither the elephants were shipped[5]; a well-equipped road ran thence to Coptos (Koft) on the Nile,[6] the main elephant park being at Memphis.[7] A fleet was maintained on the Red Sea for protection against piracy.[8]

The loss of Syria and the Aegean under Ptolemy V induced a change in Egypt's attitude toward the Indian trade; she now had to rely exclusively on the southern route. Under Ptolemy V, too, the elephant hunts began to die out, and the organisation created for them was presently diverted to the protection of trade and placed under the general of the Thebaid; in 130 his duties included supervision of shipping and the collection of topazes, and protecting those who brought incense over the Coptos route.[9] More attention was

[1] Date: Tarn, *C.Q.* 1926, 99. [2] Tarn, *J.E.A.* 1929, 22.
[3] Str. 771, 773, 815; Pithom-Stele on Ptolemais (Tscherikower 14).
[4] *OGIS* 82, 86.
[5] Pithom-Stele (Budge, *Hist. of Egypt* VII, 201 *sqq.*); *G.G.M.* 1, 172; Wilcken, *Chrest.* nos. 435, 451–2.
[6] *OGIS* 132; Str. 815; Pliny VI, 101. [7] *P. Petrie* II, 20.
[8] Diod. III, 43, 4 = Str. 777 (Agatharch.); *P. Grenfell* 1, 9.
[9] *OGIS* 132.

paid to sea-carriage up the Red Sea to Alexandria, as a rival to the Sabaean caravan trade. There was considerable activity in that sea in the second century; in the north Cleopatris near Suez was founded, in the south the southern Arsinoe, not far from Bab-el-Mandeb. Philometor also pushed the boundary up the Nile to south of Wady Halfa, and founded new settlements.[1] Probably early in the century Egyptian generals had already reached the 'Horn of the South', Cape Guardafui in Somaliland, afterwards called the Cape of Spices; they founded no factories, but discovered many strange tribes of savages to add to the only savages so far known to the Greeks, the Fish-eaters of Gedrosia discovered by Nearchus; the whole coast from the Gulf of Suez to Cape Guardafui was named Trogodyte[2] (commonly misspelt Troglodyte), and the peoples distinguished as fish-eaters, root-eaters, turtle-eaters, ostrich-eaters, and locust-eaters.

By the end of the second century the growing demand in Italy for the products of Arabia and India made this trade more important than ever to Alexandria, while the Ptolemies had two strokes of fortune: the Sabaean power broke up, and about 120–117, under Ptolemy Euergetes II, an Indian, sole survivor of his crew, was picked up half dead in the Red Sea; and under his guidance Eudoxus of Cyzicus, in Ptolemy's service, made the first (European) sea-voyage to India and back, coasting.[3] This voyage brought the discovery of the south-west monsoon,[4] associated with the name of Hippalus, but doubtless long known to Indians, which made it comparatively easy to venture outside Bab-el-Mandeb; and the ships of the later Ptolemies visited South Arabian ports, discovered Socotra,[5] did something to break the monopoly of the Arab middlemen, and sometimes sailed through to

[1] *OGIS* 111.

[2] Wilcken, *Archiv* VIII, 71.

[3] Str. 98–102 = Poseidonius, *F. Gr. Hist.* II A, no. 87 fr. 28. Cf. Str. 72, Somaliland the end of the oecumene.

[4] On this and what follows see generally Tarn, *Bactria*, 367–71; Otto-Bengtson, *op. c.* 194–218.

[5] Greeks arrived between Agatharchides (*G.G.M.* 1, 191, unknown) and *Periplus* 30.

India[1]; but the first voyages direct across the Indian Ocean to southern India were not earlier than about A.D. 40–50.[2] The later Ptolemies secured the straits of Bab-el-Mandeb by refounding Deire on the straits as the southern Berenice, while the nearer Myos Hormos began to replace the northern Berenice as the port of Coptos; and by 78,[3] if not as early as 110/9,[4] the *epistrategos* of the Thebaid had become also general of the Red Sea and the 'Indian Sea', a new name which points to regular connection with India. Indian traders on their side began to come direct to the Somali ports, and Indians appeared in Egypt[5]; a gravestone with wheel and trisula attests the presence of Buddhists in Alexandria.[6] These voyages brought the first knowledge of southern India. Pepper supplies valuable evidence of the arrival of South Indian products. Minute quantities had long found their way to Greece, though to Theophrastus it was a medical drug[7]; if then in 88 a man in Athens had *two quarts* in his house,[8] something new had happened. Eastern trade and exploration thus show a steady evolution throughout the Ptolemaic period, and when Cleopatra VII suggested abandoning the Mediterranean and ruling the Indian seas instead she was not talking folly; she might have anticipated Albuquerque.

Whether anyone at this time ever went south of Cape Guardafui depends on another story told by Poseidonius.[9] He says that in a later voyage Eudoxus coasted along Africa 'beyond Ethiopia' and brought back the prow of a wrecked ship identified as belonging to Gades in Spain; he then went to Gades and tried to sail round Africa to India in the track of the Gades ship, but turned back just south of Morocco owing to trouble with his crew. The story is quite possible; but it is disfigured with absurd details—for instance, it makes Eudoxus ignorant of the Ptolemaic regulations

[1] Contested; but Str. 101 and 118 are explicit, and 798 not against it. See Wilcken, *Z. f. ägypt. Sprache* 1925, 88.

[2] Tarn, *Bactria*, 369.

[3] *OGIS* 186, 190.

[4] Otto-Bengtson, *l.c.*; see Tarn, *J.H.S.* LIX, 1939, 324.

[5] Wilcken, *Grundzüge* I, 264.

[6] Petrie, *JRAS* 1898, 875.

[7] Athen. 66, C–F.

[8] Plut. *Sulla* 13.

[9] Fr. 28=Str. 99.

concerning imported spices—and Poseidonius was hardly the man to sift truth from falsehood, nor does he say why he believed it when he disbelieved Herodotus' story of the Phoenician circumnavigation of Africa. The Eudoxus part may be accepted, but as to the voyage of the Gades ship the verdict must be 'not proven'.

The chief rival of the Ptolemies in this later period was the wonderful Nabataean city of Petra, 'dwelling in the clefts of the rocks'. After the Parthians occupied Babylonia and controlled the central route from India, Petra became one of the greatest marts in Asia; beside land caravans, her people were now getting sea-traffic through Aelana (Akaba), and they cut out Egypt's direct imports from Dedan through her Arabian port of Ampelone, probably by capturing Ampelone and renaming it Leuce Come.[1] They extended north as well as south, and even for a time, from 85, ruled Damascus.[2] The Nabataeans had a genius for trading, and Greeks remarked upon the strange fact that they never went to law with one another[3]; probably, like Chinese merchants, they always honoured their word.

When we come to the details of trade, we are met at the outset by the fact that among all the vast literature of Hellenism no work is recorded professedly dealing with its commerce, important as this was.[4] Hellenistic trade is largely a palimpsest, buried under that of the Roman Empire as the Hellenistic road system beneath the Roman; and one cannot merely argue backwards from the better-known Roman phenomena. Some of the material in later compilers is undoubtedly Hellenistic; but these require careful analysis.

The Persians had excluded Greek traders from inner Asia; and the opening up of this continent by Alexander and his successors, the growing wealth and population of Asia and Egypt, the mass of new cities and settlements, an enhanced

[1] Tarn, *J.E.A.* 1929, 21–3; further on Dedan and the Lihyanite inscriptions, H. Grimme, *Le Muséon*, 50, 1937, 269.

[2] *Syria* VI, 218 no. 2, and coins.

[3] Str. 779.

[4] Greeks, still a ruling race in the new kingdoms, never came to think of trade in itself as a thing that could possibly be worth writing about.

standard of living in the upper classes, all gave trade a tremendous impulse. The size of merchant ships increased till it culminated in Hiero's unmanageable Syracosia,[1] with a load capacity of 4,200 tons, while the new habit of sailing direct from point to point instead of coasting increased the speed and scope of commercial operations. Many cities in the third century improved their ports, and the book of Timosthenes of Rhodes *On Harbours* filled the place now held by the *Mediterranean Pilot.* Many Greek cities signed conventions for the regulation of contractual disputes between their citizens, a movement fostered by Rhodes, and something was done towards filling the place now occupied by our banking and credit systems; letters of credit were known, though not bills of exchange.[2] Every Hellenistic king (unless the Antigonids) was a great merchant, and some Greek cities followed their example and instituted municipal trading; mines of course had never been private property, but now Rhodes, Cnidus, and others made and stamped their own jars from their own claypits,[3] Priene and Uruk owned salt-works,[4] Miletus had municipal sheep-runs and wool factories.[5] Merchants too were free of one modern anxiety; demand normally outran supply, and if you could get a thing you could certainly sell it; judging by Delos, retailers' profits were considerable, even 100 per cent. being known, though 20 per cent. to 30 per cent. was more usual.[6]

The amount of money actually in circulation increased enormously after Alexander instituted his international coinage, as was necessary for the increased trade; and by the third century the world was divided into two main currency spheres.[7] The Alexander-drachma was identical with the Attic, and this standard was used by Athens, Macedonia and her dependants, the Seleucid Empire and the Far East, Pergamum, Bithynia, Cappadocia, the Black Sea (through Lysimachus' money), and Epirus; it invaded Aetolia and

[1] Athen. 206 D; see Beloch IV, 1, 299. [2] See *ante*, p. 116 n. 4
[3] List, Wilcken, *Archiv* VI, 400; cf. Glotz, *Ancient Greece at Work*, 1926, 353. [4] *I. Priene*, 111 l. 112; Clay, *Babylonian Records* IV, 53 no. 54.
[5] Glotz, *op. c.* 351, 354. [6] Glotz, 363. [7] Beloch IV, 1, 307–12.

Boeotia, and eventually Rome, by making her denarius equivalent to the Attic drachma, joined this standard too. Ptolemy I at first adopted the Rhodian standard, owing to the close trade relations between Egypt and Rhodes; but after acquiring Phoenicia he changed to the Phoenician standard, to which Rhodes also subsequently adhered; this standard ruled in Egypt and her dependencies, Carthage and her empire, Rhodes, Syracuse, and Marseilles. The two international standards thus reflected the old opposition of Athens and Phoenicia. The Aeginetan standard was still used at Delphi and elsewhere, but had little importance; Corinth too maintained her old standard, but her coinage would pass with the Attic. Carthage experimented with token money.

In the third century the trade preponderance definitely shifted from Greece to Egypt, Rhodes, and the coast of Asia; but too much has been made of this, and the prosperity of Messene *c.* 100 (p. 112) shows the difficulty of talking about the poverty of Greece before Sulla's time. Athens' commerce certainly decayed, until the revival in the late second century; but Corinth,[1] with the transit trade between Asia and Italy, could in the second century perhaps vie with Ephesus; in 205 Heracleides said Chalcis had the best equipped market in Hellas,[2] while Boeotia was full of money[3]; Aetolia notoriously grew wealthy,[4] Ambracia[5] flourished as the port of entry from Italy till Rome diverted the traffic to Dyrrhacium, and the art of Pagasae (p. 321) attests a prosperous existence. What did happen was that much of the great *increase* went to the new countries; in 170 the 2 per cent. import and export duty produced at Rhodes a million drachmae (p. 175), as against 200,000 at Athens in 401. But it is curious that most of the wealthiest cities of the world—Seleuceia, Antioch, Rhodes, Ephesus, Cyzicus, Corinth, Delos—were fed by *transit* trade; Ephesus, a transit centre, gained steadily on her rival, manufacturing Miletus; the fact suggests the dominant part played in

[1] Beloch IV, 1, 271. [2] *F.H.G.* II p. 260. [3] Polyb. XX, 6.
[4] *Ib.* XXI, 26, 9; Agatharch., *F.H.G.* III, 192.
[5] Hatzfeld, *Les trafiqu ants Italiens*, 22; cf. Polyb. XXI, 30, 9; Str. 325

international trade by oriental produce and manufactures. Beside Miletus, the chief exceptions were Alexandria and Pergamum, with their serf and slave factories, and Tyre; but Alexandria and Tyre did great transit trades also. It is interesting to compare Alexandria, the greatest Hellenistic port, with Puteoli in Campania, when after 88 the latter became Italy's port of entry for the eastern trade.[1] Alexandria imported[2] all timber, all metals, wool, purple, marble, fine wines, spices, and horses, a formidable list; nevertheless her exports[2]—wheat, papyrus, glass, linen, woollen goods, ointments, perfumes, ivory, and luxury articles generally—far exceeded her imports; hence came part of the Treasure of the Ptolemies. But at Puteoli imports far exceeded exports[3]; and as Rome did not flood the Aegean with coin, the balance represented a new thing in the world, the plunder of the Roman tax-farmer.

We turn to objects of trade. As regards metals,[4] the general outline is clear; except for iron, copper, and to some extent silver, the eastern Mediterranean was becoming worked out, especially as regards gold. The gold of Pactolus and Tmolus in Lydia, and of Asia Minor generally, belonged to the past,[5] as did the alluvial deposit of Scaptesyle[6] and the gold mines of Mount Bermion and Pieria in Macedonia[7]; some mines along the Strymon survived,[8] but no Antigonid king coined gold. Eastward, the Hyctanis in Carmania is said to have brought down gold[9]; how far this was exploited cannot be said. The gold of the Persian empire had come through Bactria from the main Asiatic source of supply, Siberia, from which had also come the 'ant-gold' of western India[10]; but by the middle of the third century both the Siberian gold routes had been cut, and little gold came to western Asia. The gold of Spain,[11] down to 202, probably

[1] Str. 793.

[2] Wilcken, *Schmoller's Jahrbuch* XLV, 105; *Grundzüge* 1, 266; E. Leider, *Der Handel von Alexandria*, 1935. For horses, Rostovtzeff, *Large Estate* 167–8; cf. *P. Cairo Zen.* 59075.

[3] Str. 793.

[4] Blümner, *Eisen, Gold, Kupfer, Silber* in P.W.

[5] Str. 591, 626, 680.

[6] Perdrizet, *Klio* X, 1.

[7] Str. 680.

[8] *Ib.* VII, fr. 34.

[9] *Ib.* 726; Pliny VI, 98.

[10] Fully in Tarn, *Bactria*, 105–8.

[11] Str. 146.

went to, and through, Carthage. But the Ptolemies, pushing southward, opened up valuable gold mines in Nubia and in the mountains above Berenice the Golden,[1] and probably got some gold from Arabia[2]; they had a gold coinage from the start. Silver was mined in some quantity by both cities and kings in Asia Minor,[3] and Mount Pangaeus in Macedonia was worked throughout the period,[4] though Laurium failed steadily, and by Augustus' time only the dumps were being worked over.[5] But a very large amount came eastward from Spain, the Treasury of Empire, where silver was 'nowise accounted of'; it must have come from Gades to Carthage or Phoenicia, and when Jonah about 300 desired to fly to Tartessus (*i.e.* at that date Gades) he at once found a ship going there. The world required silver in masses for coinage and luxury goods, but the supply was ample; the Ptolemies could put Egypt on a silver basis and amass a great treasure, and in 91 silver plate was common at Messene, a little town in a backwater (p. 112). Copper was almost monopolised by the Ptolemies through their hold on Cyprus, which was probably too rich in copper[6] to fear even Spain's rivalry; but they never worked the mines of Sinai,[7] which indeed was becoming Nabataean.[8] Euboean copper was worked out,[9] but the Attalids had some local mines.[10] Iron was still found everywhere; and if certain mines, like the Laconian, closed down, there were valuable deposits in the islands never even touched. The finest quality (*i.e.* approaching steel) which came by sea to Cyzicus,[11] was produced by the Chalybes (p. 343),[12] now scattered about Pontus and Armenia; in the first century Chinese iron, imported into Parthia through Merv, was highly spoken of.[13]

[1] Pliny VI, 170; Agatharchides, *G.G.M.* 1, 123.
[2] Tarn, *J.E.A.* 1929, 15. [3] Rostovtzeff, *SEH passim.*
[4] Str. VII, fr. 34. [5] Str. 399. [6] Str. 684.
[7] Rostovtzeff, *SEH* 297, 1173, and Excursus II (Sinai).
[8] B. Moritz, *Gött. Abh.* XVI no. 2. [9] Str. 447.
[10] *Ib.* 607, 610; Rostovtzeff in *Anatolian Studies* 367.
[11] Rostovtzeff, *ib.* 365. [12] Str. 549.
[13] Pliny XXXIV, 145; cf. Ssu-ma-ch'ien, *Shi-ki,* ch. 123 § 103 (tr. Hirth, *l.c.* 108). Imported: Oros. VI, 13, 2 + Plut. *Crassus* 24. The theory that Seric iron came from the Cheras of southern India is unfounded.

Tin came from Cornwall and Brittany, at first through Gades and Carthage, but after 300 in increasing measure up the Loire and Garonne and overland to Marseilles.[1] Possibly there was some in Spain, but the Tin Islands are either a myth or a misunderstanding.[2] Quicksilver, in the form of cinnabar, chiefly used to make vermilion, was obtained from three sources[3]: the Cappadocian mines which had once supplied Sinope with her 'Sinopic earth', the new Zizima mines near Laodicea the Burnt, and a deposit near Ephesus; the whole supply now came to Ephesus.

Speaking generally, mining was the gravest blot on Hellenism. There are shocking stories of the mortality in the Laurium and the Cappadocian quicksilver mines[4]; but it must suffice to quote Agatharchides' description of the Nubian gold mines,[5] which the Ptolemies worked, not only with slaves and criminals (the usual practice), but with prisoners of war, who might be free Greeks. The younger men, crawling with lamps on their foreheads, tunnelled the quartz by hand, following the veins of gold. The hewn quartz was dragged out by the children, and the older men broke it small with hammers; the fragments were then, preparatory to washing, ground to dust in spar-mills, turned, not by oxen, but by the women, three to a spar and naked. They were guarded by armed Nubians; all were fettered and flogged, and were worked without rest or care for their bodies; and all, says Agatharchides drily, welcomed death when it came.

As to foodstuffs, corn[6] was probably the greatest of all trades, not excepting raw silver; Athens, Corinth, Delos, many islands,[7] Ionia,[8] and perhaps other cities, were normally importers, while the great producers were Egypt (with the Cyrenaica),[9] and the Crimea. Greece was supplied from Egypt and the Crimea; when in the second century the latter

[1] M. Cary, *J.H.S.* 1924, 166. [2] Haverfield, *Kassiterides* in P.W.
[3] W. Leaf, *J.H.S.* 1916, 1. [4] Str. 562. [5] *G.G.M.* 1, 123.
[6] A. Jardé, *Les céréales dans l'antiquité grecque* I.
[7] *I.G.* XII, 5, 1010 and 1011; 7, 40; *OGIS* 4. Str. 684, Cyprus self-supporting is a curiosity.
[8] *OGIS* 9; Ditt.[3] 354, 344 ll. 73–100. [9] For Cyrenaica, *SEG* IX, 2.

source began to fail,[1] Numidia was ready to take its place, and in 180 Masinissa sent Delos corn at a cheap rate.[2] Whether Babylonia competed with Egypt in supplying Ionia, or what happened to Babylonia's surplus, is unknown; our ignorance of the whole Seleucid interior is profound. Some Sicilian corn came to Greece[3]; but in any case Egypt's supremacy in the wheat market was unquestioned. The depôts of the international corn trade were Rhodes[4] and Delos (p. 264). Wine was produced everywhere, but the finest wines were a speciality of two countries: North Syria, whose wine was exported from Laodicea on the Sea,[5] and Ionia with the coastal islands (except Samos); Lesbos, Chios, Cos, Cnidus, Ephesus, Smyrna, Tmolus, and the volcanic Katakekaumene were all famous.[6] Alexandria insisted on Syrian and Ionian wines, whatever the duty,[7] as London insists on champagne, while Laodicean wine travelled even to South Arabia[8]; it was the vineyards which prevented Ionia growing enough corn, for vines gave roughly five times the profit of wheat off the same acreage.[9] Of other foodstuffs, Athens exported the finest oil, Athens and the Cyclades honey,[10] Byzantium salt fish[11] (partly Euxine re-exports), Bithynia cheese,[12] Pontus fruit and nuts,[13] Babylonia and Jericho dates[14]; the dried figs of Antioch on the Maeander,[15] the raisins of Cos and Berytus,[16] and the prunes of Damascus[17] were celebrated. Indian sugar was known, but was used only as a medicine.[18]

[1] Polyb. IV, 38, 5; Rostovtzeff, *Iranians and Greeks in South Russia*, 147; Ramsay, *Asian elements in Greek civilisation*, ch. XI.
[2] *I.G.* XI, 4, 1115, note.
[3] *I.G.* II², 408 (330 B.C.); *SEG* III, 92; Diod. XXVI fr. 8; Polyb. XXVIII, 2, 5.
[4] Dem. LVI, 9 *sq.*; Polyb. XXVIII, 2, 5, XXXI 31, 1, cf. V, 89; Diod. XXVI fr. 8.
[5] Str. 752.
[6] Str. 628, 637, 657.
[7] Many papyri; see Wilcken, *Archiv* VI, 400.
[8] Assuming *Periplus* 28 + 49 indicates an older trade.
[9] Jardé *op. c.* I, 187.
[10] Str. 399. 489; *P. Cairo Zen.* 59426, 59012 l. 30.
[11] *Ib.* 59012; Wilcken, *Archiv* VII, 82.
[12] Str. 565.
[13] *P. Cairo Zen.* 59012.
[14] Str. 763, 800, 818; Pliny XIII, 44; Jos. *Ant.* XV, 96.
[15] Str. 630.
[16] Pliny XV, 66.
[17] Athen. 49 D *sqq.*; Charlesworth 47.
[18] Str. 694; said to occur in medical prescriptions.

As to textiles. Alexandria was the principal exporter of linen,[1] her only rivals being bat-eating Borsippa[2] and Colchis[3]; the flax industries of Elis and Judaea were much later. Aeolis[4] and the Cyrenaica[5] both produced wool, and Pergamum[4] and Alexandria[6] exported woollen goods, but the real centre of the wool industry was Miletus[7]; her home-grown wool was as yet the best in the world, though all Lydia and Phrygia wove wool; the district about the salt Lake Tatta, where water was sold for money, and the Katakekaumene, whose wool was woven at Laodicea on the Lycus, carried great flocks.[8] Doubtless too there was a large wool industry in Syria, for it cannot have started full-blown under Rome. Several places had specialities, like the curtains and gold-woven cloth of Pergamum,[9] the carpets of Aeolis,[9] and the rough cloaks of Cilicia[10]; while Alexandria also turned out cheap goods to trade to African natives.[11] Cotton, once cultivated in Assyria,[12] was only known as a curiosity,[13] though Indian muslins must have been imported, at least in the first century.[14] Chinese silk never came westward till Chang-k'ien in 115 opened up the Central Asian caravan route, after which it certainly reached Parthia[15]; possibly Chinese silk fabrics were known in Egypt in the first century B.C.,[16] but, speaking generally, all the silk in use came from the wild silk-worm of Western Asia.[17] Cos throughout the period imported the cocoons and wove the thread into diaphanous stuffs for women's wear[18]; between wine, silk, and faith-healing, Cos prospered

[1] Wilcken, *Grundzüge* 245. [2] Str. 739. [3] Str. 498.

[4] Rostovtzeff in *Anatolian Studies* 379.

[5] Pindar, *P.* 9, 11. [6] Schubart, *Einführung*, 418.

[7] *P. Cairo Zen.* 59142, 59195, 59430; *B.C.H.* 1922, 307 no. 1; Pliny VIII, 190; Theoc. XV, 126; Athen. 540 C, D; Ezek. XXVII, 18 (LXX).

[8] Str. 568, 578, 630; Pliny *l.c.* [9] Rostovtzeff, *l.c.*

[10] Livy XXXVIII, 7, 10; Varro *R.R.* II, 11, 12, a trade-name.

[11] Wilcken, *Grundzüge*, 267. [12] *C.A.H.* III, 77.

[13] Str. 693. See however Olck, *Byssos* in P.W.

[14] Arr. *Ind.* 16, 1–3; Lucan III, 239 (probably); Warmington 210.

[15] Ssu-ma-ch'ien, *Ski-ki*, (Hirth *l.c.*, esp. pp. 103, 133); cf. Florus III, 11, 8.

[16] Sir A. Stein, *Burlington Mag.* XXXVII, 1920, 3.

[17] Blümner, *Serica* in P.W.; so the *Hou Han Shoo* (Chavannes, *T'oung Pao* 1907, 184 n. 1). [18] Arist. *H. An.* 551 b, 13; Pliny VI, 54; XI, 76.

enormously, but 'Coan garments' were only a trade name, and there must already have been a large silk industry in Phoenicia (which worked up 'Arabian' imports),[1] for silk became so common that in 91 the women at Messene had to be prohibited from wearing transparent dresses during initiation.[2] But Cleopatra's silks were possibly Chinese,[3] whether they came through Parthia or by sea from India.

A complete list of the known specialities of different places, produced or manufactured, would be a long one.[4] Alexandria supplied the world with paper (papyrus),[5] Alexandria[6] and Sidon[7] with glass, though glass-making is said to have been rare in Egypt before the Roman period.[8] Parchment, from the second century, was Pergamum's monopoly, but the story that Eumenes II invented it is untrue; it had long been known, and what he did was to utilise his wealth in cattle and leather, and his slave factories, to organise mass production.[9] Macedonia and Mount Ida in the Troad competed in supplying the world with pitch[10]; the Antigonids had some system of export duties or licences under which they lowered the price to their friends and raised it to their enemies.[11] Egypt drew her bitumen for embalming from the Dead Sea fisheries,[12] and it was plentiful in Babylonia[13]; bituminous earth, used for protecting vines from insects, was exported from Rhodes and Seleuceia in Pieria.[14] Alexander's discovery of petroleum on the Oxus[15] was never followed up. Parian marble held its own everywhere, and after 166 Athens was doing a large trade in Pentelic[16]; many others were used, sometimes only locally,

[1] Agatharch., *G.G.M.* 1, 189. [2] Ditt.[3] 736 l. 22. [3] Lucan X, 141.

[4] See for one group of commodities, A. Schmidt, *Drogen und Drogenhandel*, 1924. [5] Wilcken, *Grundzüge*, 255, &c.; cf. Str. 800.

[6] Schubart, *Einführung*, 418; de Bissing, *Rev. Arch.* 1908, i, 211.

[7] Str. 758; Pliny V, 76. [8] Cumont, *L'Égypte des Astrologues*, 108.

[9] Pliny XIII, 70; Cumont, *Doura* ch. V.

[10] Theophr. *H. Plant.* IX, 2 *sqq.*; Pliny XIV, 128; Polyb. V, 89, 6.

[11] Glotz, *Rev. E.G.* 1916, 281, 324.

[12] Diod. XIX, 98 *sq.*; Str. 763. [13] Str. 743; Isidore § 1.

[14] Poseidonius, *F. Gr. Hist.* II A no. 87, fr. 93.

[15] Arr. IV, 15, 7; Str. 518; Athen. 42 F; Plut. *Alex.* 57.

[16] Ferguson, *Hell. Athens* 376.

but the taste for and trade in coloured marbles from Euboea and Thasos and serpentine from Egypt and Tenos must be largely Roman,[1] for it was they who opened up the green marble of Taygetus[2] and exploited the red-veined marble of Docimeum, only sparingly worked in Hellenistic times.[3] Macedonia supplied Greece with timber,[4] and treeless Egypt drew on the cedars of Lebanon (always a royal domain), the pines of Cyprus, and the oaks of Bashan, while through Arsinoe in Cilicia she tapped the Taurus forests[5]; by the time she lost her northern empire she was ready to import timber from the Trogodyte coast. Rare woods came from Pontus[6] and Somaliland, and ebony,[7] known at Delos and in Egypt, from India. The world's windows were made of Cappadocian talc.[8] Egypt exported some granite, for about 130 it was used for the new docks at Delos.[9] Purple mussels and sponges were fished for at many places in Greece,[10] but the manufacture of purple was still the principal industry of Phoenicia, where Tyre and Aradus became exceedingly prosperous; dyeing was also a great industry in Ionia and western Asia Minor.[11] Ivory from India was a Seleucid monopoly until between 269 and 250 Ptolemy II threw enough African ivory on the market to break the price[12]; with the decay of the Mauryas and the exploitation of Ethiopia African ivory must have gained steadily on its rival, and in the first century the Ptolemies made magnificent gifts of ivory to the temple of Didyma.[13] Throughout the third and early second centuries there was a steady influx of slaves into the Greek cities from Thrace, Syria, and Asia

[1] Charlesworth 123. [2] Str. 367; Pliny XXXVI, 55.

[3] Str. 577; Calder, *J.R.S.* II, 1912, 245.

[4] Plut. *Dem.* 10; Diod. XX, 46, 4; Ditt.[3] 334 l. 29; Polyb. V, 89, 6; Pliny XVI, 197. [5] Str. 669. [6] *Ib.* 546.

[7] Durrbach, *Comptes des Hiéropes*, 320 B l. 68, 351 l. 4; Athen. 201 A.

[8] Str. 540. [9] Ferguson *op. c.* 362.

[10] The list Charlesworth 125 are not all new industries. For Delos, refs. Durrbach *B.C.H.* 1911, 82.

[11] Athen. 539 F–540 A; Str. 630; *B.C.H.* 1922, 307 no. 1; *I. Hierapolis* no. 342; Wilcken, *Chrest.* no. 2; *Acts* 16, 14.

[12] *I.G.* XI, 2, 163 l. 7; 203 A l. 71; 287 A l. 118.

[13] *OGIS* 193; Wiegand, *Siebenter Milet-Bericht* p. 50.

Minor (p. 105); even before 200 there was *possibly* a slave market at Delos, though on a modest scale.[1] Lastly, Pontus, whose great wealth was not really exploited till the first century, was the chief source of medical drugs.[2]

Of the luxury articles, gems[3] came largely from India and Arabia, though Egypt produced amethysts[4] and obtained topazes from the Red Sea[5] and emeralds from Talmis in Ethiopia[6]; India and the Persian Gulf sent pearls, unknown before Alexander, but now highly valued by women as ornaments.[7] But whether women used precious stones much seems doubtful[8]; diamonds were unknown, rubies extremely rare, and (except for pearls) Theophrastus deals only with the use of stones for gem engraving; the sards of Sardes and Babylonia were noted,[9] and gem engraving flourished at Alexandria. One trade, amber, was dead; the Gallic migrations had destroyed the machinery of the old amber route from the Baltic to the Adriatic, and amber was a curiosity only till the route was re-established in Nero's reign.[10] Tortoiseshell[11] came from India and the Trogodyte coast, and Alexandria was a great centre of goldsmith's work; but the real luxury trade was in spices.[12] The demand was vast. India sent cinnamon and cassia, spikenard from the Himalaya, nard and bdellium (the two latter also came from Gedrosia)[13]; Arabia, beside frankincense, chiefly sent myrrh.[14] Pisidia produced styrax and various gums,[15] which probably made the prosperity of Selge; Lake Gennesareth supplied scented rushes[16]; Jericho had a monopoly of balsam, the

[1] *I.G.* XI, 4, 1054; see Roussel, *Délos colonie athénienne*, 19.

[2] Str. 163; Crateuas' work (ch. IX, *post*).

[3] Now done scientifically, Warmington, *op. c.*, Pt. 2 ch. 3.

[4] Pliny XXXVII, 121.

[5] *OGIS* 132; see p. 245.

[6] Olympiodorus, *F.H.G.* IV, 66; cf. Str. 815.

[7] Arr. *Ind.* 8, 11; Theophr. περὶ λίθων 36; Lucan X, 139; Babelon *Margarita* in *D.S.*

[8] Theophr. *l.c.*, 'the expensive necklaces' are pearls.

[9] Pliny XXXVII, 105.

[10] Blümner, *Bernstein* in P.W.

[11] Str. 72, 773.

[12] Scientifically classified (India): Warmington pt. 2 ch. 2.

[13] Arr. VI, 22, 4; Str. 721.

[14] *P.S.I.* VI, 628; Rhodokanakis, *Z. f. Semitistik* 1924, 113.

[15] Str. 570; Pliny XII, 125; Athen. 201 A.

[16] Theophr. *H.P.* IX, 7; Str. 755; cf. Polyb. V, 45, 10.

plant having been uprooted (as the Dutch once treated the clove) everywhere but in the famous balsam gardens, which Antony later presented to Cleopatra[1]; possibly the balsam plants were divine, like the frankincense trees (*post*), for they had to be cut with a stone knife,[2] which implies some old religious rite. Cinnamon was highly prized, but the trade was so entirely in Arab hands that Greeks believed it grew in Arabia and Somaliland.[3] Alexandria was the centre of the spice trade,[4] with Rhodes as her depôt for export[5]; spices were a royal monopoly, supervised by an official[6] to whom all spices entering Egypt had to be delivered; the working up of these imports into ointments and perfumes,[7] and the export of the finished article, constituted a great industry. What an ointment now meant may be illustrated by that used at the coronation of the Parthian kings,[8] which contained 27 separate ingredients, as against four in that used to anoint the High Priests at Jerusalem. What India took at this time in exchange for her exports seems unknown. But South Arabia[9] was supposed to take little but styrax,[10] Laodicean wine (p. 255), and Alexandrian glass and cloth; hence arose the legend that South Arabia was bursting with accumulated money,[11] a legend which played its part in Gallus' ill-fated expedition under Augustus.

One commodity, frankincense, stood apart from all others; for it was as much a religion as a trade. No worship, Greek, Jewish, or barbarian, could be carried on without it, and it smoked on every altar of the 'inhabited world'. The quantities required were great; Alexander captured more than 500 talents weight at Gaza,[12] and the altar of Bel at Babylon alone consumed 1,000 talents annually.[13] The

[1] Theophr. *H.P.* IX, 6; Str. 763, 800; Diod. XIX, 98; Plut. *Ant.* 36; Jos. *Ant.* XV, 96; *B.J.* 1, 361; Justin XXXVI, 3, 1; B. Laufer, *Sino-Iranica* 429.

[2] Jos. *Ant.* XIV, 54.

[3] W. H. Schoff, *Periplus* p. 82, settled this problem.

[4] Wilcken, *Grundzüge*, 249, and *Z. f. Äg. Sprache* 1925, 86; Rostovtzeff, *Archiv* IV, 313; Collart and Jouguet, *Raccolta Lumbroso*, 109.

[5] *I.G.* XI, 2, 161 A l. 92, Durrbach, *Comptes* 354 l. 67 (myrrh).

[6] *P.S.I.* VI, 628; Wilcken, *Archiv* VII, 82.

[7] List, Pliny XIII, 8–17.

[8] Pliny XIII, 18.

[9] Arguing back from the *Periplus*.

[10] Cf. Pliny XII, 81.

[11] Str. 780.

[12] Plut. *Alex.* 25.

[13] Herod. I, 183.

frankincense country was the coastal district of South Arabia from the Yemen mountains eastwards through the Hadramaut to beyond the plain of Dhofar.[1] The trees were sacred; only men of certain families might tap them,[2] and then only with religious rites, for they were drawing the life-blood of a divine creature; the trees themselves were propitiated during tapping by burning styrax incense to them, as to gods.[3] In the factories at Alexandria where frankincense was handled the workpeople on leaving work were stripped and searched like Kaffirs in the Kimberley diamond mines.[4] Yet so little luxurious was Greek luxury that this most valued of all products, after all the expense and danger of its long caravan journey, fetched on reaching the Aegean a price per lb. roughly equivalent to a week's wages of a skilled worker.[5] Whether Egypt ever succeeded in obtaining frankincense direct through Somaliland without Arab intermediaries does not appear.

The great trading races, beside the Greeks, were the southern Arabs and Nabataeans, already noticed, and the Phoenicians; Phoenician merchants had even followed Alexander's terrible march through Gedrosia, and their later settlements on Delos show that their keenness remained unimpaired. There is no evidence that the Jews played any particular part in commerce; Josephus says truly that they were not a commercial race.[6] Two cities, Rhodes and Cyzicus, kept out non-Greeks[7]; but this was unusual. Foreign traders who settled in a city generally formed an association of their nationals, and probably brought their own gods; the type may be seen in the Phoenician Poseidoniastae at Delos, whose establishment comprised a temple, porticoes for displaying merchandise, and ancillary buildings.[8] Associations are found, however, whose basis was not nationalism but a particular trade, as the Italian oil-traders on Delos,[9] or

[1] Tkač, *op. c.*
[2] Pliny XII, 54.
[3] Herod. III, 107; Schoff, *Periplus*, 130–1, and his citations.
[4] Pliny, XII, 59.
[5] Averaging *I.G.* XI, 2, 287 A ll. 43 and 73.
[6] *c. Ap.* 1, 60; Fuchs *op. c.* 56 has scarcely a name.
[7] Hatzfeld, *Les trafiquants Italiens dans l'Orient hellénique*, 116, 156.
[8] Picard, *B.C.H.* 1920, 263; *Délos* VI.
[9] Ferguson *op. c.* 405.

the associations at Athens and Alexandria of all export merchants.[1] The later Hellenistic period saw a new phenomenon, the appearance in the Levant of the Roman trader, encouraged by the creation of the free port of Delos in 166 and the formation of the province of Asia in 130.

'Roman' traders[2] included all of Roman allegiance, some being Italian Greeks; the first recorded at Delos are Serdon, a 'Roman', in 259,[3] Novius in 250,[4] and Minatus a Campanian in 220,[5] and by 230 there were some in Epirus. By 130 they were numerous in Greece, were much the largest body on Delos, and were pouring into Asia; their way was made easy by the denarius (p. 251). By 74 they were plentiful in Bithynia, but did not penetrate further eastward in Asia Minor; but after Pompey annexed Syria a strong body settled in Antioch, and under Augustus they reached Petra,[6] but only when Petra was almost a Roman protectorate. In Alexandria they appear from 127 onwards, but were of small account[7]; Rome's chief contribution before Augustus to Egyptian business was the creation of a tourist traffic up the Nile.[8] The Roman trader was not at first unpopular, either in Greece or Asia; he often became a citizen, married a Greek wife, owned land, took part in the city life, perhaps held a magistracy, and sent his son to the gymnasium and through the ephebate; some, as Zosimus at Priene,[9] imitated the wealthy Greeks by spending money freely on municipal benefactions. They formed regular business houses with branches. But many were not free; out of 231 Romans of known condition at Delos, 88 were free (27 being Italian Greeks), 95 freedmen, and 48 slaves,[10] and this is said to be a high proportion of free. They were expected, and sometimes even ordered by the Roman Senate, to conform to the laws of the city they settled in, but they had one enormous advantage over their Greek and Oriental competitors: they

[1] *I.G.* II², 1012; *OGIS* 140.
[2] J. Hatzfeld, *op. c.*, 1919, from which much of what follows is taken.
[3] *I.G.* XI, 2, 115 l. 25.
[4] Durrbach, *Comptes*, 287 l. 58.
[5] *Ib.* 351 l. 5.
[6] Str. 779.
[7] Durrbach, *Choix des inscr. de Délos*, I, ii, nos. 105–8.
[8] As *P. Tebt.* 33.
[9] *I. Priene* 112–14.
[10] Hatzfeld 241

could, and often did, appeal from the city law to Roman law, and got the benefit of edicts or allowances from complacent Roman governors; the dice were, politically, weighted in their favour, one reason why they clung to countries under Roman rule. This ended, especially in Asia, by arousing a discontent which commercial rivalry would not have done; for the Greek, given fair play, could hold his own in *that* field.

In 166 Rome broke Rhodes' power by making Delos a free port, *i.e.* abolishing import, export, and harbour duties; and though Rhodes remained commercially prosperous, Delos soon took her place as the centre of international transit trade in the Aegean. The destruction of Corinth in 146 gave Delos a further opportunity. Mommsen's view, that Rome destroyed Corinth for commercial reasons, has now been questioned [1]; for it is unlikely that Corinth excluded Romans from participation in her trade, and though her destruction was ultimately of advantage to the Romans on Delos, it is doubtful whether Mummius really looked so far ahead; probably the act was merely a warning to Greece. Something can be learnt about the trade of Greece itself after 146 by noting where Roman traders settled; the strong body at Thespiae suggests that Thespiae secured some of Corinth's transit trade, and they invaded Epirus because the desolated country was now given over to breeding cattle and horses. It seems that the modern ports of Salonica (Thessalonica) and Patras (Patrae) now did little trade; Thessalonica fell with the Antigonids, and Macedonia's commercial centre was again Amphipolis, while Italian traffic still crossed from Brindisi to Ambracia, as in Pyrrhus' day; Patras only became important when Augustus made it a colony. The one business the Romans perhaps created was the supply of trade statuary to Italy (pp. 317–8).

Delos [2] in the third century had still been the holy island;

[1] Hatzfeld 367.

[2] Besides the works cited in the notes, see P. Roussel, *Délos colonie athénienne*, 1916; Durrbach, *Choix des inscr. de Délos*; Rostovtzeff in *C.A.H.* VIII, XX, with bibliography, and in *SEH* 788 *sqq.*; also on Delos generally, W. A. Laidlaw, *A history of Delos*, 1933, and J. A. O. Larsen, *Roman Greece*, in T. Frank's *Economic Survey of Ancient Rome*, IV.

but her trade had steadily increased with the increasing prosperity of her Asiatic background, as is shown by the continued fall in agricultural rents after 250 and the enormous rise in house rents (pp. 116, 120), and she was already a great corn-market, to which came the Antigonid officials from Thessalonica[1]; probably she owed part of her prosperity to Antigonid help.[2] Many kings adorned her with buildings; such were the houses built by Ptolemy I for the ship he dedicated,[3] and the porticoes of Antigonus Gonatas,[4] Attalus I,[5] and Philip V,[6] this last certainly meant for the use of merchants. When Rome gave her back to Athens in 166 she was not badly equipped, in spite of her poor harbour, for an international commercial centre; and under the rule of Athens and the Athenian cleruchs who expelled the Delians and settled on the island there was a vast influx of foreigners; Romans flocked thither to meet the Orientals, as did the Orientals to meet the Romans. Her prosperity reacted on her mistress, and down to 88 Athens enjoyed an Indian summer[7]; shipping again sought the Piraeus,[8] wealth increased, business men supplanted the old landowners, and larger families became not uncommon; beside her exports of Pentelic marble and statuary, Athens manufactured articles of domestic use—vases, lamps, beds. But this aftermath of prosperity originated in a great injustice to the Delians, and was partly due, not to Athenians, but to the Roman and the Phoenician who had worked in under Athens' skin.

In 130 the slaves on Delos rose; the Athenian cleruchs were helpless, and the rising was suppressed by the whole business community. Thereon the rule of the cleruchs ended, and Delos became a unique kind of state-form, the state-form composed of *politeumata* taken one step further:

[1] *I.G.* XI, 4, 1055, 666, 680, cf. 664–5, 1053.

[2] Roussel, *op. c.*, 10; R. Vallois, *Délos* VII, i, 166.

[3] Couchoud and Svoronos, *B.C.H.* 1921, 270, with *ib.* 1922, 473, 476.

[4] *I.G.* XI, 4, 1095; F. Courby, *Délos* V.

[5] R. Vallois, *Le portique de Philippe*, *Délos* VII, i, 162–3; E. V. Hansen, *The Attalids of Pergamon*, 268.

[6] *I.G.* XI, 4, 1099; Vallois *op. c.*

[7] Ferguson, *Hell. Athens*, 373.

[8] Ditt.[3] 706.

the foreign business associations became 'settlers', and in their totality apparently constituted 'Delos', seemingly without any city forms at all, but under an Athenian governor[1]; that is, political precedents were subordinated to the requirements of trade. If gold can make a golden age, Delos[2] now enjoyed one; she had part of Rhodes' transit trade, most of Corinth's, and all that she created for herself from the growing Italian demand for luxuries. Building was taken up on an extensive scale by individuals and corporations; existing houses were divided into tenements, and new warehouses erected along the sea-front, with quays lined with Egyptian granite; by 125 the artificial harbour, long in hand, was completed, and there rose a mass of temples, magazines, meeting-places for the various nationalities and their worships, culminating at the end of the century in the market-place of the Italians; cheap building, much of it, adorned with uninspiring statues and mosaics copied from an older art. Every Asiatic people met there—Egyptians, Phoenicians, Syrians, men from Pontus and Bithynia; Minaeans from South Arabia brought their god Wadd[3]; by 100 there were Jews, who built a synagogue. Between the third and first centuries the Phoenician associations steadily became less religious and more mercantile.[4] Greeks were represented chiefly by Athenians and cosmopolites like Simalos of Cyprus,[5] who acquired Tarentine citizenship and enrolled his son in an Attic deme; few came from Greece itself, Macedonia, the Islands, or the old Greek cities of Asia. Far the strongest element now was the Romans; they were favoured by the Athenian governors, Athens having consistently been Rome's friend, and became the real power in the island.

Delos was purely a place of transit trade, and as such received every kind of traffic, while the big motley population crowded on the little island made her of necessity still

[1] Following Ferguson, *ib.*, 380, against Hatzfeld, *B.C.H.* 1912, 189; *Trafiquants*, 130.

[2] Described, Ferguson, *ib.*, ch. IX; Roussel, *Délos* ,1925.

[3] Clermont-Ganneau, *C.R.Ac.I*, 1908, 546.

[4] Picard, *B.C.H.* 1920, 263.

[5] Hatzfeld, 308.

an emporium of foodstuffs; but much of her wealth was due to a less reputable cause. The growing plantation system of great estates in Italy and Sicily demanded masses of slaves, while Rhodes, politically weakened, was no longer an effective check upon piracy; and Delos and the pirates, in unholy alliance, undertook to supply what Italy required. Delos became the greatest slave-market yet known, and as the eastern governments began to grow weaker their subjects were drained away; Bithynia[1] is said to have been half depopulated. Few Greeks were guiltless where slavery was concerned, but the decadence of Delos under Roman influence here stood confessed; for while Apollo in Greek Delphi was doing what he could to free slaves, Apollo in cosmopolitan Delos looked down on such iniquity as no Greek soil had yet seen: the once holy island, within whose bounds none had made war on another, now boasted that she could easily handle over 10,000 slaves a day.[2] The gold of the golden age was indeed tainted. The shame of Delos was reflected upon Athens; but, except for Athenians, it does not appear that any Greeks had much part in this disgraceful traffic, which was mainly conducted by Romans and Orientals. Finally the power and audacity of the pirates, organised as a regular state in western Cilicia, compelled the Roman government to interfere, and the hospitality of Delos to the scourge ceased; but it was only historical justice that the city, after being sacked in 88 by a general of Mithridates, the ally of the pirates, was in 69 finally destroyed as a trade centre by a pirate captain.

Of trade after the great catastrophe of 88 and the massacre of the Roman traders in Asia (p. 42) there seems little to say here. Greece and Delos never recovered; Puteoli, the 'lesser Delos', took Delos' place as the emporium for eastern imports into Italy; the Orientals followed the trade, and in Puteoli were settlements of Nabataeans, Phoenicians, and Syrians from Heliopolis and Palmyra. Roman traders flocked back to Asia after Sulla's settlement, and large bodies are known in many places, while Nabataeans settled

[1] Brandis in P.W., *s.v.*

[2] Str. 668: 'could', not 'did'.

in Miletus.[1] Alexandria was not affected by the catastrophe; but Phoenicia must have suffered from the disintegration of her Seleucid background, and the troubles of Asia generally at the hands of the contending generals in the Roman civil wars must have been reflected in trade depression; and it seems probable that in this sphere, as in many others, the re-establishment of peace and decent government by Augustus came none too soon.

[1] *Milet* 1, 3, 387 no. 165.

CHAPTER VIII

LITERATURE AND LEARNING[1]

It was natural that, after the great upheaval of civilisation caused by Alexander's career, the number of those who tried in some fashion publicly to express themselves should increase enormously. Education, as the age progressed, became widely spread, but formed, as to-day, not one public but two: one of the highly educated, and a larger one which had education enough to read greedily but not to read seriously; both publics were catered for accordingly, one by the specialist, the other by popular literature. The systematisation in Greek hands of the production of papyrus, and subsequently of parchment, combined with the employment of educated slaves, enabled books to be produced on a scale heretofore unknown; and therewith presently appeared two new phenomena, the literary man, who wrote, not because he had something to say, but because to write books about other books was a pleasant thing to do, and the bibliophile, like Apellicon of Teos (*c.* 100)[2] who made the romantic discovery of part of Aristotle's library hidden in a cellar. The great Hellenistic capitals enabled writers to concentrate in or for certain centres where there was a numerous public; while the improvement of communications, and the spread of a common civilisation and the 'common speech' over a large part of the 'inhabited world', meant that even the man from an outland city, like

[1] Generally. F. Susemihl, *G. d. griech. Literatur in der Alexandrinerzeit*, 1891 (still indispensable); W. von Christ, *G. d. griech. Literatur* II, ed. 6 by W. Schmid, 1920 (Müller's *Handbuch* VII, ii, 1); Wilamowitz, *Die griech. Literatur*[3], 1924; Beloch IV, 1, chs. XIII, XIV; J. U. Powell and E. A. Barber, *New chapters in the history of Greek literature*, 1921, 1929, and 1933; Barber in *C.A.H.* VII ch. VIII; H. J. Rose, *A handbook of Greek Literature*, 1934.

[2] Str. 609.

Borysthenes or Artemita, was secure of an audience; a considerable list can be made of writers from the Euphrates provinces and even farther east[1]; a city like Susa, for example, as fully in the Greek culture-sphere. The rulers of the new kingdoms were generally helpful and sometimes enthusiastic; learning became a power, and was for a time rated above wealth. Poets or historians might be the friends of kings, philologists or architects their ambassadors; an apt quotation once turned the fate of a treaty.[2] Writers began to obtrude, instead of concealing, their personalities; no one can guess what Thucydides was like, or the author of the story of Ahab and Elijah, but we all know Polybius and the Preacher.

Above all, the kings established libraries[3] in their capitals. The idea of a library had probably come down from Assyria and Babylon, but in the Greek world before Alexander only an occasional tyrant had had the money to collect books; and if Aristotle formed the first private library on any scale, Alexander supplied the means. State libraries now appeared at Antioch and Pergamum, and later at Rhodes,[4] Smyrna,[5] and probably other cities[6]; but everything was eclipsed by the famous library in the Brucheion at Alexandria, founded by Ptolemy I and arranged under Ptolemy II, who founded the 'daughter' library in the Serapeum, perhaps for duplicates. Besides the Library, Ptolemy I founded the Museum; whether or not Demetrius of Phalerum gave him the idea, the foundation was in Aristotle's spirit. Henceforth, though Athens kept philosophy, Alexandria eclipsed her as the world's centre of science and literature, which sucked in workers from every quarter. Little is

[1] Ed. Meyer, *Blüte und Niedergang*, 24; add Herodicus of Babylon, and Herodorus of Susa (Cumont, *Mém. Délég. en Perse* XX, 89 no. 6). See now Tarn, *C.A.H.* IX, 596, and fully in *Bactria*, 39–55; also, on rather different lines, F. Altheim, *Weltgeschichte Asiens in griech. Zeitalter*, II, 1948, 137–69.

[2] Sext. Emp. *adv. Gramm.* 662; *C.A.H.* VII, 714.

[3] Dziatzo, *Bibliotheca* in P.W.; Beloch IV, 1, 425; and the works on Egypt.

[4] De Sanctis, *Riv. fil.* 1926, 63; Powell and Barber, II, 83; M. Segre, *Riv. fil.*, 1935, 214 (fragment of the catalogue).

[5] Str. 646.

[6] Gift of a library and 100 books to Cos, L. Robert, *B.C.H.* 1936, 421.

known of the Museum, an association of learned men, at their head a priest of the Muses, who lived and laboured in the building at Ptolemy's charges, freed by him from all worldly cares; Timon the Sceptic called them 'fatted fowls in a coop'.[1] It was broken up by Euergetes II, but seemingly re-formed again.[2] The Library was in charge of an official Librarian, who was also the crown prince's tutor. Ships from every country dumped book rolls on the quays, and it was well on in Ptolemy II's reign before they were sorted out and arranged; by the first century the Library had grown to perhaps 700,000 rolls, though the figure is uncertain. What Caesar burnt was not the Library but either some book-dump on the quay or books stacked there to be carried off; in compensation Antony gave to Cleopatra the 200,000 rolls of the library of Pergamum, though it is not known if they were ever transferred. The Alexandrian Library was broken up and partly destroyed in A.D. 272, when Aurelian burnt the Brucheion.

The known librarians who covered the great period were Zenodotus of Ephesus, Apollonius 'the Rhodian', Eratosthenes (p. 302), Aristophanes of Byzantium, another Apollonius, and Aristarchus of Samothrace; it is possible, though far from certain, that Callimachus was librarian between Zenodotus and Apollonius.[3] Of these men, four at least were philologists; philology, already started by Theophrastus' pupil Praxiphanes of Mytilene, was at Alexandria to find new scope and become the basis of her achievement. Zenodotus invented textual criticism by comparison of MSS., and the Alexandrian school established and handed down the texts of the Greek classics and also introduced accentuation. Zenodotus settled a text of Homer, expunging many interpolated verses; Aristophanes and Aristarchus worked on his text, and our vulgate text is largely Aristarchus'; many other writers were similarly treated. Zenodotus also began arranging the books; he took the epic and lyric poets, and

[1] Athen. 22 D. [2] *OGIS* 172.

[3] *P. Oxy.* X, 1241; Körte, *Archiv* VII, 243; Wilamowitz, *Hell. Dichtung* 1, 206 (excludes Callimachus); Beloch IV, 2, 592 (includes Callimachus).

his helpers, the poets Lycophron and Alexander the Aetolian, the comedies and tragedies respectively; Callimachus arranged the prose works and made and published the catalogue, a stupendous work called *Pinakes* which formed a guide to the authors, with biographies and other information; Aristophanes wrote a Supplement, while a similar work was afterwards compiled for the library at Pergamum, probably by Crates of Mallos. These men made philology a science at which many worked down to Roman times, producing commentaries, criticism, and a whole literature of rare words, the foundation of lexicography, like the list of Macedonian words compiled by the Macedonian Amerias. Part of the commentary on Demosthenes by Didymus of Alexandria (*c.* 40) has been recovered; it is really a substantive work on Demosthenes, full of citations from historians and supplying useful historical material. Didymus wrote on most authors, and is said to have produced more books (3,500 rolls) than any man before or since; he earned his nickname Chalcenteros (Brazen-Guts).

Including science and philosophy, over 1,100 Hellenistic writers are known, but most are little but names; for the great bulk of Hellenistic literature has entirely perished. We possess only wreckage, though the sands of Egypt are steadily increasing the amount. How came so few Hellenistic writers to reach Constantinople? The accepted explanation, that the Attic reaction of the second century A.D. made men contemptuous of Hellenistic work, seems inadequate; for the worst of all Hellenistic styles, the Asianic, was still alive two centuries later. Third-hand compendiums, no doubt, ultimately killed off the original historians; Hellenism was itself responsible for the modern fallacy of the short cut to knowledge. Many writers too perished because they were not read in schools; one school in 3–2 B.C. was using Eudoxus' out-of-date astronomy.[1] But, generally speaking, the causes of the great wreck, and the part played by Rome, are still obscure.

[1] C. H. Oldfather, *Greek literary texts from Graeco-Roman Egypt*, 20 no. 314.

We may take the poets first.[1] Poetry, by Alexander's day, had been almost crushed to death by the weight of the great masters; none could approach them, and it was hardly worth trying. The one name of repute since Euripides was Antimachus of Colophon; his *Lyde*, a collection of short poems on love themes addressed to his mistress, was imitated by Asclepiades of Samos (*c.* 300; lyrics rather than elegiacs), who invented the verse called 'Asclepiad', by Hermesianax of Colophon (*c.* 290), who enumerated various people of importance who had been in love in their time—very poor stuff, and by Philetas of Cos (*c.* 300). Philetas' elegies to his wife Bittis were prized by the Augustans; but the tutor of Ptolemy II and author of the first Greek lexicon really lived through the circle of scholars he formed, among them Zenodotus, Herodas, Callimachus, and Theocritus. This sort of love poetry did in form influence Propertius; but in Greece its future was to be the epigram, of which Asclepiades was a master.

Tragedies continued to be manufactured in quantities, for quantities were required for the festivals, new and old; seven writers of the early third century had enough temporary repute to be called the Pleiad, but the only one worth notice is Menedemus' young friend Lycophron, who went back to Phrynichus and wrote on contemporary subjects: a play on the sufferings of Cassandreia under its proletariat dictatorship, and a satyr play on his master Menedemus, where doubtless, as with the carved Sileni in Plato, the grotesque shell was meant to reveal the divinity within; we possess from this play a charming account of Menedemus' famous suppers, banquets of wit rather than of wine.[2] Comedy, on the other hand, flourished throughout the century, though Philemon's death in 262 marked the end of its best period. Its form, the so-called New Comedy, or

[1] A. Rostagni, *Poeti Alessandrini*, 1916; J. W. Mackail, *Lectures on Greek poetry*[2], 1926; Barber in *The Hellenistic Age*; Wilamowitz, *Hellenistische Dichtung*, 1924; A. Körte, *Hellenistic Poetry*, 1929; A. Couat, *Alexandrian poetry under the first three Ptolemies*, transl. James Loeb, 1931; H. Herter, *Bericht* on Hellenistic poetry in Bursian, 255 (1937).

[2] On Menedemus' circle see Tarn, *Ant. Gon.*, 22.

comedy of manners without a chorus, lineally descended from Aristophanes, was the most living style of art at Athens at this time—about 70 writers are known—but it was so typically Athenian that all attempts to transplant it to Alexandria or elsewhere failed; Philemon's death dramatically coincided with the end of Athens' political importance. The great name of the New Comedy is Menander (d. 292–1)[1]; enough has now been recovered from Egypt to enable us to study him directly, and not merely through Terence. His importance to his age is undoubted; also he was tremendously quotable, which helped him to live; three of his lines have become English proverbs.[2] Witty, elegant, more at home with men's mistresses than with their wives, he set a mark on literary history which lasted till Shakespeare and Molière; and it was not his fault that what he drew from life (of a sort) became for centuries a stereotyped convention. It is usual to praise him without stint; certainly he would act well, while occasionally something better—Davus in the *Hero*, Glycera in the *Perikeiromene*—does glimmer through his facile tolerance. But to the writer he and his imitators seem about the dreariest desert in literature. Life is not entirely composed of seductions and unwanted children, coincidences and recognitions of long-lost daughters, irate fathers and impertinent slaves. Doubtless he had met these things; but, though his characters were types, the life was not typical. The world, however, has decided that it *was* typical, and on material drawn from the New Comedy is chiefly based the traditional belief in Athens' decadence; it is perhaps too late to get the verdict reversed. But anyone who wished could draw from the London stage of the 1920's and 1930's a much more exciting picture of England's decadence. We should rate the latter at its true value; why accept the former?

Except for comedy, the revival of poetry largely centred

[1] A. W. Gomme, *Essays in Greek history and literature*, 1937, 249 *sqq.*; T. B. L. Webster, *Studies in Menander*, 1950.

[2] Whom the gods love die young. Evil communications corrupt good manners. Conscience makes cowards of the bravest.

on Alexandria. Men's aim everywhere was rather to keep poetry alive than to challenge the great masters, and for this purpose to utilise the manifold interests of the enlarged life of the time and bring poetry into touch with what men were doing and thinking. This took many forms; the principal ones were the poetry of instruction, the idyll and epigram (both of which included elegiacs), and the romantic epic. It is curious that instructive poetry, allied to science, was the one form not domiciled at Alexandria, the home of science. Its chief name is Aratus of Soli, Antigonus Gonatas' friend, who passed his time between Athens and Pella, and wrote the hymns[1] for Gonatas' marriage (276). His *Phaenomena*, a versification in hexameters of Eudoxus' old star-catalogue, was one of the most read and bepraised poems of the age; it helped to inspire Vergil's *Georgics*, and its influence lasted into the Middle Ages. The popularity of this dry astronomical work is a puzzle. One critic thinks it appealed to the public which desired knowledge conveyed in an easy form[2]; another, that men welcomed its plain straightforwardness as a relief from poetic conceits.[3] Both may be true; but I would rather attribute its success mainly to its illustration of the Stoic doctrine of Providence, drawn from the utility of the stars to sailor and husbandman—a note struck at once in the noble prelude, akin to Cleanthes' great hymn; and it was as an appeal to Stoics that St. Paul quoted it. Aratus set a fashion; his contemporary,[4] Nicander of Colophon, versified a scientific treatise on poisons and antidotes, which was translated into Latin, and also works on agriculture and bee-keeping, which Vergil read, while Ovid used his collection of *Metamorphoses*. Various poems by others on astronomy, geography, and fishing are recorded; they probably had little to do with poetry. One historical poem remains, the *Alexander*, attributed to Lycophron but certainly later than Cynoscephalae[5]; it belongs to no class. It survived because

[1] On the second hymn, Tarn *J.H.S.* 1920, 149.

[2] Wilamowitz, *Griech. Lit.*[3] 203.

[3] Mackail, *op. c.* 197.

[4] Date: Beloch IV, 2, 574; R. Flacelière, *Rev. E.G.* 1928, 83.

[5] Ziegler, *Lykophron* in P.W. makes it 196, which is accepted here. See Tarn, *Alexander* II, 29, cf. 24.

the utter obscurity of its diction interested philologists; but it handled in small compass a big theme, the struggle between Europe and Asia from Troy to Rome.

The characteristic Alexandrian form was the Idyll, which means a little picture complete in itself; it might take many shapes, and was sometimes intended for recitation. The master of the idyll, to his contemporaries, and the most typical Alexandrian poet, was Callimachus of Cyrene (*c.* 310–245), courtier and philologist. He had been Philetas' pupil, and he made the elegiac the fashionable vehicle it was to remain. We possess now some of his hymns, and parts of the *Coma Berenices*, known from Catullus' translation, of the little epic *Hecale*, of a poem on Arsinoe's death, and of his most important work, the *Aitia*—'causes' of various usages and cults.[1] But, were it not for his epigrams, one might almost say he was not a poet but a learned man writing verses. All that care and polish could do, he did; and one gratefully admits that he avoided sentimentality and rhetoric. He was indeed scrupulous in avoidance; a later critic called him 'the faultless', perhaps his sufficient condemnation. For he could not let himself go; and in all his fastidious variations on a dead mythology—dead even in his day to the educated—there is scarcely a line with a human touch, and certainly not a line which ever made anyone's pulse beat. He is form without substance. He set a standard, and influenced many; in form, he influenced Catullus; but in spirit he had no spark of the fire which burst out in *Odi et amo.* But curiously enough his younger contemporary Euphorion had more effect later than he, though what of him has been recovered seems an inferior imitation of Callimachus. Euphorion lived at the court of Alexander of Corinth (*c.* 250), and afterwards became librarian at Antioch; he played a part in the Augustan age and at one time affected Vergil.

Callimachus' epigrams, however, are on a different level; there he can sometimes touch us. The beautiful lines on the death of his friend Heraclitus are familiar to many through Cary-Johnson's version in *Ionica*; as good in another

[1] R. Pfeiffer, *Callimachus*, I, 1949.

vein is the man deterred from marrying out of his station by hearing the children, at play with their tops, calling to one another 'Keep to your own line'; the little speech of the nautilus shell is unsurpassed for grace. But indeed a feature of the age was the widespread mastery of the epigram and the fact that in it writers were not ashamed to show their feelings. It flourished from Leonidas and Asclepiades in the early period to the Syrian group—Antipater of Sidon, Meleager and Philodemus of Gadara—who lived in the political decay of the first century; indeed it outlasted every other form of poetry and perished only with the Greek language. Meleager's love-poems in their grace and tenderness recall the flowers he so loved; he compiled for one of his friends what was thought to be the first anthology or 'flower-garland' of poetry until earlier examples were discovered in Egypt.[1] Philodemus merely illustrates the luxurious sensuality of a Syrian city; it is strange to recognise in him the laborious philosophic compiler of the Herculaneum papyri.

Callimachus was the arbiter of his day. But one man put the idyll to another use: Theocritus of Syracuse (born *c.* 315–312). Hints he may have got from earlier Sicilian poets; something he owed to the peasant songs of the Mediterranean; but the pastoral idyll of literature is his and his only —so entirely his that from him derives the modern sense of 'idyllic'. He seemingly spent his boyhood in Sicily and his youth with Philetas at Cos (his Coan friend Aratus, now known from inscriptions,[2] was not Aratus the poet); about 276–270 he was in Alexandria. How long he remained there is unknown; one likes to think he was homesick for the trees and flowers of Sicily, and that it was he, not his Menalcas, who called on 'Etna, my mother', and thought wealth and power nothing if he could sit with his beloved in the shade of a rock and watch the blue home-sea. He indeed experimented with various forms of the idyll, and in his hands even an official ode in praise of Ptolemy, or the talk of the vulgar

[1] Schubart, *Einführung* 131.
[2] *I.G.* XI, 2, 161 B l. 66, 203 B l. 38, 287 B l. 43.

women at the show in Alexandria, became poetry. But it is for the pastorals that men have treasured him—the singing matches of shepherd and goatherd, the forsaken girl trying to charm back her lover, the two old fishermen in their reed cabin,[1] the Coan harvest festival with Lycidas' beautiful song—for these and for his love of plants and animals, the cicadas chirping in the sun, the dog dreaming of a bear-hunt, the little fox manœuvring round the boy's dinner. His men and girls are living peasants. He perfected the pastoral, and left nothing for others; his successors are far below him, and Vergil's *Eclogues* seem artificial copies, an artificiality which grew until the end was Watteau and powdered shepherdesses in hoops. Alone of the Alexandrians he has become a classic, because, alone of the Alexandrians, he could throw off all that Alexandria stood for and get back to Nature. A great poet of Nature he was not, for he could not see behind her; to him 'the yellow bees in the ivy bloom' would have been only bees, delightfully buzzing. For her grandeur, too, he betrays no more feeling than other Greeks; for that, in the Hellenistic age, we must turn to the unknown Jew who wrote the *Song of the Three Children*, and knew that the Lord was praised in the wind and the storm, the flood and the snow.[2] But for the sweetness and mere beauty of natural things Theocritus had a feeling such as no other Greek possessed; and he can never die while every burn on the moor sings as he sang.[3]

Epics continued to be written; and one at least was exciting, Rhianus' story (*c.* 250) of the Messenian war and the heroism of Aristomenes, a story which, through Pausanias' use of it, still had its place in the histories of our youth; we are the poorer without it, legendary though it be. Epic indeed had a certain future as a vehicle of local patriotism; for, as the city lost power before the monarchy, so pride grew in its past and its legends, and much poetry, often called epic, was written to glorify cities and peoples; any poet who came to a city and recited his poem on its history was liberally

[1] If *I.G.* XI, 21 be Theocritus'.

[2] Cf. S. A. Cook, 206 and n. 3.

[3] κατειβόμενον κελάρυσδε.

fêted and honoured. But there was one epic of a different type, the *Argonautica* of Apollonius of Alexandria, called the Rhodian. The reason and the details of the quarrel[1] between Callimachus and Apollonius remain a mystery; but certainly the *Argonautica* expresses a revolt against Callimachus, who said of it that a big book was a big nuisance. He polemised against its author; but it may be doubted if Apollonius really quitted the empire on that account. But Callimachus and Apollonius' successor Eratosthenes were Cyrenaeans, and Ptolemy III married a princess of Cyrene; was the cause political, Cyrene against Alexandria? In any case Apollonius' epic stands alone. As a whole, it is a learned man's failure. He could draw a picture, but could not tell a story; the celestial machinery creaks badly, and the language is troublesome. But one part of it—Medea's love-story in book III—is quite extraordinarily good; for the first and the last time in Greece someone had dared to draw a girl honestly in love, and she was a particular Colchian girl, not a type. Apollonius had no successor till Vergil used him as a model; but the Medea of book III is far better done than Dido. Whatever Alexandria did to him, he has had his revenge; while none but scholars will ever read Callimachus, Apollonius (though the chain was broken) is the precursor of half modern literature.

But the idyll and epic were for the educated; the half-educated too required amusement, and were catered for by the Mime, both spoken and sung; the former ultimately derived from Sicily, the latter from the loose 'Ionian songs' of Asia Minor; in the third century wandering companies of Mime actors were well established. The spoken Mime was a sketch of some incident of daily life, literary or otherwise; Theocritus' famous 'Syracusan women' is an example. We now have from Egypt a whole selection of the literary Mimes of Herodas (*c.* 240), apparently another member of Philetas' circle, written in scazons; many are on unpleasant subjects, clever photographs of things not worth photographing, but

[1] Wilamowitz, *Hell. Dicht.* 1, 206; add *P. Oxy.* XVII, 2079, 2080, and see Powell and Barber II, 4.

valuable as illustrating how common people talked. Allied to this form, apparently, was cinaedology, compositions whose point lay in their indecency; Sotades' verse on the marriage of Ptolemy II, for which Ptolemy's admiral Patroclus drowned him, is unprintable. The singing mime was divided into hilarody and magody, parodying tragedy and comedy respectively; but if the now famous *Maiden's Lament*[1]—the passionate appeal of a girl outside the door of a faithless lover—be really a mime, it was neither, but a piece for stage recitation. One example of hilarody has been recovered, the skeleton, to be filled out with gag, of a parody of the *Iphigenia in Tauris*, in which the barbarian king talks some Indian gibberish and the brother and sister escape by making him drunk.[2]

Parody was of course employed in better literature than the Mime; Timon the Sceptic wrote an entertaining skit called *Silloi*[3] on other philosophers, living and dead, which naturally appealed only to a select few; and Crates the Cynic produced a really good parody of Homer in the *Beggar's Wallet*,[4] in which he glorified that symbol of Cynic poverty as the one refuge for an honest man, rising like an island from the wine-dark sea of universal humbug. But Crates' poem, though in form a parody, was serious enough, and possibly led to philosophy reviving the long-dead fashion of using serious verse as a vehicle. The best example is the fine *Hymn to Zeus* of the Stoic Cleanthes,[5] the high-water mark of Greek religious poetry, very different from the orthodox hymns and paeans written to order, of which a number are now known; but almost as notable in its way is the poem in which Cercidas of Megalopolis, a politician with 'Cynic' leanings—everyone dissatisfied with the existing order was called a Cynic—exhorted his friends to meet the threat of social revolution by healing the sick and giving to the poor[6];

[1] Powell, *Collectanea Alexandrina* p. 177.

[2] *P. Oxy.* III, 413 is 2nd c. A.D., but the piece, if not Hellenistic, is of Hellenistic type. The Indian language: Rice in Powell and Barber II, 215 and refs.

[3] Fragments in Diels, *Poet. philosoph. fragmenta.*

[4] Diels *ib.* fr. 4.

[5] *S.V.F.* I, no. 537.

[6] Powell, *op. c.* fr. 4 ll. 46 *sqq.*

it stands out from the commonplace moralising poetry of the time—*e.g.* Phoenix of Colophon, *c.* 286—which has no depth. Lastly, we possess one popular (political) song, sung in the streets of Athens in 290; very catchy it is.[1]

The influence of Alexandrian poetry on Roman was great. Some well-known points have been noticed, and new ones continually come to light; a modern discovery has revealed, in a treatise preserved in Philodemus' work *On Poems*, the Hellenistic original of the doctrine and much of the detail of Horace's *Ars Poetica.*[2] But Hellenism only gave the Romans form, and subjects to treat; it did not give them the vital matter of poetry itself, the essential difference between the poet and the painstaking literary man; for that, the great poets—Lucretius, Catullus, Vergil—looked into their own souls.

Before turning to prose proper, the spoken word must be noticed. The judicial commissions killed forensic oratory —no great loss—but political oratory flourished for a century after Alexander. Deinarchus and Demosthenes' nephew Demochares were indeed only relics of Demosthenes' age, though Demetrius of Phalerum (317–307) perhaps took his own line; but Aratus of Sicyon (271–213) was obviously a great orator, for during a long career he consistently swayed the Achaean Assembly as Demosthenes never did the Athenian. As no speech of his remains, it is not known how he did it; but Plutarch says[3] he disdained the forms of art, *i.e.* rhetoric, and possibly he spoke extemporarily and said just what he thought; the effect on men accustomed to rhetorical artifices might be startling. The most important speech of which Polybius gives a précis, Agelaus' appeal[4] for Greek unity at the conference of Naupactus (217), with its two unforgettable images, must have been really good; Pyrrhus' minister Cineas was ranked by contemporaries with Demosthenes.[5]

But political oratory ultimately died also; and from the

[1] Athen. 253 D (see p. 53).
[2] C. Jensen, *Philodemos über die Gedichte*, 93; *Neoptolemos und Horaz.*
[3] *Arat.* 3. [4] Polyb. V, 104. [5] Plut. *Pyrrh.* 14; App. *Samn.* 10.

second century everything was swamped by the growth of rhetoric. It is not worth enumerating the professors of this art, increasingly numerous down to Roman times. Hegesias of Magnesia-under-Sipylos (*c.* 250) helped to popularise the flowery Asianic style, whose laboured rhythms can be cut up into lengths resembling modern *vers libre*[1] (it is uncertain whether he or Timaeus invented it); Hermagoras of Temnos (*c.* 150), whose *Handbook* became authoritative, marks a stage on the road back to Atticism. Rhetoric was capable of some good, by teaching men to arrange their thoughts clearly; but it became one of the curses of Hellenism. Men concluded that style was everything and substance nothing; what you said was immaterial provided you said it according to rule and avoided hiatus. For some reason rhetoric intoxicated Greeks; it took the place filled to-day by cheap journalism and the cinema; men flocked to rhetorical displays as to a theatre. It debased everything it touched. Petronius said it taught people much about pirates and so forth but little about life[2]; and Martial summed it up in his bitter jibe at an advocate who could make fine speeches about Hannibal but was useless in a petty larceny case.[3]

In prose, history took first place.[4] Under the stimulus of the opening up of Asia, the two generations after Alexander witnessed a large output; but all these historians have perished, though some are partially known through their use by later writers. The vice of writing for effect, introduced by Isocrates and his pupils, was not dead or going to die; but there was a sense of reality in the new world which led some, especially in circles which had known Alexander, to react against rhetoric. When Ptolemy I (probably between 288 and 283) wrote his history of Alexander from the official *Journal* and other official documents, supplemented by his own notes and recollections, he was doing a new thing—he was the man of action writing down what he knew and had

[1] Specimen in J. B. Bury, *Ancient Greek Historians*, 171.
[2] *Satirae* 1.
[3] *Ep.* 286 (VI, 19).
[4] Generally, Bury *op. c.*; also my bibliographies, *C.A.H.* VI chs. XII–XIII, XV. For the fragments, Jacoby, *F. Gr. Hist.*

seen; it is well for us that he did. Similarly Nearchus, in the account of his voyage (before 312), produced perhaps the most trustworthy chronicle in Greek; both these men had been Alexander's friends from boyhood and had felt his directness.[1] Aristobulus of Cassandreia, who wrote about 294–288, was one of Alexander's Greek technicians, with an outlook rather different from Ptolemy's military one; a sober writer, he knew much about Alexander personally, and was good on geography. These three are represented for us by Arrian; Aristobulus also stands behind much of the primary (the favourable) portrait of Alexander in Diodorus. Aristotle's nephew, Callisthenes of Olynthus, wrote (*c.* 330) a book full of absurd adulation, intended to advertise Alexander; but it exercised little influence on the tradition. Books produced in the outer circle, as by Chares the chamberlain or Ephippus the gossip-monger, were full of worthless trivialities, for a man can only see what he is big enough to see; but Onesicritus the sea-captain does not belong here and hardly merits the wholesale appellation of 'liar', for he was writing, not a history of Alexander, but a romance on the lines of Xenophon's *Cyropaedeia*. Reaction, begun by two of the philosophic schools, Peripatetics and Stoics, was taken up by a secondary writer, Cleitarchus of Alexandria, a man of whom no serious critic in antiquity had anything good to say save that he was clever, and who wrote (not before 280–270, and possibly later) a rhetorical history of Alexander, thoroughly unfavourable in tone; it made of him an imitative character who massacred, cheated, and lied to heaven, though this last was possibly only passed on by him.[2] Cleitarchus' extravagances caught Roman tastes later, and Pliny calls him 'much read'; he used and garbled Aristobulus, and relied a good deal on stories told by the poetasters who accompanied Alexander, on Alexandrian gossip, and a vivid imagination. He is the source of the secondary (the unfavourable) portrait of Alexander in Diodorus, and was used to some extent by Curtius.

[1] See Tarn, *Alexander* II, part 1, for what follows.
[2] Tarn, *Alexander* II, 265.

Soon after 264 Timaeus of Tauromenium completed at Athens his big history of the Western Greeks to that year; this for two centuries exercised much influence. He was learned and industrious, well travelled, and diligent in collecting epigraphic evidence, but his mind had no depth, and he did not really understand Dionysius and Agathocles; he wrote as a rhetorician in the Asianic style, and related wonders and legends, though he introduced the clumsy dating by Olympiads, which gained some vogue and was employed by Polybius and Castor. Diodorus' Agathocles goes back to him. An innovation was attempted by Duris, sometime tyrant of Samos, who wrote a history of the period from Leuctra to 280; he aimed at making history interesting by dramatising characters and motives and using the accessories of the theatre; what can be traced of his work is tolerably remote from fact. A better man, Nymphis of Heraclea Pontica (active 280), wrote a history of Alexander's Successors which has perished without trace; but his history of Heraclea, represented by Memnon, seems to have been good and vivid. Diyllus at Athens wrote a history of Greece from the Sacred War to Cassander's death in 298, favourable to Cassander, which is thought to have left traces in Diodorus; Demetrius of Phalerum left a history of his rule in Athens, besides much other work; Demochares wrote a rhetorical history of his own times from the nationalist standpoint; Demetrius of Byzantium narrated in minute detail the Gallic invasion of Asia; Proxenus wrote on Pyrrhus' Epirus; and Pyrrhus himself left a volume of *Memoirs* dealing with his wars, if indeed the work was not merely an edition of his official *Journal*.

But the great history of the half-century after Alexander, probably one of the greatest histories Greece produced, was written by Hieronymus of Cardia, the friend, possibly the relative, of Eumenes of Cardia, who after Eumenes' death served Antigonus I, Demetrius, and Gonatas as general and administrator; it ran from the death of Alexander to (probably) that of Pyrrhus. It stands behind Diodorus XVIII *sqq.* and Arrian's *Diadochi*, was partly used by Plutarch in his *Lives* of Eumenes and Demetrius, and exercised a steadying force on the whole of our broken tradition of the period; the more that period is studied, the stronger the conviction grows of the presence of a great lost writer behind it. He dated by campaign years, like Thucydides, and his figures seem to have been trustworthy, a rare phenomenon. He neglected style, and consequently perished; but he was careful to tell the truth as he saw it—and he had played an active part in the history he related—and there are indications enough that he could draw both pictures and characters; indeed the astonishing fact that, even now, we can trace some *development* in the character of Demetrius, if due to him (as it must be), would set him in this respect above any previous historian; for to Greeks generally character was static.[1] He illustrated what Polybius emphasised,[2] that in Greece only men of action could write good history. The Antigonid dynasty were fortunate in his services, and he makes it possible for a time to understand Macedonia a little. Neither Seleucid Asia nor Ptolemaic Egypt ever produced a competent historian; the early Seleucids, at least, deserved a better fate.

The interval between Hieronymus and Polybius was, as regards Greece, covered by Phylarchus, who wrote in Athens and continued Duris' history to Cleomenes' death (219); he is represented by Plutarch's *Lives* of Agis and Cleomenes, and colours a good deal else. It is usual to treat him merely as another Duris, partly for his dramatic introductions of female characters; but though he was a convinced partisan of Cleomenes, he grows in importance the more his period is analysed, and where he clashes with Polybius it is not always Polybius who is right.[3] Aratus of Sicyon covered much of the latter half of the century in his *Memoirs*, really his autobiography; strongly partisan, and unfair to opponents, he yet enables us to know the Achaean League, and he was frank about his own failings; he is represented

[1] Wilamowitz, *Hell. Dicht.* I, 75 says *no* Greek drew development of character. Apparently Aratus did too.

[2] XII, 28.

[3] Instance, *C.A.H.* VII, 761.

by Plutarch's *Life*, and was Polybius' primary source for this period. Sosylus' history of Hannibal is a real loss, as the one fragment shows[1]; for he was with Hannibal in Italy.

The second century belongs to Polybius of Megalopolis (*c.* 198–117), a man who played his part in the politics and warfare of the Achaean League, was carried off to Rome after Pydna, became the friend of Panaetius and Scipio Aemilianus, and returned to Greece in 146. His great history told the story of the 'inhabited world' from 221 to 146. Only the first five books remain, with long extracts from others; but Livy represents him, though mixed with inferior material. He treated Ephorus and Timaeus as his predecessors, and gave a preliminary account of Greece and Rome to bridge the gap between Timaeus and 221; he was attracted by the wide field they covered, though he properly hated rhetoric and, as became Panaetius' friend, discarded all wonders. Hieronymus, unhappily, he ignored, as he disliked Macedonia; and the development in Aratus' character probably comes from Aratus. Polybius is not pleasant reading; his style is that of rescripts and despatches, and desperately long-winded; like Timaeus, he interrupts his narrative with polemical discussions which to-day would form appendices. In military matters he compares badly with Hieronymus; and Livy knew more about ships than the Arcadian could teach him. He used official archives where he could, and utilised many sources of evidence, but he was deficient in scientific training; his mind was a politician's, and for politicians he wrote; he believed the present could learn from the past, and on politics he is solid, if dull, though he has queer gaps, like his omission to describe the Achaean constitution. He is not impartial; his own party among the Achaeans resembles 'God's Whigs' in certain English writers, and his attitude to Aetolia and Macedonia calls for constant mental adjustment on the reader's part; but though a partisan of Rome, he makes some effort to be fair to Hannibal, though not to Carthage. But if one emphasises

[1] *F. Gr. Hist.* II A p. 903.

his defects, it is because he is almost big enough to carry them off. He had a great subject and gave it full scope; his hero is Rome, and his theme Rome's expansion over the Mediterranean world; all his rivulets run into that river. His history is the epic of Rome's heroic age. He understood the time, and the men it produced; he knew both Greece and Rome from the inside. He could draw fine pictures when he chose; he did try, though not deeply enough, to understand the causes of events; and he was not afraid of ethical judgments. Above all, he emphasised that history's sole concern is truth.[1] Mommsen's way of regarding the second among Greek historians remains the right one: contrast the darkness before and after him with the period when his sun scatters the clouds.

Polybius' history was continued by Poseidonius[2] (p. 349). He was picturesque and full of detail, but as an historian quite superficial. He related many marvels, and his much praised picture of the Celts[3] reveals little insight into Celtic character; if Caesar really went to him for their psychology no wonder Caesar had trouble. His standpoint was that of the Roman optimates, and comparative darkness falls on Rome between the Gracchi and Sulla; nowhere do we feel a great writer behind the extant tradition. His quality is shown by his long surviving account of Athens joining Mithridates[4]; instead of explaining the nature and reason of the hatred Rome evoked, he relates that a little people, secure and peaceful, who had waged no war for a century, suddenly rose and fought to the death against her as they had against Xerxes, because—a plausible sophist told them to. A better historian may have been Nicolaus of Damascus, philosopher and historian at the court of Herod I, with some practical knowledge of affairs. He wrote a universal history; the section on Herod survives in substance in Josephus, and is the reason so much is known about Herod, while greater men are forgotten. Of the general history of the world by Agatharchides of Cnidus (*c.* 120) nothing is known; and it is quite

[1] I, 14, 6; XXXVIII, 4, 5.
[2] Fragments, *F. Gr. Hist.* II A, no. 87.
[3] Frs. 15, 116.
[4] Fr. 36.

uncertain whether the book of Timagenes of Alexandria (*c.* 20) called *Of the kings* was really a history of the Macedonian monarchies.[1] Apollodorus of Artemita wrote a Parthian history, from which a few fragments on the Graeco-Bactrians survive. Lastly, a tribute of thanks must be paid to Diodorus of Sicily, who wrote his *Historical Library* early in the reign of Augustus. As an historian, he was not equal to the work he undertook; his book, always pleasant to read, is good or bad according to the writer he is summarising at the time. But he has thus preserved much that would otherwise have perished, Iambulus for instance; and it is primarily to him that we owe our knowledge of Hieronymus.

There were other forms of historical writing beside the formal histories. Early in the third century two priests, Berossus of Babylon[2] and Manetho of Egypt, attempted to make their countries' history available to Greeks; but few cared to study barbarian history seriously, though Theopompus knew of the Avesta,[3] and Berossus' astrology was welcomed; the Calendar of Sais,[4] a calendar of the Egyptian year and festivals written in Greek about 300, is however notable, while Callimachus seemingly knew and imitated a Babylonian fable.[5] Under Ptolemy I Hecataeus of Abdera wrote on Egypt as a Greek saw it; later one Menander worked up some Phoenician chronicles. Alexander Polyhistor of Miletus (*c.* 50), who collected the literature about many countries, Greek and barbarian, has preserved some Jewish propaganda (p. 233). The local patriotism which influenced poetry also influenced history, and a long list of local or town chronicles is known[6]; such chronicles might also embody the labours of the antiquarian and epigraphist, like the *Atthis* or Athenian Chronicle of the learned Philochorus[7] (d. 261), which gave much information on the constitution, festivals, and ceremonies of Athens; doubtless there were works which

[1] Ed. Meyer, *G. d. Altertums* II, 23, burst the Timagenes bubble.
[2] P. Schnabel, *Berossos und die babylonisch-hellenistische Literatur*, 1923.
[3] *F. Gr. Hist.* II, no. 115, p. 64 (71).
[4] *P. Hibeh* I, 27.
[5] E. Ebeling, *Die babylonische Fabel*, 1927; not necessarily at first hand.
[6] List, Christ-Schmid[6], 215.
[7] New frs. *Klio* V, 55.

rendered similar service for other cities. Craterus, whom tradition identifies with Gonatas' half-brother (this is doubtful),[1] compiled a corpus of Athenian decrees with a sound historical commentary; but the outstanding name in the antiquarian field is Polemon of Ilium (second century). He spent half his life studying inscriptions in many countries; having acquired his knowledge, he then wrote voluminously on the foundation, antiquities, and customs of many cities, and on epigraphy itself, together with critical *adversaria* of every kind. He was regarded as very trustworthy; but nothing of his remains, and he is probably our worst loss after Hieronymus. Many imitated his travels (*periegesis*) and writings, though not his great knowledge; Pausanias probably used him more than he admits. Eratosthenes (p. 302), who beside his other activities was a genuine historical critic,[2] founded the study of chronology; Apollodorus of Athens in 144 worked his chronology into a rhyming chronicle, whose fragments are for that reason of value, and Castor of Rhodes (d. 42) used Apollodorus in compiling a set of synchronised chronological tables which were in turn used by Varro and by Eusebius' predecessor, Julius Africanus; there is thus a chain linking Eratosthenes with Eusebius' ambitious chronological scheme.

The Peripatetic school, with their love of collecting facts, naturally handled historical work from the start. Theophrastus wrote a history of scientific studies, others wrote histories of medicine and mathematics; two of Theophrastus' pupils, Duris the historian and Chamaeleon of Heraclea Pontica, produced the first histories of art and poetry respectively, and were to have many followers. Dicaearchus (*c.* 300) wrote an important work called *The Life of Hellas*, probably a history of culture. All these works are lost, as is Dicaearchus' important *Constitution of Sparta*; Theophrastus' little sketches of human types, called *Characters*, of some interest for social history, alone survive. But the Peripatetic influence on history proper was to become

[1] Br. Keil, *Hermes* XXX, 199, 214; Jacoby, *Krateros* in P.W.
[2] Reuss, *Rh. Mus.* LVII, 568; De Sanctis, *Riv. fil.* 1928, 53.

thoroughly bad[1]; they created, or fixed, that doctrine of Fortune which gained such vogue (p. 340), and from their diligence in collecting every scrap of everything sprang the so prevalent habit of mixing up truth and legend without discrimination, a habit which quickly enough became nothing but a passion for scandal. There is no more unpleasant feature of the time than the propaganda they carried on against Alexander and his house; they had not even the wit to avoid mutually exclusive allegations,[2] and this the first known propaganda campaign was typically unwholesome. They specialised in biography, which the individualism of the third century inevitably brought into prominence; but their habit of mixing up true and false, which already appears full-blown in a very early work, Clearchus of Soli's *Lives*, was to be its curse. Biographers of influence at Alexandria were Satyrus (*c*. 220), whose recovered *Life* of Euripides,[3] written in dialogue form, is better than one expected, and Callimachus' pupil Hermippus of Smyrna; and in their footsteps Alexandria piled up masses of biographical material, but so uncritically that when later Plutarch took the material and with its help produced great works of art, truth and falsehood had become hopelessly fused; for instance, no one yet has succeeded in analysing Plutarch's *Life* of Alexander. Hellenism, however, produced one serious and competent biographer to whom we owe much, the sculptor Antigonus of Carystus (d. after 225), who wrote the lives of the third-century philosophers; he partly survives, together with much inferior material, in Diogenes Laertius.

Hellenistic geography begins in science (Chap. IX) and ends in literature. Eratosthenes' great *Geography* gave a description of the world he knew, good for the Mediterranean and for what Alexander, Patrocles, Megasthenes and Pytheas (whose voyage he wisely recognised as true) had made known (Chap. VII); the fringes were conjectural, for he naturally knew nothing of the African and Indian

[1] Cf. Powell and Barber I, 145.
[2] For the worst case see Tarn, *Alexander* II, App. 18.
[3] *P. Oxy*. IX, 1176.

peninsulas, the world east of the Ganges, or northern Europe and Asia; but his account of Asia beyond Euphrates for long held the field. But it was Polybius' utilitarianism which chiefly turned men's thoughts to descriptive geography. His younger contemporary Agatharchides of Cnidus has left an excellent account of the Red Sea coast and its strange peoples, based on Egypt's penetration southward (Chap. VII); Apollodorus of Artemita wrote on Bactria and Chinese Turkestan; the much-travelled Artemidorus of Ephesus (*c.* 100) produced an important general work, utilising his predecessors and rich in detail, known only from Strabo's use of it. Poseidonius' works (p. 349) were full of descriptive geography, brilliant and picturesque; it is now thought that from him come Strabo's accounts of the peoples of western Europe and of the mineral wealth of Spain, of the volcanic districts of Asia Minor and elsewhere (which Strabo might well have known himself), and of the strange Cran d'Arles at the Rhône mouth, and also Diodorus' flaming description of the wonders of Arabia.

Though Strabo of Amaseia published his *Geography* under Tiberius he must be mentioned here, for there are few writers to whom we owe more. His book is the swan-song of Hellenism; through his eyes we survey that world as a whole as it passed away. He is no original geographer; he embodies his predecessors, but he writes well and is a tolerably sane critic; to suggest that we should value him less had we Artemidorus and Poseidonius is true but ungrateful. One might wish that the world around him, which he knew so intimately, had been the Hellenistic kingdoms in their bloom; that we had more of the Bactrians and less of Roman client-kings. But the mass of information he has collected on the serious matters—geographical theory, Greek cities, economics—is great; while he had learnt more about the interior of farther Asia (not the coast) than anyone was to know again till Marco Polo. His book is shot through with pictures. Here we have the glory of Alexandria and Rhodes and the social system of Bengal; Cappadocian priest-kings, Indian fakirs, German priestesses, Gallic Druids pass before us; he tells of the strange festivals of Thrace and Persia, the couvade of the Iberians, the head-hunters of Carmania; in his company we can discover Britain with Pytheas or explore the Caspian with Patrocles, watch the mongoose killing the crocodile, or gather crocuses in the Corycian grotto; we can fish for fresh water in the Phoenician sea, spear sword-fishes off Sicily, stalk ostriches in Nubia, or ferret rabbits in Spain. No more picturesque book remains since Herodotus.

The underside of geography was the 'traveller's tale'; its type was settled by Antiphanes of Berge, author of the story about the country where it was so cold that in autumn a man's words froze in the air and you did not hear what he was saying till they thawed in the spring; 'Bergean' became Greek for 'fish story'. Hecataeus on the Hyperboreans and Amometus on the Uttara Kurus (Attacori) of the Himalaya were books of this type, and a surviving specimen is Lucian's amusing *True Story*, lineal ancestor of *Sindbad the Sailor*. The underside of history, which was occupied with mythical and romantic tales, was even more prolific; among other things the Aeneas legend and the story of the founding of Rome were worked up in Hellenistic circles, where Geoffrey of Monmouth would have been welcomed as a brother craftsman. But the principal achievement was the Alexander-Romance, a compound, sometimes self-contradictory, of material from Egypt, Babylon, and Greek tradition, and of stories from many sources; the Greek text in the best version, A′, contains some genuine historical items. A′ became known as Pseudo-Callisthenes, though it has nothing to do with that writer: and though it has been argued that its text did not attain final shape till *c.* A.D. 300, many of its items are certainly Hellenistic,[1] and the most famous story of the Romance, though not in A′, was known in Greece in the third century B.C.[2] The Romance, with endless variations, ultimately spread over Asia to Malaya and Siam, and came

[1] Dates: A. Ausfeld, *Der griech. Alexander-roman*, 1907; W. Kroll, *Kallisthenes*, pt. 2, in P.W., and text of A′, *Historia Alexandri Magni*, 1926; Tarn, *Alexander* II, Index *s.v.* Alexander-Romance.

[2] The journey to the Well of Life: Tarn, *Alexander* II, 364 n. 1.

westward to France and Britain. History itself tended to become more and more a thing of textbooks and compendiums, boiled down from the greater writers and repeated from one to another, gradually growing worse; Justin and Orosius, though later, will illustrate the type.

Indeed the forms and content of prose writing were endless; for there was no branch of human thought or activity which was not a subject for literature. The Utopias have already been mentioned (p. 122). The letter became a serious vehicle, used by philosophers; but letters, forged or doctored, also played a part both in the spread of literary history and in the war of pamphlets and propaganda which accompanied the military struggles after Alexander's death; of the published correspondence of Alexander, Olympias, Antigonus Gonatas, and others, only part at best was genuine.[1] Imaginary conversations between historical personages were written (two have now been found)[2]; and the satires of Menippus of Gadara (*c.* 280), much used by Lucian, written in prose and verse mixed, were also sometimes cast in dialogue form, as were Satyrus' *Lives*. A large class desired short and easy reading, and there grew up a whole literature of snippets on every subject[3]—history, war, banquets, theatres, moral philosophy, miscellaneous gossip; they ranged from genuine historical extracts to the most untrustworthy anecdotes. Polyaenus and Aelian exhibit the type, and Athenaeus' vast hodge-podge, invaluable for all the otherwise unknown writers whose names it has preserved, is only a glorified example. Alexander's supposed *Plans* were a first-century compilation of the kind, combining a little truth with much falsehood[4]; Ptolemy Euergetes II seemingly published his own commonplace book. Greeks

[1] Every letter must be considered separately (cf. Kaerst, *Phil.* LI, 602).

[2] Demades and Deinarchus, *Berl. Kl. Texte* VII, 13; The 'Macedonian Dialogue', *Gött. Nachr.* 1922, 32 (*P. Freiburg* 7 and 8). Cf. Lucian, *Δημοσθένους ἐγκώμιον*.

[3] Such collections were called *ὑπομνήματα*, which also means (*a*) a king's official *Journal*, (*b*) what we call Memoirs. List of Memoirs, Christ-Schmid[6], 212; list of Miscellanies, index to Müller's *F.H.G.* IV, p. 697, cf. *J.H.S.* 1921, 10.

[4] Tarn, *Alexander* II, App. 24.

had no feeling about plagiarism, and to copy out a predecessor was a compliment; the end can be seen in Augustus' protégé, Juba II of Mauretania, who would buy any forgery and compiled large uncritical works on many subjects by the simple use of paste and scissors; Pliny's *Natural History* is only a better example of the same type. Of course such writers preserved many true things as well as false, but the two became so fused that it is now often impossible to distinguish them.

Others compiled lists; the ten Attic orators, the seven wonders of the world, more than one list of 'inventors',[1] are all Hellenistic; Phlegon gave a list of centenarians,[2] and somebody made one of teetotallers.[3] There was a whole literature of wonders and marvels, often attributed to great names of the past, as indeed were many sorts of books. The romantic love-tale (not serious attempts at portraying love, like Apollonius') appears in many places and contexts—Hero and Leander, Sappho and Phaon, Pyramus and Thisbe, Antiochus I and Stratonice—and paved the way for the so-called Greek novel of Roman times; Parthenius of Nicaea in 73 brought a book of such love-stories to Rome. There was much literature on special subjects, some good, like the book of Timosthenes of Rhodes *On Harbours*; Poseidonius' pupil Asclepiodotus has left a pedantic book on drill and tactics; we hear of works on agriculture, bee-keeping, fruit-trees, gardens, horse-breeding, fishing, precious stones, the interpretation of dreams; there were descriptions of special festivals, or of the great ships of Ptolemy IV and Hiero; a whole literature on gastronomy and the demi-monde. A work on cosmetics was naturally attributed to Cleopatra.[4]

One work must be named for the evil it did: the late third-century book *On the wantonness of past times*.[5] The object of the writer, who called himself Socrates' pupil Aristippus,

[1] Diels, '*Laterculi Alexandrini*', in *Antike Technik*², 30; a longer list used by Pliny. [2] *F. Gr. Hist.* II, no. 257, fr. 37.

[3] Athen. 44 B *sqq.* must derive from a Hellenistic list.

[4] Susemihl II, 417; *C.A.H.* X, 39 and n. 6.

[5] Wilamowitz, *Philol. Untersuchungen* IV, 48; Hense, *Teles*², Prolegomena LXIV.

was to attach to every honoured name as much scandalous matter as he could invent; there is plenty of him, now universally discredited, in Diogenes Laertius' *Lives* of the philosophers. It was scarcely the only book of the kind; and anyone who wants to understand Hellenism must be prepared to treat as it deserves the scandal-mongering he will meet with in some extant literary sources. Philip II, no model character, might have shamed many a writer when after Chaeronea he gazed on the Sacred Band of Thebes lying dead in their ranks and cursed those who had spoken evil of such men.[1]

[1] Plut. *Pelop*. 18.

CHAPTER IX

SCIENCE[1] AND ART

It was after Alexander that Greek science came into its own. A good beginning had been made long before his time in mathematics and medicine; the Pythagoreans and Plato and his school had brought geometry to an advanced stage—the inscription over Plato's Academy, 'Let none enter who knows not geometry', is famous—and Hippocrates, whose oath the modern doctor still takes, had laid solid foundations of the science of medicine; while Aristotle, for whose work Alexander had liberally provided, had not only systematised the whole province of learning, but had settled the principle governing research, the collection of a mass of data from which deductions could be drawn. Everything was ready for an outburst of activity, which came as soon as Alexander had in effect quadrupled the size of the known world. He himself provided the material for an increase of knowledge on many lines, botany, zoology, geography, ethnography, hydrography; but it was probably of greater importance that he brought Babylon into the Greek sphere. The result was that for a few generations after his death there was such a growth of true science as the world was not to see again for very many centuries; the supremacy of this period, till quite modern times, is unquestionable. But it contained also one of those queer contradictions of which Hellenism was full; we regard science as essentially European, but Hellenistic astronomy was partly due to Babylonians.

We may take astronomy first.[2] Babylon had for long

[1] Generally, Gercke-Norden II, 5 (1933), *Exakte Wissenschaften*, by A. Rehm and K. Vogel; M. R. Cohen and I. E. Drabkin, *A Source Book in Greek Science*, 1948.

[2] Generally, Sir T. Heath, *Aristarchus of Samos*, 1913; *Greek astronomy*, 1932; Hultsch, in P.W. *s.v. Astronomie*; O. Neugebauer, 'The history of

collected empirical observations of the heavens, and the Greek picture of the sky with its planets and constellations was, like our own, Babylonian, while the Babylonian constellations had before 523 even reached China[1]; but in the Persian period[2]—it is dated to 523—scientific astronomy, in the sense of the *use* of recorded observations, started in Babylonia, where there were three schools, those of Uruk, Sippar, and Babylon with Borsippa.[3] The great name after Alexander's time is Kidinnu of Sippar (Kidenas),[4] though whether he was late fourth or third century seems uncertain. P. Schnabel in 1923 attributed to him the exciting discovery of the precession of the equinoxes, though this has been disputed[5]; and he makes his calculation of the year 365 days 5 hours 41 minutes 4·16 seconds, only 7 minutes 16 seconds too short on modern calculations for 300 B.C.

Among Greeks the accepted view of the universe since Eudoxus (fourth century) had been that sun, moon and planets revolved round a fixed earth in concentric spheres; but Aristotle's younger contemporary, Heracleides of Heraclea Pontica, had discovered that the earth turned on its axis and that Mercury and Venus revolved round the sun.[6] These views were accepted by Aristarchus of Samos (*c.* 310–230), a pupil of Strato the Peripatetic, who followed them up with the discovery that the sun was far larger than the earth—some 300 times its mass, he thought. It was probably this which to him made the geocentric theory impossible; and he propounded the view that the earth and all the planets revolved round the sun in circles, while the sun and fixed

ancient astronomy: problems and methods', *Journ. Near East Stud.*, IV, 1945, 1 (with good bibliography). For Babylon, modern literature down to 1933 in W. Gundel's *Bericht* on *Astronomie, Astral religion, Astralmythologie und Astrologie*, in Bursian, 242, 1934, ii, 1–153, especially 25–6, 98–9, 101; add J. Bidez, 'Les écoles chaldéennes sous Alexandre et les Séleucides', *Mélanges Capart*, 1935, 41.

[1] C. Bezold, *Ostasiatische Z.* VIII, 42.

[2] P. Schnabel, *Berossos*, 238.

[3] Str. 739; Schnabel 212.

[4] Schnabel 219, 237–9.

[5] Schnabel *ib.* and in *Z. Assyr.* 1927, 1. Largely accepted; rejected by F. X. Kugler, *Sternkunde und Sterndienst in Babel* II, 582–630, and see now Neugebauer, *J.A.O.S.* 1950, 1, who reinstates Hipparchus.

[6] Heath, *Aristarchus*, 249.

stars were stationary, the latter being an enormous distance away. In the realm of thought the suggestion, though he could not prove it, should have been epoch-making; but the great geometricians who followed him—Archimedes, Apollonius, Hipparchus—naturally could not make observed phenomena agree with the sun as centre of a circle, and therefore rejected his system; Hipparchus was right enough, from the geometrical standpoint, in saying one must 'save the phenomena', *i.e.* stick to observations. Unfortunately this did not lead to the discovery of elliptical orbits, but to the further evolution of Heracleides' idea of epicycles; and someone in the third century, very likely Apollonius,[1] produced Tycho Brahe's system—the planets went round the sun and the sun round the earth; this also was not fated to endure. Among other third-century astronomers Archimedes' friend Conon of Alexandria must be mentioned, for he named the constellation *Coma Berenices* after the lock of hair Berenice dedicated for the safety of her husband Ptolemy III,[2] one of the few constellations in our sky which do not go back to Babylon. Meanwhile a group of Babylonians—Sudines is notable among them—were translating into Greek, and by the second century rendered available to Greeks, much Babylonian material, including Kidenas.[3]

The great name of the second century was Hipparchus of Nicea (*c.* 146–126).[4] His contemporary the astronomer Seleucus,[5] a Greek of Seleuceia on the Persian Gulf and an intriguing figure, was defending Aristarchus' heliocentric theory and striving to find proofs for it; Hipparchus took up epicycles and eccentric circles, handled them better than Apollonius, and produced that geocentric system which, copied later by Claudius Ptolemy, was to rule the world till Copernicus; Seleucus lost his battle, Apollonius' system

[1] Heath 267.

[2] Pfeiffer, *Callimachus*, I, fr. 110, cf. Catullus 66; Susemihl I, 721.

[3] Cumont, *Astrology and religion among the Greeks and Romans*, 11.

[4] Add Rehm, *Hipparchos* 18 in P.W.; Susemihl I, 765. All figures following from Heath and Hultsch; see esp. Hultsch's table, Heath p. 350.

[5] Cumont, *Syria*, 1927, 83. Called a Chaldaean, Str. 739; possible meanings of this, Tarn, *Bactria* 43 and refs.; Bidez, *op. c.* 76.

expired, and the world settled down to the sun, moon and planets revolving round the earth. Hipparchus got the sun's apparent movement right, but could never quite manage the moon. The pity of it was that, could heliocentricism have been established, it should have killed astrology and saved the world infinite trouble. Hipparchus used to be supposed to have discovered the precession of the equinoxes; his calculation made the equinoctial point go forward 36″ a year (really 50·3757″). Whether he was the real discoverer or not depends on Kidenas' alleged priority (p. 296); for some time, on balance, modern opinion inclined to Kidenas. Hipparchus certainly used Babylonian eclipses and a good deal of other information[1]—it is doubtful where his debt to Babylon was going to stop[2]—and he knew Kidenas' work, for an express statement is said to have come to light showing that he took from Kidenas the equation 251 lunations=269 anomalistic months.[3] His calculation of the year, however, differed from that attributed to Kidenas, being 6 minutes 14·3″ longer than the mean tropic year; but the fact which they established, that the year was not 365¼ days, was neglected in practice till the Gregorian calendar. Hipparchus' calculation of the length of the mean lunar month was less than 1″ out, and his figures for the moon's distance and diameter approximated closely to reality; he made the sun's mass 1,880 times that of the earth, and began to recognise its enormous distance, making it 1,245 earth-diameters away against Aristarchus' 180; unfortunately Ptolemy went back to 605. In his observations he used parallax, already known to Archimedes. His greatest work was his catalogue of over 805 fixed stars, placed by latitude and longitude and divided into three classes of brightness, a catalogue somewhat enlarged by Ptolemy. He was the last of the scientific astronomers, unless Ptolemy be included; he already faced a new world, that of astrology (pp. 345 *sqq*).

One first-century name, however, must be given here,

[1] Cumont, *op. c.* (astrology), 57, 61; Kugler, *op. c.* II, 17.

[2] E. F. Weidner (cited Kugler II, 621) even denies him *any* originality.

[3] Cumont 63; Schnabel 291. But see now Neugebauer (p. 296, n. 5).

because of two brilliant guesses. Poseidonius[1] (p. 349) made the sun's diameter $39\frac{1}{4}$ earth-diameters against Hipparchus' $12\frac{1}{3}$ and Aristarchus' $6\frac{3}{4}$, and its distance from the earth 6,545 earth-diameters against Hipparchus' 1,245; that is, respectively three-eighths and five-eighths of the true figures. But he got the distance by taking from Archimedes the diameter of the sun's apparent orbit as *equal to* 10,000 earth-diameters, whereas Archimedes had been showing, for another purpose, that it must be *less than* 10,000—a good example of Poseidonius' methods.[2] Ptolemy unhappily took for the sun's size and mass much smaller figures even than Aristarchus; and Ptolemy was to be authoritative for very many centuries.

Mathematics[3] were closely allied to astronomy, and the same men were often active in both fields. Probably the third-century achievement in mathematics was actually far greater than that in any other science. Geometry had to be the foundation of everything, figures for numerals being unknown; probably it was the very perfection of their geometry which prevented Greeks inventing a numeral notation. Euclid (*c.* 300) was not an original mathematician, though he wrote on many subjects, and his famous geometry, though he tightened up some proofs, was really a textbook of existing learning; but he was a wise man, who like Plato and Archimedes believed in knowledge for its own sake, and he once told Ptolemy I that there was no 'royal road' to geometry. His book was the world's textbook of geometry through Greek, Roman, Arabian, mediaeval, and modern times, down to a generation still living. Greek geometry had always included much that would now be treated as algebra, but it is thought that quadratic equations were already applied to finding numerical values in Euclid's time; the first step toward an algebraic notation was, however, not

[1] Beside Heath, see Reinhardt, *Poseidonios* 198.

[2] Heath 348.

[3] This section mainly from Heath, *A history of Greek mathematics*, 1921; cf. *id.*, *A manual of Greek Mathematics*, 1931; J. L. Heiberg, *Mathematics and Physical Science in classical antiquity*, 1922; *Gesch. der Mathematik und Naturwissenschaften im Altertum*, 1925; Ch. Singer, *A short history of Science*, 1941, ch. II.

to be taken till Diophantus in the third century A.D. Eratosthenes handled mathematics among his other activities; Archimedes dedicated to him his book *On Method*, and when the gods demanded, as a condition of staying a plague at Delos, that an altar there, cubic in form, should be doubled, it was Eratosthenes who discovered how to duplicate a cube.[1] Apollonius of Perge, of Euclid's school, somewhat younger than Archimedes, is probably the second name in pure mathematics; his great work on Conic Sections, of which the latter part was dedicated to Attalus I, marked such an advance in knowledge that seemingly it left little for others to do, and it was possibly he who made a beginning with trigonometry, though the first systematic use of trigonometry was due later to Hipparchus, who (among other things) employed triangulation in his criticism of Eratosthenes' map.

The greatest name of all is Archimedes of Syracuse (d. 212). He wrote monographs on very many subjects, and the mere list of his technical achievements is a long one; among other things, he calculated limits for the value of π (the ratio between the circumference of a circle and its diameter), though Apollonius subsequently got a little closer; invented a terminology for expressing numbers up to any magnitude; laid the foundations of the calculus of the infinite; and founded the whole science of hydrostatics. On his tomb, which was lost and rediscovered by Cicero, there was engraved at his wish the figure of a sphere within a cylinder, indicating that he considered his proof of the relation of the volume of a sphere to a circumscribing right cylinder his finest achievement. He was also the greatest theoretical mechanician of the ancient world; and though he held with Plato that a philosopher should not put his knowledge to practical use, it was in fact the practical use he made of his knowledge which caught the world's imagination. He made a planetarium, worked by water, to represent the motions of the heavenly bodies (the planets must have been moved by hand); he invented the compound pulley, the *baroulcos* or windlass for moving heavy weights,[2] and the endless screw,

[1] Knaack, *Eratosthenes* in P.W., 362. [2] Dindorf's Stephanus *s.v.*

used to pump out ships and drain the fields after the Nile flood, which survives in our Archimedean drills. Everyone knows the stories about him: how he was too absent-minded to remember to eat; how one day he discovered specific gravity by noticing the water he displaced in his bath, and jumped out and ran home naked, shouting *Eureka*, 'I have found it'; how when difficulties arose over the launching of Hiero's great *Syracosia* he launched the ship by himself, and told the king, 'Give me where to stand and I will move the earth'; and how during the siege of Syracuse the solitary geometrician kept the whole strength of Rome at bay for three years with his grapnels and improved catapults. He is the only mathematician who ever became a legend.

Archimedes apart, practical mechanics (as distinct from engineering) came to little, and chiefly meant siege-engines and catapults,[1] on which various treatises remain, and mechanical toys; labour was too cheap for much thought to be given to machinery, though Ctesibius invented a catapult worked by compressed air[2] and a water-clock, someone else invented a water-mill, and the younger Ctesibius[3] a water-organ,[4] used in the early Church. Aristarchus made an improved sun-dial. Heron of Alexandria had some idea of the expansive power of steam[5]; but some place him after A.D. 200, though the first century B.C. is more probable.[6] The most useful invention was the *dioptra* or portable water level, which took the theodolite's place in land surveying; Hipparchus constructed a more elaborate form for astronomical use, it is thought on Babylonian models.[7] Mathematics remained vigorous, but the first-century attitude is shown by the Epicurean Zeno of Sidon attacking the very foundations of geometry; Poseidonius refuted him, and the period closes with a vast history of mathematics written by

[1] Diels, *Antike Technik*[2] 1920; Schramm in Kromayer and Veith, *Heerwesen und Kriegsführung*.
[2] Described, Diels *op. c.* 106.
[3] Orinsky, *Ktesibios* in P.W., would identify the two.
[4] Athen. 174 B; Ditt.[3] 737 n. 2; Tittel, *Hydraulis* in P.W.
[5] Diels *op. c.* 59.
[6] The date controversy: Diels, 57 n. 2; Hoppe, *Hermes* LXII, 79 (c. 130 B.C.); Hammer-Jensen *ib.* LXIII, 34 (late); Gercke-Norden, II, 5, 74.
[7] Hoppe *l.c.* 91; Hultsch, *Dioptra* in P.W.

Poseidonius' pupil Geminus, a summary of the results obtained.

In scientific, as distinct from descriptive, geography,[1] there was great activity, which revived again under the Antonines. The beginning was the series of measurements made by Alexander's surveying section (bematists), which for long formed the basis of the geography of Asia; and about 300 the Peripatetic Dicaearchus,[2] with pecuniary help from Cassander or Lysimachus,[3] made a map of the world, calculated the heights of various Greek mountains, and (probably) calculated the earth's circumference; using Syene-Lysimacheia as base line, he made it 300,000 stades, considerably too large, but meritorious for the first attempt. But the great geographer of the third century, and one of the greatest men it produced, was Eratosthenes of Cyrene[4] (275–200), a pupil of Ariston the Stoic heretic at Athens, who worked at Alexandria, but whose affinities were with the Academy.[5] He almost rivalled Aristotle in the number of fields of learning he covered; beside his studies in historical criticism and chronology, he published works on mathematics and philosophy and a history of comedy which superseded Lycophron's, and he wrote poetry; his nickname was *Beta* (Number Two), meaning that on a poll of learned men he would have gained the 'vote of Themistocles' in every branch of study. He measured the circumference of the earth by calculating what fraction of an arc of meridian equalled the known distance from Alexandria to Syene, and made it 252,000 stades; the length of the stade he used is unknown, so certainty is unattainable, but the most probable calculation makes his measurement 24,662 miles, the true mean circumference being 24,857 miles.[6] His actual

[1] H. Berger, *Gesch. d. wissenschaftlichen Erdkunde der Griechen*², 1903; F. Gisinger, *Geographie* in P.W.; J. Oliver Thomson, *A history of ancient geography*, 1948.

[2] Beloch IV, 1, 463.

[3] His use of Lysimacheia identifies the 'kings' of Pliny II, 162.

[4] Susemihl I, 409; Knaack in P.W. *s.v.*

[5] Tarn, *A.J. Phil.* LX, 1939, 53.

[6] Heath, *Aristarchus*, 339; Hultsch much the same; other calculations, Beloch IV, 1, 465; Gisinger *l.c.*; Viedebantt, *Klio* XIV, 207; J. O. Thomson, *op. cit.* 159–62.

error, whatever it was, arose from his not possessing the means of determining whether Alexandria and Syene had precisely the same longitude (they have not); but it was an amazing feat, and never improved upon till modern times. The 'inhabited earth' he made some 8,910 by 4,340 miles, divided latitudinally by the parallel of Rhodes (36°), which he treated as equivalent to the Taurus-Hindu Kush line[1]; this latter division he took from the gazetteer[2] of Alexander's empire made shortly before Alexander's death. He also drew certain parallels of latitude and longitude.

The question of whether India and Africa joined or not, which had so perplexed Aristotle, had been settled by Alexander, and Eratosthenes' strongly critical mind never doubted that all the oceans were one and that the inhabited world, Europe-Asia-Africa, was an island[3]; he pointed to the similarity of the tides in the Indian and Atlantic oceans, and rightly deduced that one could sail from Spain round Africa to India,[4] a voyage which was not actually made before Vasco da Gama, though the philologist Crates of Mallos (*c.* 168), in his controversy with the philologist Aristarchus over Homer's geography, made Menelaus take it,[5] and Poseidonius utilised the idea in the Eudoxus story (p. 248). Eratosthenes was also the first to see that one could sail westward from Spain to India.[6] In some ways he had juster views than any of his successors; but his weakness was his difficulty over longitudes, and Hipparchus, with improved knowledge, was able to subject his map to serious criticism in this respect. Hipparchus himself had the fine idea of getting the latitude and longitude of a large number of places astronomically fixed by the co-operation of different observers all over the world[7]; the political position made it impossible, but that it ultimately bore some fruit is suggested by the number of places for which latitude and longitude is given in the later geography of Claudius Ptolemy,

[1] Str. 84, 86.
[2] Diod. XVIII, 5–6; Tarn, *J.H.S.* 1923, 93; *Alexander* II, App. 14 and 17.
[3] Str. 32, 56, 113.
[4] *Ib.* 38.
[5] Str. 38, περιπλοῦς, so not across the Atlantic as Susemihl II, 6.
[6] Str. 64.
[7] Capelle, *N.J. Kl. Alt.* XLV, 306.

which was to dominate the world till Columbus, though in the Farther East, at any rate, Ptolemy's co-ordinates are guesswork.

Polybius did much to render Greek geography after him descriptive, as being the only sort useful to the historian; and the only advance in scientific geography between Hipparchus and the Roman period came from Poseidonius[1] (p. 349), whose curiosity about the things of the earth was boundless, and who wrote on meteorology and volcanic phenomena beside his famous work *On the Ocean*, a title taken from Pytheas. Neither scientific nor critical, he nevertheless rendered services to science. His huge collection of phenomena, volcanic and aqueous, to illustrate changes in the earth's surface showed what his idea of evidence was; myth or history, the destruction of Atlantis or the destruction of Helice, were all one to him, but out of it all there did emerge the European-Anatolian earthquake belt as a whole. He employed some strange assumptions in calculating the earth's circumference[2]; what stade he used is unknown, but in any case he made the earth too small.[3] He is the author of our five zones,[4] for Polybius had made six, and Eratosthenes seven by dividing the tropic zone into two burning belts and a habitable equatorial belt between them, a wonderfully good guess at the actual desert belts; Poseidonius took the midday shadow as the criterion, whether during the year it fell one way, both ways, or all round. Luckily he followed Eratosthenes' conviction that all the oceans were one,[5] a belief which was to be lost again to the world owing to its rejection by the astronomers Hipparchus and Seleucus; and he made a famous journey to Gades (Cadiz), where he studied the Atlantic tides. Aristotle and Dicaearchus had thought the sun made the tides by raising a wind, and it was that very great traveller Pytheas who first showed it was the moon. Seleucus,

[1] Capelle *op. c.* and *N.J. Kl. Alt.* XXI, 616; Reinhardt, *Poseidonios*, 61–123; the fragments. [2] Heath, 344; Gisinger *l.c.*; Reinhardt, 196.

[3] He took 140,000 as the circumference of the paralle of Rhodes, see *infra*. [4] Frs. 28, 76. [5] Frs. 28. 82.

observing the Persian Gulf, discovered the inequality of the tides (spring and neap tides) and attributed this to the moon's position in the zodiac; Poseidonius took the observation of inequalities further, and attributed them to the moon's phases. But for agent he went back to Aristotle's wind, whereas Seleucus thought that the interaction of moon and earth set up some form of pressure or current[1]; he may have been groping in a direction which, if followed up, might have led to the discovery of gravitation.

However, Poseidonius' journey threw light on more than the tides; it ultimately led to the discovery of America. Someone, probably Eratosthenes, had suggested that the Atlantic might be divided longitudinally by land (*i.e.* America),[2] a suggestion which inspired Seneca's famous prophecy of the discovery of a New World.[3] Poseidonius, however, not only rejected this idea, but, having got the size of the earth too small, believed that, on the parallel of Rhodes (36°), the 'inhabited world', which he made 70,000 stades across from east to west, was half the circumference; so, looking at the Atlantic, he very naturally remarked that a man sailing west for 70,000 stades would come to India.[4] This remark, passed on by (among others) Roger Bacon,[5] was the ultimate foundation of Columbus' confidence; and it was only historical justice that he should set sail for India from Poseidonius' Cadiz.

In medicine,[6] the two great names of the early third century were Herophilus of Chalcedon and Erasistratus of Iulis in Ceos, who founded rival schools; Herophilus worked in, and his school became identified with, Alexandria, though it invaded Asia; of Erasistratus' life and place of work little is known, for the stories about him, especially that which

[1] Aetius p. 383, Diels.

[2] Str. 65; Berger *op. c.* 398.

[3] *Medea* 375.

[4] Str. 102=fr. 28 § 6 (p. 239 in *F. Gr. Hist.*) 140,000 stades altogether; the other measurement he gives, fr. 28 § 2 (p. 234) 180,000 stades, is the corresponding N–S circumference.

[5] A. G. Little, *Roger Bacon*, Proc. Brit. Acad. 1928, offprint p. 16.

[6] Heiberg *op. c.*; Ch. Singer, *Greek biology and Greek medicine*, 1922; Susemihl I chs. 24, 34; W. H. S. Jones, *C.A.H.* VII, ch. IX.

makes him Seleucus' physician, have no value.[1] Both made important advances in anatomy and physiology. Herophilus discovered the nerves, previously unknown, which he understood ran from the brain and the spinal cord, and distinguished the cerebrum and cerebellum; he also found out that the arteries carried blood, not air (as had been believed), and pulsed, not of themselves, but from the heart; therewith he practically discovered the circulation of the blood, lost again till Harvey. Some of his names for parts of the body, as the duodenum and the torcular Herophili, are still in use. Erasistratus improved on the anatomy of the heart, but his chief discovery was the distinction between the motor and the sensory nerves; unfortunately he went back to the belief that the arteries carried air. Both men performed serious operations, and dissected corpses. Vivisection of animals was already known to Aristotle; but Celsus, a sober and competent writer, has a horrible story[2] that Herophilus vivisected criminals given him by Ptolemy I (anaesthetics were unknown), and the same is implied of Erasistratus.

Their schools made no great advance on the two masters, and were ultimately eclipsed by a third, the empiric, founded by Herophilus' pupil Philinus of Cos, which, influenced perhaps by the scepticism of the Academy, is supposed to have neglected anatomy and to have held that disease was curable without a knowledge of physiology; but its best known member, Heracleides of Tarentum, did practise dissection, and its concentration upon medicines did much for the study of drugs. One interesting personality, Asclepiades of Prusa, appeared in the first century; he was not a trained physician, but he undertook to cure disease without drugs by dieting, walking, massage, and cold baths, and achieved such success that a legend grew up that he (like Empedocles) had raised a man from the dead; the origin of this legend can, for once, be traced, for Celsus says that he once recognised that a man being carried out to burial was

[1] Wilamowitz, *Hell. Dichtung*, 163 n. 3, thought that he too worked in Alexandria.

[2] I p. 4 l. 37, Daremberg; but see *C.A.H.* VII, 286.

still alive.[1] Under Augustus, Celsus closes the age with a medical encyclopaedia, a summary of the advances made in knowledge since Hippocrates, parallel to Geminus' history of mathematics. Naturally all through the period scientific medicine had its half-world, the cures in the temples of Asclepius and Sarapis, where the patient slept in the precinct and was healed in a dream by the god; some of the recorded cures are amusing stories,[2] but doubtless some patients really were healed by suggestion. By the first century the wandering magician was a serious rival to both doctor and priest.

Zoology and botany did little more than make a start, Theophrastus and his successor Strato wrote on zoology. but essentially the science remained where Aristotle had left it, and all that was done was to familiarise the Greek world with various new animals; Seleucus sent an Indian tiger to Athens,[3] and Ptolemy II had a zoological garden[4] containing, besides 24 great lions, leopards, lynxes, and other cats, Indian and African buffaloes, wild asses from Moab, a python 45 feet long, a giraffe, a rhinoceros, and a polar bear[5] (whose journey south must have been exciting), together with parrots, peacocks, guinea-fowl, pheasants, and many African birds.[6] Botany fared rather better; Theophrastus' great *History of Plants*, which incorporated the results of Alexander's expedition, was for long the high-water mark of that science; all that was added to it was more precise knowledge of plants like the Arabian frankincense tree, and of drugs. The empiric school of medicine did much for the knowledge of drugs, and there was a whole literature of poisons and antidotes, in which Attalus III and Mithridates Eupator were specially interested; Attalus had a garden of

[1] Cf. Pliny VII, 124 with Celsus II p. 38 l. 15.

[2] Ditt.[3] 1168–9. Cf. R. Herzog, *Die Wunderheilungen von Epidauros* (*Philol.* Suppl. Bd. XXII, 3), 1931.

[3] Philemon, *Neaira* fr. 47 (Kock II, 490); Alexis, *Pyraunos* fr. 204 (*ib.* 372).

[4] Agatharch. *G.G.M.* I, 111.

[5] Callixenus ap. Athen. 201 C calls it μεγάλη, which refutes any idea that it was an albino.

[6] Athen. 201 C, cf. 200 F; Diod. III, 36, 3 *sqq.*; *P. Cairo Zen.* 59075.

strange plants for his study of the subject. But botany never attained to a classification and nomenclature, though Mithridates' physician Crateuas did something to diminish the uncertainty of verbal description by introducing the method of representing plants pictorially.[1]

Too much must not be made of Hellenistic science, exciting as it is, since of the two sciences which to-day bulk so large, physics and chemistry, chemistry (except for alchemy[2]) never got started and physics died with Strato, who made a limited use of Democritus' atomic (really molecular) theory; for the adoption of that theory by Epicurus had nothing to do with science (p. 328), though in Lucretius' account of evolution, based on Empedocles' idea that many ill-adapted animal forms had perished, there was the germ of a true evolutionary hypothesis, had science taken it up. The Greek got no further than he did because he had no scientific instruments, and, except in surgery, rarely experimented; he had, perhaps for his happiness, no gift for instruments and machines, and probably he went about as far as was possible without the telescope, the microscope, and the test-tube. Cornford said that if some Archimedes had overcome the Greek prejudice against mechanical crafts and invented optical glass the whole course of history would have been changed.[3] But several things—Nero's eye-glass,[4] references to burning-glasses,[5] and above all 'Alexander's mirror' on the Pharos,[6] which enabled ships to be detected beyond the range of vision—show that the properties of the concave lens were at least suspected; but this was not followed up, for the bent of the Greek mind was to try to think the thing out by itself; philosophy rather than science was the goddess to be served, and of the sciences mathematics, for this reason, far surpassed the others.

[1] Singer, *J.H.S.* 1927, 1.

[2] Wellmann, *Bolos* in P.W.; Diels, *Ant. Technik.*[2] ch. VI; F. S. Taylor, *A survey of Greek Alchemy*, *J.H.S.* L, 1930, 109.

[3] *C.A.H.* IV, 577.

[4] Plin. XXXVII, 64.

[5] Ar. *Clouds* 766; Plut. *Num.* 9, see L. R. Farnell, *Cults*, V, 353.

[6] Stories collected, A. Hilka, *Studien zur Alexandersage*, 1911, p. 5. H. Thiersch, *Pharos*, 91, suggests a Hellenistic telescope.

The transition from science to art[1] was formed by architecture[2] and town-planning[3]; for in some respects Hellenistic architecture was an alliance of the older Greek architecture with engineering, which perhaps first came definitely to birth with Philo's arsenal and dockhouses at Athens in Alexander's reign. If mass of construction counts for anything, the century or so after Alexander was one of the great blossoming times of architecture, with its multitudes of new cities, each of which, so far as it was Greek, would now contain a theatre, market-place, town hall, gymnasium, and at least one temple; the theatre at Ephesus held 24,500 people,[4] and the Council-Chamber at Miletus was superb. Some description of Alexandria and Pergamum has already been given and Antioch and Seleuceia on the Tigris were ultimately not much less populous than Alexandria. Antioch was four distinct walled towns or 'quarters' enclosed in a general ring wall; Demetrias (p. 68) was a double city, one ring wall enclosing Demetrias and Pagasae. The great advance in siege machinery due to Alexander's engineer Diades[5] and still more to Demetrius had led to corresponding improvements in the city wall; the magnificent fortifications of Heraclea-Latmos, a city of the second class, can still be traced,[6] going straight across mountain and ravine with towers at intervals; the little Melitaea in Oeta had walls no ladder could scale.[7] Normally the wall followed the city contour on the flat and took in part of the hill behind; it

[1] Generally, see B. Ashmole, *C.A.H.* VIII, ch. 21, and Bibliography; *C.A.H.*, *Vol. of Plates III*; W. Zschietzschmann, *Die hellenistische und römische Kunst*, 1939.

[2] Generally: M. Collignon and E. Pontremoli, *Pergame*, 1900; Th. Wiegand and H. Schrader, *Priene*, 1904; Wiegand, *Milet*; Pontremoli and B. Haussoullier, *Didymes*, 1903; A. R. Schütz, *Das Typus des hellenistischen Hauses*, 1936; D. S. Robertson, *A handbook of Greek and Roman Architecture* 2nd ed., 1943; W. B. Dinsmoor, *The architecture of ancient Greece*, 1950 ch. VII.

[3] I owe much here to A. von Gerkan, *Griechische Städteanlagen*, 1924. Cf. F. Haverfield, *Ancient Town Planning*, 1913; A. Boethius, 'Roman and Greek town architecture" in *Göteborgs Högskolas Arsskrift*, LIV, 1948, 3.

[4] Brückner, *Ephesos* in P.W., 2816.

[5] *Laterculi Alexandrini* (p. 293 n. 1); Athenaeus περὶ μηχανημάτων.

[6] Krischen, *Milet* III, 2.

[7] Polyb. V, 97, 5.

left no room for expansion, which explains why Antioch, for example, as it grew, became a cluster of towns with separate walls. No Hellenistic city ever challenged the 17-mile circuit of the wall of Syracuse. Alexandria's huge wall was possibly 10 miles round, Ephesus' 7½, Miletus' 7[1]; but the extraordinary wall-circuits of some Acarnanian towns, meant to shelter the country population, might rival Ephesus.[2] Of course at Alexandria and Seleuceia there was a great native population outside the wall.

The characteristic of the Hellenistic city was its rectangular streets, which cut it up into blocks like a chess-board; Hippodamus of Miletus had introduced the system at Piraeus in Pericles' time, but it now became usual.[3] Polybius[4] compares the Hellenistic city to the camp of a Roman legion, with two main streets crossing at right angles, dividing the town into four quarters, with four gates at each end of the main streets. Some cities in Syria of this type are known,[5] and probably Alexandria, Seleuceia,[6] and others were such; but the only one whose extant literary description corresponds to this formation is Antigoneia-Nicea in Bithynia.[7] But some cities were naturally conditioned by the lie of the ground: Priene may be typical of the usual form on the slope of a hill, and there, though the chess-board pattern is maintained, the two main streets both run parallel to the long axis; at Miletus, on the flat, the plan seems to consist in distributing the public buildings to the best advantage. Smyrna was a horseshoe round a hill,[8] built in three separate blocks, each with rectangular streets but differently orientated, which may explain the number of kings who are said to have 'built' it; Seleuceia in Pieria rose in terraces up a cliff[9]; Delos just grew anyhow. In fact there was no stereotyped planning; the architects achieved beauty by adapting things to their ends; for example, the main street usually formed one side of the market-place, but the street

[1] Gerkan 110; for the splendid fortifications of Miletus, see Wiegand, *Milet* II, Heft 3, 1935.
[2] Noack, *Arch. Anz.* 1916, 215.
[3] For Egypt, Schubart, *Einführung*, 437.
[4] VI, 31, 10.
[5] Cumont, *C.A.H.* XI, 634.
[6] Air photographs.
[7] Str. 565.
[8] Str. 646.
[9] Ruge in P.W. *s.v.*

was planned to lead to the market, the market did not grow out of the street.[1] There is, however, some evidence that orientation was so arranged as to secure the greatest amount of sun for the houses in winter,[2] except of course in Babylonia, where at Seleuceia the houses naturally faced north.[3]

Alexandria apart, where the main street is called 100 feet broad, the streets were not yet as wide as the Roman. At Pergamum the main streets had by law to be 33 feet wide; the broadest street at Priene is about 24 feet, at Magnesia 26½. Cross streets run about 14 to 15 feet wide, though 10½ is known[4]; the cheapness of labour is illustrated by little Assos cutting streets through the living rock. Smyrna boasted that she was the first city to pave her streets[5]; but Hellenistic paving, though known, is rare, and Miletus, Antioch, and Alexandria were not paved at all. The first known covered colonnade alongside a main street, common in Roman times, was built by Herod I at Antioch.[6] Great attention was paid to the water supply; where possible, the water was merely led downhill by gravitation into a reservoir and thence distributed; but, judging by Priene, the distribution of water to single houses was only very occasionally done. The underground cisterns at Alexandria were a thing apart, and the statement that every house in Antioch had water laid on belongs to a far later period; but the extremely severe penalties imposed by the Pergamene Public Health law for fouling the town water illustrate a new regard for health.[7] Where a gravitation supply was impossible, pressure was well understood; the supply for the hill at Pergamum was forced up the last two miles through metal pipes under a pressure of 18 atmospheres.[8] Baths became common, and were in every well-equipped gymnasium[9]; at Pergamum there were apparently public lavatories[10] and drains from the houses had by law to be covered in,[11] as at

[1] Gerkan 95.

[2] N. E. Manasseh, in *Second Preliminary Report upon the excavations at Tel Umar*, 29.

[3] *Ib.* 79.

[4] Manasseh, *ib.* 82.

[5] Str. 646.

[6] Jos. *Ant.* XVI, 148; *B.J.* 1, 425.

[7] *OGIS* 483.

[8] Water-supply: Gerkan 87.

[9] Hepding, *Ath. Mitt.* 1907, 273.

[10] *OGIS* 483 l. 221.

[11] *Ib.* ll. 60–75, 222.

Athens[1]; but probably open drains, as at Priene, were the rule till the Romans built sewers.

Architectural technique altered little. The arch and the vault, long known in Babylonia, and the cupola came in during this period to reinforce the older forms of construction derived from wood, but are only occasionally met with; arches occur at Pergamum and Didyma, but the buttressing necessitated by the outward thrust of the arch seems to have been foreign to Greek instincts; the vaulting of the Alexandrian cisterns is said to be Arab. The Corinthian capital gained steadily in popularity at the expense of the older orders; mixture of Ionic and Corinthian is found in Asia. Otherwise architectural innovations related to the forms of buildings. Private houses were still of the type which opened on a central court, but were greatly improved and more luxurious; in the second century the peristyle—a colonnade round the court—begins to occur at Delos.[2] Building had to vary with the available material; it was said Alexandria could never be burnt because there was no wood anywhere,[3] while the absence of marble in Egypt led to the invention of 'incrustation', the panelling of inner walls with thin slabs of that material; walls too were painted to look like marble, while on the other hand there were cities like Mylasa where the abundant local marble was used even to build private houses.[4] Sometimes, too, the wall-panels of a room were painted with gardens or colonnades, so that you seemed to be in a hall open on all sides.[5] At Tyre and Aradus, whose island sites afforded no lateral space, houses ran up many stories high[6]; and this was perhaps so at Alexandria within the wall by *c.* 100, for the city began with houses only half the distance apart that was compulsory at Athens, and seemingly the intervening space could be built over upon payment.[7]

One would like to illustrate Hellenistic architecture by

[1] Arist., *Ath. Pol.* 50, 2.

[2] J. Chamonard, *Délos* VIII, 1.

[3] Hirtius, *Bell. Alex.* 1.

[4] Str. 658.

[5] The Villa Boscoreale at Pompeii.

[6] Str. 753, 757.

[7] *Dikaiomata* 95 *sqq.*; Wilamowitz, *Hell. Dicht.* 1, 156; V. Ehrenberg, *Alexander und Ägypten*, 95.

describing the palace quarter at Alexandria; but nothing is known about it, except that the palaces stood in gardens. Ptolemy's abode must be figured, not as an oriental palace, but as strictly Greek, a cluster of juxtaposed halls and living rooms; Philopator's house-boat, a magnificent villa of halls and shrines surrounded by a colonnade and mounted on a barge, may illustrate the type,[1] and imported marble must have been freely used. It was an age of pillared colonnades, especially for the use of merchants; king's gifts often took this shape, like the porticoes of Antigonus Gonatas, Attalus I, and Philip V at Delos (p. 264), and of Antiochus I at Miletus.[2] The normal type of market-place had colonnades round three sides, the fourth abutting on the road, and the great cities began to separate its mercantile and political functions,[3] as they separated the mercantile and military functions of the harbour; the double harbour of Alexandria was copied where the lie of the land permitted,[4] and an important city would be able to close one of its harbours with chains, though perhaps no other city, unless Cyzicus,[5] ever rivalled the advantage Athens had had in being able to close *all* her harbours.[6] But Sostratus' lighthouse on the Pharos at Alexandria,[7] built as a tower of three diminishing stories, nearly 400 feet high, was unique; the third story was the 'lantern', eight columns supporting a cupola, under which burnt a fire of resinous wood, the light possibly being thrown out by convex mirrors; a lift ran up to it. It perhaps gave Arab architects the idea of the minaret. The amphitheatre, though not common, certainly goes back to Hellenism, which had some fancy for circular buildings, as the Philippeion at Olympia and the Arsinoeion at Samothrace; a Doric temple at Samothrace has a rounded apse like a Christian basilica.[8]

[1] Athen. 204 D; Caspari, *J.D.A.I.* 1916, 1. Cf. Fr. Studniczka, *Das Symposion Ptolemaios II*, 1914.

[2] *OGIS* 213; *Milet* 1, 7 no. 193a and p. 31; *SEG* IV, 442.

[3] Gerkan 103.

[4] K. Lehmann-Hartleben, *Antiken Hafenanlagen*.

[5] Str. 575.

[6] Michel 1465 l. 40; Schol. Ar. *Pax* 144.

[7] *OGIS* 66–8; Poseidippus, no. 1 (Schott); Eusebius, Schöne II, 119; Breccia, *Alexandrea* 107; Bevan 95; Thiersch, *Pharos*, and *J.D.A.I.* 1915, 213.

[8] Conze and Hauser, *Samothrake* I, Pls. XI, XVII.

The number of temples built was very great, as, beside the new cities, many settlements and associations required one; but the Serapeum at Delos[1] shows that these last must, inevitably, have often been poor cheap work; clubs of 50 members could not afford much of a chapel. At Doura-Europus a room with raised tiers of seats like a theatre was annexed to the temple of Artemis-Nanaia (*c.* 32 B.C.) and to two later temples, presumably for some cult purpose; a sacred dance has been suggested.[2] Among the great temples of the time the most notable were the great Serapeum at Alexandria, where a Roman pillar still marks the site of the Sarapis column, and the temples of Zeus Olympius at Athens, completed under Hadrian, and of Apollo at Didyma near Miletus, never really finished at all; most beautiful[3] was said to be that of Artemis Leukophryene at Magnesia on the Maeander, planned by Hermogenes[4] and completed in 129. The Artemision at Ephesus, the wonder of the world, can hardly be included here, as it is essentially fourth century; but a short description of Didyma may be given.[5] Strabo calls Didyma the greatest of Greek temples,[6] but in fact Sicily has the honour, the dimensions in feet of the five largest being: Zeus at Acragas, 363 by 182; Apollo at Selinus ('G'), 360 by 163; Didyma, 354 by 160; Artemis at Ephesus, 342 by 164; Zeus at Athens, 354 by 135.

The old temple at Didyma had been burnt in the Ionian revolt,[7] and Miletus began the new one about 300. Didyma could only be reached by sea, and the Sacred Way from the landing-place to the temple was still bordered by the original archaic figures of worshippers[8]; this idea, which came from the sphinx-bordered temple avenues of Egypt, now returned again to Egypt from Didyma, the approach

[1] Roussel, *Les cultes égyptiens à Délos* 264.

[2] Cumont, *Doura* ch. III; cf. *Excavations at Dura-Europos*, fifth season. 132 (C. Hopkins).

[3] Str. 647.

[4] Vitruv. III, 2, 6; Ditt.[3] 1156.

[5] Cf. J. D. Beazley and D. S. Robertson, *C.A.H.* VI, 555; R. C. Bosanquet, *Dublin Lectures on Archaeology*, Oct. 1924.

[6] Str. 634.

[7] The Susa knucklebone (Haussoullier, *Mém. Déleg. en Perse* VII, 155) is conclusive that the later story of Xerxes and the Branchidae is untrue.

[8] Haussoullier, *Cinquantênaire de l'École pratique des Hautes Études*, Paris, 1921, 85.

to the Serapeum at Memphis being bordered by statues of distinguished Greeks.[1] The precinct of the temple was shaped like a stadium, and some believe races were run round it, Greek athletic sports being always part of a festival primarily religious. The temple was dipteral and decastyle, that is, it was surrounded by two rows of columns and was ten columns in breadth along the front, no other temple being more than eight. Instead of the usual two columns *in antis*, *i.e.* in the recess between the cella walls, there were twelve, in three rows of four each; the impression made on the approaching visitor was of a forest of slender Ionic columns, which suggested some Egyptian or Persian hall, and was intended to divert his mind from the fact that he could see no *naos*, the roofed room which held the temple statue. For when he entered the *prodomos* (vestibule), before him rose a screen of stone, blocking all further view, and in its centre the great door of the 'oracle-bureau', which Ptolemy XI covered with ivory,[2] and from which oracles were probably handed out. At either side were staircases with arched roofs; passing down one, he entered what replaced the *naos*, a court fourteen feet below the floor level and open to the sky. At the far end was the shrine of Canachus' Apollo, carried off by Darius I and sent back in 295 by Seleucus; but the visitor, turning his back on Apollo, saw before him the grand stairway of 22 steps, leading back the way he had come and up to the chamber between the court and the *prodromos*, the 'oracle bureau'; at the head of the stairway were three doors, two leading to upper rooms, possibly treasuries. Didyma thus differed absolutely from the well-known form of every other Greek temple. But the sculptured bases of its columns, and still more the twelve columns *in antis*, went back to the sixth-century Artemision at Ephesus, just as the Sacred Way belonged to an older world; while one of the architects of Didyma, Paeonius, had worked on the new Artemision and probably desired to avoid repeating himself. Didyma thus became a unique combination of audacious novelty and conscious archaising.

[1] Wilcken *J.D.A.I.* 1917, 149.

[2] *OGIS* 193.

With Hellenism, art changes its character. Classical restraint goes; there are no longer limitations, for it is a time that tries all things and explores many new paths. All the tendencies of the time are in its sculpture[1]: lack of repose, for indeed the age knew little; self-consciousness, expressed in the theatricalism which has left its mark at Pergamum; romanticism, and realism even to ugliness. Individualism breaks through in the outburst of portrait statuary, the brotherhood of human beings in the representation of old working people, like the rather wonderful old shepherdess and fisherman of the Conservatori palace at Rome. The Fortune of Antioch reminds us that Fortune was the typical worship of the third century, just as the Isis of Delos introduces the new world of the first; Struggle is personified in the Pergamene frieze, and Triumph is glorified, as never before or since, in the Victory of Samothrace. Happily every attempt to express something otherwise than had been done by Phidias or Praxiteles is no longer condemned offhand, and no one need feel a sense of guilt in admiring some Hellenistic work. Decadence ultimately showed, of course; things like the Alexandrian grotesques, the degradation of Eros into a cupid, the transition from Theocritus to the artificial 'nature' of the pastoral reliefs, statues like the once-admired Laocoon, all illustrate tendencies at work. Idealism gradually declined, and inspiration began to be drawn, not from the artist's soul, but from the past. But even so, technical skill never failed till sculpture at the end became a trade; and the continuing love of beauty may be illustrated by the fact that the Aphrodite of Melos (Venus of Milo) and the Aphrodite Anadyomene of Cyrene have both been assigned to the late second century.[2]

[1] Generally. Collignon, *Hist. de la sculpture grecque*, 1897; W. Klein, *Die Kunst der Diadochenzeit*, 2 vols., 1905–7, *Gesch. d. gr. Kunst* III, 1907, and *Von Antiken Rococo*, 1921; E. A. Gardner, *A handbook of Greek sculpture*², 1924; G. Dickins, *Hellenistic sculpture*², 1920; C. Picard, *La sculpture antique* II, 1926, 193–310; A. W. Lawrence, *Later Greek sculpture*, 1927; J. D. Beazley and B. Ashmole, *Greek Sculpture and Painting*, 1932; E. Buschor, *Das hellenistische Bildnis*, 1949.

[2] G. Bagnani, *J.H.S.* 1921, 232; G. Krahmer, *Röm. Mitt.* 1923–4, 138.

Much work has been done on the tendencies of these three centuries; local schools have been traced, or the time has been divided into periods without regard to locality, sometimes labelled with terms of an alien art, baroque or rococo; perhaps one who is not an art-critic may be pardoned a certain distrust in face of a science of criticism which during the last few years has succeeded in placing the Victory of Samothrace everywhere from 322 to 31, including dates which, to the historian, are frankly absurd.[1] That sculpture was a living force is shown by the enormous output and the occasional prices paid; though about half a talent was a usual price for a good statue,[2] Attalus II is said once to have paid 100 talents for one[3]; Philip V found 2,000 statues at Thermum[4] and the Romans took a great many from Ambracia,[5] both places which were certainly not art-centres. The considerable mass of Hellenistic work still known, in originals, fragments, and copies, bears no relation at all to what once existed; for this was the age of the honorary and votive statue, and every Greek city set up considerable numbers, some doubtless good; but the known families of sculptors by heredity illustrate the gradual transition from art to craft in this matter. The final step came after the Roman conquests, when the plunder of a Mummius or a Verres induced at Rome a taste for Greek statuary in bulk, as a self-made man furnishes a library. Athens' commercial resurrection after 146 was partly due to her supplying Rome's need, both by original work based on older statues and by good copies, and other cities imitated her; the better things of the sort can be seen in the over-muscled Farnese Hercules and the over-graceful Apollo Belvedere. Ultimately a Roman firm, the Cossutii, set up branches throughout Greece

[1] Lawrence, *J.H.S.* 1926, 213 (322); Beloch IV, 1, 524 (306–300); Dickins *op. c.* (c. 250); Krahmer *op. c.* (c. 150); Lippold, *Röm. Mitt.* 1918, 94 (some Roman victory); Klein, *Rokoko*, 106 (Actium). The American expedition now excavating the temples on Samothrace has put forward "the decades around 200 B.C." (*Times*, Oct. 23, 1950); but full evidence and reasons must be awaited. For the date taken in this book, *i.e.* after the battle of Cos, c. 258, see *post* p. 320.

[2] Wilhelm, *Neue Beiträge* VI, 2.

[3] Plin. VII, 126; XXXV, 100.

[4] Polyb. V, 9. 3.

[5] *Ib.* XXI, 30, 9; Livy XXXVIII, 9, 13.

wherever there was marble and engaged Greeks to turn out statues wholesale for the Roman market[1]; and sculpture, which began as a religion, ended as a trade.

There was seemingly a school at Alexandria,[2] though she was primarily a collecting centre; but the work so far found in Egypt is chiefly second-rate,[3] and the Alexandrian grave-reliefs are hardly even that, unless for the one generation when Athenian artists, quitting Athens because Demetrius of Phalerum's prohibition of grave-reliefs had spoilt their livelihood, settled in Alexandria[4]; it was in Egypt that the practice arose of putting on statues' hair in stucco. Praxiteles' influence remained great, and not only at Alexandria, but the smoothness of his skin-texture became exaggerated; the beautiful Cyrene Aphrodite illustrates the style, which sometimes merely covered slack work. Alexandria's real strength was in the smaller arts; probably she invented mosaic[5] and cameo-cutting. Curiously, though idealism fared badly in Alexandrian art, the city contained one strongly idealist work, the cult-statue of Sarapis.[6] This may really have been the work of Scopas' pupil Bryaxis, wherever Ptolemy I brought it from; it was coloured dark blue, and the eyes were jewelled, to gleam through the darkened temple from the richly decorated and lighted cella; the face is described as mild, majestic, and mysterious, as befitted the god of the underworld, and on the head was a *modius* or corn-measure, significant of that great granary, Egypt.

Lysippus' influence lived on at Rhodes, where his pupil Chares of Lindus, to commemorate Rhodes' resistance to Demetrius in 304, carved that colossal statue of the Sun which was one of the wonders of the world; it was destroyed by the earthquake of 225, and nothing remains to suggest

[1] Hatzfeld, *Trafiquants* 227. [2] Lawrence *contra*, *B.S.A.* XXVI, 67.

[3] Lawrence, *J.E.A.* XI, 179.

[4] *Contra*, A. J. B. Wace, *J.H.S.* 1930, 154, who denies any Attic influence in Egypt. [5] Mosaics: Cumont, *L'Égypte des Astrologues*, 101 n. 1.

[6] Weitz, *Sarapis* in Roscher; Amelung, *Rev. Arch.* 1903, ii, 177; Lippold, *Festschrift Paul Arndt*, 1925, 115; the works on Egypt. It has recently been contended that the head was golden; see Brady, *Harvard Stud. in Class. Philol.* LI, 1941, 61 (*post* p. 356 n. 1).

what it was like.[1] The Rhodian was a virile school, a school of athletic men and carefully draped women; the well-known Praying Boy of Berlin and the so-called Hellenistic Ruler at Naples may illustrate its best period, and even in the first century, when it had declined to the tortured forms of the Laocoon and the Farnese Bull groups, its technical mastery remained astonishing. But the most influential work of Lysippus' school was the famous Fortune of Antioch,[2] made for Antioch by his pupil Eutychides, a gracious and charming woman with a pensive face, seated on her mountain with the river-god Orontes at her feet; she was fully draped and wore a turreted crown, thenceforth the universal mark of the city-goddess, and held a palm-leaf in her hand. To say with Brunn that she has not the dignity or austerity of an older goddess is otiose, for she was not a goddess (though she became one); she was the personification, the individuality, of the group of men and women who were Antioch (p. 340). The type, with many variations to suit local circumstances, was copied by innumerable cities throughout Asia.

The earlier history of the school of Pergamum is only of technical interest, and Pergamene great art,[3] in which Scopas' influence lived again, dated from the two victories of Attalus I over the Gauls (before 230). Some marble copies, probably contemporary, remain of Gallic figures from his monument of victory, the best known being the Dying Gaul of the Capitol, immortalised by Byron as the Dying Gladiator, and the group of the Gaul who has killed his wife and is stabbing himself. They are rated highly; the artists of the monument have found a new kind of realism in rendering the strange type and rough-hewn features of the barbarians, fearless of death though impatient of defeat; they have caught more of the Celtic spirit than the literary men ever did. The second phase of this art is shown in the titanic frieze of the altar of Zeus at Pergamum,[4] more than 400 feet

[1] C. Robert, *Chares* 15 in P.W.

[2] P. Gardner, *New Chapters in Greek Art*, 1926, ch. XII.

[3] E. V. Hansen, *The Attalids of Pergamon*, 1947, ch. VIII.

[4] A long, detailed description in Hansen, *op. c.*, 292–30[illegible]

long, which exhibits, with vast learning, the battle of the gods against the Titans. The strange shapes of the Earth-born, some ending in serpents, the multiplied attitudes and incidents of every form of contest, some impressive, some theatrical, the wild turmoil and motion of the whole, are like nothing else in Greek art; whatever else the frieze was, it must have been enormously effective, and Christian literature was not far wrong in calling the altar 'Satan's seat', for it expressed Hellenism as nothing else ever did; the whole tumult of the age, the meeting of civilisation and barbarism, the conflict of good and evil, the striving with unfamiliar ways of expression, knowing no rest—all is there. It inevitably calls to mind another altar, the beautiful restful figure of Earth with her fruits on Augustus' *Ara Pacis*, when the struggle that was Hellenism had worn itself out, and the world asked of the Roman victor one boon only, peace.

The artistic affinities of the masterpiece of the age, the Victory of Samothrace, are, like her date, disputed[1]; but *some* connection with the Victory of Demetrius' coin, set up to commemorate his naval victory over Ptolemy I at Salamis in 306, seems assured, and the most satisfying view to the historian, and the only one which will explain Samothrace,[2] is that of Professor Studniczka[3] and Professor Ashmole,[4] which sees in her a monument set up in filial piety on Arsinoe II's own island[5] by Demetrius' son Antigonus Gonatas to commemorate *his* naval victory over Ptolemy II at Cos (*c.* 258). Viewed from the side as she stands in the Louvre, her mighty wings seem almost too large, which leaves little question that she was slightly tilted forward to balance them; she was not standing, but alighting, on the galley's prow, and if Cos were really her battle her upraised right arm bore the Isthmian victor's crown.[6] In this attitude her drapery is correct; it shows the sweep of the sea-wind through it as she stays her flight.

[1] See p. 317 n. 1. [2] *C.A.H.* VII, 714 n. 2. [3] *J.D.A.I.* 1923–4, 125.

[4] In *C.A.H.* VIII, 675; H. Thiersch, "Pro Samothrake", *Wien, S.B.* 212, 1930, Abh. 1, 21 *sqq.* [5] *OGIS* 15.

[6] The American expedition (*ante*) found the missing right hand of the statue; abrasions on the fingers may show that it bore a (metal) wreath.

Little imaginative work came from the Greek mainland, where inartistic peoples, Achaeans and Aetolians, were supreme; but Damophon's attempt (second century), in his colossal group of Despoina and Kora at Lycosura in Arcadia, to recapture the detached serenity of the older gods is interesting. Lysippus' portraits of Alexander, however, gave a tremendous impulse to portraiture, which spread outward from the mainland; Polyeuctus' well-known Demosthenes (*c.* 280) is good, and conjecture to-day has a fair field among the great number of extant portrait-heads, some striking enough. But to realise what could be done we must go to the coins, where among much conventional work is found some of the very best, like the beautiful idealised Alexander-heads on Lysimachus' pieces, or that artistic mystery, high-water mark of Greek portraiture, the heads of the Graeco-Bactrian kings. Much relief work exists beside coins, but Schreiber's long series of Hellenistic reliefs[1] belongs only in part to Hellenism; a very beautiful set of early high reliefs, painted, are those on the Sidon sarcophagus depicting a battle and lion-hunt of Alexander. With relief, sculpture and painting join hands and mutually influence each other; beside grave-reliefs painted over there stand other gravestones only painted.

These gravestones—those from Pagasae, though second-rate, are the best[2]—are the only Hellenistic paintings extant in the original; for vase-painting was over. The repute of the great masters shows that Greeks thought their painting[3] as valuable as their sculpture; what it was at its best can barely be guessed, for easel pictures have perished, and nothing remains of the historical painting of Apelles and his time except literary notices and one copy, the mosaic of Alexander's battle. All we have is wall decoration, an art essentially Hellenistic; except for one or two tombs, it means

[1] *Die hellenistischen Reliefbilder*, 1889.

[2] A. S. Arvanitopoullos, *'Εφ. 'Αρχ.* 1908, 1; *Γραπταὶ Στηλαὶ Δημητρίαδος-Παγασῶν*, 1926, especially 142, and Plates.

[3] Generally: E. Pfuhl, *Malerei und Zeichnung der Griechen*, 1923; *Masterpieces of Greek drawing and painting* (abbreviated; trans. J. D. Beazley), 1926. Pfuhl is not responsible for my view of Pompeii.

Pompeii, where the first period derives from Alexandria. But Pompeii rarely even furnishes copies; much of it is trade work, itself adapted from cheap trade copies—mythological subjects, grotesques, vapid cupids; there are graceful little pieces of flowers and landscape, but they tell no more of great art than the Greek Anthology of great poetry. It seems possible to trace how the painted figure gradually shook itself free of its fourth-century affinity to sculpture—perhaps the real work done by Hellenistic painting—and how a knowledge both of perspective and of landscape emerged[1]; but though the Greek loved sun and air, his poetry shows little feeling for landscape; the Pompeii landscapes are conventional and devoid of atmosphere, and probably landscape in painting was never much more than a setting for figures.

Two sets of figures, however, at Pompeii stand right out from the mass, and can be looked at for their own sakes and not as antiquarian curiosities. One is the beautiful group of women on the extreme right of the long scene of Dionysiac ritual (or myth) in the Villa Item, which Pfuhl holds[2] must go back to some great fresco; the other, even more important, is the frescoes of the Villa Boscoreale, which give us portraiture, otherwise known only from the dreadful Fayum mummy-cases.[3] These frescoes are supposed[4] to be true copies (first century) of fine early third-century work representing the family group of Demetrius I; their affinities are with the school of Lysippus. The rugged figure of the philosopher, with grand head and streaming white beard—a figure of painting, not of sculpture—might be some mediaeval John the Baptist grown old; the sad thoughtfulness in the eyes of the woman called Eurydice is not easily forgotten. Above all, even the copy conveys the suggestion that these were in truth great men and women.

Except perhaps for certain influences on the temple at

[1] R. Pagenstecher, *N.J. Kl. Alt.* XLVII, 271; Pfuhl II, 883; Beloch IV, 1, 528.
[2] II, 878.
[3] Girard, *La peinture antique*, 250; Pfuhl II, 840, 847.
[4] Studniczka *l.c.*, 68 *sqq.*

Didyma, the art here considered is purely a Greek development. Some interaction took place between Greek and Oriental art in this period; but this difficult question is essentially one for experts, and most of the material, such as the architecture of Syria, the paintings from Doura, the important Gandhāra school of sculpture in India, the necropolis of Kom-el-Chougafa in Egypt, belongs to the Roman Imperial age, whether its roots in any case go back to Hellenism or not. The sculptures of the monument of Antiochus I of Commagene (p. 170) show local stone-cutters imitating late Greek work.[1] The massive remains of the Tobiad stronghold at Arâk il-Emîr near Heshbon (second century), whether a temple or a fortress, reveal a Greek building with certain Persian and Phoenician borrowings.[2] The Nabatean tomb of Hamrath at Suwêdā in the Haurân (*c.* 85–60) is also Greek,[3] but the great Nabatean temple of Balsamem (Ba'al Shamin) at Sî in the Haurân (*c.* 33) shows little that is Greek[4] beyond some inscriptions and the influence of the Corinthian column, an influence also traced in the arrangement of the palm-leaves on the capitals of the Egyptian (Ptolemaic) temples at Edfu and Esneh.[5] Some Alexandrian grave-steles exhibit Egyptian influence; and in the first century a revived native Egyptian sculpture began to turn out portraits under Greek influence.[6] But most striking, if it really belongs to this period, is the tomb near el Amarna of the Egyptian official Petosiris, discovered in 1920.[7] It resembles some Greek Heroön, though the architecture is Egyptian; the motives of the reliefs are purely Egyptian, but Greek influence in execution is strong, notably in the sacrifice for the hero and the mourning

[1] Humann and Puchstein, *Reisen in Kleinasien*, 1890.

[2] *Syria II A* (Princeton expedition): *Architecture of Southern Syria*, by H. C. Butler, p. 1.

[3] *Amer. Arch. Exped. to Syria: Architecture*, by H. C. Butler, 325.

[4] *Syria II A*, 365. [5] K. D. McKnight, *Art and Archaeology* 1924, 43.

[6] Lawrence, *J.E.A.* XI, 190.

[7] G. Lefebvre, *Le tombeau de Petosiris*, 1924 (c. 300). P. Montet, *R.E.A.* 1926, 62, *Rev. Arch.* 1926, 161 (Persian period); so Jouguet, *L'Impérialisme macéd.* 330. But C. Picard, *Mélanges V. Loret*; *Bull. Inst. arch. orient.* XXX, 1930, 201, has confirmed Greek influence, not Persian.

women; also the women and peasants wear Greek costume, and the artist, who knows something of perspective, has tried to introduce Greek realism into the attitudes. The blending of Hellenistic and Asiatic elements in what remains of Parthian art, and the influences which ultimately carried Greek motives to India and across Central Asia, lie outside the sphere of this book.

This chapter must remain incomplete; for nothing can be said here of Hellenistic music [1] except that it played as great a part as to-day, and its appeal was not confined to the educated. Two hymns, written in five time, have been recovered from Delphi,[2] and one is very beautiful; but music is a lost world, not merely because it has perished, but because, if we had it, few would now understand it, since Greek music was based on the employment of finer intervals than the semitone.

[1] Generally, J. F. Mountford in Powell and Barber, II, 146 (with bibliography).

[2] Powell, *Collect. Alex.* 141–69.

CHAPTER X

PHILOSOPHY[1] AND RELIGION[2]

THE philosophy of the Hellenistic world was the Stoa; all else was secondary. What we see, broadly speaking, as we look down the three centuries, is that Aristotle's school loses all importance, and Plato's, for a century and a half, becomes a parasite upon the Stoa in the sense that its life as a school of scepticism consists wholly in combating Stoic doctrine; Epicurus' school continues unchanged, but only attracts small minorities; but the Stoa, which meanwhile has taken under its shield both popular and astral religion and many forms of superstition, finally masters Scepticism, in fact though not in argument, and takes to itself enough of a revived Platonism to form that modified Stoicism or Eclecticism which was the distinguishing philosophy of the earlier Roman empire.

Athens was the centre of philosophy throughout the entire

[1] Generally: Lives of the Philosophers in Diogenes Laertius; the general works of Wendland, Kaerst (bk. V, ch. 2), and Beloch ch. XII. E. Zeller, *Stoics, Epicureans and Sceptics*, trans. 1880. Stoa: H. v. Arnim, *Stoicorum veterum fragmenta* (*SVF*); Sir A. Grant's essay in his *Aristotle's Ethics*, 1885; G. H. Rendall, *Marcus Aurelius* (introduction), 1896; W. L. Davidson, *The Stoic creed*, 1907; E. V. Arnold, *Roman Stoicism*, 1911 (bibliography); E. R. Bevan, *Stoics and Sceptics*, 1913; M. Pohlenz, *Die Stoa*, 1948. Epicurus: Usener, *Epicurea*, 1887; C. Bailey, *Epicurus*, 1926, *The Greek atomists and Epicurus*, 1928; A. J. Festugière, *Épicure et ses dieux*, 1946. Cynics: D. R. Dudley, *A history of Cynicism*, 1937; Tarn, *Alexander* II, App. 25 § II. Sceptics: Arnim, *Arkesilaos* and *Karneades* in P.W.; M. M. Patrick, *The Greek Sceptics*, 1929.

[2] E. R. Bevan, *Later Greek Religion*, 1927; U. v. Wilamowitz-Moellendorf, *Die Glaube der Hellenen* II, 1932, 261 *sqq.*; A. D. Nock, *Conversion*, 1933, chs. II–IV; W. Schubart, *Die religiöse Haltung des frühen Hellenismus*, 1937; O. Kern, *Die Religion der Griechen* III, 1938; M. P. Nilsson, *Greek Piety*, 1948; *Gesch. d. griech. Religion* II, 1950. For the thought of the period more generally, N. H. Baynes, *The Hellenistic civilisation and East Rome* (James Bryce Memorial Lecture), 1946.

period, though later on two great Stoics did work in Rhodes. Soon after 317 Demetrius of Phalerum procured for Aristotle's successor, the alien Theophrastus, the right to hold land and form Aristotle's school (the Peripatetics) into a legally organised association, like Plato's Academy; in 306 the Athenian Epicurus came from Lampsacus and set up his school in his garden; Zeno came to Athens after 317 and began to teach in the Painted Porch, the Stoa, in 302; and the early third century saw the four schools, like great colleges, working side by side. Aristotle's school had its brief day of power from 317 onwards; Cassander favoured it, Theophrastus inspired the laws of Demetrius of Phalerum, and Demetrius himself after his fall helped Ptolemy I to found the Museum. Theophrastus was a many-sided man of great learning; but after the death of his successor Strato the school abandoned its founder's search for theoretic knowledge, and by the middle of the third century its work was over; it had rendered much service to science and much disservice to history, but it did nothing more for the world except to contribute a few elements to eclecticism. Like Aristotle himself, it was alien to Athens and usually antipathetic to the Antigonids; it might have had a better chance had it moved to Alexandria with Demetrius. Plato's school could not die, for it was Athenian of Athens; but it also abandoned the search for knowledge, and when Arcesilaus revivified it, it was to be on lines which, though they might go back to Socrates, had little to do with Plato.

The small local schools died out or merged in the Middle Academy of Arcesilaus, though Menedemus[1] of Eretria, the teacher and friend of Antigonus Gonatas, was a notable and attractive figure, a man of strong sense and character and the centre of a brilliant literary circle; his friends compared him to Socrates, but he left neither writings nor successor, and his influence, which depended on his personality, died with him. The Cynics, however, remained an active body. They had no established centre, as became their profession of poverty; but their appeal was largely to

[1] Th. Gomperz, *Greek Thinkers* (trans.) II, 205; Tarn. *Ant. Gon.* 22

the poor, and their roughness and studied neglect of ordinary decorums and courtesies rather discounted the manliness of their attitude toward life, though they did affect the early Stoa. But Zeno's teacher the Cynic Crates, the 'physician of souls', seems to have been a man; he had much wit and more earnestness, stripped himself of a large fortune to lead the life of a beggar and a preacher, and, though ugly, so won the devotion of his pupil Hipparchia that she too gave up everything to marry him and share his way of life; a man who in that age attacked sexual immorality as scathingly as he did was something of a portent. But the weakness of the Cynics was precisely that 'beggar's wallet' which Crates glorified: they saved their souls by living on common people who had no time to save their own. That strange creature Bion of Borysthenes,[1] another friend of Antigonus Gonatas, was also three parts Cynic. He had risen from a lowly origin, and was vain of his wit and with something of the vulgar mountebank about him; but beneath the outer husk lay humanity and a sort of simple manliness, and his influence was great, for he was the first of a long line of wandering teachers who popularised philosophy and whom Origen afterwards compared to the wandering Christian preachers; they gave the age a sort of spiritual background. Though no original thinker, he had force enough to make men listen; and even at the Rhodian docks he drew the sailors in crowds with his usual message—do your duty, be content with little if so it be, and face your fortune like a man. To understand what that feat meant, translate it to the London docks of yesterday.

The two new philosophies, those of Epicurus and Zeno, were both products of the new world which Alexander had made, and primarily of the feeling that a man was no longer merely a part of his city; he was an individual, and as such needed new guidance. The two philosophies both aimed, not at the discovery of truth, but at the satisfaction of practical needs; and they accordingly had certain things in common. The aim of philosophy was the happiness of the

[1] Hense, *Teles*², Prolegomena; Tarn, *Ant. Gon.* 233.

individual; and what mattered was conduct. Both therefore went back behind Plato and Aristotle to Socrates. Both were content to take sense-impressions as true, Epicurus saying that all were true, while Zeno made the criterion of truth the impression which so grips you that disbelief is impossible; both treated the universe, including man's soul, as composed of something material (though to the Stoics, who were really intensely spiritual, this was a mere matter of words) and adopted existing physical explanations, Epicurus that of Democritus, Zeno that of Heraclitus. Both desired the avoidance of passions and emotions, which bring the unhappiness of unsatisfied desire. Both laid their full stress on ethics, morality, which they absolutely divorced from politics; neither cared for science or learning. But there the resemblance ends; in essentials they were as far asunder as the poles. The new world was affecting men in two ways. The majority felt that they belonged to it, but were sailing an uncharted sea; this the Stoa set out to chart. But a minority felt oppressed and fearful, and desired escape; and for them Epicurus pointed a way.

The world they dreaded, he said, was only a machine. No gods, good or evil, affected it; it was not made or guided by design; it came into being through certain mechanical principles. He revived Democritus' atomic theory: atoms (he meant molecules) fell in a ceaseless rain through the void, and their clashing formed the world. But at once he met two difficulties. Atoms falling in a straight line through the void could not, as he understood it, clash. Also he cared nothing for atoms, and very much for ethics; and there could be no morality without free-will. He solved his two problems together: the atoms had the power of deliberately swerving a little, in order to meet; that is, he gave them free-will. His mechanical world, then, had something more than mechanics in it from the start; the materialist could only make a world at all by denying his own principles. The rest was easy, and Empedocles' idea that many less adapted animal forms had been tried and had died out helped him; the result can be seen in the wonderful description of the evolution of life on the earth in the supreme monument of this school, Lucretius' poem *On the Nature of Things.* Epicurus' aim was, by constructing a world on scientific principles, to free men from fear of the gods and the evils of superstition; man's soul at death dissolved again into the atoms which made it. His school did render good service by refusing to touch divination and astrology. But he conceded this much to popular belief, that gods existed; only they *did* nothing, except exhibit an ideal happiness. They were a little company of Epicurean philosophers, of extreme tenuity, living in intra-mundane space, and conversing perpetually, probably in Greek; one slides insensibly into Cicero's parody[1] that their sole occupation was to say to each other 'How happy I am'.

But his ethics were serious enough. Happiness was the aim; and happiness meant pleasure; pleasure was the one true good. But not the physical or sensual pleasures of his predecessors the Cyrenaics; intellectual pleasure primarily, for the mind matters most. And passive pleasure rather than active—repose, freedom from passions, desires, needs, above all absence of pain; the keyword of man's effort was to be *ataraxia*, escape from worry. Virtue was vital, but not, as the Stoics taught, for its own sake—that had no meaning; it was vital because without it happiness could not be. This constituted a doctrine of renunciation, a renunciation of active effort and positive happiness, and his followers formed little isles of quietude apart, bound together by the friendship he so stressed; except that they lived among their fellows and enjoyed family life, one might call them, spiritually, the first monks. They never influenced the great world; they had no wish to. They never altered or added to what their founder taught. But they met a perpetual human need, and they never died out; in the second century A.D. an unknown Diogenes at Oenoanda in Lycia set up their teaching in a long inscription on a stone[2] because it had brought him a happiness and peace which he wanted his fellow-men to share. Epicurus himself, who died in 270,

[1] *De Nat. D.* 1, XLI (114). [2] Ed. William, 1907 (Teubner).

was a gentle frugal man, who bore his last painful illness with quiet fortitude; his personal success in Athens was considerable, and the lives of his own circle, which included women, were not only exemplary but a fragrant oasis in a stormy age; and if his doctrine of pleasure was sometimes abused, this was not done by those who really followed his teaching. The real reproach against his philosophy was that it taught men to shirk living; it was a running away.

Very different was the gaunt ascetic Phoenician[1] who founded the Stoa, Zeno of Citium in Cyprus, the noblest man of his age. Shy and silent, a foreigner who spoke and wrote indifferent Greek, he made headway but slowly; he had no centre for his followers like Epicurus' Garden, and talked to those who came in a public colonnade, the Painted Porch, a forecast of the fact that the Stoic teachers were never to be tied to a centre at Athens, but were to spread throughout the world. But early in his career he attracted Antigonus Gonatas, who became his pupil and his life-long friend, doubtless a help to him in the worldly sense, and long before his death his personality had conquered Athens, especially the young men, over whom his influence is said to have been great; though Antigonus' friend, he kept clear of politics, and when he died after the war between Antigonus and Athens, which must to him have been acute torture, Athens gave him a public funeral and one of the most beautiful testimonials any man ever received; for the striking decree which accompanied the honours voted to him after death ended with the words, 'He made his life a pattern to all, for he followed his own teaching.' He left a notable circle of pupils, among them Ariston, who taught Eratosthenes; Persaeus, who went to Antigonus as spiritual adviser; and Sphaerus, who helped Cleomenes' revolution at Sparta. Zeno's successor, Cleanthes of Assos, author of the greatest religious hymn in Greek, was to bring out the religious side of his doctrine; Cleanthes' successor Chrysippus of Soli, a

[1] Phoenician to contemporaries: Diels, *Poet. Philos. Fr.*; Timon, 193 fr. 38; Crates, 215 no. 27. Zeno a Phoenician name: Herzog, *Koische Forschungen* 71 no. 42. Zeno may have had some Greek blood.

voluminous writer, got the tenets of the school elaborately laid down in many books; Panaetius and Poseidonius we shall meet later. Unhappily the writings of Zeno and Chrysippus are lost, except for fragments, and no Stoic writings survive in completeness till we come to the Eclectics of the Roman Empire—Seneca, Marcus Aurelius, Epictetus; though Cicero's *De Officiis* represents Panaetius' treatise *On Duties*. Zeno at the start owed something to Heraclitus, possibly something to Babylon (p. 347), and much to the Cynics; but the great system of ethics developed by himself and his successors was very different from anything the Cynics ever envisaged.

The Stoic idea of brotherhood and a World State has already been noticed (p. 79). Their Universe was in fact one great city; and it was ruled by one Supreme Power whom the Stoics envisaged under many aspects and names—Destiny, Zeus, Providence, the Universal Law, Nature. From this Power, conceived of in their material terminology as a fifth element or divine Fire, came all that exists, heaven and earth and all that is therein, including the soul of man; everything was a derivative of God, and in a derivative sense *was* God; the spark in man's nature was akin to the divine. The universe, at the end of every world-period—a recurring cycle of enormous length—was reabsorbed into the divine Fire, and then started afresh to run an exact repetition of its course; ages hence another Socrates would teach in another Athens, and there was no new thing under the sun; all had happened before, and history merely repeated itself, a strange idea but familiar to us from the superb lyric at the close of Shelley's *Hellas*. Hence the Power that ruled the universe was Destiny; but it differed from the terrible Babylonian Fate, for it was all-wise, and that which it decreed for men was best for them. Indeed it was God, for the universe was the product of design, and He had made the laws which ruled it, summed up in that Universal Law which was really Himself; He too obeyed the law He had created. He was not a God devoid of moral attributes, for His design was all-wise and all-good; the stars did not turn blindly in their courses, but illustrated His Providence for sailor and husbandman. In the hands of the religious Cleanthes He is even a merciful God: He makes all the odds even, and that which is dear to none other is dear unto Him. Still, everything was determined; and in Determinism the Stoics encountered the usual difficulty, for first and foremost their system was a moral one, and without free-will there could be no morality; the logical outcome of Determinism is antinomianism—I may do what evil I will, for that too is fated.

Another difficulty they met was in the practical bearing of the idea of a World State. As all men were citizens of one City, all ought to be equal. But in fact men differed in character, ability, circumstances; in Chrysippus' metaphor, nothing could prevent some seats in the theatre being better than others; all men therefore were not and could not be alike, and equality was only a theory. Also their World State was in practice unrealisable; for the world was composed of ordinary men, ruled by people who were not philosophers and had no knowledge of the Universal Law. Fortunately the Stoics were content to do what they could; they stood behind the king's throne and advised; like other philosophers, they wrote treatises on how States should be governed[1]; they were ready to fight against bad governments, notably tyranny, or, like Sphaerus at Sparta and Blossius at Pergamum, to work for any reform which promised greater equality to the people, any step towards their own form of Communism, which meant Concord and the abolition of class-war.

Consistently with their principles, then, they seemingly could not admit either free-will or inequality, and yet they had to accept both. Their solution of both dilemmas was to go back to the root principle of Wisdom or Mind. Human minds were sparks of the divine Fire, but the human body was clay; therefore the body mattered nothing. Zeno said

[1] On what survives of these Treatises περὶ βασιλείας see, on the fragments in Stobaeus, Goodenough, *Yale Class. Stud.* I, 1928, 55, and Tarn, *Alexander* II, 368, 410; on the kernel of the *Letter to Aristeas*, Tarn, *Bactria*, 426, and literature cited; cf. Schubart, *Archiv* XII, 1936, 4; new fragments and generally, Rostovtzeff, *SEH* 1379 n. 83.

that all that had to do with the body—strength and weakness, sickness and health, wealth and poverty—was matter of indifference; and this, in theory, remained their attitude throughout. The Stoic sage, the Wise Man, would neglect such things, and turn only to the things of the soul. But these were, or could be, the same for all men; the slave in the silver mines, brutalised in body, might still in his soul follow after Wisdom and be the peer of the philosopher or the saint. Men then *were* equal after all, for all, if they wished, could be equal in their souls; in that realm the beggar might be king.

Through Wisdom they also solved Determinism. Certainly their Wise Man was a monster, passionless, pitiless, perfect; he would do good, but without feeling for others, for his calm must remain unruffled; in St. Paul's words, he would give his body to be burnt, but he had not love, and it is strange that Zeno, who had based his Ideal State upon Love, gave no place to love of others in the Wise Man's composition. But man reads what he will into his ideal, and that the Wise Man acted as an ideal is unquestionable; he was something to aim at, but never (fortunately) to reach. But Wisdom was of the Divine Power; true wisdom therefore on earth must be coincident with the Divine, and the wise man would desire that which God or Destiny in its wisdom had ordained for him. Therewith, for Stoics, the contradiction of determinism and free-will was transcended by a new philosophic concept, duty; man *had* free-will, but it was his imperative duty so to employ it as to approximate to the Divine Will. Whether he submitted to Destiny, or kicked against the pricks, made no difference in the material sphere; he had to go the way marked out for him. But in proportion as he attained to wisdom, so would he recognise that that way was the right way, and find peace of mind, and the truly wise would need neither driving nor leading; he would see, and gladly anticipate, that which Destiny intended; the free exercise of his own will would simply bring him into unison with the will of God. The ideal man, when he came, would say 'Thy will be done'.

Therewith too, for himself, the Stoic solved the ancient problem of happiness. Unhappiness usually arose from wanting something you had not got or could not get; the way to be happy, then, was to want what you got, that is, to go in accord with the Divine will. This is what they meant by 'living according to Nature', and not the rather material sense in which the Cynics employed that phrase; for Nature too was God. Certainly they used this conception to discard from consideration luxury and pleasure, wealth and success, the complexities of civilisation, which were no part of the Divine plan. But accordance with the Divine will meant far more than neglecting these material things: the Stoic will not grieve for his son's death, for the decree is all-wise, and nothing better could have happened. For the Supreme Power is not only all-wise but all-virtuous; what it does is best. To reach harmony with that Power, therefore, the thing most necessary is Virtue; and virtue, and nothing else, is therefore happiness; virtue *is* its own sufficient reward. For centuries many men believed this, and some practised it.

Virtue was the central point of Stoic ethics. On this Zeno was uncompromising; the intention to do evil, he said, was equivalent to doing it.[1] At first he said that all that was not absolute virtue was vice; but this rule was so unworkable that he had to modify it himself before he died by granting a middle sphere of things indifferent, which subsequently became divided into things to be preferred and things to be rejected, the Stoic being bound to choose the former; on these lines the main Stoic conception of duty was strongly reinforced. That you *ought* to follow the moral course was to them not an assumption, for Stoicism's first postulate was that it was itself a moral system, and it could claim that the contrary course must be wrong because it introduced discord into the cosmic order, which was a bigger thing than mankind. Now man's means of getting into harmony with God were wisdom and virtue, and in both these matters progress was possible; the Stoic was thus led to examine the progress

[1] *S.V.F.* I, fr. 251 must mean this.

he was making, and the idea arose of conscious moral growth. Moreover the Supreme Power had had forethought for men. and they had an aid on the path; there now first appeared in philosophy the conception, heretofore a popular one, of conscience. Conscience and Duty were the corner-stones of Stoic ethics.

The influence of those ethics on the world and on Christianity was to be great. Critics might carry the outworks of the system, or wits riddle the Wise Man with their arrows, but the central fortress, the philosophy of conduct, was to stand firm. Stoicism in fact was as much a religion as a philosophy, and a virile one, as it was to show. Strength was needed to despise the things of the body, and on strong natures it acted as a tonic; the true Stoic, whatever else he was, was captain of his soul, or, in their phrase, *autarkes*, sufficient to himself. And he was master of his fate; fate could not hurt him, for what it brought him was what he would have chosen. But to all, strong and weak, it had a message, its insistence on the things of the soul. Whatever the world did to you, in one sphere the world had no power; you could withdraw into your own soul, and there find peace; for none could harm you *there* but yourself.

The Sceptic school started with Pyrrhon of Elis, who in youth accompanied Alexander to India; but he wrote nothing, and is known only through his disciple Timon the 'sillographer' (p. 279). Timon's doctrine was simple. The source of trouble is contradictory knowledge, but nothing can be known, therefore suspend your judgment and never dogmatise; remember too that nothing matters, not even whether you live or die; thus you will attain the goal, imperturbability. He attained to a good deal of money by preaching this throughout the world, but he did not attain to imperturbability, for much of his life was spent in attacking Arcesilaus for poaching on his preserve; and he left no successor, for with Arcesilaus (*c.* 264–242) Scepticism passed over to the Academy. Arcesilaus was a patriotic Athenian of fine character, but as a philosopher he was a negative force; he too believed that knowledge was impossible, and thought that he had demonstrated this merely by overthrowing the Stoic theory of knowledge, the 'irresistible impression', a tribute to the position the Stoa had attained. His greater successor Carneades (213–129) was so occupied in fighting the Stoa that he said of himself that he would never have been anybody but for Chrysippus. He did good service by attacking the Stoa's shadow side, divination and astrology, and forcing Panaetius to modify his position in this regard; and it was not difficult to destroy the 'irresistible impression'. But Carneades produced no real effect; he could not touch the essentials of Stoicism, and the world simply passed him by. For the world had somehow to live and act, and here Carneades had nothing to offer. Knowledge being impossible, Arcesilaus had said the guide of action must be Reasonableness, which meant nothing; Carneades substituted Probability, but could only interpret it to mean 'Do as your neighbours do'. He also laid himself open to much misconstruction by his habit of arguing for or against any thesis indiscriminately, as an intellectual exercise; he tried this at Rome in 156, and plain Romans were shocked at such immoral levity; even his pupil, the Carthaginian Hasdrubal-Clitomachus, who composed 400 rolls in an attempt to reduce Carneades' oral teaching to writing, confessed that he sometimes did not know which was Carneades' real view. But Carneades, though he had a sort of passion for destruction, was a man of good personal repute, and one of the acutest minds Greece ever produced; and some of the difficulties he raised have never been answered. Scepticism died with him, but revived again with Cicero's contemporary Aenesidemus, and again under the Antonines; it did supply a want, for it was useful that someone should criticise and prune dogmatic philosophy.

It has been truly said that in the religious sphere the only vital things in Hellenism were philosophy and the Oriental religions. Twilight was indeed falling on the Olympians, in spite of external show—new epiphanies,[1] new

[1] Lindian Chron. A ll. 3, 7; *SGDI* 3086; Pfister, *Epiphanie* in P.W., § 22 *sq.*

oracles,[1] new festivals, the attempted religious revival in Greece after 146 (p. 39); and the great temples that were built and completed were generally to some alien deity, like Sarapis of Alexandria or the Fair-browed goddess of Magnesia, successor of the Dindymene Mother. What was happening can be seen in the one great temple a Greek city planned to a Greek god; Apollo's temple at Didyma was still unfinished four centuries later, not for lack of money at Miletus, but for lack of that living faith which had formerly enabled cities to complete their temples in a generation. Once Zeus at Dodona had himself spoken to his devotees as a god might, in the wind in the oak tree, the bubbles on the spring; at Didyma oracle-giving was a business, conducted from a bureau. Many things conspired to decide the fate of the Olympians. They belonged to, and fell with, the city state; philosophy killed them for the educated, individualism for the common man; he was no longer part of the city, content with whatever its corporate worship might be, but wanted something that spoke to himself. But perhaps what settled the matter was the conquest of Asia and Egypt; for it was a conquest by the sword alone, not the spirit. Greece was ready to adopt the gods of the foreigner, but the foreigner rarely reciprocated; Greek Doura freely admitted the gods of Babylon, but no Greek god entered Babylonian Uruk.[2] Foreign gods might take Greek names; they took little else. They were the stronger, and the conquest of Asia was bound to fail as soon as the East, in the religious sphere, had gauged its own strength and Greek weakness; for what Greece could give to Asia, science and philosophy, only a chosen few could take; these things were never for the mass. Had Ptolemy I enthroned Zeus in Alexandria and persecuted Osiris, Egypt would have fought but would have understood; that the Ptolemies instead built temples to Egyptian deities meant to Egyptians not toleration but weakness—the invader had no faith in his own gods. From the second century Hellenism was between the hammer and the anvil, the sword of Rome and the spirit of Egypt and Babylon. One man saw it—

[1] Ditt.[3] 635 B, 735, 1157. [2] Schroeder, *Berl. S.B.* 1916, 1180.

Antiochus Epiphanes—and has been called a madman ever since. But his attempt to unify his realm on a basis of Greek religion and culture failed; and Greek religion got no second chance.

Individualism showed itself in the enormous outburst of private associations after 300 (p. 93). They were the regular channel by which foreign worships entered a Greek city[1]; a few foreigners settled there would club together to worship their own god, and Greeks might join them. These associations probably made for diversity in cult-practice; for example, many a Dionysus club in Egypt had its own *hieros logos* or ritual book.[2] A foreign club might worship the god of the city in which it settled, as the Haliastai at Rhodes worshipped Helios; but a Greek club, though it often worshipped some Olympian, never worshipped its own city-god. The Muses came into prominence as the official deities of the great corporations of learning, the four philosophic schools at Athens and the Museum at Alexandria; a whole class of helping or protecting demons was worshipped—Amynos,[3] Hypodectes,[4] and Dexion[5] (who was Sophocles) at Athens, Pasios[6] at Cos, Anthister[7] at Thera; family clubs would worship their ancestor as a hero.[8] But one thing, in the third century, the clubs never did: they never worshipped the deified king, a strong indication that king-worship in its inception was a purely political phenomenon. The first case of such king-worship by a club was when the Asiatic branch of the Dionysiac artists, under the lead of Craton of Teos, worshipped Eumenes II, and Craton founded the club of Attalistai[9]; for the Egyptian Basilistai only appear as making a dedication to some god for the king.[10]

Far the most important Greek god of the age outside

[1] Foucart, *Les associations religieuses*; Ziebarth, *Gr. Vereinswesen*; Poland *op. c.*; Nock, *C.R.* 1924, 105.

[2] *B.G.U.* 1211; Schubart, *Einführung* 352.

[3] Ditt.[3] 1096, Michel 1548.

[4] *I.G.* II, 1061.

[5] Ditt.[3] 1096.

[6] Ditt.[3] 1106 l. 148, but see Hiller's note.

[7] *I.G.* XII, 3, 329.

[8] Michel 1001; Ditt.[3] 1044.

[9] *OGIS* 325–6; Michel 1015–16; *I.G.* XI, 4, 1061.

[10] *OGIS* 130; *I.G.* XII, 3, 443; San Nicolo, *Äg. Vereinswesen* I, 26; Launey, *op. c.* II, 1026 *sqq.*

Greece was Dionysus, whom the Dionysiac artists carried all over the world; art and literature gave him a triumphal progress across Asia on the model of Alexander's.[1] His name Sabazios was equated with Sabaoth, and he thus affected the Jewish Diaspora (p. 225); the Orphics identified him with very many deities, and in Egypt he was identified with Sarapis through the Osiris element in the latter. He became ancestor of the Ptolemies, as well as of the Attalids, and possibly his enthusiastic devotee Ptolemy IV dreamt of making him the chief god of his composite empire (p. 212). Certainly if any Greek god was to conquer the world, Dionysus was the only one possible. But great as the influence of the Orphics subsequently became, it was not on these lines that things were to shape themselves.

A dominant factor of the time was the striving after one god. Alexander had transcended national states, which implied transcending national cults; and though there was no longer one empire, there was one 'inhabited world' and one culture, which imported (it seemed) one god, an idea to which philosophy had accustomed the educated. This might take the form of the national god claiming to be god of the whole earth, as Yahweh in Judaea; but another movement, very typically Hellenistic, was a great expansion of syncretism, the equation or fusion of one god with another as being alike forms of the one divinity behind them.[2] Men would worship any god impartially; when Stratonice, wife of Antiochus I, enriched Apollo of Delos (p. 98), rebuilt the temple of the Syrian Atargatis at Hierapolis,[3] and joined a club at Smyrna which worshipped the Egyptian Anubis,[4] she doubtless saw in them merely forms of one deity. The process was assisted by Stoicism. The Stoics did not reject the gods of the people; they brought them into their pantheistic system by allegorising all the myths, however barbarous; they sought to explain, not destroy, for the gods too

[1] Nock, *J.H.S.* 1928, 21.

[2] Fullest instance, Isis (*post*); fullest account, Kaerst *op. c.* p. 208; see also Festugière's study cited p. 359 n. 3.

[3] Lucian, *De Dea Syr.*, 17, 19.

[4] Michel 1223.

were part of the beneficent world-order, veils mercifully granted to the common man to spare his eyes the too dazzling nakedness of truth.

One deity, however, stood apart; even the Stoics could not assimilate Fortune. Fortune was a thoroughly Hellenistic conception. The first Peripatetics, Demetrius of Phalerum[1] and Theophrastus,[2] moulded her form; Menander suggested she might be Providence[3]; an unknown poet compared her to Iris, the messenger of the gods.[4] She dominated the third century, and even Polybius[5] and Poseidonius later did not disdain the concession to popular belief implied in the use of her name. She was not blind chance, but some order of affairs which men could not comprehend. But all could see her. Fortune had brought this general of Alexander's to a throne, that to a grave; Fortune had decreed that Macedonia should strike down Persia and would herself (so Demetrius prophesied)[6] fall in turn; after Cynoscephalae the Greeks sympathised with Philip V because Fortune had reversed her wheel.[7] She was not altogether an unkindly goddess, for she did not deprive men of hope: to-day to thee, but to-morrow to me. Each man had his own Fortune, his *daimon*[8]—Romans called it his *Genius*; it was almost his individuality. Cities and citizens alike swore by the king's *daimon*,[9] men had an implicit belief in the 'Fortune' of Alexander or Antigonus Doson,[10] and the great influence of Eutychides' statue of the Fortune of Antioch ultimately made of a city's Fortune the city goddess.

For the educated, the place of religion was being taken by

[1] Polyb. XXIX, 21, 1–9. [2] His *Kallisthenes*: Cic. *Tusc.* III, 10, 21.
[3] *Κωνειαζόμεναι* ll. 13 *sqq.* [4] Powell, *Collect. Alex.* 196 no. 34.
[5] Another view; W. Siegfried, *Studien z. gesch. Anschauung des Polybios*, 1928; but see Laqueur, *Woch.* 1929, 961.
[6] Polyb. *ante.* [7] App. *Mac.* 9, 1.
[8] Identical: Bouché-Leclercq, *L'astrologie grecque*, 288; Wilamowitz, *Hell. Dicht.* 1, 74, *Hermes* LXII, 290.
[9] By his *daimon*: *P.S.I.* IV, 361; *P. Cairo Zen.* 59462; *B.G.U.* VI, 1257; *P. Dem. Zeno* 4, in Spiegelberg, *Demotischen Urkunde des Zenon-Archiv*, 1929, 11, cf. Wilcken, *Archiv* IX, 239. By his Fortune: *OGIS* 229 l. 62; Str. 557. [10] Athen. 251 C.

philosophy and science. But these hardly affected the common man; he must worship something, and, as the Olympians faded, a more real religious feeling began to develop, and the appeal of the intimate and confident oriental worships became irresistible. In this sphere the East led its conqueror captive; and though the movement did not perhaps culminate till after the Christian era, it was gathering strength all through the Hellenistic period. One must, however, distinguish between the countries. Of Persia, ultimately so great a force, nothing can be said here[1]; the subject is intricate and obscure, but certainly the day of Mithras the Unconquerable was not yet, though the Cilician pirates worshipped him in the first century[2]; the Mithraion mentioned in Egypt was only a local chapel of some Persian mercenaries.[3] The two world-influences came from Babylon and Egypt; the cults of Syria and Anatolia exercised much local influence, but were hardly of equal importance, though Syrian cults invaded Greece (p. 342) and Egypt,[4] and Anatolian penetrated far (p. 344).

In Syria[5] the old religions grew in power, though partly under Graecised forms; the coins, especially of the Roman period, reveal a very medley of cults and syncretisms.[6] But though several old priest-states of the Anatolian type are known, there was no really dominant deity, doubtless because Syria had always been politically divided into several kingdoms or spheres of influence. The most powerful god was Hadad of Damascus[7] (Rimmon of the Old Testament), who absorbed many local Baals; he became

[1] Cf. Bidez-Cumont, *Les mages hellénisés*, 2 vols., 1938. The date of Reitzenstein's documents is most uncertain; see Baynes, *Israel among the nations*, 289–94. Cf. Kaerst *op. c.* 218, 239.

[2] Plut. *Pomp.* 24.

[3] Wilcken, *Archiv* VII, 71.

[4] Schubart, *Einführung* 353; add *Archiv* VIII, 287; Wilcken, *Zu den 'Syrischen Göttern'*, Festgabe für A. Deissmann, 1927, 1; Rostovtzeff, *Kleinasiatische und syrische Götter im römischen Aegypten*, *Aegyptus* XIII, 1933, 493.

[5] S. A. Cook, *op. c.*, chap. 3, esp. 217–19; Cumont, *Les religions orientales*[4], 1929.

[6] Hill, *B.M. Coins, Phoenicia*, and *J.H.S.* 1911, 56; Wroth, *B.M. Coins, Galatia &c.* (Syria).

[7] Dussaud in P.W. *s.v.*; *Syria* III, 219.

Zeus of Damascus and Zeus of Heliopolis (Baalbek), but his chief temple was at Hierapolis-Bambyce (Mabbog), where he was Zeus before 150. His consort at Damascus and Hierapolis, Atargatis,[1] Lucian's 'Syrian goddess', was originally a pointed stone (*betyl*), but had long since become a woman under the influence of the invading Persian goddess Anahita (Anaïtis); subsequently she often became a Greek city-goddess,[2] and by the time of her marriage to Antiochus Epiphanes she was the greatest goddess in Syria.[3] Her most famous temples were those at Hierapolis, whither at the biennial festival men came from all over Asia to be purified in her sacred pool and where tame lions and bears lived in the precinct, and at Ascalon, where she was a mermaid, with the local name of Derceto; wherever she went she brought her sacred pool and sacred fish, the fishes of the Euphrates who had assisted at her birth and been rewarded with a place in the Zodiac; her fish-pond, eunuchs, and lions relate her to Artemis of Ephesus and the Anatolian goddess, the 'Lady of the Wild'. Her temples were the home of clouds of pigeons, as some mosques to-day. Hadad had reached Delos before 100, but Atargatis went further; she was one element of that 'Syrian Aphrodite'—the other being the Phoenician Astarte—who travelled all over Greece and even reached Macedonia,[4] and whose club at Athens shared the precinct of her kinswoman the Anatolian Mother.[5]

Atargatis was not the only betyl in Syria. There were, among others, a famous pair at Tyre.[6] The black stone at Emesa, Elagabal, was to play a great part at Rome later and another stone throws some light on a Seleucid city, Seleuceia in Pieria. For the two gods of Seleuceia's worship were a thunder-god, Zeus Keraunios[7] (probably Balsamem,

[1] Lucian, *De Dea Syr.*; Dussaud *l.c.*; Cumont, *Dea Syria* in P.W.; Honigmann, *Hierapolis, ib.*; Str. 748.

[2] Cumont, *Mon. Piot* XXVI, 14; coins.

[3] Tarn, *Bactria,* 193.

[4] List in Cumont, *Dea Syria*; 'Αρχ. Δελτ. II, 144 no. 1 (Macedonia).

[5] Poland 478.

[6] S. A. Cook 160.

[7] Cumont, *Balsamem* in P.W.; *Études syriennes* 221; Cook 217, H. Seyrig, *Syria* XX, 301.

the 'Lord of Heaven'), and Zeus Kasios,[1] a conical stone enshrined on the neighbouring Mount Kasios; Seleuceia therefore had officially adopted the local native worships, as Doura officially adopted Adad and Nanaia from Babylon. Zeus Kasios travelled to Egypt, and thence to Delos; but at Seleuceia he remained a stone, and did not achieve human form till Hadrian's time. Similarly the Ammonite Milcom (Moloch) survived throughout as a god of the hellenised Rabbath-Amman (Philadelphia).[2] And Marnes, 'our lord', at Gaza, must not be forgotten; he was the doughtiest champion of paganism against Christianity, and held his ground till the Marneion was destroyed in 401.[3] But the most interesting god of all was the local deity of the little town of Doliche in Commagene,[4] who lived 'where the iron grew'[5]; for he was really Teïsbas (the Hittite, or Hurrian, Teschub), god of that strange broken people the Chaldi or Chalybes, the greatest iron-smiths of the world west of China, who had once ruled the kingdom of Van in Armenia, but had scattered in groups wherever there was iron to enable them to set up their forges and practise their inherited technique; later, as Juppiter Dolichenus, their little iron-god with his hammer, in which some see the Hittite double axe, was to spread throughout the Roman Empire in the track of the Roman sword.

The temple states of Asia Minor have already been described (Chap. IV). How old the worship of the Anatolian nature-goddess and her son and consort was cannot be said; but Greeks had a persistent tradition that the 'Phrygians' were the oldest race on earth[6] and their religion older than the Egyptian. The true Anatolian worship was probably far older than Phrygians or Hittites, but it cannot be said to what lost people it goes back, or what were the original

[1] Salač, *B.C.H.* 1922, 160; Roussel, *Les cultes égyptiens à Délos*, 95 no. 16; Cook 157.
[2] Hill, *B.M. Coins, Arabia* XXXIX.
[3] Cook 180–6.
[4] Cumont, *Ét. syr.* 196.
[5] Inscriptions in Cumont; Suidas, *Χάλυβες*; Schol. Ap. Rhod. 1, 1323 (cod. Paris). Cf. Str. 223–4 (iron 'growing'); Plin. XXXVI, 125 (marble); Hippolytus, cited Reitzenstein, *Poimandres* 85 (all minerals).
[6] Herod. II, 2; cf. Hippolytus, *l.c.* p. 83.

names of the goddess and her son, which may always have varied locally; perhaps Ma looks as old as anything. The original worship had been overlaid and syncretised by layer after layer of invaders; the Hittites apparently contributed a peasant deity, who reinforced the god; the Indo-European Phrygians brought their sky-god, who in the sanctuaries he invaded elevated the god at the expense of the goddess and took the respectable name of Zeus[1]; the Persians brought Anaïtis, who reinforced the goddess. The temple prostitutes also occur in Babylonia, but it cannot be said which borrowed from which, or if both go back to some earlier world. Certainly, though the Greeks brought their own gods to the cities, many of the Greek names in Anatolia are modern appellations of native gods. The connection of the Anatolian goddess with Greece may be extremely old; but as regards Hellenism, though as Meter—the Anatolian Mother—she had had her associations for worship in Athens[2] from the fourth century onwards and as Ma or Cybele ultimately reached Macedonia,[3] Susa,[4] and Rome, and though Attis and Adonis penetrated the Hellenistic clubs,[5] the Anatolian religion on the whole remained rooted to the soil of Anatolia. But in its own land it was enormously strong; even at Ephesus Artemis maintained herself as a State within the State till Lysimachus' time. Valuable statistics have been collected for the most hellenised province, Lydia,[6] outside the Greek cities; 117 inscriptions refer to Greek cults and 237 to Asiatic, of which 112 relate to the Anatolian goddess and her son; the figures show how completely the Greek spirit failed to master Anatolia, and, as they comprise the whole Roman period, statistics for Hellenism alone would be even more unfavourable.

The history of Mēn Askaenos,[7] who was the Anatolian

[1] Cf. Calder, *J.H.S.* II, 247. [2] Poland 214.
[3] Baege, *De Mac. sacris* 113; *'Αρχ. Δελτ.* VIII, 267.
[4] Cumont, *Mém. Déleg. en Perse* XX, 80 no. 2.
[5] Michel 982; Ditt.[3] 1098. [6] J. Keil in *Anatolian Studies* 239.
[7] Ramsay, *C.R.* 1905, 418; *B.S.A.* XVIII, 37; *J.H.S.* 1912, 151; *J.R.S.* VIII, 107; Anderson, *J.R.S.* III, 267; M. M. Hardie (Mrs. Hasluck), *J.H.S.* 1912, 111.

god probably syncretised with the Babylonian moon-god Sin, is notable in this respect. When the Seleucids built Pisidian Antioch it was found necessary, for the sake of the native settlers, to establish on Mount Karakuyu near the city a new sanctuary of Mēn; the Sacred Way and Hall of Initiation have now been excavated, and the inscriptions show that Greek Antioch also was worshipping Mēn in the first century. Augustus replaced the priest by his own procurator, and thus became himself the god of the god's peasants; but Mēn, though he lived beside a large Hellenistic city, long resisted every attempt to displace him. The symbol of his initiates, the moon-god's crescent, is in its horseshoe form identical with the oldest form of horseshoe found in Scotland; it may be a pleasing conceit to see in those who hang up horseshoes for luck the last practitioners of a pagan cult which was hoary when Greece was born.

Babylonia's great contribution was star-worship, which we call astrology.[1] Its roots go very far back; and though in the Seleucid age many Babylonian astronomers refused to touch it, it had developed in Babylonia into a full-grown system. The stars, and above all the planets, obviously moved in the vault of heaven according to fixed laws; and a doctrine of 'correspondence' had arisen—this was the vital matter—according to which the heavens above and the earth beneath were the counterpart of each other, and what happened in the sidereal world was reproduced on earth. But the movements of the sidereal world were fixed; if then there was correspondence, what happened on earth was also fixed; and men's actions too were fixed, for man was a microcosm, a little world, the counterpart of the great world or universe, and his soul was a spark of that celestial fire which glowed in the stars. From this sprang one of the most terrible

[1] Bouché-Leclercq, *L'astrologie grecque*, 1899; Cumont, *Astrology and Religion among the Greeks and Romans*, 1912; Fr. Boll and C. Bezold, *Sternglaube und Sterndeutung*, 3rd ed. by W. Gundel, 1926; H. Gressmann, *Die hellenistische Gestirnreligion*, 1925; Gundel, *Sternbilder und Sternglaube* in P.W. See also the works by Gundel and Bidez cited p. 295 n. 2, and Gundel, *Neue astrologische Texte des Hermes Trismegistos*, Abh. Bay. Ak. Heft 12, 1936; Cumont, *L'Égypte des astrologues*, 1937.

doctrines which ever oppressed humanity, the Babylonian *Heimarmene* or Fate, which ruled alike stars, earth, and men; all their motions were fixed by an immutable Power, non-moral, which neither loved nor hated, but held on its course as inexorably as the planets across the firmament.

Greeks had heard of astrology by 400; Plato shows some acquaintance with it in his later period, and Eudoxus and Theophrastus knew that Chaldeans cast horoscopes.[1] Effective knowledge of Babylonian star-worship was brought to Greeks by Berossus, *c.* 280, but its time really came in the second century, when science was beginning to fail, and the irresistible advance of Rome might well seem Fate's counterpart upon earth. It ultimately penetrated and coloured many religions. Astronomy might have killed it; instead, by the end of the second century, it had killed astronomy (Chap. IX), and thenceforth it had a free field till Copernicus. It had reached Egypt also by the second century, when those writings appeared (before 150) which attributed the discovery of astrology to a mythical Egyptian king Nechepso and his priest Petosiris; and it was from the accessible Alexandria as a secondary centre that it spread over the Mediterranean world. The details of star-worship were probably further elaborated all through the Roman period. There was more than one system; in one the planets were most prominent, in another the twelve signs of the Zodiac, developed in Egypt into the 36 decans, corresponding to the 36 decades of the Egyptian year, and ruled by 36 demons with extraordinary names[2]—Chnumen and Chnachnumen, Smat, Srat, and Sikat—who also governed the 36 parts of the body. But planetary astrology had the greater power; the seven planets—Sun, Moon, Mercury, Venus, Mars, Jupiter, Saturn—were the interpreters of Fate, the seats of the awful Cosmocrators or 'rulers of this world', who subsequently became definitely evil and hostile to man's soul. To the seven planets were assigned their own colours, corresponding to the seven stages of a Babylonian temple, their own minerals, plants and animals; the seven vowels of the Greek

[1] W. Capelle, *Hermes* LX, 373. [2] Bouché-Leclercq 222.

alphabet became their signs; and from them came that persistent use of 'seven'[1] which survives in our (Hellenistic) week,[2] and appeared in the seven sleepers, the seven wonders of the world, the seven ages of man (which Shakespeare took from astrology),[3] the seven stoles of Isis, the seven-stepped ladder of Mithras, the seven joys of the righteous in the Salathiel apocalypse, the seven angels and vials of *The Revelation*, the seven gates of hell, and the seventh heaven.

The Zodiacal signs governed the destinies of various peoples[4] and cities[5]; coins testify that Antioch and Nisibis were under Aries, Edessa under Aquarius, Singara and Rhesaena under Sagittarius. But what mattered to men was that *their* destinies were fixed at birth by their stars, and a competent practitioner could foretell them by casting horoscopes. The English language is full of the terminology of this outworn creed; men are still jovial, mercurial, or saturnine, talk of fortunate conjunctions of events, believe in unlucky numbers, and thank their stars. By the first century Fate was in a fair way to oust the more kindly Fortune as the arbiter of men's lives. Later, probably under Stoic influence, some were to welcome Fate as an escape from the caprices of Fortune and the deceptions of Hope; but to the majority Fate was the negation of freedom, an impossible tyranny,[6] and the pressure on men's minds would have become unbearable but for certain ways of escape which will presently be indicated.

It was unfortunate, but perhaps inevitable, that the Stoa, many of whose chief exponents came from Asia, should take up astrology[7]; the weakness of Stoicism was its detachment from the scientific spirit, and astrology was to be its shadow side. It has been said that Zeno was influenced by astrology from the start[8]; certainly Chrysippus regarded the Chaldeans as allies,[9] and the resemblances of the two systems were

[1] Some believe this antedates astrology.
[2] F. H. Colson, *The Week*, 1927.
[3] Given Bouché-Leclercq 501.
[4] Cumont, *Klio* IX, 263.
[5] Hill, *B.M. Coins, Arabia* &c., *s.v.*; Cook 207, 166 n.
[6] Boll-Bezold 22, 79.
[7] Cf. M. Pohlenz, *N.J. Kl. Alt.* 1926, 257.
[8] Nilsson, *G.G.A.* 1916, 44.
[9] *S.V.F.* II, fr. 954=Cic. *de fato* 11 *sqq.*

patent. To each the universe was an organic whole, ruled by one almighty Power and bound together by something which the Stoic called Sympathy[1] and the Babylonian correspondence; to each, man was a microcosm and his soul a spark of the ethereal fire; the destruction and identical renovation of the world at the end of each world-period was, in some form, common to both. But there was one crucial difference: the Babylonian Fate was a non-moral Force, the Stoic Destiny a moral Providence, which at the start had taken forethought for men. Stoicism struggled hard to mould Fate into the semblance of Providence. It was illogical, but men's need was great; possibly the continuing repute of Aratus' *Phaenomena* (p. 274) was partly due to its argument that Providence had created the stars. Epicurus' school, to its honour, rejected astrology. Carneades attacked it as he attacked the Stoa, and propounded the crux: 'Why do men fated to die at different times die in the same shipwreck?'[2] But astrology was to escape from worse difficulties than that, and slipped away on a theory of general influences which overrode the special ones. But the great Stoic Panaetius of Rhodes, the friend of Polybius and Scipio, did discard astrology and the popular gods from his system; and it was important that it was Panaetius' Stoicism, rationalist and strongly moral, which through Scipio's circle found its way to Rome; what Rome first took from the Stoa was the philosophy of conduct alone. The man who might have done more than Carneades was the Greek astronomer Hipparchus (p. 297); had he used his enormous mathematical ability to amend instead of to destroy Aristarchus' heliocentricism, he might have saved the world many centuries of astrology; for to astrology heliocentricism meant (or should have meant) death. As it was, he merely reversed the traditional rôles of Europe and Asia; while on the Persian Gulf Seleucus the pupil of the Chaldaeans (p. 297), was defending heliocentricism, Hipparchus was championing the connection of the soul and the stars.[3] But whatever

[1] K. Reinhardt, *Kosmos und Sympathie*, 1926. [2] Cic. *De Fato* 11 *sqq.*
[3] Pliny II, 95; Rehm, *Hipparchos* in P.W., 1680.

Hipparchus' responsibility, the man who did most to establish astrology and its kin firmly in Europe was Panaetius' successor Poseidonius.

Poseidonius[1] of Apamea in Syria (135–51), who worked in Rhodes and there held high civic office, was the last great intellectual force which Hellenism, untouched by Rome, produced; his learning ranged over many fields, Cicero was his pupil, and he dominated the first half of the first century as Eratosthenes had dominated the end of the third. His work as historian, geographer, and descriptive writer has been noticed; it reveals his strength and weakness, a mind of great scope and boundless desire for knowledge, but quite uncritical and without the scientific spirit. As a philosopher, he blended some Platonism with the Stoa; but he blended much more than that. In his religious-philosophic activity he is a most difficult figure to grasp; nothing of his remains, and but little of the mass of material in later writers is definitely attributed to him. It has been usual to call everything which exhibits certain tendencies Poseidonius, and to represent him as a double mind, standing between east and west and drawing from both, a philosopher and man of science, an astrologer and oriental mystic and what not, author of a great system which combined all the floating tendencies of the time, science and superstition, star-worship and popular worship, heaven and earth, men, gods, and demons; one in whom all things met and from whom they passed out to influence the future. Is this Poseidonius, or only a label for the spirit of the first century? He is perhaps too shadowy to dogmatise overmuch about; the compound of influences often called Poseidonius can perhaps hardly be disentangled. It is certain that he set Zeus above Destiny instead of identifying them[2]; that is, his world was a religious world, ruled by Reason and Will. It seems likely that he was working on a scheme; he wanted to prove the

[1] Bevan, *Stoics and Sceptics*; Reinhardt, *Poseidonios*, 1921 (emphasises the Greek side of his thought); usual view summarised, Wendland, *Hell. röm. Kultur* 134, Otto, *Kulturgesch.* 128. Life: Jacoby, *F. Gr. Hist.* II, C, p. 154.

[2] Aetius p. 324, Diels.

close interrelation of earth and heaven. So far, science and philosophy had run separate courses; he would blend them, but science was to serve his philosophy. For it is not true to say that, in science, he wanted to find out the reason of things; he wanted to find there *his* reason for things, the connection of earth and heaven; he took trouble to show that the moon governed the tides, that climate affected races, that the sun painted the peacock of India or ripened the beryl in the Arabian mine, because all these things were useful for his thesis, his doctrine of vital force by which heaven acted on earth and which pulsated through the universe. His vast collection of data to illustrate the changes in the earth's surface was meant to prove the parallelism of earth and man, the fire and water which ran through the veins of the earth as blood and air through the veins of a man; block the vein, and both suffer alike—the volcano explodes, the man's vein bursts.

But what else came into his cosmic system beside heaven and earth, Zeus and man? The gods we know did; astrology is fairly certain.[1] He would have repudiated the accusation of superstition; his pantheistic deity, immanent in every portion of the Universe, *was* Nature; everything that exists is equally in Nature. The trouble is the number of things he accepted as existent. He believed in, and wrote on, divination[2]; it was in Nature. He wrote on daimons[3]; and there is just enough to show that he did believe the soul became a daimon and inhabited the upper air.[4] And supernatural beings spoke to men in dreams.[5] His own system, then, lofty in some respects as were his ideas of the correlation of the universe under the rule of a divine Providence, was not so very far from what we have called the spirit of the time; his Universe admitted too much, for he did not distinguish between what existed and what men believed to exist. He opened the door to demonology

[1] Cumont, *Astrology and religion*, 84.

[2] *περὶ μαντικῆς*: Cic. *de Div*. 1, 6; cf. Susemihl II, 132 n. 166.

[3] *περὶ ἡρώων και δαιμόνων*: Macrob. *Sat*. 1, 23, 7.

[4] Assuming Sext. Emp. *adv. math*. IX, 71–4 be his; so Bevan 108, Reinhardt 473.

[5] Cic. *de Div*. 1, 64; Reinhardt 467.

and much else. That he did not enter the open door with the crowd matters little; what the crowd saw was that his presence made their proceedings respectable; for if a daimon appeared in dreams, why not in a crystal, and if in a crystal . . . there is no halting on *that* slope. Every forsaken lover or speculative trader who hired some wandering Egyptian to call down a demon for him with an ibis' egg and a bit of garlic might claim that he was only carrying out to its logical conclusion the teaching of the great Poseidonius.

We come to the ways by which man could escape from Fate. One was provided by the heavens themselves; certain phenomena, such as comets, could not be brought under any fixed order, so there was something at work beside the fixed revolutions of the spheres. Correspondingly, astrology itself admitted many quite illogical elements; it managed to incorporate Fortune,[1] and it presently provided a doctrine of 'opportunities', fortunate planetary conjunctions which might be seized on by one bold enough. But, speaking generally, there were three main lines on which man sought to escape from his stars, all depending on a belief that some god was really more powerful than that Fate which ruled the gods; it was the human mind reacting for itself, as it always has done, against the dead weight of Determinism, and declaring that there should be no such thing; its weapon was the ineradicable belief of men in some helping deity, could they but find him. These three lines were Gnosis, magic, and the eastern mystery-religions. Gnosis means knowledge, but not the knowledge of the philosopher; some god had once directly revealed the secret key of the universe to some chosen soul, and could a man find that knowledge, hidden from other men, he was immune from Fate; he had short-circuited the stars. They might torment his body, but his soul was beyond their reach; for Reason was above Fate.[2] Gnosis was to produce some elevated doctrines, but though its roots go back to

[1] Bouché-Leclercq 288.

[2] *Corp. Herm.* XII, 9 (=Nock-Festugière, *Hermès Trismégiste* I, 1945, 177, and App. E, p. 193); cf. Reitzenstein *Mysterienreligionen*³, 300, 408.

Hellenism its day was not yet; all the great systems are essentially later than the Christian era.

No time or country has ever yet been free of magic.[1] But in the second century a fresh flood from Asia poured into the Greek world at astrology's heels; all the rivers—Assyrian, Babylonian, Anatolian, Persian, Jewish—met in Egypt as in a reservoir, and from Egypt[2] went out to water the earth, Its root idea was, that by employing proper means the hands of the gods could be *forced*; a formula to compel the Moon says, 'You have to do it, whether you like it or not'.[3] To some it was almost like the old Greek will to freedom come to life again in another sphere; the god or demon could be compelled to alter your fate. But to the mass of people, to whom star-worship meant, not a great oppressive system, but some wandering Chaldean and his horoscopes, magic was merely a short cut to getting some material thing you wanted. Many magic papyri are known, with formulae and ceremonies for every sort of personal advantage; they will give success in love or money-making, cure disease, exorcise devils, destroy an enemy; among them are omnibus charms, good for any purpose. All sorts of materials were in vogue, from the humble onion to the formula, probably seldom used, which begins, 'Take an emerald of great price and thereon carve a beetle'[4]; the sacred ibis, and the baboon, discoverer of Osiris' corpse, naturally played a large part. The demon called might come in many ways; the magician would see him for you in water or ink or crystal, suggestion playing a considerable part, but he might also be produced in person; if properly equipped you were for the moment his master, but he might hurt you afterwards, and beside protective charms there are formulae for getting the demon quietly back to his own place again, the side in which mediaeval magic

[1] Generally: Th. Hopfner, *Griech.-ägyptische Offenbarungszauber*, 1921 and 1924, and *Mageia* in P.W.; cf. Weinreich, *Phil. Woch.* 1925, 795; K. Preisendanz, *Papyri graecae magicae* I, 1928; II, 1931.

[2] Our texts are Roman period, but the material is Hellenistic; cf. A. J. Festugière, *La révélation d'Hermès Trismégiste* I, 1944.

[3] C. Wessely, *Griech Zauberpapyrus von Paris und London*, p. 31 no. 2242, see p. 32 ll. 11, 16.

[4] *Ib.* p. 132 l. 231.

was so lamentably weak. Usually you summoned one of the demons or spirits from the intermediate air; but a great god could also be called, as in the famous invocation of Typhon.[1] Your best hold over a demon was to utter his true name; but he probably concealed it with some care, and to make sure you pronounced a vast number, corrupt forms from every language in Asia, with strings of meaningless vocables; Typhon is called in the power of the 'hundred-lettered name',[2] Jewish magicians did not scruple to use the name Yahweh, and most potent of all, if a man could learn it, was that Ineffable Name with which Solomon had once sealed up in bronze jars 19,999 demons of the congregation of the Evil One.[3] Some formulae indeed contain nothing but names; and the Jewish Essenes were sworn never to reveal the names of the angels,[4] which means that they used them for magic. Magic almost became a religious system; many honestly believed in it, and the papyri contain prayers for deliverance from one's stars.[5] It had relations with the lower forms of Gnosis; you could compel the god to impart to you his secret knowledge. But Gnosis in its higher forms rejected magic; Fate, says a Hermetic writing, is not to be compelled.[6]

But far more important than magic were the Hellenistic mystery-religions.[7] Magic might alter your fate, but initiation lifted you above the sphere of Fate altogether; the god could and would look after his own, and though the stars might work their will on your body, your soul, even in this life, was beyond their reach, and after death would rise above their spheres to the sphere of the divine and dwell with the gods; you were in fact 'saved'. The universal

[1] C. Wessely, *Griech. Zauberpapyrus von Paris und London*, p. 49 ll. 179 *sqq*.
[2] *Ib*. p. 51 l. 252; p. 79 l. 1380.
[3] Reitzenstein, *Poimandres* 295 n. 1.
[4] Jos. *B.J.* II, 142.
[5] *Poimandres* 78 n. 1.
[6] Cited Reitzenstein, *Myst. rel.*[2] 301 (said to be lost).
[7] Generally: W. R. Halliday, *The Pagan background of early Christianity*, 1925, ch. VIII; S. Angus, *The mystery-religions and Christianity*, 1925; Reitzenstein, *Mysterienreligionen*[3], 1927; O. Kern and Th. Hopfner *Mysterien* in P.W. XVI; W. K. C. Guthrie, *Orpheus and Greek Religion*, 1935, esp. ch. VIII; I. M. Linforth, *The arts of Orpheus*, 1941.

basis of the mystery-religions was that you sought this *soteria*, 'salvation', by personal union with a saviour god who had himself died and risen again; to employ the well-known Orphic phrase, you ceased to be a worshipper, a rod-bearer, and became a Bacchus—you were as the god himself. Mysteries were an old phenomenon in Greece; what was new was the tremendous appeal which, with the break-down of Greek religion, they now made. Accusations of charlatanry and sensuality were freely levelled against their followers, but a religion is not judged by the bad men among those who profess it. These religions brought to the aspirant a new sense of sin, a new conception of holiness; and the rite of initiation, culminating in the knowledge that you were saved, was undoubtedly an intense emotional experience. From the second century onwards men's religious sense deepened. There were many mystery-religions, each claiming to possess the original initiation and to be of universal force; each claimed that the others merely worshipped its own god under other names. The older forms persisted, and certain phrases of Orphism, with its religious ecstasy and its ideas of purity and the antagonism of flesh and spirit, obtained considerable vogue; probably the Orphic hymns took shape at Pergamum. But what must be noticed here are the new forms which entered the Greek world through the occupation of Anatolia and Egypt.

The regular form of the Anatolian mysteries, as practised at Karakuyu (p. 345), was reconstituted by the late Sir W. Ramsay[1] from various sources; but scholars have differed greatly as to its value. Leaving Karakuyu aside, in some mysteries the initiates witnessed the death and resurrection of the god, and heard the priest pronounce the message of consolation: 'Be of good cheer, mystae, the god is saved; even so shall we after our troubles find salvation.'[2] In some mysteries there was shown a mystic representation of the divine marriage of the god and goddess; while in some, on the analogy of the Isis-ceremonial (*post*), the

[1] *B.S.A.* XVIII, 37; *J.R.S.* VIII, 132. Cf. Picard, *Ephèse et Claros*, 1922. [2] Firmicus Maternus *de err. prof. rel.* 22 *sqq.*

rite of initiation must have concluded with the recognition of the new initiate as himself a god. Ramsay laid great stress on the phenomenon of the sacred marriage in these mysteries as typifying the growth of morality, civilisation, the higher law, over against the temple prostitutes. This view has been contested,[1] on the ground that communism of women is not historical; but a thing need not have existed to exercise enormous influence—the *Contrat Social*, for instance—and the point is simply, did men think there was, or had been, such a thing? It seems that they did; Greeks attributed promiscuity impartially to the first Athenians[2] and to contemporary savages,[3] as did Egyptians to mankind at the start.[4]

But of all the mystery religions that invaded the Aegean world far the most important was the Egyptian. The Serapeum at Delos has revealed that the triad who were so to influence Hellenism were not Isis, Sarapis, and their son Horus or Harpocrates, but Isis, Sarapis, and Anubis,[5] the god who conducted souls to the realm of immortal life; the religion from the first stressed the fact that its great gift to men was immortality,[6] though Isis also made it clear that she was above Fate,[7] and that over those who came to her Fate had no more dominion. By the first century it must have seemed that if there was to be a universal religion, it could only be this. Everywhere men turned to Sarapis and Isis as saviours; their worship had spread far, and its penetrative power was such that Isis alone of foreign deities succeeded in entering Babylonian Uruk,[8] while Sarapis reached India.[9] Sarapis[10] has been supposed to be the only

[1] Farnell, *Greece and Babylon*, 277.
[2] Clearchus, *F.H.G.* II, 319
[3] Agatharc. *G.G.M.* 1, pp. 130, 133, 143, 153. Cf. Plut. *Mor.* 328 C.
[4] Marriage invented by Isis, Ditt.[3] 1267, see p. 359 and n. 3.
[5] Roussel, *Les cultes égyptiens à Délos*, 277; add *I.G.* XII, 3, 43, and *B.C.H.* 1926, 425 no. 48 (Thespiae).
[6] Also *P. Oxy.* 1380 ll. 13, 242.
[7] Apul. XI, 6, 15.
[8] Schroeder, *Berl. S.B.* 1916, 1180, names compounded with Isi- and Esi-.
[9] Huvishka's coin: P. Gardner, *B.M. Coins, Greek and Scythic kings of Bactria and India* 149.
[10] Wilcken, *U.P.Z.* 1, 77, 82; Kaerst, *op. c.* 242; Bevan, *Hist. of Egypt*, 41; O. Weinreich, *Neue Urkunden zur Sarapisreligion*; Sethe, *G.G.A.* 1923, 106;

god ever successfully made by a modern man. Egyptians at Memphis had worshipped Osiris in his Apis form as Osiris-Hapi, to Greeks Osorapis; Ptolemy I, or those about him, combined this deity with Greek elements and therefrom made what was in effect a new god, Sarapis; possibly he was meant to unite Greeks and Egyptians in a common worship. But Egyptians would not accept him, and though he kept Osirian characteristics and Isis as consort, he became the Greek god of Alexandria, whose great cult-statue, with its golden head[1] and jewelled eyes gleaming from its darkened shrine, became one of the chief glories of that city. Sarapis and Isis were represented on earth by the divine Ptolemaic pair, and Zeus, Hades, Asclepius, and Marduk contributed elements to Sarapis' nature; he became the universal ruler, whom his worshippers almost constituted for themselves as they would.

In the third century there was a lively propaganda in Sarapis' behalf in the cities of Egypt's sphere[2]; his worship spread quickly over the Aegean world,[3] and sometimes, as at Eretria, he entered an older shrine of Isis, whose cult often paved the way for his own, as it did at Athens.[4] At first his worship, like Isis', was confined to private associations; but later it often became official, as at Athens,[5] Demetrias, Tanagra, Lindus, Dionysopolis, Chaeronea, Thessalonica,[6] and Delos. At Delos,[7] for instance, an

Roeder, *Sarapis* in P.W.; Lehmann-Haupt, *Sarapis* in Roscher; T. A. Brady, *The reception of the Egyptian Cults by the Greeks* (330–30 B.C.), Univ. of Missouri Studies X, 1935, 5. 'Serapis' at Babylon in Arr. VII, 26, 2 (see Lehmann-Haupt above) is Ptolemy I's propaganda; see Kaerst *op. c.* 244; Nock, *J.H.S.* 1928, 21 n. 2; Tarn, *Alexander* II, 70.

[1] Brady, *Harvard Stud. in Class. Phil.* LI, 1941, 61.

[2] *P. Cairo Zen.* 59034, 59168; *P.S.I.* IV, 435.

[3] Kaerst *op. c.* 255–8, with many refs. Add Paton and Hicks 371 (Cos); *B.C.H.* 1927, 219 (Thasos); *I.G.* XII, 2, 511 (? Methymna); Tod, *B.S.A.* XXIII, 86 (Macedonia); some in n. 6 *post*, and, further examples, M. N. Tod, *J.E.A.* XXXI, 1945, 104; see Brady *op. c.*

[4] *'Αρχ. Δελτ.* 1, 115; Ditt³. 280; Roussel *op. c.* Add. See now Sterling Dow, 'The Egyptian cults in Athens', *Harvard Theol. Rev.* XXX, 1937, 183.

[5] Paus. 1, 18, 4; many priests known.

[6] *I.G.* IX, 2, 1101, 1107; Michel 890; Ditt.³ 765 (5); 762; 1207; *B.C.H.* 1927, 228. [7] *I.G.* XI, 4, 1299; generally, *ib.* 1215–95, and Roussel *op. c.*

Egyptian priest, Apollonius, introduced him before 300, and after the god had lived in lodgings for two generations Apollonius' grandson built him a house; by 166 he had three temples, and that year (or earlier) one was taken over by the city; this official Serapeum was greatly enlarged later. In Egypt 42 temples to him are said to have been known [1] (perhaps an exaggeration), but his main seats were the temples at Alexandria and Memphis: and Ptolemy I is said to have brought from Athens the Eumolpid Timotheus to inaugurate his mysteries on the lines of the Eleusinian. The papyri often allude to some mysterious people called *catochoi* [2] who lived in the precinct of the Memphis Serapeum. Professor Wilcken's explanation, that they were religious devotees possessed by the god, hardly explains why they could not leave if they wished; Woess' view is perhaps more probable, that they were refugees in the temple asylum who, being unable to leave (through fear of blood feuds or some such reason), did sometimes, to avoid expulsion, dedicate themselves to the god (a thing known elsewhere) [3] and even seek initiation. A more recent and perhaps [4] better suggestion is that the civil power may have prevented them leaving, as later it was to do with monks. The destruction of the Alexandrian Serapeum and its statue in A.D. 391 by the bishop Theophilus was taken by the world as the outward sign that Christianity had definitely triumphed.

But important as Sarapis became, he hardly equalled his consort; and while he was never invoked without her, she was often invoked alone. [5] Of all the deities of Hellenism, Isis [6] of the Myriad Names was probably the greatest. She was identified with practically every goddess and deified woman of the known world; she was the one reality which

[1] Aristides *εἰς τὸν Σαρᾶπιν*, 1, p. 96 (ed. Dindorf).

[2] Wilcken, *Archiv* VI, 184; VII, 299; *U.P.Z.* 1, 52. Sethe, *Gött. Abh.* XIV, 5; *G.G.A.* 1914, 385; 1923, 106. Woess, *Asylwesen* 140–64. Reitzenstein, *Myst. rel.*[3] 198. Bevan *op. c.* 296.

[3] New fr. of Alexis, cited Woess 164.

[4] Cumont, *L'Égypte des Astrologues*, 149 n. 1.

[5] Roussel *op. c.* 276.

[6] Meyer and Drexler, *Isis* in Roscher, is fullest. Cf. Roeder, *Isis* in P.W.; F. Legge, *Forerunners and rivals of Christianity* I, 56. See the works by Brady and Dow cited *ante*.

they all imperfectly shadowed forth. She was Lady of All, All-seeing and All-powerful, Queen of the Inhabited World; she was Star of the Sea, Diadem of Life, Lawgiver and Saviour; she was Grace and Beauty, Fortune and Abundance, Truth, Wisdom, and Love.[1] All civilisation was her gift and in her charge. Her statues portrayed a young matron in modest dress with gentle, benevolent features, crowned with blue lotus or the crescent moon, and sometimes bearing in her arms the babe Horus. Sacrifice was offered to her daily, as to Atargatis at Bambyce[2] and to Anaïtis at Ecbatana[3]; but only at great festivals was her actual image shown to worshippers, gorgeously robed and blazing with jewels, for her black-stoled priests understood every ceremonial art that might attract men. The November festival, Isia, represented the passion of Osiris—his death at Typhon's hands, Isis' faithful quest for his body, his divine resurrection; more magnificent was the spring festival of the Launching of the Ship, when, to celebrate the opening of navigation, the gorgeous procession so vividly described by Apuleius made its way from the temple to the seashore to launch the symbolic ship of the goddess.[4] Her service was typified as warfare; the initiates were the soldiers in her army. That initiation was no light matter; the novice might serve for many years before the goddess 'called' him, and to enter her shrine uncalled was death.[5] It was death too to enter it after call and due instruction by the mystagogue; but it was death to the novice's old life and birth to a new life, the life of salvation. In the ceremony itself the aspirant was first purified with water, and then wandered in the dark places of the underworld as Osiris had done between his death and resurrection, submitting to certain trials—possibly he actually 'died' and was 'buried', and probably suggestion played a considerable part; at the end he came out into a blaze of light, and with the sacred garments on him and a torch in his hand was exhibited to

[1] *P. Oxy.* XI, 1380.
[2] Lucian, *de Dea Syr.* 44.
[3] Isidore 6.
[4] Apul. XI, 8 *sqq.*, 16.
[5] Paus. X, 32, 13–18; Reitzenstein, *Myst. rel.*[3] 254.

the congregation as himself a god, his soul henceforth free from the dominion of fate and of death.[1]

But there was more in Isis-worship than ceremonial, or even than the mysteries, important as these things were. Isis was a phenomenon which had not appeared in the Mediterranean in historical times, but which, having once appeared, has never since quitted it; she was the woman's goddess. Half the human race had been badly off for a friend at the court of Heaven. Athena was uniquely a man's goddess; and if women cried to Artemis in childbirth it was largely because there was no one else. To the ordinary decent woman the main facts of life were that she was wife and mother; she had little in common with a virgin warrior who patronised art, or a virgin huntress, cold as her own moon; little with the fertility goddess of an old matriarchal age, and even less with Aphrodite, though doubtless people can spiritualise anything. But now she had a friend, and the greatest of them all; one who had been wife and mother as she was, one who had suffered as she might suffer; one who understood. Isis herself leaves no doubt on the point; she is the 'glory of women', who gives them 'equal power with men'.[2] 'I am Isis' runs her creed, the Isis-hymn found at Ios[3]; 'I am she whom women call goddess. I ordained that women should be loved by men; I brought wife and husband together, and invented the marriage contract. I ordained that women should bear children, and that children should love their parents . . .' In that strength Isis swept the Mediterranean. When finally Christianity triumphed, and Zeus and Apollo, Sarapis and the star-gods, were hurled from their seats, Isis alone in some sense survived the universal fall; the cult of the Virgin had been introduced before the Serapeum was sacked, and Isis' devotees passed

[1] Apul. XI; Reitzenstein *op. c.* 19.

[2] *P. Oxy.* 1380 ll. 130, 214. More crudely, Diod. 1, 27.

[3] Ditt.[3] 1267 = Werner Peek, *Der Isishymnus von Andros und verwandte Texte*, 1930, 123; so also in the Cyme version and the Andros hymn. The other documents in Peek, and Isidorus' hymns to Thermuthis-Isis as *ἀγαθὴ τύχη*, *SEG* VIII, 548–51, are not in point here. See further A. J. Festugière, 'À propos des arétalogies d'Isis', *Harvard Theol. Rev.* 1949, 209.

quietly over to the worship of another Mother—how quietly sometimes may be seen from this, that various instances are said to be known of her statues afterwards serving as images of the Madonna.[1]

The interest of the Hellenistic religions is that they depict the world in which Christianity arose. That world provided more than the medium of the common civilisation in which Christianity was to spread; it to some extent paved the way. Men were seeking the unity which must lie behind the different deities and their worships, even as Alexander had once called all men sons of one Father; while the terrible upheaval of the Roman civil wars greatly strengthened the already strong desire for a saviour, for whom many were already looking beyond the sphere of mankind. But though Hellenism supplied the longing, and probably in some a quickened sense of purity (even if only ceremonial) and of faith, there were to be two vital things in the new religion which were not in Hellenism, quite apart from the figure of the Founder, Whose spirit Hellenism did not touch. Plato had declared that all souls were immortal, and a few Jews had grasped the same general idea, while the Stoics gave the souls of the virtuous a limited survival till the end of the world-period; but to Hellenism generally immortality was only for certain benefactors of their kind or the initiates in some mystery-religion; it was not for the mass of men, as their epitaphs reveal pathetically enough. And of all the Hellenistic creeds, none was based on love of humanity; none had any message for the poor and the wretched, the publican and the sinner. Stoicism came nearest; it did transvaluate some earthly values, and Zeno, at least, gave offence by not repelling the poor and the squalid who came to him; but it had no place for love, and it scarcely met the misery of the world to tell the slave in the mines that if he would only think aright he would be happy. Those who laboured and were heavy laden were to welcome a different hope from any which Hellenism could offer.

[1] Meyer and Drexler 431, cf. 428–30; C. W. King, *The Gnostics and their remains*[2], 173 (the 'Black Virgins'), but see L. Brélier, *C.R.Ac.I.* 1935, 379.

LIST OF GENERAL WORKS

K. J. Beloch, *Griechische Geschichte* IV, ed. 2, Berlin-Leipzig 1925–7; H. Bengtson, *Griechische Geschichte*, 1950; E. R. Bevan, *The House of Seleucus*, London 1902, and *A history of Egypt under the Ptolemaic Dynasty*, 1927; A. Bouché-Leclercq, *Histoire des Lagides*, Paris 1903–7, and *Histoire des Séleucides*, 1913; J. B. Bury and others, *The Hellenistic Age*, Cambridge 1923; *Cambridge Ancient History* (*C.A.H.*), VI, 1927 to X, 1934; M. Cary, *A history of the Greek world from* 323 *to* 146 B.C., 1932; E. Cavaignac, *Histoire de l'Antiquité* III, Paris 1914; R. Cohen, *La Grèce et l'hellénisation du monde antique*, 1934, with excellent bibliographies; G. Colin, *Rome et la Grèce de* 200 *à* 146 *av. J.C.*, Paris 1908; J. G. Droysen, *Geschichte des Hellenismus*, ed. 2, Gotha 1877; W. S. Ferguson, *Hellenistic Athens*, London 1911, and *Greek Imperialism*, London-New York 1913; G. Glotz, P. Roussel and R. Cohen, *Histoire grecque* IV (*Alexandre et l'hellénisation du monde antique*), 1938; Fr. Heichelheim, *Wirtschaftsgechichte des Altertums*, 1937; M. Holleaux, *Rome, la Grèce, et les monarchies hellénistiques au* IIIe *siècle av. J.C.* (273–205), Paris 1921; A. H. M. Jones, *The cities of the Eastern Roman Provinces*, 1937, *The Greek city from Alexander to Justinian*, 1940; P. Jouguet, *L'Impérialisme macédonien et l'hellénisation de l'Orient*, Paris 1926 (Trans. as *Macedonian Imperialism*, 1928); J. Kaerst, *Geschichte des Hellenismus* II, ed. 2, Leipzig 1926; J. A. O. Larsen, *Roman Greece*, in T. Frank, *An economic survey of ancient Rome* IV; M. Launey, *Recherches sur les armées hellénistiques*, I 1949, II 1950; B. Niese, *Geschichte der griechischen und makedonischen Staaten* II and III, Gotha 1899, 1903; W. Otto, *Kulturgeschichte des Altertums*, Munich 1925; M. Rostovtzeff, *A history of the ancient world* I, Oxford 1926, *Social and Economic History of the Hellenistic World*, 1941, with very full notes; P. Roussel, *La Grèce et l'Orient*, Paris 1928; F. Schroeter, *De regum hellenisticorum epistulis in lapidibus servatis quaestiones stilisticae*, 1932; C. B. Welles, *Royal Correspondence in the Hellenistic Period*, 1934; P. Wendland, *Die hellenistisch-römische Kultur*, ed. 3, Tübingen 1912; U. von Wilamowitz-Moellendorf, *Staat und Gesellschaft der Griechen*, ed. 2, Leipzig-Berlin 1923.

INDEX